College Financial Aid For Dummies® 2nd Edition

Cheat Sheet

Who Does What in the Financial Aid Process

Student	College Financial Aid Office	College Student Accounts Office	U.S. Department of Education	State
Completes FAFSA*	Publishes financial aid information in college catalog	Reconciles student bill/account with the financial aid office for posting award amounts	Distributes FAFSA documents to high schools, colleges, and libraries in early winter	Distributes information and state aid applications to students and high schools
Completes CSS Profile*	Distributes financial aid information packets to applicants	Credits student's bill/account with all outside funding	Accepts FAFSA documents for processing after Jan.1	Receives results of FAFSA
If transfer student, asks previous college(s) to send transcripts and other documents+	Requests verification information (tax forms, W-2s, and untaxed income documents) from student's family	Refunds excess aid to student	Notifies students of FAFSA results on Student Aid Report (SAR)	Assesses student's demonstrated need based on cost of attendance
Completes college aid application*	Assesses student's eligibility for aid	Prepares adjustments for early student withdrawals	Notifies colleges regarding student's SAR on an Institutional Student Information Report (ISIR)	Notifies colleges and students of award funds and recipients
Completes college verification form+	Sends award letters to students	Receives Stafford and Parent loan checks from lenders and credits student's account or credits the Direct Student or Parent loan administered by the college	Notifies state scholarship agencies regarding SAR results	Disburses scholarship funds to colleges to credit student accounts
Returns award letter to college financial aid office	Certifies student loan application for Direct (or) Stafford and Perkins (or) other student loans	Prepares student's college Work-Study checks and/or credits student's account with earnings	Accepts SARs and student and age results	
Applies for campus Work-Study position	Certifies PLUS loans (parent loans for undergraduate students)	Administers deferred tuition plans to pay students	Notifies colleges of federal funds they will be receiving to award to students (for such programs as Perkins, Supplemental grants, and Work-Study)	Notifies regarding prepaid and college savings plans
Reapplies for federal aid in January	Makes college Work-Study and job assignments	Notifies student and parents at end of year regarding the tuition and fees paid by student for the Hope Scholarship program		Administers reciprocity agreements between states for tuition adjustments
Applies for private scholarships in January	Reconciles financial aid awards with student accounts office to assure proper crediting in student's bill			Establishes residence criteria for tuition and state scholarship eligibility

* = always required; + = may be required by college

...For Dummies®: Bestselling Book Series for Beginners

College Financial Aid For Dummies, 2nd Edition

Cheat Sheet

College Money Pocket Calendar

High School

FIRST YEAR

Begin drafting a four-or-more-year college financing plan.

SOPHOMORE YEAR

Start a college scholarship resource file. Collect information.

JUNIOR YEAR

October: Research financial aid opportunities and lenders. Take the PSAT.

November: Attend financial aid workshops and college fairs. Collect information on colleges and financial aid resources.

December: Complete asset structuring and position student for maximum financial aid eligibility. See PSAT results.

February: Register for May or June SAT. Plan to visit college campuses.

March: Discuss colleges with counselors.

April: Research scholarships for free in the career center and online.

May: Write to college admission offices requesting entrance and scholarship information. See college Web sites.

Summer: Visit college campuses. Request applications for private financial aid.

SENIOR YEAR

September – October: Update college list based on research. Complete and send admission applications.

October – December: Request scholarship applications. Prepare CSS Profile. Attend college fairs for costs and forms.

November: Take SAT. Get a Free Application for Federal Student Aid (FAFSA). Attend financial aid workshops. Mail CSS Profile. Complete school aid applications.

January: Complete and send early income taxes, FAFSA, and other aid applications.

February: Review and save Student Aid Report (SAR). Add any updates and return. Send tax information to school financial aid offices.

March: Complete scholarship applications. Apply for Federal Stafford and Federal PLUS loans.

April: Compare each college's award package. Send admission acceptance and award acceptance letters to schools.

May: Send any appeal letters and negotiate with colleges. Choose a college; notify those you're not interested in.

June: Send deposit and apply for loans. Work to save money. Begin scholarship research for next year.

College

FIRST-THROUGH-SENIOR YEAR

September: Interview for on-campus jobs.

October – December: Apply for private scholarships.

January: Renew FAFSA.

February: Complete and send taxes. Resubmit SAR with updated data. Send tax information to financial aid office.

March: Send returned, updated SAR to financial aid office.

May: Sign and accept renewal award letters.

...For Dummies®: Bestselling Book Series for Beginners

Praise, Praise, Praise for Dr. Herm Davis, Joyce Lain Kennedy, and this book

"The best of the financial aid books ...thorough, cutting-edge research, and clear, careful advice set this book above the rest."
— *Richard L. Tombaugh,* Former President, National
Association of Student Financial Aid Administrators

"I've seen several excellent sites on the Web discussing financial aid for students. None, however, are on a par with your exceptional book. I learned so much and I thank you so much."
— *Evonne Weinhaus*, Parent, St. Louis, Mo.

"A lot of student financial aid books cross my desk for review. *College Financial Aid For Dummie*s is by far the best."
— *George Chamberlin,* Newspaper Financial Columnist
and Radio Host, San Diego, Ca.

"Dr. Herm Davis's work, *College Financial Aid For Dummies*, is unmatched in the quality of its information, scope and timeliness. If there were an 'Oscar' or an 'Emmy' for the best financial aid book in the world, this book would sweep the awards. Lots of authors research and report; Dr. Davis really knows the financial aid field all the way through — from research and application to winning the means to make college dreams come true. Co-author Joyce Lain Kennedy makes the learning enjoyable.
— *Audrey Hill,* Past President, National Association of
College Admissions Counselors

"I appreciated reading your book, *College Financial Aid For Dummies*. I found your book well researched and well written...I am confident that your book will help others in making one of the largest and most important family investments of a lifetime — a college education."
— *Leon Litow,* Parent, Burtonsville, Md.

"I have been a college admissions counselor for more than 30 years. Your *College Financial Aid For Dummies* book is the book that answers the bottomless well of students' financial aid questions with authority — and, yes, even with humor. This book is a standout and we thank you for giving us a reliable resource our students can count on."
— *Joseph A. Monte*, Counselor, Einstein High School,
Kensington, Md.

"Your book is fabulous! I was bummed about how I would ever understand all this financial aid stuff and then a friend told me about your book. The negotiation chapter alone is a gold mine, a real eye-opener. You've given me hope."
— *Ben Carr*, Student, Wheaton, Md.

"I just wanted to take the time to say thank you for such a comprehensive and useful book."
— *Iris Kipnis*, Director of Guidance and Counseling, St. John Neumann High School, Naples, Fl.

"I thought your book was great! You've taken a heavy topic and given it humor and made it interesting as well as educational. You must have spent a lot of time writing this excellent book. I especially liked The Part of Tens."
— Bradford Hill, Oceanside, Ca.

"Your *College Financial Aid For Dummies* is absolutely the best book on college financial aid I've ever read — and believe me, I've read quite a few! I recommend your book to all my clients. It is comprehensive, timely and fun to read. Your supportive and friendly advice eases parents' and students' anxieties, and provides them with workable and practical options. Thanks for this book — we need it!"
—*Lori Potts-Dupre,* Educational Consultant, Takoma Park, Md.

"I have been reading your book and I've been devouring it. It's great! Of all the student financial aid books I've read, I appreciate *College Financial Aid For Dummies* the most."
— *Linda Blakeman*, Parent, Glenside, Pa.

"Thanks for giving me my life back. I dreaded the thought of paying for professional school until I read your book, *College Financial Aid For Dummies*, and found out about loan forgiveness. It's information of great interest to me."
— *Brian Opensky*, Student, Cleveland, Oh.

...FOR DUMMIES™

References for the Rest of Us!™

BESTSELLING BOOK SERIES

Do you find that traditional reference books are overloaded with technical details and advice you'll never use? Do you postpone important life decisions because you just don't want to deal with them? Then our *...For Dummies®* business and general reference book series is for you.

...For Dummies business and general reference books are written for those frustrated and hard-working souls who know they aren't dumb, but find that the myriad of personal and business issues and the accompanying horror stories make them feel helpless. *...For Dummies* books use a lighthearted approach, a down-to-earth style, and even cartoons and humorous icons to dispel fears and build confidence. Lighthearted but not lightweight, these books are perfect survival guides to solve your everyday personal and business problems.

> **"More than a publishing phenomenon, 'Dummies' is a sign of the times."**
> — *The New York Times*

> **"A world of detailed and authoritative information is packed into them..."**
> — *U.S. News and World Report*

> **"...you won't go wrong buying them."**
> — *Walter Mossberg, Wall Street Journal, on IDG Books' ...For Dummies books*

Already, millions of satisfied readers agree. They have made *...For Dummies* the #1 introductory level computer book series and a best-selling business book series. They have written asking for more. So, if you're looking for the best and easiest way to learn about business and other general reference topics, look to *...For Dummies* to give you a helping hand.

IDG BOOKS WORLDWIDE®

1/99

COLLEGE FINANCIAL AID FOR DUMMIES®
2ND EDITION

by **Dr. Herm Davis**
&
Joyce Lain Kennedy

IDG BOOKS WORLDWIDE

IDG Books Worldwide, Inc.
An International Data Group Company

Foster City, CA ♦ Chicago, IL ♦ Indianapolis, IN ♦ New York, NY

College Financial Aid For Dummies®, 2nd Edition

Published by
IDG Books Worldwide, Inc.
An International Data Group Company
919 E. Hillsdale Blvd.
Suite 400
Foster City, CA 94404
www.idgbooks.com (IDG Books Worldwide Web site)
www.dummies.com (Dummies Press Web site)

Library of Congress Catalog Card No.: 99-63194

ISBN: 0-7645-5165-5

Printed in the United States of America

10 9 8 7 6 5 4 3 2 1

2B/SY/QW/ZZ/IN

Distributed in the United States by IDG Books Worldwide, Inc.

Distributed by CDG Books Canada Inc. for Canada; by Transworld Publishers Limited in the United Kingdom; by IDG Norge Books for Norway; by IDG Sweden Books for Sweden; by IDG Books Australia Publishing Corporation Pty. Ltd. for Australia and New Zealand; by TransQuest Publishers Pte Ltd. for Singapore, Malaysia, Thailand, Indonesia, and Hong Kong; by Gotop Information Inc. for Taiwan; by ICG Muse, Inc. for Japan; by Norma Comunicaciones S.A. for Colombia; by Intersoft for South Africa; by Eyrolles for France; by International Thomson Publishing for Germany, Austria and Switzerland; by Distribuidora Cuspide for Argentina; by Livraria Cultura for Brazil; by Ediciones ZETA S.C.R. Ltda. for Peru; by WS Computer Publishing Corporation, Inc., for the Philippines; by Contemporanea de Ediciones for Venezuela; by Express Computer Distributors for the Caribbean and West Indies; by Micronesia Media Distributor, Inc. for Micronesia; by Grupo Editorial Norma S.A. for Guatemala; by Chips Computadoras S.A. de C.V. for Mexico; by Editorial Norma de Panama S.A. for Panama; by American Bookshops for Finland. Authorized Sales Agent: Anthony Rudkin Associates for the Middle East and North Africa.

For general information on IDG Books Worldwide's books in the U.S., please call our Consumer Customer Service department at 800-762-2974. For reseller information, including discounts and premium sales, please call our Reseller Customer Service department at 800-434-3422.

For information on where to purchase IDG Books Worldwide's books outside the U.S., please contact our International Sales department at 317-596-5530 or fax 317-596-5692.

For consumer information on foreign language translations, please contact our Customer Service department at 1-800-434-3422, fax 317-596-5692, or e-mail rights@idgbooks.com.

For information on licensing foreign or domestic rights, please phone +1-650-655-3109.

For sales inquiries and special prices for bulk quantities, please contact our Sales department at 650-655-3200 or write to the address above.

For information on using IDG Books Worldwide's books in the classroom or for ordering examination copies, please contact our Educational Sales department at 800-434-2086 or fax 317-596-5499.

For press review copies, author interviews, or other publicity information, please contact our Public Relations department at 650-655-3000 or fax 650-655-3299.

For authorization to photocopy items for corporate, personal, or educational use, please contact Copyright Clearance Center, 222 Rosewood Drive, Danvers, MA 01923, or fax 978-750-4470.

About the Authors

Dr. Herm Davis spends the majority of his time consulting with students and parents on paying for college. One of the nation's top student aid authorities, Dr. Davis heads the National College Scholarship Foundation, a nonprofit organization providing information to students. Additionally, he directs College Financial Aid Counseling and Education Services Inc. (CFACES).

A resident of Rockville, Maryland (a Washington, D.C. suburb), Dr. Davis is a 30-year veteran in financial aid and scholarship information for higher education. He was, for 15 years, Director of Financial Aid at Montgomery College in Rockville, Maryland, before leaving to devote all of his time to financial aid counseling and scholarship information management.

Dr. Davis has served on several government and professional boards concerned with financial aid. He is the financial aid advisor to the nonprofit Special Operations' Warriors Foundation, an organization that provides college planning for children of men and women who died or became disabled while serving the nation in special military operations.

Dr. Davis presents financial aid programs to such high profile groups as the Department of Justice, Department of Defense, Department of State, The Washington Post Scholarship Incentive Program, The American Legion's Boys Nation, and the Fannie Mae Foundation — Futures 500C Club.

Each year Dr. Davis presents college financial aid programs in more than 70 high schools as a community service, including ten schools that feature English as a Second Language programs. In addition to his work with middle-income students, he has helped more than 3,000 low-income and minority students receive financial aid totaling more than $4,000,000.

His doctorate in higher education administration in 1978 from George Washington University in Washington, D.C. featured a dissertation on *Financial Aid and Academic Progress*. Dr. Davis was born in Indiana, is a U.S. Navy veteran, and graduated from Indiana State University in Terre Haute with a bachelor's and a master's degree in education.

Joyce Lain Kennedy is the author or co-author of eight books. Her most recent are *Resumes For Dummies, Cover Letters For Dummies,* and *Job Interviews For Dummies* (IDG Books Worldwide), which recently received a Ben Franklin award as the best careers book of the year. She also writes a Los Angeles Times Syndicate column, CAREERS. Kennedy's column, now in its 31st year, appears in more than 100 newspapers. Kennedy was for 20 years the executive editor of *Career World*, a national magazine for secondary and college students, where she became interested in student financial aid. Writing from Carlsbad, California (a San Diego suburb), Kennedy is a baccalaureate business graduate of Washington University in St. Louis.

ABOUT IDG BOOKS WORLDWIDE

Welcome to the world of IDG Books Worldwide.

IDG Books Worldwide, Inc., is a subsidiary of International Data Group, the world's largest publisher of computer-related information and the leading global provider of information services on information technology. IDG was founded more than 30 years ago by Patrick J. McGovern and now employs more than 9,000 people worldwide. IDG publishes more than 290 computer publications in over 75 countries. More than 90 million people read one or more IDG publications each month.

Launched in 1990, IDG Books Worldwide is today the #1 publisher of best-selling computer books in the United States. We are proud to have received eight awards from the Computer Press Association in recognition of editorial excellence and three from Computer Currents' First Annual Readers' Choice Awards. Our best-selling ...For Dummies® series has more than 50 million copies in print with translations in 31 languages. IDG Books Worldwide, through a joint venture with IDG's Hi-Tech Beijing, became the first U.S. publisher to publish a computer book in the People's Republic of China. In record time, IDG Books Worldwide has become the first choice for millions of readers around the world who want to learn how to better manage their businesses.

Our mission is simple: Every one of our books is designed to bring extra value and skill-building instructions to the reader. Our books are written by experts who understand and care about our readers. The knowledge base of our editorial staff comes from years of experience in publishing, education, and journalism — experience we use to produce books to carry us into the new millennium. In short, we care about books, so we attract the best people. We devote special attention to details such as audience, interior design, use of icons, and illustrations. And because we use an efficient process of authoring, editing, and desktop publishing our books electronically, we can spend more time ensuring superior content and less time on the technicalities of making books.

You can count on our commitment to deliver high-quality books at competitive prices on topics you want to read about. At IDG Books Worldwide, we continue in the IDG tradition of delivering quality for more than 30 years. You'll find no better book on a subject than one from IDG Books Worldwide.

John J. Kilcullen
Chairman and CEO
IDG Books Worldwide, Inc.

Steven Berkowitz
President and Publisher
IDG Books Worldwide, Inc.

*Eighth Annual
Computer Press
Awards ≥1992*

*Ninth Annual
Computer Press
Awards ≥1993*

*Tenth Annual
Computer Press
Awards ≥1994*

*Eleventh Annual
Computer Press
Awards ≥1995*

IDG is the world's leading IT media, research and exposition company. Founded in 1964, IDG had 1997 revenues of $2.05 billion and has more than 9,000 employees worldwide. IDG offers the widest range of media options that reach IT buyers in 75 countries representing 95% of worldwide IT spending. IDG's diverse product and services portfolio spans six key areas including print publishing, online publishing, expositions and conferences, market research, education and training, and global marketing services. More than 90 million people read one or more of IDG's 290 magazines and newspapers, including IDG's leading global brands — Computerworld, PC World, Network World, Macworld and the Channel World family of publications. IDG Books Worldwide is one of the fastest-growing computer book publishers in the world, with more than 700 titles in 36 languages. The "...For Dummies®" series alone has more than 50 million copies in print. IDG offers online users the largest network of technology-specific Web sites around the world through IDG.net (http://www.idg.net), which comprises more than 225 targeted Web sites in 55 countries worldwide. International Data Corporation (IDC) is the world's largest provider of information technology data, analysis and consulting, with research centers in over 41 countries and more than 400 research analysts worldwide. IDG World Expo is a leading producer of more than 168 globally branded conferences and expositions in 35 countries including E3 (Electronic Entertainment Expo), Macworld Expo, ComNet, Windows World Expo, ICE (Internet Commerce Expo), Agenda, DEMO, and Spotlight. IDG's training subsidiary, ExecuTrain, is the world's largest computer training company, with more than 230 locations worldwide and 785 training courses. IDG Marketing Services helps industry-leading IT companies build international brand recognition by developing global integrated marketing programs via IDG's print, online and exposition products worldwide. Further information about the company can be found at www.idg.com.   1/24/99

Dedication

This book is dedicated to the countless members of the **professional financial aid community** who have spent their lives serving students and parents.

It is dedicated to those from whom I have been privileged to learn, especially the late **Dr. Doug McDonald,** who served as the director of financial aid at the Community College of Baltimore, the University of Delaware, and was the executive director of the Maryland State Scholarship Board. Dr. McDonald provided leadership as president of the Eastern Association of Financial Aid Administrators, and as a board member of the National Association of Financial Aid Executives.

It is dedicated to my family for the enduring support they've given in allowing me to take time away from family happenings to grow into a committed financial aid professional as I attended endless financial aid meetings and family workshops, took college courses on higher education issues, and worked on this book. To my daughter, **Shauna Davis,** to my son **Craig Davis,** and to my friend and wife **Sara Jo Davis,** I thank you.

And it is dedicated to **each of you readers** whose need for funding to pay for the next leg of your life's journey inspired me to focus my attention on cutting-edge financial aid practices.

— Dr. Herm Davis

Authors' Acknowledgments

Turning out a book like this takes a championship team. We appreciate the contributions of all the good men and women who helped, including legions of selfless individuals in a multitude of scholarship sponsoring organizations.

Most sincere thanks to *Dummies Trade Press* stars for making this book worthy: **Kathleen M. Cox,** project editor, and **Ted Cains,** copy editor, and the people in Production who took such care in making this book look nice. For putting this book into print: **Kathleen A. Welton,** Vice President and Publisher, and **Mark Butler,** Senior Acquisitions Editor. Once again, a special yellow Dummies rose to superpublicist **David Kissinger.**

Many thanks also to technical reviewer **Ellen Frishberg,** Director of the Office of Student Financial Services, *John Hopkins University*, who meticulously reviewed this entire work and made numerous contributions.

In the Washington, D.C. area, **Josey Vierra** worked like a gold-medallist in producing resource data. At *College Financial Aid Counseling and Education Services Inc.,* **Gus Gekos, Craig Davis, Nver Mekerdeegian,** and **Maria Limarzi** gave stellar performances in researching and verifying data, as did *Sun Features Inc.'s* **Walter Tamulis** in California.

Steve Carter, Mary Miller, Amy Luyex, Anita Gross, and **Mike High** in the *U.S. Department of Education* worked overtime to get us tomorrow's federal newspaper today.

Kathy Tyson at the *College Savings Plan Network* went all out to help us frame qualified state tuition plans.

Additionally, we were fortunate to find top experts who painstakingly reviewed various chapters for accuracy and timeliness of data: Investments and savings: Certified financial planners **David Dondero, Rich Wagner, Karen and Rick Shaeffer,** and **Lois Fishman.** Loan repayments: **Gary Spoales,** *Bank of America*. Government bonds: **Sheila Nelson,** *U.S. Treasury*. Lottery funding: **Terry Olson-Hatch,** *Florida Prepaid College Program*. Statistical updates and information: **Larry Gladieux,** *College Board;* **Bill Miller,** *College Scholarship Service;* **Dr. Dallas Martin's Staff,** *National Association of College Financial Aid Administrators*.

William Witbrodt of *Washington University*, **Dr. John Brugel** of *Rutgers University*, **Dr. Barbara Schneider** of *University of Colorado* and **Lorne Robinson** of *Macalester College* came through with sample award letters.

Cartoons at a Glance

By Rich Tennant

"It's part of my employer tuition assistance agreement with the 'Pizza Bob' corporation."

page 79

"and here's our returning champion, spinning for her 3rd & 4th year college tuition..."

page 5

"My daughter's college education is costing me an arm and a leg and over 60 noses a year."

page 183

"I really can't have a relationship now - I'm afraid it might impact my 'needs analysis form'."

page 257

"Someone put a financial aid form in our tip cup."

page 325

"Our plan is to buy the rest of it when we pay off our college loan."

page 297

Fax: 978-546-7747 • E-mail: the5wave@tiac.net

Publisher's Acknowledgments

We're proud of this book; please register your comments through our IDG Books Worldwide Online Registration Form located at http://my2cents.dummies.com.

Some of the people who helped bring this book to market include the following:

Acquisitions, Editorial, and Media Development

Project Editor: Kathleen M. Cox

Acquisitions Editor: Mark Butler

Copy Editor: Ted Cains (*Previous Edition:* Tamara S. Castleman)

Technical Editor: Ellen Frishberg, Director of Student Financial Services, Johns Hopkins University

Editorial Manager: Seta K. Frantz

Editorial Assistant: Jamila Pree

Production

Project Coordinator: Regina Snyder

Layout and Graphics: Steve Arany, Linda M. Boyer, Angela F. Hunckler, Barry Offringa, Brent Savage, Jacque Schneider, Michael A. Sullivan, Brian Torwelle

Proofreaders: Nancy Price, Nancy L. Reinhardt, Marianne Santy, Rebecca Senninger

Indexer: Ty Koontz

General and Administrative

IDG Books Worldwide, Inc.: John Kilcullen, CEO; Steven Berkowitz, President and Publisher

IDG Books Technology Publishing Group: Richard Swadley, Senior Vice President and Publisher; Walter Bruce III, Vice President and Associate Publisher; Steven Sayre, Associate Publisher; Joseph Wikert, Associate Publisher; Mary Bednarek, Branded Product Development Director; Mary Corder, Editorial Director

IDG Books Consumer Publishing Group: Roland Elgey, Senior Vice President and Publisher; Kathleen A. Welton, Vice President and Publisher; Kevin Thornton, Acquisitions Manager; Kristin A. Cocks, Editorial Director

IDG Books Internet Publishing Group: Brenda McLaughlin, Senior Vice President and Group Publisher; Diane Graves Steele, Vice President and Associate Publisher; Sofia Marchant, Online Marketing Manager

IDG Books Production for Dummies Press: Michael R. Britton, Vice President of Production; Debbie Stailey, Associate Director of Production; Cindy L. Phipps, Manager of Project Coordination, Production Proofreading, and Indexing; Shelley Lea, Supervisor of Graphics and Design; Debbie J. Gates, Production Systems Specialist; Robert Springer, Supervisor of Proofreading; Laura Carpenter, Production Control Manager; Tony Augsburger, Supervisor of Reprints and Bluelines

Dummies Packaging and Book Design: Patty Page, Manager, Promotions Marketing

◆

The publisher would like to give special thanks to Patrick J. McGovern, without whom this book would not have been possible.

◆

Contents at a Glance

Table of Contents

Introduction

This edition of *College Financial Aid For Dummies*, 2nd Edition is for the academic year 2000-2001.

Welcome. You've been kind in your comments about the first edition of *College Financial Aid For Dummies,* and we two authors feel the same way about you: Through these covers pass some of the world's finest readers.

For those of you new to this book, here's a bit about who we are and how we know what you need to do. One of us — Dr. Davis — has been immersed in the college financial aid profession for 30 years. For the last 18 of those years, he has worked with syndicated careers columnist Joyce Lain Kennedy — the other of us — to produce an annual booklet on the topic of college financial aid. We live on two coasts: Herm on the east and Joyce on the west. We work together online, by fax, and by telephone.

Why This Book? Lotsa New Stuff

Just as we did in the first edition, we've slaved over hot computers to bring you the latest and most useful information about paying for college or vocational-technical school. When we added up all the revisions, we were struck by the magnitude of change occurring since this book first saw daylight in 1997.

Before you plunge into the details of the financial aid changes that we've incorporated throughout this second edition, here's a little tease of what's new:

- ✔ Hope Scholarships and Lifetime Learning tax credits make the first two years of college universally available. (See Chapter 1.)
- ✔ State college tuitions are leveling off and even rolled back. (See Chapter 1.)
- ✔ Students are rushing online to apply for admission and financial aid. (See Chapters 1 and 12.)
- ✔ New college savings plans offer tremendous tax breaks — a sleeper benefit likely to gain big fans. (See Chapters 8 and 15.)
- ✔ Education IRAs mean parents can sock away a tax-favored $500 into a fund in their child's name to meet future college costs. (See Chapters 1 and 15.)

✔ Pell grants are much improved and will become more generous, perhaps reaching the level of buying power they held in the late 1970s. (See Chapters 1 and 7.)

✔ Elite colleges are boosting financial aid to recruit middle-and-lower-income students they really want — the "one-tenth of 2 percent of the student population" that all top-tier schools chase. (See Chapter 1, 6, 10.)

✔ "Dialing for dollars" is no longer rare, especially at some elite schools, as parents and students telephone colleges with better offers from other schools hoping to coax more aid by playing one college against another. (See Chapter 9.)

✔ Colleges can now credit a student's work-study earnings to pay their bills. (See Chapter 7.)

✔ Debt repayment is liberalized in several ways: Borrowers with more than $30,000 in student loan debt must be given the option of repaying over longer periods of time rather than the standard 10 years; forbearance for 60 days is allowed to a borrower requesting deferment, loan consolidation, or a change in repayment plan. (See Chapter 23.)

✔ Form requirements are changing in a move toward "one-stop" instruments. The Federal Stafford and Federal Direct loans no longer require a separate loan application, but include loan application space on the FAFSA, the main federal financial aid form. Parents must now sign the FAFSA and include their social security numbers. (See Chapters 7 and 20.)

✔ A parent can no longer automatically boost a child's demonstrated financial need by attending college at the same time as a family member, but there's still a way to benefit. (See Chapter 1.)

✔ Additional deductions are available to reduce the amount a family must contribute to the cost of college (Expected Family Contribution on the FAFSA), including child-care costs and private school tuition for elementary and secondary school. (See Chapter 20.)

✔ Loan forgiveness is further liberalized. Teachers in various settings can now wipe out $5,000 in debt. (See Chapter 22.)

✔ Distance education — chiefly online education over the Internet — is now eligible, within strict limitations, for federal financial aid programs. (See Chapter 1.)

✔ Loan consolidation funneled through the U.S. Education Department, at cheaper rates than the original loans, is now possible. (See Chapter 23.)

Despite all the changes, this book continues to have a dual focus:

1. **What you must know to navigate the financial aid system to your advantage.** Using information rooted in Dr. Davis's extensive experience, we share with you the kinds of insider knowledge that most guidebooks just can't deliver.

2. **What you must know to create a financial plan for four or more years of college.** You should not merely scrabble together a quick fix to pay for the next semester (although we do tell you what to do if school's about to start and you're cashless and clueless).

We identify some of the best private scholarships available, and coach you on how to work the system to shake loose gift money. We tell you what to watch out for when taking out loans. We reveal how much you can really count on work aid. We tell you how a tiny blunder on your forms can mean a giant loss of money.

We tell you how to negotiate with school financial aid counselors without ticking them off. We dissect little-known options such as using the state National Guard to collect on the GI Bill.

We focus on the undergraduate financial aid challenge but look too at the graduate financial aid scene. We continue to hear extreme stories of graduate students finishing their studies with more debt than a condo would cost, so we've paid special attention to the issue of debt. We hope you will too as you thread your way through the financial aid system.

A glance through the Table of Contents tells you that this rich and informative book is a leading light in the guidebooks to find college money. And quite immodestly, we think it's the best of the bunch and challenge anyone who disagrees to a sit-down arm-wrestling match.

Icons Used in This Book

A helpful feature of the *...For Dummies* series is the liberal use of cute pictures called icons that draw your attention to information too useful to ignore. These are the icons used in this book and what they signify:

New developments or trends you should know. This helps you to avoid moldy, old info.

Pay rapt attention to this data. You could get flagged if you don't.

The bare essentials of student financial aid you absolutely, positively, for sure must understand. Or else the universe blows apart.

Look for this icon to identify the authors' expert tips on getting the most money without selling a sibling.

This icon identifies niches of riches — outstanding sources of college money.

Despite what you may have heard, this icon directs your attention to myths and realities about college aid.

This icon shows it's important for you to record a fact for future reference in your indelible memory.

When you think you make too much money (but not enough to pay school bills), read what this icon highlights and be reinspired to nab that money you need.

This icon highlights information useful to international students who'd love to hop a jetliner to earn a college education in the United States.

If you're not fresh out of high school but want a chance at a college education, these tips will help you achieve your goals.

Away you go on the great hunt for the college gold. Good fortune be yours!

Part I
Who Qualifies for Financial Aid?

The 5th Wave   By Rich Tennant

"and here's our returning champion, spinning for her 3rd & 4th year college tuition..."

In this part . . .

Few students understand the financial aid system well enough to navigate its complex ins-and-outs, let alone plan paying for four years in advance. Because the earnings premium attached to a college degree may be as high as 80 percent, more people are enrolling than ever. To beat the rising competition for financial aid, you need to combine an in-depth understanding of the college money system and good old-fashioned resourcefulness.

This part helps you steer through the aid-finding maze. You find stockpiles of information on qualifying for college money, the intricate workings of college funding, and the cost of higher learning. You also learn how to get financial aid when your circumstances are unique. And you get tips on highlighting your most aid-worthy attributes. Read on to find out how to help the financial aid system help you.

Chapter 1

Affording the American Dream

● ●

In This Chapter

▶ Easing up on crushing tuition stress

▶ Rising: Middle-income-favored policies

▶ Shifting assets to qualify for maximum aid

▶ Making a realistic four-year financial plan

● ●

A big part of the American Dream is premised on college. According to a new report by the American Council on Education entitled *Too Little Knowledge Is a Dangerous Thing,* Americans are convinced that higher education is essential for economic success, although the report admits that "everyone knows someone who did well without going to college."

To a majority of Americans (58 percent), a college education is so intertwined with economic success and "the good life" that these parents will make sure their children go to college no matter what it costs — and it costs plenty. Financing the higher education part of the American dream is a nightmare that won't go away.

But the dream is still within reach. Although college isn't getting any cheaper, new financial aid rules *are* making it more affordable. You'll be glad to know about a raft of revisions in federal and state financial aid policies that are easing the hardship for middle-income and working-poor families struggling to provide a postsecondary education for their kids.

Here's a snapshot of the new affordability emphasis brought about by official policies in the higher-education reauthorization law (1998 Amendments to the Higher Education of 1965) and the revised tax law (Tax Relief Act of 1997).

New Federal Laws Cut Your Tax Burden

Congress has approved a number of laws designed to help meet college costs. In most instances, these laws can be used by families with annual incomes of up to $100,000.

The tax credits described here will be of the greatest help to middle-income families that do not receive enough gift (free) money to pay for tuition and fees, and students who attend pricey colleges that offer little gift money. Families that pay minimum taxes will not receive maximum benefits. Low-income, non-taxpaying families and high-income families receive no benefits from the new tax credits.

Each of the tax breaks has its own set of regulations and restrictions, so to take maximum advantage of what you are legally entitled to, check with your tax preparer, financial planner, or the IRS (800-829-1040). The source of the following examples in tax credits is the U.S. Department of Education.

Hope Scholarship tax credit

Aimed to benefit students starting college, this tax break permits you to deduct up to $1,500 from your family (or independent student) income tax if you spend that much during each of the first two years of college. Only money spent for tuition and required fees counts (less grants, scholarships, and other tax-free educational assistance).

> ***Family of two students:*** *A married couple with an adjusted gross income of $60,000 and two children in college at least half-time, one at a community college with a tuition of $2,000 and the other a sophomore at a private college with $11,000 tuition, would have their taxes cut by as much as $3,000.*

The Hope credit is phased out for joint filers between $80,000 and $100,000 of adjusted gross income, and for single filers between $40,000 and $50,000. The credit can be claimed in two tax years for students who are in their first two years of college or vocational-technical school and who are enrolled on at least a half-time (six credits) basis for any portion of the year.

The Hope Scholarship tax credit is not of value to the families too poor to have a tax obligation or too affluent to qualify but for everyone else, Hope helps make the first two years of college available.

Lifetime Learning tax credit

This tax credit is especially helpful for adults who want to go back to school to upgrade their skills and to college juniors, seniors, graduate and professional students, and mid-career changers who want to take a course or two. A family receives a 20 percent tax credit for the first $5,000 of tuition and required fees paid each year through 2002, and for the first $10,000 thereafter, not to exceed $1,000 per year.

Unlike the Hope Scholarship, this tax credit can be used for any undergraduate or graduate year beyond the second year of college.

> ***Returning to school full time to become a teacher:*** *A homemaker, whose family has an adjusted gross income of $70,000 wants to attend a graduate teacher-training program at a public university ($3,500 tuition) after being out of college for 20 years. Her family's income taxes would be cut by as much as 20 percent of tuition paid.*

> ***Auto mechanic:*** *A married man, whose wife works part time, and who has two grown children and an adjusted gross income of $32,000, is going back to a local technical college to take some computer classes with a tuition of $1,200. This family would have its taxes cut by as much as $240.*

The Lifetime Learning credit is available throughout your lifetime on a per-taxpayer (family) basis, and is phased out at the same income levels as the Hope Scholarship tax credit. Your family can claim the Lifetime Learning tax credit for some members of your family and the Hope Scholarship tax credit for others who qualify in the same year.

Education IRAs

Parents and grandparents can create Education IRAs and make penalty-free withdrawals from other IRAs. You can put up to $500 a year into an Education IRA for the higher education expenses of yourself (the taxpayer), a spouse, a child, or a grandchild. Earnings accumulate tax-free and can be used for tuition and required fees, books, equipment, and eligible (school approved) room and board if used before the age of 30.

Your ability (as a taxpayer) to contribute to an Education IRA phases out when your adjusted gross income reaches $150,000 and disappears at $160,000 per year for joint filers. The comparable figures if you're a single filer are $95,000 and $110,000. You can't, in the same year, use tax-free distributions from an Education IRA and benefit from the Hope Scholarship tax credit or the Lifetime Learning tax credit.

Tax break for loan repayment

This tax break reduces the burden of student loan debt repayment by allowing students or their families to take a deduction for interest paid in the first 60 months of repayment on student loans.

> **Workforce rookie:** *A new college graduate finds a job paying $25,000 a year (and has no other income). The newbie, who is in the 15 percent federal income tax bracket, has racked up a total debt of $13,500. The monthly payment for this student's loans is $166. The total amount of payments for the year is $1,992, over half of which is interest ($1,080) which can be deducted. The newbie's maximum tax benefit can be calculated by multiplying $1,080 by 15 percent for a savings of $162.*

The maximum annual deduction in 2001 and beyond is $2,500. It is phased out for joint filers with adjusted gross incomes between $60,000 and $75,000, and single filers between $40,000 and $55,000. The deduction is available for all educational loans made before August of 1997 (when the tax cuts became law), but only to the extent that the loan is within the first 60 months of repayment. Congress is dicussing expanding this deduction at the time of publication.

State Qualified Prepaid Tuition Plans

More liberal provisions allow you to use state qualified prepaid tuition plans (see Chapter 8) to cover room and board expenses as well as tuition. Grandparents and others can now contribute to your educational prepayment plan.

Community Service Loan Forgiveness

This provision excludes from your (the graduate's) income tax liability the student loan amounts forgiven because you take a job that addresses unmet needs provided by nonprofit, tax-exempt, charitable, or educational institutions.

Employer Tuition Assistance

The tax code (Section 127) allows you as a worker to exclude up to $5,250 of employer-provided undergraduate education benefits from your income tax — until June 1, 2000. Based on the history of this deduction, it probably will be extended another few years.

New Federal Laws Ease College Financing

The federal government is by far the dominant dispenser of financial aid to students and their families. (See Chapter 7.) Glance over these other recent developments that make college more affordable:

- ✔ **Student loan interest rates:** The higher-education reauthorization bill of 1998 lowers the interest rate on student loans to 7.46 percent — the lowest rate in nearly two decades. A student borrowing $13,000 would save about $700 in interest payments over ten years.

- ✔ **Pell grants:** The monies available in Pell grants, the basic federal gift program that opens access to a college education to low-income students, are going up. Now programmed to max out at $4,800 for the 2000-2001 academic year (you can't be sure until the annual Congressional appropriation of funds although $3,525 is most likely), a Congressional bill (Affordable Higher Education-Through-Pell Grants Act of 1999) has been introduced to raise Pell grants' maximum award level to $6,500 and to increase the eligibility pool for the grants, which would greatly help middle-income families with more than one child in college at the same time.

- ✔ **Distance education:** In what may turn into a far-reaching benefit with enormous portents, Congress has removed the ban on federal financial aid programs for some distance learners. In a split-second-changing-workplace, adults who need to keep their day jobs but increase their skills can now study interactively online and meet both objectives. The 1998 higher-education reauthorization amendments waived regulations that largely deny eligibility for aid to students participating in distance-education programs. Initially, the waivers take effect at 50 colleges or consortia of colleges.

New State Trends Promote Affordability

State officials also have heard the message that college is too expensive. Because they'd like to keep their college graduates within their borders, many states have taken more generous innovative measures:

- ✔ **State spending on higher education rises:** With the South taking the lead — especially Florida, Georgia, Kentucky, Mississippi, and Virginia — state budgets for higher education are the healthiest they've been in nearly a decade. Total state coffers for college operations and student aid rose to a record $52.8 billion for fiscal 1998–1999, a jump of 6.7 percent, or $3.4 billion, over the previous year. Community colleges, distance learning, and student aid enjoy large gains.

✔ **Scholarships for students with good school records:** Growing numbers of states are rewarding students who have good school records (a B average or better) with merit scholarships, including Louisiana, Mississippi, Florida, Kentucky, and West Virginia. The amounts vary, but $2,500 for four years is common. (The long-term outlook for state merit scholarships is unclear; scholarship proposals have been held up or turned down in more than a half-dozen states.)

✔ **States protesting college cost increases:** State politicians in California, Virginia, Massachusetts, and elsewhere — hearing the cries of anguished parents and students — are increasingly demanding a leveling off, or even a rollback, of state college tuitions. South Carolina's Queens College has cut the tuition rate for freshmen by 27 percent, from $12,980 to $9,410. Virginia has instituted a 20 percent cut for in-state students at the state's colleges and universities.

✔ **State-expanded tax incentives for savings plans:** In addition to the federal tax breaks for state prepaid qualified tuition programs mentioned previously, state governments are giving similar benefits. In effect, the plans that permit spending on room and board, as well as tuition and fees, double the tax advantages of the original prepaid plans. New York, under a new program, permits residents to deduct $5,000 a year from their state taxable income for contributions made to a state family tuition account — up to $100,000 per student.

Others Join the Affordability Movement

The making-college-affordable good news fans out into the private sector too. Private colleges are feeling the pain of middle-income students whose families have been paying more than the cost of a new car for a year of study; elite colleges such as Princeton, Yale, and Stanford are adding millions of dollars to their financial aid budgets with most of that money targeted to middle-income families. Some schools no longer count home equity, and others exempt up to $150,000 of a family's savings, home equity, and other assets.

The College Scholarship Service, the arm of the College Board that helps colleges evaluate the financial-aid needs of their applicants, is adjusting its formula to be more generous to families that earn $60,000 to $100,000 per year, as well as to families that have saved money for college.

Evidence is everywhere that college simply must continue along the affordability track. Students are surging to inexpensive two-year community colleges in record numbers. Increasing numbers of top students are choosing cheaper second-tier colleges, saving their money for graduate school, or refusing to go into debt. Not only are parents asking what institutions fit their child's academic and social interests and educational objectives, but — how much can they commit financially to help their child meet his or her educational goals?

The basic argument among financial aid professionals and public planners continues to be whether to reserve virtually all financial aid for students in the lowest income families or to distribute aid up the income chain to additional deserving students. But there's no argument about the fact that financial aid in the United States today *is* leaning toward middle-income and working-class families, as well as families at poverty levels.

As one financial aid director who prefers to remain nameless put it: "The country is moving away from the need-based system providing access and choice for students without family financial resources and toward a system that helps middle-income families (who vote in large numbers) feel better about public monies being spent on higher education financing by making them eligible to receive some of their tax money back as financial aid."

The majority of new programs being funded, especially at the state level, are heading in the direction of merit based (which statistically go towards affluent families disproportionately for various reasons), according to yet another observer in financial aid circles.

Still another trend giving a financial aid research edge to middle-income students, most of whom now own a computer, is the spectacular rise of the Internet. A whopping 82.9 percent of the nation's college freshmen annually surveyed (by the Higher Education Research Institute at the University of California, Los Angeles in 1998) said they use the Net for research or homework.

Without judging the pros and cons of what's happening to financial aid today, this chapter starts you on the knowledge journey necessary to get your fair share of aid and reduce the financial strain on your family. We begin with the concept of finding free money that you need not pay back.

Sniffing Out Gift Money

Here's a sampling of potential "keeper" perks that middle-class families and others can take advantage of:

✔ Schools feeling the competitive heat are in bidding wars. They use financial aid as a powerful marketing tool. Even famous schools woo fence-sitters whom they really want with honeyed offers that are hard to refuse.

✔ Organizations, civic groups, and corporations hand over private scholarships.

✔ Looking for help close to home — from local businesses and civic groups, for instance — will reveal a raft of small but valuable awards to local students.

✔ Certain majors (such as health, science, and engineering) get more than their share of student aid.

✔ Military commitments (ROTC) pay tuitions and more.

In addition, more than half of all students hold down jobs while attending college (which gives them valuable work experience to use after graduation).

And remember, state schools and community colleges themselves constitute aid in the sense that taxes keep their tuitions below market rate for local residents. So explore all your options; college can be in your future regardless of your income.

Pricey Schools May Not Be Out of Reach

A four-year education at elite schools is costing out at $130,000 to $150,000. Do you feel a vow-of-poverty attack coming on? Should you forget about an expensive education? Not necessarily.

Don't write off expensive schools just because their tuitions leave a space as big as the Grand Canyon between your will and your wallet. Make the effort if that's what you want, because your costs may be roughly the same whether you attend a college topping $25,000 or one dropping as low as $5,000 a year.

The amount that your family is expected to pay remains about the same no matter where you enroll. The more expensive the college, the more aid for which you are eligible. All you need to do is apply and qualify academically. At least, that's the way the system is supposed to work — and, very often, it does. Academically speaking, however, schools have fallen on difficult economic times.

Although most schools still insist that they hew to a *need-blind admissions policy,* which means that the decision to accept or turn down an applicant is made without regard to that student's financial need, many educators admit privately that students who can pay have the edge over equally qualified students who are less able to pay.

In practical terms, all but the most selective and well-endowed schools tilt toward students who can pay their way without dipping into the institutions' coffers. (For a list of colleges and universities with deep endowment pockets, see Chapter 6.)

Keeping your nose in the books is the key to snagging merit scholarships. The people handing them out are GPA groupies. They love applicants who emerge from high school in the upper regions of their class and demolish SAT and ACT tests as if they were child's play.

Some colleges, for example, knock 40 percent off tuition to students who graduate in the top 5 percent of their high school class and are selected for a grant; others give the best students whatever money they need to attend — the best students being those graduating in the top 2 percent of their class, with a GPA of 3.9 out of 4.00 and SAT scores higher than 1450.

The bar is high, too, for those who leap over it to win sports, music, drama, or art scholarships: Both talent plus academic achievement often must be stellar.

But what if talented applicants have only so-so grades? They may still make the scholarship cut. Sometimes talent outweighs academic records by a country mile — just ask any football coach.

Colleges frequently aim their merit scholarships toward students they want but who may not show up without the inducement of serious aid. Aid offers are designed with an eye toward the school's diversity mix of brains, talent, and cultural composition.

If you're lucky enough to be in the most-wanted category — with some combination of great grades, leadership activities, fine arts ability, desirable major, geography, or minority status — don't let the school know that your enrollment is a done deal or its limited aid budget may go to those who need persuasion.

Suppose your talent is nonexistent. Your grades are in the "not bad" category, and the processional line between you and the valedictorian is 200-people deep. You may get admission but probably no federal grant aid whatsoever from elite schools, regardless of how strapped you are. If your middle-class family's income tops the federal and state aid caps (adjusted to about $40,000), you can still try for funds from the college's own resources. If you come up empty, shop for low-interest loans.

Qualifying for Financial Aid

Question: Who qualifies for college financial aid?

Answer: Surprise! You and most of the people you know!

If you and your family do each financial aid task (1) correctly and (2) in a timely manner, you will receive student financial aid of some kind.

Although each aid program defines its own special criteria, certain eligibility requirements are common to virtually all programs:

- ✔ You must be enrolled in an eligible program at an eligible institution. The financial aid program defines what is eligible.

- ✔ You generally must show satisfactory academic progress toward a degree or certificate to keep financial aid.

- ✔ Typically, you must be "in good standing" with the institution you attend.

- ✔ For federal student aid programs, you must be a United States citizen, or a noncitizen who is a permanent resident. Refugees or those granted political asylum may be eligible.

- ✔ Aid programs sponsored by colleges and private organizations may require that you be a U.S. citizen or permanent resident.

- ✔ As a rule, you must be a legal resident of the state from which you seek financial aid to receive it. Out-of-state residents may be able to participate in state-backed loan programs.

- ✔ Many financial aid programs require that you be at least a half-time student (six semester hours of courses per semester, or the equivalent).

- ✔ Some programs sponsored by schools and private organizations require that you attend college on a full-time basis (12 semester hours minimum).

- ✔ International students qualify for special programs sponsored by colleges and private organizations. (See Chapter 2 for more information.)

Federal aid programs usually apply to more than 9,000 eligible colleges, universities, and vocational-technical schools (which teach everything from computer repair to cosmetology). You can also use federal aid money at hospital schools of nursing and two-year colleges.

Rarely are less-than-half-time students eligible for federal funds. The exception is Pell grants, which can be used for less-than-half-time students; you just won't receive as much as if you were enrolled full-time.

Unlike federal programs, state aid programs may not consider vocational-technical school students eligible for some aid programs. Other types of study that may not qualify for aid from various programs include religious studies and vocational-technical programs of less than six months' duration.

Perceived versus demonstrated need

Need means the amount of money your family *can't* afford to pay for your education — it's the difference between the cost of your college education and the dollars your family is expected to ante up for college expenses. Need does not mean poverty status.

The concept of need has a particular meaning in financial aid offices, however. You may tell your college financial aid counselor you have need just because you're on thin shoe leather, and bill collectors are hot on your trail. While that's not a good position to be in, aid givers consider that type of informal reporting as *perceived need*. It doesn't mean a thing to them.

What you have to do is show *demonstrated need*, as explained in Chapter 3. You do so by filling out a mass of paperwork supported with financial documents. The complex paperwork evaluates families' income and assets to determine how much of the overall college tab individual students and their parents can afford.

Financial aid personnel at various schools put approximately the same ceiling on how much they expect a family to pay, regardless of costs at their college. Once you're accepted for admission, they try to offer an aid package that makes up the difference.

Expect aid packages to be a mixed bag

The aid package, described in greater detail in Chapter 3, is comprised of self-help money and gift money. *Self-help money* includes work-study jobs and loans that must be paid back. *Gift money* includes grants (based on demonstrated need) and scholarships (based on merit), which aren't paid back. Gift money is also called *free money*. Once you grasp the concept of demonstrated need, you can act to increase your eligibility for aid by following the advice given throughout this book.

Playing the Aid Game: Asset Control

The key to getting aid based on your financial status is clear: *The more impoverished you look, the more aid you get.*

For example, aid-analysis programs require you to count your savings in regular taxable accounts as wealth, not the savings you have in your home equity, retirement accounts, and cash-value life insurance policies. (Some schools, however, do throw all of a family's wealth into one big pot to measure how much aid the student's entitled to receive.)

Even Washington politicos are concerned that, with the exception of unsubsidized loans, the middle-income student gets the short end of the financial aid stick. The president and the Congress have responded by creating a huge new (mostly middle-class) entitlement in the form of tax breaks worth an estimated $400. At press time, they had not yet come to a meeting of the minds. The end result is likely to be a compromise of some sort, giving middle-class students more than they have but less than they want.

Financial aid for students with disabilities

Students with disabilities may face such additional expenses as special equipment related to the disability and its maintenance, expenses of services such as readers, interpreters, note takers or personal care attendants, special transportation requirements, and medical expenses relating to the disability but not covered by insurance.

Scholarships specifically designated for students with disabilities are very limited (see the Resource Guide at the end of this book). If you have a disability, be sure to pursue scholarships available for qualities other than disability.

In addition, the state vocational rehabilitation agency, as well as organizations of and for people with disabilities, may be able to help you realize your college goal.

Moreover, at each college, students with disabilities should ask about financial support not only at the financial aid office, but at the Office of Student Services, 504 coordinator, or Office of Disability Support Services.

For a fuller discussion of available resources for college students with disabilities, obtain an annually revised information paper, *Financial Aid for Students with Disabilities.* The paper is free. Order from:

HEATH Resource Center
American Council on Education
One Dupont Circle NW, Suite 800
Washington, DC 20036
V: 800-544-3284
I: www.acenet.edu (click on HEATH)

Play or pay?

Autumn was just beginning and Shawn, an outstanding California high school senior with a GPA of 4.9 (out of 4.0 — extra points for advance placement college courses), was trying hard to get into Stanford on an early-decision basis. As the son of a single mother, inexpensive macaroni-and-cheese casseroles were a popular supper in Shawn's home.

When early February rolled around, Shawn was overjoyed to receive The Acceptance Letter. But he was surprised to find that, while the aid package was good, it was far less than he had expected given his mother's financially lean situation. The aid deficiency was due to a legacy of $20,000 his grandfather willed jointly to Shawn for school and to his mother for retirement.

If Shawn had had a four-year college-financing plan in place, his family could have taken steps prior to *December 31 of his junior year* to arrange the family's finances in ways that would increase the amount of financial aid Shawn would receive — steps to increase his demonstrated need. Shawn, for example, could have bought a computer or car for college, both legitimate expenses.

What can Shawn do to improve his aid eligibility as he begins his first year of college?

Shawn should spend the legacy dollars on college tuition, books, supplies, room and board, and transportation. While a formal list of unacceptable expenditures doesn't exist, college aid officers will frown on blowing the money on such nonessential items as an expensive car or clothing, gifts, or luxury student housing.

Timeline for moving student assets

The year before you attend college is the *base year* that colleges use to measure what you can afford to pay.

For first-year college students, the base year is:

the last half of your high school junior year (January – May)

the first half of your high school senior year (June – December)

In the year before the base year, your *pre-base year,* you should try to line your pockets: restructure assets, take capital gains from selling assets, and rake in bonuses or commissions before your base year begins.

During the first half of your base year (January through May), scale down your affluent image on financial aid applications by buying big ticket items with cash, paying off your credit card balances, and taking other capital losses to slim down income and assets like bonuses, commissions, and inheritances. Unless you're pushed into a financial corner, avoid taking money out of your retirement funds because financial aid offices don't calculate that money when deciding how much you can contribute to the tuition pot.

Timely financial fix-ups

Table 1-1 provides a simple chart of when to redraw your financial picture. We assume you're applying for aid for the 2002-2003 school year.

Table 1-1	When to Redraw Your Financial Picture
Pre-Base Year (January–December 2000)	*Base Year (January–December 2001)*
Fatten your bank account by December 31, 2000.	Slim down your bank account.
Sell and shift assets.	Take unavoidable losses on assets.

To increase your aid eligibility, you can make these other short-term strategic moves. All of them should be accomplished *prior to December 31 of your junior year in high school.* (Or, if a nontraditional student, the year before you intend to apply for aid. See Chapter 2 for more about nontraditional students.)

Because need-analysis standards vary from school to school, make anonymous calls to target schools asking what specific assets are included in their calculations.

A key point to remember: Your ability to pay *this* year's tuition is based on your income and assets of *last* year. That's because colleges can't see into the future and verify your family's financial status this year.

Curious rules of college aid

Though the rules vary widely among schools, financial aid logic isn't always self-evident. Here are a few hypothetical illustrations of what seems odd to the financial aid novice, followed by explanations.

1. Godparent puts $8,000 in a high school senior's account, causing the senior to lose a low-interest college loan. **Aid loss: $2,800.**

2. Parent moves $40,000 from a $100,000 savings account to an annuity or life insurance account. **Aid gain: $2,145.**

3. Sally has $12,000 in a saving account. The system (federal formula) requires that Sally contribute $4,200 toward college bills. Al has $12,000 in a savings account, but the system doesn't require Al to contribute a cent. **Aid gain: $4,200.**

Explanations

1. When a student has assets (savings, bonds, stocks, and so on), the student is expected to kick in the cash equivalent of 35 percent of those assets; in this illustration the amount is $2,800.

2. Financial aid need estimators must ignore $38,300 of the average parents' assets due to an asset protection allowance. After $100,000 savings shrink to $60,000, financial aid need estimators must still ignore that $38,300, leaving them just $21,700 to skim a meager 5.6 percent contribution from. Before shifting the $40,000, the parents were expected to contribute $3,360. After the shift, they only had to contribute $1,215, a difference of $2,145.

3. Al's parents earn under $50,000 a year and filed a short tax form (IRS 1040EZ/A). Parents whose income is under $50K and file the short tax form don't have to reveal asset information on the standard federal financial aid application form. Presto! Payment isn't required because no valuation of assets exists for the parents or student. Sally's parents didn't take this approach because they earned $65,000 a year and were ineligible for this benefit.

Federal need analyzers don't count assets like the value of your car or home when they figure how fat a cat your family is. Nor do they subtract debts from your assets. But they seem to smell money in the bank, and they count every cent as an asset after the asset protection allowance. (Remember, the more assets, the less aid.)

Most of the following tips suggest that you shift cash into assets that aren't counted or pay off debts that don't help you look poor on paper. For instance, suppose you have $50,000 in a savings account but owe $20,000 on a consumer debt. The federal formula recognizes the $50,000 in your bank account loud and clear. Frustratingly, they ignore the $20,000 you owe. By withdrawing the money from savings and using it to pay your debt, and because you have a $30,000 asset protection allowance, your assets drop from $50,000 to zero. Presto! You qualify for more financial aid.

Here are pointers for parents to help reframe your aid eligibility. All of them are legal and legitimate. As an East Coast financial planner says: "There is no reward in heaven for paying extra money for college."

- ✔ **Spend down and pass over.** Any asset keeps you from receiving maximum aid dollars. Getting rid of the money by paying tuition and other legitimate college-related expenses is to your advantage as it can increase the amount of financial aid you'll receive every year after that.

- ✔ **Reduce a child's kitty.** Financial aid administrators expect parents to spend 5.65 percent of their assets (and that's *after* subtracting an asset protection allowance), but they expect students to spend 35 percent of their savings each year for school with no asset protection allowance. If you're thinking of a tax savings, forget it — the tax benefits of putting money in a child's name are small compared to the big cut in family financial aid.

- ✔ **Pay off consumer loans and home mortgages.** Home equity loans generally reduce assets; so consider taking out a home equity loan to pay off automobile loans, credit card debt, or other consumer loans. Watch out: Although most schools don't count home equity as an asset, some do count it to determine eligibility for institutional aid only.

- ✔ **Time your purchases.** If you have assets of $50,000 or more, make major purchases before December 31 of a child's junior year in high school. If you are 45 years or older, for every $1,000 you withdraw from savings, the amount you're expected to fork over for college decreases by about $120.

- ✔ **Time your income.** If you plan to cash in high-performing stocks or other investments to pay for college, do so before December 31 of the year before you are evaluated for your aid award. That is, if you want aid in the 2002-2003 school year, try to report the big money before December 31 of 2000; remember that 2001 is the base year on which your income and assets will be evaluated. The same timing applies to extravagant bonuses or commissions — although this timing is harder to arrange. Capital gains can inflate your income dramatically, and if you sell after December 31, that boost in income will slash your aid eligibility the next year.

✔ **Put assets off-limits.** Rules are far from universal, but schools do not include retirement funds, such as 401(k)s and individual retirement accounts, when totaling a family's assets for federal need analysis, but some higher-cost colleges use these assets to measure a family's ability to pay.

✔ **Start your own home business.** Some parents, who have always wanted to operate a little business from home, reduce assets by making capital investments in their enterprise. The business, which is unlikely to make money in the initial years, probably will result in a tax deduction as well as more aid for their child. (*Warning:* Some colleges discount paper losses.)

Caveats when shifting assets

Keep the following caveats in mind when applying for financial aid:

✔ **Some of the preceding strategies carry risk.**

You could lose your investment in your home business, for instance.

✔ **Tax accountants and financial planners can slash your aid eligibility.**

Accountants and planners who lack in-depth knowledge of college financing can torpedo your chances to receive aid. Certain income strategies, such as shifting money to a child's account, may work well for long-term tax reduction planning but are ill-advised for the college years unless your income precludes grant aid eligibility.

✔ **Before moving money out of a kid's name and stashing it in the parent's name, double check that the transfer passes two acid tests:**

- Do not transfer any asset until you determine that the action will give you the increased-aid-eligibility results you seek.

- Is the move legal with the IRS? Ask your accountant or the bank involved to be sure that no rules are broken.

A Plan for the Long Haul! Way to Go!

When you get into the college financial aid game, approach it with a four-year plan that allows you to shift assets and avoid eating beans when tuition deadlines strike, as the following story illustrates.

Both of Hilton's parents worked and were proud that they could send their son to an Illinois name-brand university. But last year, when Hilton, a sophomore, returned home to Maryland for the December break, they broke staggering news:

> *Mom lost her job. We can't afford to send you back to your school for the spring semester. Sorry, we'll try again in the fall.*

Hilton's family had not sought college financial aid when he graduated from high school, assuming that their family income — $78,000 — was too high to qualify for more than good wishes. And Hilton was neither scholar, jock, nor talented musician, so the idea that a "good" school would offer Hilton a bundle of money to grace its campus was unlikely. What's more, the family found the complex financial aid process to be just too much trouble.

Hilton's parents had saved a few dollars and assumed that with their jobs and careful money management, they could handle Hilton's college. They would deal with the tuition year by year.

All went as anticipated until Mom lost her job and Hilton's college costs threatened to sink the family. Good news: Mom landed another job within a few months, and Hilton returned to his college in the fall. Bad news: Hilton unnecessarily lost a semester of school because he failed to file an emergency appeals letter with his school. He didn't know he could.

The moral to Hilton's story is apparent:

- ✔ Learn as much as you can about the college financial aid system.

- ✔ Use that knowledge to plan how to pay for all your college years.

- ✔ Ask questions; don't assume.

Beyond an unexpected financial crunch and lost time, you need a four-year family college financial plan for other reasons, too — not the least of which is to allow yourself adequate time to plan how you will shift assets and increase your family's share of the aid money.

Devise a four-year plan (a computer-generated spreadsheet is useful) that realistically addresses your anticipated cash flow over the next four years based on your best estimate of three factors: your income from all sources, your family's expected school and living costs, and your hoped-for financial aid (based on your research after reading this book). If glaring gaps appear between what you think you need for college and your financial resources, start now to think of solutions. Waiting until the midnight hour to solve your problem is an invitation to trouble. To review the essential ingredients in the financial aid process, see the Cheat Sheet at the front of this book.

The Aid Chase: It's Not Over until It's Over

Here's why you should ignore the advice of financial aid nonprofessionals who come to the party dressed as experts: When school financial aid counselors award aid, they consider every situation individually. Awards depend on the size of the college's aid kitty at the time you apply and your specific circumstances. Would you have guessed that families with six-figure incomes could get aid? They do.

At Amherst, for instance, where yearly tuition and living costs are in the $30,000 neighborhood, 50 families earning between $90,000 and $105,000 last year received about $13,000 each, of which about half was gift money that doesn't need to be repaid. The remainder was given in low-interest loans and work-study jobs. That's not all. Sixteen families that earn more than $135,000 scored an average of $11,000 in aid per year, about half in gift money. Being called "needy" when you belong to a six-figure family isn't all that unusual at Amherst. Nearly 80 percent of applicants in the $90,000-plus group received aid; in the higher bracket (up to $135,000), 32 percent scored awards.

In the curious process of college financial aid, assuming that you don't qualify for assistance for any price range of college is a big mistake. Assuming that you're out of the running is a sure way to cheat yourself. In the financial aid game, our advice is:

Play out your hand until the game is over.

Chapter 2

What If You're Adult, Part-Time, International, or Other?

Moving forward on a financial aid journey when you're a part of the traditional crowd — attending full-time college on campus in your home country in your teens or early 20s — is difficult enough, even though your pathway is well marked and you know what to expect.

However, seeking aid funds when you're a nontraditional learner set apart from the crowd is a more challenging task altogether, because you may not know where your pathway *begins*, much less how it twists and turns.

This chapter is for learners who don't fit the traditional mold.

Who Are Today's Typical College Students?

Colleges today are filled with students who don't fit yesteryear's stereotype of "teenaged high school graduates entering college full-time for studying and partying." And contemporary college students don't necessarily congregate on the ivy-leafed campus your father knew (although your father and your grandfather may be on campus along with you!). Consider the new scenarios:

✔ **Adult at risk:** At 47, Dan is a successful and talented craftsworker in the construction trades. But Dan frets about the future, worrying that he's getting too old to continue the heavy lifting that his work requires. Is construction management the answer? Can Dan afford to go after the construction-focused college degree that many companies now demand?

✔ **Part-time wake-up call:** Twenty-seven-year-old Kelly's two children are now in school. Kelly dropped out of a community college after high school because she said, "I wasn't sure what I wanted to do." She traveled around the country working as a waitress; she fell in love, and married a coworker. Kelly plans to stay home for another few years but worries that her beginner's skimpy accounting skills, acquired at the community college, are inadequate for today's tough job market. She'd like to study part time, but her family's budget is stretched as thin as the rubber band that keeps her bills together. The cost of babysitters, as well as tuition, is more than Kelly can handle. Can Kelly receive financial aid to study part time?

✔ **College without a campus:** David's on an unsuccessful archaeology dig in a remote mountainous area. He knows he needs graduate credentials to advance in his field, so he's been looking into using his computer as a distance-learning campus. David's earnings are as sparse as the expedition's findings. Paying for college online has him stumped. Can David reap aid for virtual study?

✔ **World-class student:** Chang's family has decided that he would benefit from obtaining a graduate engineering education in the United States. Chang's Korean family can get most of the money together for his studies but they are short about $10,000. Is all financial aid for U.S. colleges saved for U.S. citizens? Or is help available for this international student who wants an American graduate college education?

✔ **American in Paris:** Ever since she was a young girl of eight, Rosemary had her heart set on studying art in Paris. But her father, a high school teacher, and mother, a paralegal, were responsible for the nursing-home bills of Rosemary's grandmother, as well as bringing up Rosemary and her brother. For Americans, studying overseas is an unrealistic goal unless you're well-heeled. Or is it? Can student aid save Rosemary's dream?

Dan, Kelly, David, Chang, and Rosemary represent the new faces in higher education today. for lack of a better term, we'll call them *nontraditional*, though they're certainly not uncommon.

Exploding numbers of nontraditional students are changing the profile of the prototypical American student. Collectively, the majority of all American undergraduates now fit nontraditional descriptions — they're not in the bloom of youth, not full time, not campus-bound, not hailing from within the borders of the United States, and not staying on their side of an ocean to study. Part-time students alone now account for more than 30 percent of the nation's undergraduates.

Although some overlap is unavoidable, nontraditional students generally fit into one of five categories:

- ✔ **Full-time adults,** for whom a workplace focus often spurs an effort to seek new skills or make a career change.

- ✔ **Part-time students,** holding onto their day jobs or family duties as they slog it out in the halls of academe.

- ✔ **Off-campus students,** who crack the books in distance-education programs, sitting in front of a computer or learning via television, telephone, or postal mail.

- ✔ **International students,** who recognize that the borderless economies of the world translate into a need for education beyond borders; often their learning destination of choice is the United States.

- ✔ **American students who travel outside the United States,** finding that an educational exchange of ideas flows two ways. Privileged families of old sent their offspring to spend a "junior year abroad." Now, society's rank and file think that an international experience may be just what the competitive workplace ordered.

Nontraditional students have a catalog of special problems, from getting off work in time to study, to child care, to getting a visa, to getting health insurance. But for all five groups, no problem looms larger than paying for college. We discuss the money angle one group at a time.

Adult Students: Paying the Back-to-College Tab

Jerry Fushianes, PA-C, is a certified physician assistant who recently graduated from the University of Detroit Mercy, a private Catholic institution. Jerry entered graduate school to build on his old career of paramedic.

Here's how he describes his quest for higher education: After being in the workplace for several years, Jerry became "very excited" about going back to school. "Until I learned what it cost!" he adds. "The University of Detroit Mercy is one of the most expensive PA (physician assistant) schools out there. The cost is $470 per credit hour, making my tuition bill over $6,500 per semester, including books and fees."

The hard realities of coming up with that kind of money sent Jerry scurrying to the university's financial aid office: "No two ways about it, I just couldn't afford retraining."

Jerry's first clue that his dream was reachable was when he received a $2,000 grant from the state of Michigan, a benefit available to all the state's students who attend a private university. The eligibility requirements for the state grant were, according to Jerry, "a pulse and an acceptance letter from a college."

Next, Jerry began to look at other opportunities. He found Harper Hospital in Detroit, which would trade $6,000 per year for two years' service after graduation. Jerry took that as well and revved up his financial aid hunting: "I looked at civic and religious organizations for sponsorship. I came up dry. So I took out both subsidized and unsubsidized loans."

Then he received a scholarship from the Physician Assistant Foundation for $2,000. Jerry's aid hunt was a hit! He totaled up his costs and income.

How does Jerry feel about his experience? "Student aid for adults is real and very attainable. And I had a job waiting for me when I graduated," he says.

The newly minted physician assistant doesn't seem worried about paying back the $50,000 in student loans. He jumped right in and took two jobs to pay his loans off quickly, working nights at Harper Hospital and days at The Family Doctor, a family medical practice. Good thinking!

Jerry is one of the nearly half of today's college students who are over the age of 25, a figure up from one-third in 1974. Jerry already had a bachelor's degree when he began his return trip for a master's degree to become a physician assistant. Some students need only a stray course or two to flesh out workplace skills, but most are angling for the bachelor's degree they didn't take seriously when they dropped out years ago.

Whatever the motivation or career field, here's the key fact to remember if you are an older student headed back to college: The mechanics of obtaining student financial aid are exactly the same for adults 25 years or older as for younger students in the traditional age group of 18 to 22.

In fact, you can get in on the new college savings plans, too. Suppose that you're a 20-something single. Open an account for yourself, claim state income tax deductions, and use the money for graduate school. If you change your mind, skip school, and start a family, you can name your child as beneficiary.

Jerry's total two-year PA education costs:

Tuition	$33,480
School expenses	$2,500
Living expenses	$33,000
Total costs	$68,980

Jerry's financial aid figures:

State tuition grant ($2,000 x 2 yrs.)	$4,000
Harper Hospital ($6,000 x 2 yrs.)	$12,000
PA Foundation	$2,000
Student loans	$50,000
Total financial aid	$68,000

How to receive more than the standard Stafford loan in a calendar year

Jerry's loan amounts are more than the norm. Briefly, here's what happened: The U.S. Department of Education requires postsecondary educational institutions to establish a *standard academic year (AY)* for awarding federal aid.

Colleges have two choices. They may choose to standardize with a calendar year, in which all students begin and end at the same time; this type of AY is called a *scheduled academic year (SAY)*.

Or they may choose another type of AY that permits students to start when they wish and progress at their own speed, which is called a *borrower-based academic year (BBAY)*. After the student completes the required number of credit or clock hours, the student can be considered for the next grade level of loan eligibility, which permits a second loan to be awarded within a shorter time period than is true for a student in a SAY program.

Thus, when a college uses the BBAY, a graduate student can indeed receive an additional $9,250 within a 12-month period of time.

In neither SAY nor BBAY programs can a student receive more than the total allowed under the federal student loan program — for undergraduate studies, the total is $23,000, and for graduate studies, $65,500.

Beware of phony college degrees

People who are stalled in their careers because they lack a needed educational credential and can't find the money to pay for it may be tempted to take the easy way out — buying a degree facsimile from a degree mill.

Degree mills usually claim to have libraries, classrooms, and other essential facilities, but the truth is that they have a couple of desks and telephones. Their professors are untrained or nonexistent. Admission requirements are such that anyone who breathes can earn a doctorate (highest academic degree).

Fake colleges often advertise in small ads that look legitimate in magazines and newspapers. Some mills advertise on the Internet. Sometimes they claim to be "accredited." The so-called accrediting agency is a work of fiction concocted by mill operators.

Employers are smarter about degree mills than you may suspect. At the hiring stage, if you try to float a worthless degree, you'll be passed over; later, discovery of your questionable credentials may result in job termination.

Here are two ways to separate the bogus from the beautiful:

- If you're studying to get or upgrade a job or obtain a license to work, call a few employers' human resource departments and ask if the company ever hires graduates of the school in question.

- Be sure the school is accredited by a recognized accrediting body. The U.S. Department of Education maintains a list of these bodies and you can verify your school's accreditation by calling 1-800-4FEDAID.

Part-Time Students: Aid Is Uphill but Climbing

When your numbers are high enough, people listen more attentively to your needs. Now that part-time students warm nearly one-third of college undergraduate seats, more states pay attention to giving grant money to this long-ignored group of students. Funding the part-timers — still a fraction of student aid spending — seems to be gaining political support.

More than a dozen states have recently considered proposals to juice up financial assistance to part-timers, reports the *Chronicle of Higher Education*. Maryland, Indiana, Massachusetts, and Missouri have continued or expanded fledgling financial aid programs aimed at part-timers. Others — Florida and South Carolina — are focused on ensuring that part-timers can collect on some scholarship programs. Still other states are in the talking stages of making aid accessible to people whose job or family obligations limit the time they can spend on studies.

Not all states are so enlightened, despite the fact that in a technology-driven world, adults must run faster and faster just to stay in place. Your argument (it's true): This nation *needs* better educated workers.

Part-timers — who are typically women or ethnic minority students attending public community colleges — are technically eligible for most financial aid programs if they attend college at least half time (even less for Pell grants). In real life, financial aid officers favor full-time students, disbursing only leftover dollars, if any, to students who take less than a full load of classes.

Our advice to part-timers: Don't be easily discouraged if a school tells you to fend for yourself. Hang on and seek scholarships/grants from employers and private loan organizations to lift you out of the hole you find yourself occupying.

Uncovering the Money for Distance Learning

Distance education is soaring as the world marches double-time to faster and faster drummers. Funding to pay for distance learning isn't soaring to keep up; however, it is gaining altitude. The 1998 Amendments to the Higher Education Act of 1965 law says the time is here to recognize that students whose computers are their classrooms need financial help, too.

Although online computer study is driving the distance-education bus, you can also earn an undergraduate or advanced degree at honest-to-goodness accredited colleges and universities through television, telephone, videocassette, and postal mail programs. Off-campus programs vary in cost but usually compare favorably to on-campus study. A bachelor's degree at a virtual university often costs $30,000 to $40,000, but a few schools offer them for under $15,000, particularly state schools. A master's from a private institution may be priced at $15,000.

Here are key 1998 amendments to the Higher Education Act — a sign-of-the-times federal legislation:

✔ For a pilot study involving a limited group of institutions, the amendments waive federal regulations that disallow student aid for distance-education programs. To start, waivers affect 15 colleges or consortia of colleges for the 1999–2000 school year, and another 35 colleges or consortia two years later. Colleges must be institutions that are eligible to receive federal student aid funds (all Title IV schools). Foreign institutions can't participate. The much publicized consortium of western state colleges, Western Governors University, is included in the first batch.

✔ The Secretary of Education must annually evaluate the distance-education student aid funding and report on the number and types of students pursuing certificates and degrees through distance-education programs.

We predict that, if all goes well with the demonstration study, student aid funding for distance education will swell dramatically in the years ahead.

In the meantime, here's a quick tally of what you must know to tap federal distance-education funds today:

✔ You must be a candidate for a degree. Skipping around with a course here and there won't make you eligible for federal funding.

✔ You must sign up for at least half-time study (a minimum of six credit hours). Technically you can receive Pell grant funds if you're less than a half-time student, but in real life, you really need to be a half-time student.

✔ You must choose a course or program that is accredited by the U.S. Department of Education through an accrediting body that the DOE recognizes. The institution you choose for distance learning may not pass accreditation muster for several reasons, ranging from the quality of its offerings to the unfortunate rule that an institution doesn't qualify for federal aid if more than half of its courses are offered via telecommunications.

If you and your program meet these requirements, you are eligible for the same federal student aid programs available to resident students, except for a few fine-print qualifiers that your potential school's financial aid chief should know.

You begin your quest for financial aid by applying at the school's financial aid office, just as you would if you were physically on campus (see Chapter 3).

Other than federal funds, most student aid resources, from scholarships to loans, are technically available to distance learners. The problem is the same as with part-time learners — your aid comes from the bottom of the barrel, after the school has already awarded funds to full-time, on-campus students.

Can Your Boss Send You to College?

Maybe you need a year or two more of college to finish your bachelor's degree, or you want to earn a graduate or professional degree. In these uncertain times, you can never have too many marketable skills polished by solid education and training.

If you're getting your education bit by bit over a period of years, rather than in one straight line through college, maybe you should try to find an employer who's willing to foot the bill.

Educational Aassistance programs (EAPs) are more commonly found in sizable companies than in small firms. Such industries as insurance, hospitals, and public utilities are among those that offer the most generous EAPs, according to an annual survey by the Chamber of Commerce of the United States. Fewer than half of retailers offer EAPs, and manufacturing plants aren't high on education benefits either:

- **Who pursues degrees?** Studies by the National Association of Independent Colleges and Universities show the following statistics: Of employees who go to college on the employer's nickel, 33 percent pursue associate (two-year) degrees, 23 percent pursue bachelor's degrees, 22 percent pursue master's degrees, and 13 percent pursue certificates (any post-secondary level study).

- **Must you repay tuition with service?** Employers want to be sure they get a return on their educational investments. Don't be surprised if your employer asks you to sign an agreement stating that you'll repay the company if you depart the premises before a specific period of time.

- **How many employers offer tuition assistance?** Surveys vary, but apparently a majority of employers provide some form of tuition assistance to their employees. Two studies say as many as 90 percent of employers pay for all types of education assistance programs.

  Two other recent studies say that seven out of ten employers reimburse employees for courses that are part of a degree program, with slightly more covering bachelor's degree programs than graduate programs.

- **What percentage of tuition costs are reimbursed?** Most employers reimburse employees for the tuition bill, rather than pay it outright. About half of employers return 100 percent of tuition costs, 18 percent reimburse between 50 percent and 90 percent, while the remaining 30 percent refund less than 50 percent. Almost all employers insist that you get at least a C in a course before you see a dime.

- **Do only full-time employees get EAP help?** Only one quarter of employers pay tuition benefits to part-timers.

- **How can you prospect for EAP-friendly employers?** Check company Web sites for employee benefit statements. Anonymously call human resource offices and ask about education benefits for employees.

Do you have to pay taxes when your company pays tuition?

Companies offer two kinds of EAP funding: funding for courses that are specifically job-related and funding for courses that are for general employee self-improvement (such as getting your college degree).

The first category — funds for job-related courses — are tax-free to employees and a business expense to employers. When your company says, "Go get training to do your job," you go get training, end of discussion.

But the second category — funds to complete a degree or certificate for self-improvement with some relationship to your job, or what is termed Section 127 in the U.S. Tax Code — is

the more ambiguous form of EAP. For 20 years, companies have been able to deduct employee tuition reimbursement as a business expense, and employees have been able to escape paying taxes on it as long as the annual per-student expense was no higher than a given cap. The current cap is $5,250 per year. The law granting this tax break is not permanent; Congress must reauthorized it every three years or so. The 1997 reauthorization again permits tax-free, employer-provided educational assistance for undergraduate courses that begin before June 1, 2000. Remember, the tax-free benefits don't apply to graduate courses.

International Students: Destination USA

Are you a citizen of a country outside the United States who is thinking, "Hmmmn . . . I'd love to study at a U.S. college or university if only I had the funds to do so?" With perseverance, you may be able to gather the funds you need.

Starting on the home front

Start your mission in your home country. Begin with the premise that you will gather your own money in your country before shipping out. Of the half-million students who come to the United States from abroad each year to attend college, some 80 percent of undergraduate students and nearly 50 percent of graduate students accumulate the funds from their own resources and those of their families, according to NAFSA: Association of International Educators. Some international students receive funding from their governments, which usually expect them back home when school's over.

The very few scholarships awarded from within U.S. borders to internationals may only be granted while you're in your home country; you often become ineligible once you reach U.S. shores.

Whatever methods you use to collect educational funds, have a plan to pay for the entire four years or you may have to pack up and ship out after a year or so. A few institutions of higher education require that international students provide proof of funding for the entire planned period of study.

Targeting undergraduate stateside student aid

The deepest pockets of funding for students from abroad are the colleges and universities themselves. In a recent year, the schools gave international students nearly $147 million, according to reports filed with the College Board. Table 2-1 identifies the top 15 U.S. *undergraduate* student international aid givers; collectively, they awarded more than $50 million to students from afar in the 1997–98 school year.

Table 2-1 Top Aid-Giving Schools for International Undergraduates

College	Number Students	Number Int'natl	Dollars Awarded to Int'natl	Number Given Aid
1. Harvard & Radcliff	6,630	450	$7,515,315	311
2. Massachusetts Institute of Technology	4,363	334	$5,220,054	201
3. Mount Holyoke	1,810	194	$ 4,776,117	183
4. Univ. of Pennsylvania	11,404	847	$ 3,750,000	150
5. Middlebury	2,087	141	$3,445,950	137
6. Princeton	4,600	243	$3,300,000	150
7. Dartmouth	3,932	326	$3,165,360	132
8. Macalester	1,727	193	$2,589,048	168
9. Brown	5,751	390	$2,544,594	101
10. Eastern Michigan	17,528	457	$2,210,200	430
11. Clark	2,047	339	$2,109,376	184
12. Smith	2,630	201	$1,956,816	107
13. Brandeis	2,976	153	$1,942,049	90
14. Stanford	6,427	311	$1,929,960	120
15. Franklin and Marshall	1,807	103	$1,819,125	77

(Source: Calculations by Dr. Herm Davis based on data in The College Board's College Handbook: International Student Handbook of U.S. Colleges, 1999. Data reflects schools with large international student funding programs or a significant ratio of international students who received financial assistance during the 1998-1999 academic school year.)

Financial aid information of all types is time-sensitive. The data in Table 2-1, the latest available, is significantly useful in targeting schools where you have a better-than-average chance of receiving institutional aid.

Table 2-2 provides a more comprehensive listing of more than 100 U.S. schools that provide financial aid to non-U.S. students.

Table 2-2	Undergraduates: Colleges that Award Significant Aid to International Students			
State/ College	*No. Students Enrolled*		*International Students*	
	College-Wide	*Int'natl*	*Total Dollars*	*Students Awarded*
ALABAMA				
Univ. of Alabama	14,287	435	$396,066	66
ARIZONA				
Arizona State University	32,537	1,266	$1,160,114	298
ARKANSAS				
Harding University	3,573	234	$1,166,928	168
Ouachita Baptist University	1,619	84	$334,776	74
CALIFORNIA				
California Inst. of Technology	904	84	$1,171,000	40
Menlo College	516	64	$153,506	31
Stanford University	6,427	311	$1,929,960	120
Thomas Aquinas College	219	33	$348,174	29
University of Redlands	1,415	78	$110,812	26
Whittier College	1,277	58	156,000	32
COLORADO				
Colorado College	1,999	50	$308,385	15
DELAWARE				
Wesley College	1,307	17	$10,000	5
DISTRICT OF COLUMBIA				
George Washington University	7,058	771	$796,280	68
Georgetown University	5,883	575	$400,000	20

State/College	No. Students Enrolled		International Students	
	College-Wide	Int'natl	Total Dollars	Students Awarded
FLORIDA				
Bethune-Cookman College	2,523	110	$20,000	20
Eckerd College	1,443	186	$910,296	141
Florida Atlantic University	13,589	612	$841,039	287
Florida Institute of Technology	1,820	512	$716,595	129
Florida Southern College	1,775	77	$430,716	66
Lynn University	1,638	258	$908,215	77
University of Miami	7,955	770	$846,763	103
University of South Florida	23,489	427	$738,072	162
University of Tampa	2,292	203	$83,835	23
GEORGIA				
Mercer University	3,886	174	$234,187	75
HAWAII				
University of Hawaii (Manoa)	11,782	606	$300,000	250
ILLINOIS				
Illinois Institute of Technology	1,677	241	$766,150	199
Illinois Wesleyan University	2,016	40	$103,422	11
Know College	1,149	102	$648,512	64
Monmouth College	1,036	52	$566,800	52
North Park College	1,528	112	$399,980	70
Principia College	534	70	$879,996	52
University of Chicago	3,684	194	$491,742	18
INDIANA				
Earlham College	1,025	44	$455,790	30
Goshen College	946	62	$433,000	80
Purdue University	28,607	1,296	$483,551	65
Tri-State University	1,102	140	$352,000	110
Wabash College	793	32	$520,800	31
IOWA				
Coe College	1,253	64	$269,442	37
Dordt College	1,283	172	$600,000	175
Drake University	3,368	153	$335,700	90

(continued)

Table 2-2 (continued)

State/College	No. Students Enrolled		International Students	
	College-Wide	Int'natl	Total Dollars	Students Awarded
LOUISIANA				
Louisiana State Univ. A & M	21,216	732	$1,716,352	506
Tulane University	6,699	329	$757,570	55
MAINE				
Bates College	1,611	31	$462,672	17
Bowdoin College	1,597	47	$542,904	24
Colby College	1,753	96	$872,009	53
MARYLAND				
Hood College	900	25	$161,520	16
St. John's College	455	12	$324,700	17
Univ. of Maryland	23,784	817	$460,980	195
MASSACHUSETTS				
Amherst College	1,642	64	$891,501	39
Boston Conservatory	342	75	$324,940	55
Brandeis University	2,976	153	$1,945,080	90
Clark University	2,047	339	$2,109,376	184
Eastern Nazarene College	670	29	$228,000	29
Gordon College	1,348	24	$283,140	22
Harvard & Radcliff College	6,630	450	$7,515,315	311
Massachusetts Inst. of Technology	4,363	334	$5,277,054	201
Mount Holyoke College	1,810	194	$4,776,117	183
Smith College	2,630	201	$1,956,816	107
Suffolk University	2,909	470	$431,208	106
Wellesley College	2,246	120	$969,874	38
Williams College	1,970	98	$547,350	25
MICHIGAN				
Eastern Michigan University	17,528	457	$2,210,200	430
Kalamazoo College	1,241	28	$6,000	5
MICHIGAN				
Michigan Tech. University	5,542	275	$68,328	26

State/ College	No. Students Enrolled		International Students	
	College-Wide	Int'natl	Total Dollars	Students Awarded
MINNESOTA				
Concordia College (Moorhead)	2,858	81	$346,060	52
Gustavus Adolphus College	2,418	51	$274,008	42
Macalester College	1,727	193	$2,589,048	168
St. Olaf College	2,845	66	$1,014,993	63
University of St. Thomas	4,888	53	$287,232	32
MISSISSIPPI				
University of Southern Mississippi	11,821	195	$308,884	68
MISSOURI				
College of the Ozarks	2,763	35	$312,800	34
St. Louis University	6,110	533	$142,738	46
Truman State University	5,957	140	$111,782	61
University of Missouri (Kansas City)	5,572	282	$278,635	133
Washington University	5,493	410	$463,535	55
NEW HAMPSHIRE				
Dartmouth College	3,932	326	$3,165,360	132
NEW JERSEY				
Princeton University	4,600	243	$3,300,000	150
NEW YORK				
Colgate University	2,842	66	$1,141,492	44
Columbia Univ.- Columbia Col.	3,763	146	$856,581	33
D'Youbille College	1,149	110	$404,393	97
Hamilton College	1,694	61	$868,052	41
Hartwick College	1,493	48	$418,416	23
Hobart & William Smith College	1,829	33	$363,180	30
Hofstra University	8,568	317	$70,265	23
Ithaca College	5,556	105	$877,566	74

(continued)

Table 2-2 *(continued)*

State/ College	No. Students Enrolled		International Students	
	College-Wide	Int'natl	Total Dollars	Students Awarded
NEW YORK				
Manhattan School of Music	408	126	$429,900	50
Parsons School of Design	1,788	581	$735,420	140
Rochester Institute of Technology	9,418	417	$215,028	66
St. John's University	11,960	295	$654,357	79
St. Lawrence University	1,892	123	$1,326,797	61
University of Rochester	4,533	244	$10,670	136
Vassar College	2,361	71	$1,000,316	46
NORTH DAKOTA				
Jamestown College	1,072	99	$255,956	61
OHIO				
Cleveland Institute of Music	220	43	$276,055	31
College of Wooster	1,700	123	$1,515,125	115
Denison University	2,022	91	$1,160,675	85
Franciscan Univ. of Steubenville	1,579	121	$167,915	71
Kenyon College	1,536	30	$376,442	22
Miami University (Oxford)	14,594	129	$13,600	4
Mount Union College	1,844	62	$194,712	42
Ohio Wesleyan University	1,870	192	$1,483,000	114
OREGON				
Lewis & Clark College	1,764	99	$390,984	44
Linfield College	2,427	62	$17,657	17
Reed College	1,276	42	$365,904	18
PENNSYLVANIA				
Allegheny College	1,855	28	$365,904	16
Bryn Mawr College	1,182	106	$1,047,592	56
Dickinson College	1,792	85	$522,795	21
Elizabethtown College	1,703	36	$285,384	33
Franklin and Marshall College	1,807	103	$1,819,125	77
Gettysburg College	2,102	42	$360,000	20

State/College	No. Students Enrolled		International Students	
	College-Wide	Int'natl	Total Dollars	Students Awarded
PENNSYLVANIA				
Lafayette College Shippensburg Univ. of PN	2,129	73	$959,146	46
Slippery Rock Univ. of PN	5,602	46	$220,600	25
Univ. of PN	6,337	185	$941,082	134
Swarthmore College	1,362	75	$944,580	39
Univ. of Pennsylvania	11,404	847	$3,750,000	150
RHODE ISLAND				
Brown University	5,751	390	$2,544,594	101
Columbia Bible College	476	17	$296,416	17
TENNESSEE				
University of the South	1,257	27	$375,377	17
TEXAS				
Abilene Christian University	3,840	187	$528,210	90
Ambassador University	860	177	$716,396	170
Southern Methodist University	5,314	125	$498,438	86
Texas Christian University	6,163	190	$892,186	122
University of Houston	22,367	894	$1,073,840	248
University of Texas (Arlington)	17,897	431	$240,344	355
VERMONT				
Bennington College	347	39	$879,396	38
Middlebury College	2,087	141	$3,445,950	137
VIRGINIA				
Liberty University	5,804	240	$1,181,760	192
WASHINGTON				
Whitman College	1,375	30	$291,744	18
WEST VIRGINIA				
West Virginia Wesleyan College	1,569	72	$369,600	42
WISCONSIN				
Beloit College	1,159	134	$888,624	68
Lawrence University	1,127	83	$1,226,212	90

(Source: The College Board, The International Student Handbook of U.S. Colleges, 1999)

Most of the available U.S.-sponsored financial aid that doesn't require you to be a U.S. citizen or permanent resident comes from the colleges themselves.

Graduates pull in more aid than undergraduates

Graduate students outrank undergrads when schools hand out U.S. student money. Table 2-3 lists the top 20 graduate schools that give aid to international students.

Table 2-3	Graduate Aid: The 20 Schools that Award the Most Aid to International Graduate Students			
State/ College	*No. Students Enrolled*		*International Students*	
	College-Wide	*Int'natl*	*Total Dollars*	*Students Awarded*
1. Cornell University	4,288	1,572	$21,518,000	742
2. Arizona State University	10,320	1,435	$13,212,010	1,091
3. Boston University	8,348	1,895	$13,127,918	907
4. University of California: Berkeley	7,509	1,127	$10,961,565	1115
5. University of Notre Dame	1,881	535	$10,178,244	438
6. Johns Hopkins University	1,366	459	$9,959,841	459
7. Louisiana State A & M	5,040	1,029	$7,956,000	975
8. Vanderbilt University	3,234	446	$7,120,064	365
9. Oklahoma State University	4,329	992	$6,822,730	862
10. University of Miami	3,140	636	$3,570,720	430
11. Dartmouth College	955	80	$3,430,448	109
12. New Jersey Institute of Technology	3,138	848	$3,255,917	373
13. North Carolina State University	6,083	928	$2,893,728	591

State/ College	No. Students Enrolled		International Students	
	College-Wide	Int'natl	Total Dollars	Students Awarded
14. Georgetown University	3,486	734	$2,754,430	190
15. Iowa State University	4,260	1,380	$1,856,406	1,362
16. St. John's University	3,553	433	$1,733,223	201
17. Auburn University	2,767	474	$3,063,448	334
18. SUNY at Binghamton	2,696	446	$1,585,164	226
19. Maharishi, University of	577	185	$1,380,001	137
20. Medical College of Ohio	406	124	$1,176,000	98

(Source: The College Board, The International Student Handbook of U.S. Colleges, 1999)

"By far, the most scholarship dollars go to Ph.D. students at USC," says Mary E. Randall, associate dean and director of graduate education and admissions. "We award virtually no funds to undergraduates; a small amount goes to master's candidates; the lion's share goes to doctoral candidates in the form of teaching and research assistantships. These are awarded only to the cream of the crop, the very best students. We present aid to internationals because we attract the finest minds in the world and create a stimulating environment for all our students. Our international learners add cultural richness to our student body and help prepare our graduates to work in a worldwide economy."

Table 2-4 lists U.S. schools that award significant amounts to international graduate students. Graduate aid tends to be academic-based, not need-based.

Table 2-4	Graduate Aid: Universities Awarding Significant Aid to International Graduate Students			
State/College	**No. Students Enrolled**		**International Students**	
	College-Wide	**Int'natl**	**Total Dollars**	**Students Awarded**
ALABAMA				
Auburn Univ.	2,767	474	$5,063,448	384
Tuskegee	172	23	$112,280	14
ARIZONA				
Arizona State University	10,3320	1,435	$13,212,010	1,091
CALIFORNIA				
Monterey Inst. of International Studies	761	278	$522,720	88
San Francisco Conservatory of Music	100	36	$192,593	17
University of California: Berkeley	7509	1,127	$10,961,565	1,115
University of San Francisco	2,616	315	$197,017	40
COLORADO				
University of Colorado (Boulder)	4,165	606	$523,000	40
University of Northern Colorado	2,207	68	$156,320	40
CONNECTICUT				
University of Bridgeport	1,110	142	$129,792	39
DISTRICT OF COLUMBIA				
Catholic Univ. of America	2,317	334	$1,181,620	131
Georgetown University	3,486	734	$2,754,430	190
FLORIDA				
Florida Atlantic University	3,131	234	$1,185,444	176
Florida Institute of Technology	2,292	251	$666,001	66
Florida International U.	5,876	527	$888,350	218
Florida State University	6,075	496	$345,002	133
University of Miami	3,140	636	$3,570,720	430
University of Florida	7,876	447	$751,875	266

State/College	No. Students Enrolled		International Students	
	College-Wide	Int'natl	Total Dollars	Students Awarded
HAWAII				
Univ. of Hawaii (Manoa)	4,879	911	$150,010	70
ILLINOIS				
Bradley University	945	260	$ 253,266	102
Eastern Illinois University	1,552	61	$151,970	35
INDIANA				
Rose-Hulman Institute of Tech.	170	95	$276,066	42
University of Notre Dame	1,881	535	$10,178,244	438
IOWA				
Maharishi, Univ. of	577	185	$1,380,001	137
Iowa State Univ.	4,260	1,380	$1,856,406	1,362
LOUISIANA				
Louisiana State Univ. A & M	5,040	1,029	$7,956,000	975
MARYLAND				
Johns Hopkins Univ.	1,366	459	$9,959,841	459
Johns Hopkins Univ. (Peabody Conservatory of Music)	335	157	$907,215	93
MASSACHUSETTS				
Boston Conservatory	121	50	$164,250	34
Boston University	8,348	1,895	$13,127,918	907
Suffolk University	1,491	150	$427,600	50
MICHIGAN				
Michigan Technology Univ.	628	264	$521,196	176
MINNESOTA				
Univ. of Minnesota (Duluth)	435	102	$964,972	76
MISSISSIPPI				
U. of Southern Mississippi	2,778	151	551,232	116

(continued)

Table 2-4 *(continued)*

State/ College	No. Students Enrolled		International Students	
	College-Wide	**Int'natl**	**Total Dollars**	**Students Awarded**
MISSOURI				
St. Louis University	3,003	292	142,748	46
Univ. of Missouri, St. Louis	2,563	98	$442,212	86
NEW HAMPSHIRE				
Dartmouth College	955	180	$3,430,448	109
NEW JERSEY				
New Jersey Institute of Technology	3,138	848	$3,255,917	373
NEW MEXICO				
NM Institute of Mining and Tech.	258	87	$124,504	79
NEW YORK				
Cornell Univ.	4,288	1572	$21,518,000	742
Manhattan School	426	175	$578,612	68
St. John's University	3,553	433	$1,733,223	201
SUNY at Binghamton	2,696	446	$1,585,164	226
NORTH CAROLINA				
North Carolina State University	6,083	928	$2,893,728	591
Univ. of NC (Charlotte)	2,689	227	$1,295,168	98
OHIO				
Medical College of Ohio	406	124	$1,176,000	98
Miami University	1,596	144	$643,310	115
OKLAHOMA				
Oklahoma State University	4,329	992	$6,822,730	862
OREGON				
Oregon Graduate Institute	474	120	$825,000	75
PENNSYLVANIA				
Duquesne University	2,967	280	$868,384	176

State/College	No. Students Enrolled		International Students	
	College-Wide	Int'natl	Total Dollars	Students Awarded
TEXAS				
Texas A & M University	6,774	1,942	$553,104	276
University of Houston (Houston)	6,618	3,600	$618,552	142
VIRGINIA				
Virginia Commonwealth Univ.	6,387	217	$918,222	86
WYOMING				
Univ. of Wyoming	2,207	180	$760,920	136

(Source: The College Board, International Student Handbook of U.S. Colleges, 1999)

Few major universities across the nation reported their financial aid for graduate international schools in this College Board survey, including three major California institutions with large international student populations: UC-Berkeley, University of Southern California, and UCLA. Even so, the survey shows funding to international graduate students of more than $100 million for the latest year surveyed! Who can doubt that money is available for international students?

If you're a star student, contact (by postal mail, e-mail, or telephone) the colleges in the U.S. that you'd like to attend. At each school, approach both the chairperson of the appropriate department and the director of financial aid or the international student adviser. You can get these names in education directories available at libraries and embassies. See Chapter 18 for more information about aid for graduate school education.

You can also scout out aid on the school's Web site; find a list of college and university Web sites on the Direct Hit Web site (www.directhit.com). Direct Hit is a new-generation search engine that also parks itself on various conventional search engines, such as HotBot (www.hotbot.com). Direct Hit lists the most popular Web sites for researching topics — in this case, two- and four-year colleges and universities. In the search box, type in **List of Colleges**.

Working your way through college

Don't expect to finance your study by working in the United States. The federal government has strict regulations against international students working off-campus during the first year; the rules aren't very liberal even after the first year.

Loans for international students

You may be able to find a U.S. bank that will give you a loan if a creditworthy U.S. citizen or permanent resident co-signs for the loan. Here is another source for loans:

The International Education Finance Corporation
424 Adams St.
Milton, MA 02186
888-296-IEFC (4332)
Internet: www.iefc.com

The International Education Finance Corporation (IEFC) is a unique, private firm that specializes in global loans for students. Details appear on the firm's Web site, but IEFC offers these two popular loan programs:

- ✔ **Canadian Higher Education Loan Program (CanHELP):** For Canadian citizens who wish to study at institutions in the United States
- ✔ **International Student Loan Program (ISLP):** For international students enrolled at U.S. schools

The money for both programs comes from the Bank of Boston and is guaranteed by The Education Resources Institute (TERI).

See Chapter 16 for information on becoming an educated borrower.

Information resources for international students

To find out about U.S.-sponsored aid that may be available to the international student, contact the following organizations:

✔ **The United States embassy or consulate in your home country**

✔ **Council on International Educational Exchange**
205 E. 42nd St.
New York, NY 10017
1-888-COUNCIL (268-6245)
Internet: www.ciee.org

Grants are limited to U.S. students.

✔ **Institute of International Education**
809 United Nations Plaza
New York, NY 10017-3580
212-883-8200
Internet: www.iie.org

✔ **NAFSA: Association of International Educators**
1307 New York Ave. NW, 8th Floor
Washington, DC 20005-4701
202-737-3699
Internet: www.nafsa.org

Previously called the National Association of Foreign Student Affairs, NAFSA's international educator members promote international educational exchange between the U.S. and the rest of the world. The organization offers information only and virtually no direct grants.

✔ **U.S. Information Agency**
Office of Public Liaison
301 Fourth St., Room 602
Washington, DC 20547
Internet: www.usia.gov (Educational and Cultural Affairs Bureau)

We have discussed only the highlights of aid for international students in this chapter. Other topics — exchange rates, visas, taxes, health insurance, filling out forms — are covered in various books (which we note at the end of this chapter) and on the following Web sites:

✔ **Aid for international students seeking to study in the U.S.:** EduPASS: The International Student's Guide to Studying and Living in the USA (www.edupass.org)

✔ **Aid for U.S. students seeking funding to study abroad:** FinAid's Study Abroad and Foreign Study Programs (www.finaid.com)

U.S. Students Going Abroad Can Get Traveling Money

With a few exceptions — such as Japan, Germany, and Canada — don't count on other nations' governments or private resources being too generous with their study money for noncitizens. Get your cash at home before hopping on a plane to schools abroad.

The basic guidelines for Americans who wish to be eligible for financial aid as they study abroad are the following:

> ✔ As a U.S. student who attends an accredited U.S. institution overseas as an extension of your stateside institution, you are eligible for the full range of federal financial aid programs. You may also be eligible for aid from your home school for study abroad; the home school sets its own policies for institutional aid.

> ✔ As a U.S. student who attends an international institution overseas, you are eligible for federal and private loan programs only, not for any gift aid.

The idea of an international experience thrills many American students until they find out that the old spoilsports who give out aid insist that you shoulder at least a half-time load at the foreign institution and receive credit toward your degree. You can't just coast along for enrichment.

Although only about 100,000 Americans study off U.S. shores each year, many helpful programs are available. To find out about aid that may be accessible to the American student who wants to study abroad, contact the following organizations:

> ✔ **American Institute for Foreign Study**
> 102 Greenwich Ave.
> Greenwich, CT 06830
> 800-727-2437
> www.aifs.com
>
> This organization arranges cultural exchange and study-abroad programs throughout the world for more than 40,000 students each year.

> ✔ **Council on International Educational Exchange**
> 205 E. 42nd St.
> New York, NY 10017
> 212-822-2600
> www.ciee.org

> ✔ **Institute of International Education (IIE)**
> 809 United Nations Plaza
> New York, NY 10017-3580
> 212-984-5380
> www.iie.org

✔ **NAFSA: Association of International Educators**
1307 New York Ave. NW, 8th Floor
Washington, DC 20005
202-737-3699
www.nafsa.org

Work Hard at Looking Hard for Money

Yes, even when you don't fit the mold of the traditional college student, you can pay for the education and training to end up where you want to be. Be prepared to work hard at looking hard.

Jerry Fushianes, PA-C, mentioned earlier in this chapter, recounts his first days at seeking aid, when a financial aid officer gave him superb advice:

> *Jerry, it's obvious you're going to need $20,000 a year in financial aid. If you want $20,000 in aid, you need to put $20,000 worth of effort into finding it.*

That financial aid counselor was so right.

Additional reading

✔ *A Selected List of Major Fellowship Opportunities and Aid to Advanced Education for Foreign Nationals.* National Academy of Sciences, Fellowship Office, 2101 Constitution Ave. NW, Washington, DC 20418; www4.nas.edu/nas/nashome.nsf

✔ *Financial Resources for International Study.* Institute of International Education, 1999; IIE Books, Box 371, Annapolis Junction, MD 20701, 800-445-0443; www.iie.org. Lists funding sources for U.S. students seeking support for study abroad.

✔ *Funding for U.S. Study: A Guide for International Students and Professionals.* Institute of International Education, 1999; IIE Books, Box 371, Annapolis Junction, MD 20701, 800-445-0443; www.iie.org. Lists 600 funding sources for graduate and postdoctorate international students seeking financial help for study in the U.S.

✔ *International Student Handbook of U.S. Colleges, 1999;* College Board Publications, 2 College Way, Forrester Center, WV 25438, 800-323-7155; www.collegeboard.org. Discusses financial aid facts and figures of about 3,000 colleges for international students.

✔ *Peterson's Scholarships for Study in the USA and Canada 2000* (for international students), 1999. Available at bookstores or from www.petersons.com.

Chapter 3

STARTERS: Decoding the Financial Aid System

*F*inancial aid supposedly goes to the students who need it the most. In actuality, it goes to those who best understand how to find it and apply for it, a process that has become more complicated over the years. In this chapter, we decode the financial aid application process for you. We also roll out the big pieces of the U.S. financial aid system in which the process takes place. After clearing the cobwebs from the basic structure of financial aid, the chapters following this one fine-tune the particulars of what you should know to cut the best deals you can in paying for college.

Understanding the Financial Aid Process

At first glance, the financial aid process seems simple enough:

✔ You fill out a financial aid application and send it to a central processing office in Illinois, where computers figure out how much your family can afford to pay for college.

✔ If your family's contribution is short of the mark, the government and the college help pay the difference, whether you're headed for Harvard or a bargain-priced state university.

In a perfect world, the process would be straightforward and easily deciphered. But simplicity in getting student financial aid is a myth.

Don't take "no" for an answer

If you're told "no" to something you want in your college's financial aid office by an employee (who may be no more experienced in the financial aid process than a work-study student who started this week), refuse to go away without pushing the envelope. Look at "no" as the first step on your road to "yes."

Here are three common "no" phrases to watch out for:

✔ No, you can't have an appointment.

✔ No, you haven't submitted the right information and documents to support your aid request.

✔ No, you can't appeal your case to anyone else.

You want to do your utmost to ward off those infuriating no's from office assistants by being sure that you submit all aid application documents on time and correctly filled out. When your applications are blemish-free and deadline-compliant, hold your ground if an office assistant dares utter a rude "no."

The "no" person may force you to adopt hardball tactics that we learned from Bill Murray. Or maybe it was Chevy Chase. Pleasantly mention that if someone doesn't come up with a "yes" soon, you'll have to dash home, grab your pet python, and bring it back to the financial aid office for a few cuddles. Ask them, with innocent eyes, "You do like big, wraparound snakes, don't you?"

Now we're deadly earnest: Most students don't appeal a turndown. That's their mistake. Don't let it be yours.

In fact, applying for college aid is one of the most complex and difficult financial experiences you may ever have.

An East-coast financial planner complains that he spends more time completing a college financial aid form than filling out a 1040 tax form. If you put the wrong figures in the wrong slots, or make some other innocent mistake that doesn't fully reflect an adjusted (reduced) income, your expected family contribution will be much higher than you anticipate, and you can miss out on enough aid to pay the difference.

The financial aid process is made even more difficult because of occurrences beyond your control. Your college's financial aid staff may give conflicting directives or penalize you by failing to update your account on their computers. Congress may not pass financial aid legislation quickly enough for the process to work smoothly. Your aid application may simply get lost.

Nothing about applying for college money is simple — and *you must understand the process.* When students are turned down for aid, it's often because of the following reasons:

> ✔ They failed to file an application on time — *they haven't learned the process.*
>
> ✔ They miss turning in a required document — *they haven't learned the process.*
>
> ✔ They don't know how to compete for resources — *they haven't learned the process.*

Learning the process is the real key to getting college financial aid. If you arm yourself with knowledge and make a four-year financing plan, you can get the education you want at a price that you can handle.

Demonstrated Need: The Key to Aid

What is financial need?

Need is the difference between what a student's family is expected to contribute and the total cost for one year of the college or university where a student hopes to enroll. Amazingly enough, the term for what a family is expected to contribute is called the *expected family contribution (EFC)*. Both the family contribution and the student contribution are included in the EFC.

Qualifying for financial aid depends on family income and assets, family size, how many parents work, age of the oldest parent, number of family members in college at the same time, and the cost of attendance.

To treat everyone as fairly as possible, everyone fills out the same instrument of torture, which is something like a tax form. The system used to determine the EFC is called the *Federal Methodology,* a need-analysis formula approved by the U.S. Congress. You arrive at your expected family contribution by filling in the blanks of a form called the *Free Application for Federal Student Aid (FAFSA)*, which we describe later in this chapter.

Under the Financial Aid Umbrella

In case you don't get enough freebie dollars — and face it, you probably won't — find out all you can about the disorganized, freewheeling financial aid system. Learn how the system works so that you can make the system work for you. Figure 3-1 shows a simple diagram of how the financial aid system is organized.

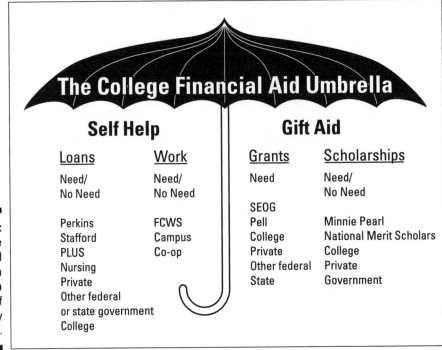

The College Financial Aid Umbrella

Self Help		Gift Aid	
Loans	Work	Grants	Scholarships
Need/	Need/	Need	Need/
No Need	No Need		No Need
		SEOG	
Perkins	FCWS	Pell	Minnie Pearl
Stafford	Campus	College	National Merit Scholars
PLUS	Co-op	Private	College
Nursing		Other federal	Private
Private		State	Government
Other federal			
or state government			
College			

Figure 3-1:
The financial aid umbrella covers a variety of money sources.

Self-help money

On the left side of the financial aid umbrella you find self-help financial aid, which includes *loans* and *work.*

Loans: Money you pay back

A *loan* for education is student financial aid that you or your parents must repay. Loans differ in their availability and repayment terms. Loans come in these three basic types:

- ✔ Federally subsidized or unsubsidized
- ✔ State subsidized
- ✔ Private or supplemental loans or lines of credit

Availability may or may not be based on your demonstrated need, as described earlier in the chapter. Here's the lowdown:

- ✔ **Need-based loans:** Loans in which the federal or state government subsidizes the interest payments require that you show financial need in order to obtain them.

> **Non-need-based loans:** You pay the full interest with no subsidies available to you or your family.

Loans come from a rich variety of sources:

- ✔ Government
- ✔ Colleges and universities
- ✔ Banks
- ✔ Foundations
- ✔ Organizations
- ✔ Employers
- ✔ Individuals

Figure 3-1 shows a sampling of loans: the Federal Perkins, Federal Stafford, and Federal PLUS loan programs, nursing, and private loan resources. We talk more about federal loan programs in Chapter 7.

Availability of a loan may or may not be related to you or your family's credit record and ability to repay. Commercial lenders usually take credit ratings and repayment potential into account before making an education loan, while government and nonprofit sources do not.

You or your family may be forced to start repayment of some loans while you're still in school, but you can delay repayment of others until you graduate and are out in the workplace making an income. For more about becoming an educated borrower, see Chapter 16.

Work: Earn as you learn

Well over half of those attending college have jobs to keep the money flowing in and to gain marketable work experience.

There's another good reason to be a working scholar: You may graduate on schedule. A new study of students who entered college in 1989 and graduated by 1994 reveals that only 59.7 percent of those who were not employed graduated, compared to 72.1 percent who worked 1 to 14 hours a week and 65.4 percent who worked 15 to 33 hours a week. (The results of the study, which was conducted by the National Center for Education Statistics, may indicate that workers have superior time management skills or the drive to finish what they start.)

The federal and state *work-study programs* are prime examples of work as student aid. The part-time (often 10 hours or less), campus-based jobs are usually for undergraduates, but graduates can sometimes arrange to join the work crowd. What kinds of jobs are on the work-study menu? Government program designers ambitiously aim to make the jobs appetizingly career oriented, but you may have to settle for a plain-fare grunt job. Students work during the academic year, and pay is usually the national minimum wage.

Other employment-based aid includes regular part-time jobs on or off campus, cooperative education that alternates classroom study with jobs, and paid internships. See Chapter 11 for more about working as your way to pay.

Gift money

Gifts — grants and scholarships — are everyone's favorite because you don't need to repay and the money is usually not taxable. Chapter 10 has more information about qualifying for gift aid.

Grants: No payback

A *grant* is based on need. Pell grants are the federal government's most ambitious gift program. Annual awards range from about $400 to $3,525 yearly, depending on the funds that Congress provides and the number of applicants. However, the Higher Education Act of 1998 has authorized, if not appropriated, the maximum Pell grant amount to $4,800 for 2000–2001, $5,100 for 2002–2003, and $5,800 for 2003–2004. Chapter 7 has more information about federal grant programs.

Scholarships: Your money to keep

Scholarships may or may not be awarded on the basis of need. *Merit* — how well you do during high school and college years in both grades and activities — is the basis for most undergraduate non-need-based awards.

Scholarships that are based on neither need nor merit may rely on uncommon criteria. As a single example, people who have a severe-to-profound bilateral hearing loss can apply for a $2,000 scholarship from the Minnie Pearl Scholarship Program administered by the EAR Foundation.

The Resource Guide at the back of this book lists a sampling of scholarship resources. Also see Chapter 8 for state aid awards.

The help comes bundled in packages

Student aid is delivered in a combination package:

- ✔ Loans (self-help)
- ✔ Work (self-help)
- ✔ Grants (gift money)
- ✔ Scholarships (gift money)

Everyone hopes for the gift side of the aid umbrella: The more free money, the better. Your aid package isn't a do-it-yourself project; your college's financial aid department puts the aid mix together.

Meet the Forms That Drive Financial Aid

Here's a list of forms you can't escape.

Free Application for Federal Student Aid (FAFSA)

The FAFSA is a universal need-analysis form. You use it to apply for all federal need-based aid. When you and your family have finished writing yards of answers to everything about your clan's financial status, you send your FAFSA to an official processor for the U.S. Department of Education (a government subcontractor in real life). A few weeks later, you receive a Student Aid Report that reveals the expected family contribution (EFC) figure. Each college to which you apply uses this information to determine your family's contribution.

To receive maximum aid, send your FAFSA form by February 15. (Each college determines its own deadline that you have to meet to receive maximum funding.)

Don't forget to fill out a renewal FAFSA for every year that you want federal aid.

The FAFSA is the only need-based application form required for federal student financial aid programs and the majority of state scholarship programs. The majority of all state institutions, as well as all two-year colleges and proprietary vocational-technical schools, use only the FAFSA for a need-analysis form.

The FAFSA is also used as the master application for Federal Stafford and Federal Direct loans (but not yet for the Federal PLUS loans).

Get a copy of FAFSA from your college's financial aid office, public library, or high school guidance counselor's office or on the Internet. Turn to the Resource Guide at the back of this book to see a real FAFSA.

Table 3-1 is a generalized guide to what a family of four at various levels of income is expected to pay to send one child to college for one year, in this case the 2000–2001 school year.

Table 3-1	Expected Family Contributions	
Income (before taxes)	Expected Family Contribution	
	1 student in college	2 students in college
$30,000	$1,200	$853
$35,000	$2,256	$1,379
$40,000	$3,313	$2,030
$45,000	$4,163	$2,440
$50,000	$5,681	$3,307
$55,000	$7,085	$4,036
$60,000	$8,777	$4,882
$65,000	$10,704	$5,845
$70,000	$11,691	$6,574
$75,000	$13,759	$7,373
$80,000	$14,605	$7,796
$85,000	$16,767	$8,877
$90,000	$17,989	$9,488
$95,000	$18,457	$9,722
$100,000	$19,679	$10,333

Source: The National College Scholarship Foundation

The figures in Table 3-1 are based on the assumption that one parent works and that the older parent is age 46 and the family has four members. If both parents work, or if one parent is older than 45, the expected contribution is lower. Net assets are presumed to be less than $43,500. If the family's assets are greater, the expected contribution is higher. Use the table as a warm-up to gain a quick idea of the amount of cash your family has to dig up for your schooling.

College Scholarship Service (CSS) Financial Aid Profile

Many high-cost colleges figure a family's expected contribution and ultimate need for aid two different ways — by using both the federal methodology system (FAFSA) and the institutional methodology system (College Scholarship Service Profile). The College Scholarship Service Profile is an institutional need-analysis service developed by members of the College Scholarship Services, a division of the nonprofit College Board. Expensive colleges

File your FAFSA on the Web

Are you a *do-it-this-very-minute* type of person? If so, you'll be glad to know that you can obtain and fill out the Free Application for Federal Student Aid (FAFSA online) and then transmit it via the Internet. The Web address is www.fafsa.ed.gov. One small detail: You still have to print out a signature page and mail it to the processor via the post office because, at this writing, the Department of Education doesn't accept digital alternatives.

What keeps your family's financial affairs hidden from snoopy hackers? The Department of Education, which originates the FAFSA, is using an encryption program to protect student data and ensures that DOE complies with the 1974 Family Education Rights and Privacy Act online.

How can you tell if your data is encoded? A quick clue is your browser. On Netscape Navigator, a picture of a key appears on screen in a lower corner; when the connection is securely coded, the key is whole, but when insecure, the key is broken. Internet Explorer shows a lock when the line is safely coded.

What's next: Until recently, the digital provision for federal student aid has flowed only one way — from you to the feds. You upload your FAFSA on the Net to the Department of Education, which responds to you by postal mail. But the transaction is going electronically interactive as the fed's *Access America for Students* program gears up to respond to your computer.

Access America for Students' one-stop service, now being piloted at a few colleges, not only e-mails you a report of your eligibility and permits your electronic signature (eliminating the need for you to send a postal-mail signature), but it also permits you to pay tuition, choose courses, buy books, file tax returns, and learn about jobs and internships — all online. See www.students.gov.

may use it for regular enrollment as well as for early-decision or early-action applicants. (See the glossary in the Resource Guide at the back of this book for definitions.)

The Profile assesses *all* assets of you and your family, such as equity in the home. Retirement accounts, insurance policy values, and the like are requested by some colleges to satisfy institutional awarding policies. The CSS Profile system also uses a different formula to assess student income and expected summer earnings contributions:

- ✔ **The bad thing** about the CSS Profile is that (unlike the Federal Methodology's FAFSA measurement of what your family can afford), the Profile count of what your clan owes doesn't overlook a dollar in assets.

- ✔ **The good thing** about the CSS Profile is that the school doesn't keep you waiting to find out how much money you have to dig up, because you mail your Profile at the same time that you file your admissions forms. You appreciate the quick response when you are college shopping and affordability is your first priority.

FAFSA and CSS Profile: The brass-tacks differences

The CSS Profile is more comprehensive in its data collection and is a tougher asset collector than the FAFSA. The CSS Profile generally results in a higher expected parental contribution than the FAFSA. But the result can be quite different depending on how the school's financial aid counselor treats special circumstances. Specifically:

✔ The CSS Profile counts the family home as an asset; the FAFSA doesn't.

✔ The CSS Profile requires a minimum student contribution, typically from savings and student jobs. The FAFSA doesn't require a minimum student contribution.

✔ The CSS Profile considers only the number of children in undergraduate school. The FAFSA considers the number of children in undergraduate and graduate school.

✔ The CSS Profile relies heavily on the *professional judgment* of financial aid counselors to shave tuition bills on the basis of such special circumstances as high medical bills and private secondary school costs. The FAFSA also allows for special circumstances, but in addition, permits financial aid counselors to use professional judgment to reduce the expected family contribution by counting into the reduction formula a parent who is legitimately enrolled in full-time college study at the same time as the parent's child.

(As a rule, parents can no longer take a few classes solely for the purpose of reducing the amount of expected family contribution; the parent-as-student strategy was recently disallowed as abuse of the system.)

College Financial Aid Application

Just when you thought you'd used up the last bit of ink in a dozen roller pens, you run into a college that requires (1) a FAFSA, (2) A CSS Profile, and (3) the college's own *financial aid application!*

Overkill? The colleges that require their own financial aid application don't think so. Their rationale: Some colleges distribute scholarship and aid programs that have special requirements and so they need more information than the two national aid application forms provide.

Here are a few examples of why colleges employ their own application forms even if they use both the FAFSA and CSS Profile:

✔ A religious-affiliated institution may need to know if you're a member of its faith to consider you for a scholarship.

✔ Colleges offer scholarships related to a student's major — business, nursing, engineering, and computer science, to name a few.

✔ Alumni sponsor scholarships for students from specific counties, cities, and high schools.

✔ Colleges may have exotic scholarships for students who

- Are left-handed. (Fred and Mary Beckley Scholarship — Fred and Mary were left-handed tennis players who met on the court. They married and established an endowment for left-handed students with need.)

- Have a last name of Murphy, Baxendale, Borden, or Smith (Harvard College).

- Have calf-roping skills (University of Arizona).

- Plan to quit smoking, drinking, or using drugs (Bucknell University).

- Are female, majoring in athletics, and graduated from Seneca Valley High School (University of North Carolina-Greensboro).

Some colleges use their own financial aid application form *instead* of the CSS Profile. Their customized application forms can become grisly in the depth of detail requested; in addition to all the other data, the college may ask about funds in siblings' accounts.

Here are examples of rationales for using a customized application form:

✔ For placement purposes in the work-study program, the college aid office may need to know about your work experience, driver's license, lifeguard experience, or other facts to make a job placement.

✔ If you've indicated an interest in a study-abroad program, the college aid office adjusts your budget depending on costs for transportation and overseas housing.

✔ When you have a special medical consideration, you may require a boost in aid for medication.

✔ If you're a graduate student, the financial aid office looks for loans that directly relate to your discipline: MedLoans (medical students), EdLoans (education students), LawLoans (law students), and MBA Loans (business school students).

✔ A married graduate student who brings the spouse to campus has extra expenses.

Why can't colleges get together and devise one comprehensive form used by all? Why do you need several different application documents to request aid? Good questions, but you won't find any succinct answers. What you have to know is that the colleges call the tune and you dance the jig.

Financial Aid Transcript (FAT)

If you're planning to jump ship from one college or university to another in the same year and want financial aid, you may need the *Financial Aid Transcript. Note:* You need the FAT whether or not you received aid at the old school. Check with your school; much of the information is available online through the Naional Student Loan Data System (NSLDS).

The skinny on the FAT is that it's free, but it's your responsibility to tell your old college to send your FAT to your new college.

Timing Help: Go with the Flow

The U.S. Department of Education distributes money to each college to disburse to students who meet eligibility requirements. The college financial aid offices also fatten their aid kitties with endowment-generated funds and awards they administer from other sources, such as general revenues.

No matter where the aid money comes from, most of your greenbacks will be awarded by your school.

You begin by completing and submitting your FAFSA to the specified Department of Education (DOE) processing center. Personnel at the center process your paperwork and return the results to you within four to six weeks. Here's how the process works:

✔ Each college you specify receives the results of your FAFSA on a document called the *Institutional Student Information Report (ISIR)*. The college receives your results electronically.

✔ You receive your FAFSA results on a document called the *Student Aid Report (SAR)*. The color of the paper used for SARs changes from year to year, and so you may hear others refer to them as "blue forms" or "pink forms" or "yellow forms." You receive your SAR in two parts.

• SAR Part I is a summary of the FAFSA information you submitted.

• SAR Part II is a form to use if you need to correct or update Part I data. Review your SAR Part I for accuracy; if you fail to spot and correct errors, you can lose thousands of dollars. Return only Part II to the specified Department of Education processor.

• *Note:* Make copies of the corrections on Part II and send them to the financial aid office of each college you've targeted and to your state's scholarship agency. If your SAR was completely accurate and you made no corrections, send nothing to the schools and state agency; they're supposed to receive the information on the Institutional Student Information Report (ISIR) mentioned earlier.

- Occasionally a college asks that you send the original Part I and Part II of your SAR. Go ahead and send it. Immediately order a duplicate SAR from the Department of Education by calling 800-433-3243. Duplicate SARS are free.

Although you get feedback from FAFSA, don't expect to be told your expected family contribution by the central processor of the CSS Profile. You get an acknowledgment, but that's all it is. However, each college that required you to provide a CSS Profile receives the results, which are then reviewed by your financial aid counselor who decides the amount of your demonstrated need.

Suppose you filled out your FAFSA, CSS Profile, and a college's own financial aid application form. Here's how one young man fared who did that very thing, according to his award notification letter from a major university.

Federal Pell Grant		$3,125
Federal Supplemental Grant		$2,000
University Grant		$12,425
Federal Work-Study Program		$2,000
Federal Subsidized Stafford Loan Referral		$2,625
Federal Perkins Loan		$4,000
	Total Aid	$26,175
Cost of Attendance (COA)		$28,607
Expected Family Contribution (EFC)		$2,432
	Total Need	$26,175

When to Apply for Aid

The $64,000 question for many students is the following: Do I apply for financial aid before or after I have been admitted to a college?

The answer is: *Apply for admission and financial aid at the same time.* You should not wait for one procedure to be completed before starting on the other.

When students apply for regular admissions, the college normally notifies them of acceptance in April, May, and June. But most financial aid priority deadlines are in February. If you wait until admission to apply, you miss the deadlines for the awarding of financial aid.

The student financial aid process is tiresome, sometimes agonizing. But if spending a few hours with some forms means the difference between an education and no education, the choice is obvious.

Not everyone gets the message. The choice wasn't obvious to the Tappedout family parents. They were too busy to research the financial aid process and fill out the forms correctly. Here's their story:

"When our son said he wanted to go to college, we threw a big party and served champagne and caviar pie. When he told us he would go on to get his master's, we had a party and served bottled water and cookies. Last week, he informed us that he wants to continue studying for his Ph.D., and we still had a party — we served tap water and sponge cake." (Thanks to humor great Robert Orben for that one.)

A Flow Chart Sums It Up

In case you have questions about how the parts fit together in the FAFSA application and processing cycle, Dr. Davis's chart in Figure 3-2 illustrates how your data goes with the flow. (Parents are indicated in parentheses when information is needed from them if you are a dependent.)

FAFSA (Free Application for Federal Student Aid) Start to Finish

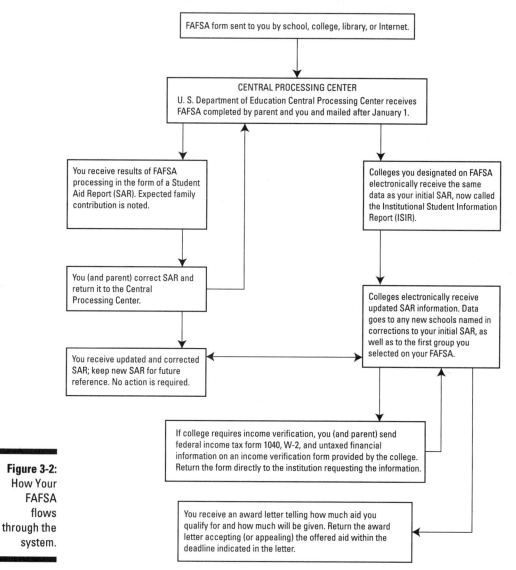

Figure 3-2:
How Your
FAFSA
flows
through the
system.

Chapter 4

Dr. Davis's Comprehensive College Money Calendar

• •

In This Chapter

▶ A timeline to secure the funds you need whether undergraduate, graduate, or nontraditional

• •

Here's a handy schedule that you can use to keep your financial aid search on track. Consider writing the action items on the actual pages of your calendar.

Note: This calendar is designed for both undergraduate and graduate students attending U.S. colleges and universities. If you plan to attend graduate or professional school, the deadlines for financial aid when you are in your college undergraduate senior year are identical to those for a high school senior in the 12th year. This financial aid calendar applies to all students, whether full time or part time, campus sited or distance learning.

Sophomore Year of High School

❏ **Continuing:** Start a college scholarship resource file. Save private scholarship sources sponsored by organizations, service groups, corporations, government agencies, and individuals.

❏ Explore career options through high school career studies and self-discovery. (Many scholarships are available from career-related professional organizations.)

❏ Join appropriate clubs or participate in activities associated with scholarships, such as Scouts, service clubs, and jobs.

❏ Parents shift financial assets if restructuring is to your advantage. January 1 in the junior year marks the start of the year that influences aid for college freshmen (see Chapter 1).

Junior Year of High School

❏ Register with your school counselor to take the PSAT, which is the National Merit Scholarship Qualifying Test, and the ACT.

❏ Apply for advanced placement to be eligible to take college courses in high school.

❏ Investigate banks, credit unions, and other institutions that make educational loans; open an account if that's a requirement for being able to borrow.

❏ **October:** Take the Preliminary Scholastic Assessment Test (PSAT).

❏ **November:** Attend financial aid workshops to get a head start on early financial aid planning and to understand the financial aid process.

❏ Attend college fairs. Gather information about colleges and financial aid resources.

❏ Review PSAT results.

❏ **February:** Register for May or June SAT II for schools that require it.

❏ Make plans to visit colleges to see the campus "in action."

❏ **March:** Visit the high school guidance and career center to discuss colleges.

❏ **April:** Do a free computer scholarship search using Internet services (see Chapter 12).

❏ **May:** Contact college admission offices where you want to enroll, asking for information on entrance and scholarships. Ask for college's admission video if one is available. Check Internet for college Web sites to see if your target schools offer an electronic admission option.

❏ Contact your state's scholarship administration (see Chapter 8) to determine state financial aid opportunities and application procedures.

❏ **Summer:** If you haven't already done so, visit colleges of interest.

❏ Request applications from private scholarship sponsors.

❏ Prepare for early decision applications.

❏ Do an estimated EFC on the Internet (www.fafsa.ed.gov).

Senior Year of High School

❏ **October:** Continue to pursue scholarship resources, including merit-based funds.

❏ Create a checkoff sheet of admissions and financial aid forms and deadlines.

❑ Send letters to scholarship providers requesting scholarship applications.

❑ Send college applications.

❑ Prepare College Scholarship Service's Profile for those colleges that require this document to award institutional funding.

❑ Attend college fairs to collect admission and financial aid information.

❑ **November:** Secure a Free Application for Federal Student Aid (FAFSA) from your high school counseling/career center.

❑ If you missed the free winter financial aid workshops in your junior year, attend free workshops (minimum of two) offered by your high school or organizational sponsors to review the correct method of completing the FAFSA. Although you have already mailed the CSS Profile, you can find out if you committed any gross errors you need to quickly correct. (You're fortunate if your school's workshop is scheduled earlier, which is ideal, but most schools can't get to them until November.)

❑ Complete institutional aid applications if required by the college.

❑ *Parents:* Prepare your income tax information to complete taxes early; this helps when completing the FAFSA.

❑ **December:** Fill out the FAFSA form but hold to mail after January 1 through February 15.

❑ **January:** Mail an original FAFSA or a renewal FAFSA form after January 1 and not before, using the self-addressed envelope that came with the form. Even if you're using estimated income, mail your FAFSA before February 15. (You can file your FAFSA after February 15, but the later you file it, the less aid you are likely to get.) You may also be required to complete an institution's supplemental form(s).

❑ **February:** Receive the results of the FAFSA, called a Student Aid Report (SAR). Keep these forms in a safe place until you (and your family) complete federal taxes.

❑ If a dependent, you and your family each complete U.S. Federal Tax Form 1040 or 1040A.

❑ Update the SAR from the information on the Form 1040 or 1040A. Make additional corrections, such as new colleges of interest that should receive the SAR.

❑ Sign, date, and return the SAR to the designated address on the SAR.

❑ Send copies of your and your family's 1040 with W-2(s) attached to each targeted college's financial aid office.

❑ Double-check that all private scholarship applications are completed and sent; thousands of private scholarships have deadlines of March 1.

❑ **March:** Receive corrected SAR, which reflects the actual tax data.

❑ Send a copy of the corrected SAR results to each college financial aid office. *Note:* Colleges should already have received the corrected results through the sometimes imperfect electronic data exchange (EDE), but play it safe and send the colleges a copy.

❑ **April:** Continue to receive admission acceptance letters. Hold all admission offers until the corresponding financial aid award letters are finalized to weigh offers.

Note: You may have to pay a deposit to hold your admission status until you have your financial aid plan intact. The deposits, usually due by May 1, are nonrefundable. Deposits at state schools typically are less than $100 but rise to hundreds of dollars at private schools.

If your award letter hasn't arrived, call the school and ask if the deadline for paying your deposit can be extended by four weeks.

❑ Receive college financial aid notification (award letters). Accept all awards by school deadlines; return award letters promptly. Prepare financial aid appeal letters as required (see Chapter 9). Remember, you are still negotiating and deciding, although you accept everything at this point.

❑ **May:** Receive outside scholarship notification.

❑ Compare all award letters and institute final negotiations with the college(s) of choice.

❑ Finalize college selection.

❑ Notify each nonselected college admission office that you have made another choice and will not be enrolling in the fall. Report to each nonselected college financial aid office that you are relinquishing your earlier aid acceptance because you will not be enrolling in the fall.

❑ Receive your award letter from your number-one school choice. Complete your family's section of the master promissory note for student, parent (FPLUS), or other loan documents that are included with the award letter. Submit these by certified mail to your prime-choice school.

❑ Complete paperwork for on-campus housing at the selected college.

❑ **June–August:** Work during the summer and earn as much as $2,200 for college expenses. (Your financial aid award is already completed so this money will not count against your funding for the year. Students are allowed to earn up to $2,200 per year before their earnings are considered a contribution toward the expected family contribution.)

❑ Complete a computerized scholarship search for the next academic year. New scholarship sponsors are available for each year that you advance in college.

❑ If you plan to work while in school, try to line up a job a few weeks before school starts. Many of the best jobs are taken before students hit the campus. You may even want to make a special trip to the campus to explore job options, starting at the college itself to see what it offers.

Freshman through Senior Year of College

❑ **September:** If you don't already have a job, meet with financial aid office's college placement coordinator to interview for a campus job as authorized in the award letter.

❑ **October–December:** Apply for private scholarships.

❑ **January:** Complete and submit new or renewal FAFSA for the next school year.

❑ Complete and submit new or renewal CSS Profile. (Many colleges only require the Profile for the freshman year.)

❑ Complete Institutional Aid Application if required by the college.

❑ **February:** Prepare federal income tax forms.

❑ Receive Student Aid Report (SAR) and update with tax information. Resubmit SAR. Send copies of your and your family's income tax forms to the college's financial aid office, if required. (Be sure that tax forms are signed or they won't be accepted.)

❑ Interview for a dorm assistant position for the next school year.

❑ **March:** Receive corrected SAR. Send copy of corrected SAR to the college's financial aid office to ensure that they have your new information.

❑ Don't overlook tax breaks. You may be able to claim a tax credit *(Hope* and *Lifetime Learning)* for some or all tuition paid. Deductional interest on education loans is another possibility. For specifics, check out these resources: IRS Help Line at 800-829-1040, IRS *Publication 970,* or www.irs.ustreas.gov.

❑ If you haven't already landed a summer job, begin your search.

❑ **April:** Do a free computer scholarship search using Internet services (see Chapter 12).

❑ **May:** Receive renewal award letter. Renewal letters are usually distributed after the spring grades are posted. Sign and return award letters promptly.

❑ You can drop into the financial aid office to discuss an unsatisfactory award renewal, but don't expect to truly negotiate — they've already got you.

Chapter 5

College Costs: Upward and Onward

· ·

· ·

*T*owering tuition increases over recent years — often double the rate of increase in the overall cost of living — have made the college tab so high that almost no one can pay the full freight at private colleges these days, and many families can't handle ramped-up bills at public institutions.

This chapter takes a look at increasing college costs and helps you plan for them.

Figuring Out College Costs

What are the costs that you face? At one extreme is a year's education at an exclusive school that now prices out at more than $30,000, including living expenses. At the other end are a very few highly endowed schools that charge no or a tiny tuition, such as Cooper Union in New York or Berea College in Kentucky. The overwhelming majority of schools are somewhere between those bookend figures.

The national average tuition increase is 4 percent annually. Surveys of actual costs are always a couple of years behind the time when you want to know what kind of money the schools require from you or your bill payer. Table 5-1 attempts to bridge that gap; it presents Dr. Davis's projections of typical college costs for the 2000–2001 academic year.

How did Dr. Davis come up with these guestimates? He first calculated the probable costs for the 1999–2000 academic year by adding 4 percent to the actual costs for 1998–1999. He then boosted those totals by another 4 percent to arrive at forecasted costs for the 2000–2001 academic year. These projections aren't meant to be precise, but they do give you a fair idea of what to expect.

Table 5-1	Projected Sample College Costs in 2000–2001			
	Public Colleges		**Private Colleges**	
	Resident	**Commuter**	**Resident**	**Commuter**
Four-Year Colleges				
Tuition & fees	$3,508	$3,508	$15,995	$15,994
Books & supplies	717	717	735	735
Room & board	4,899	2,269	6,355	2,316
Transportation	662	1093	603	949
Personal expenses	1,526	1,613	1,153	1,360
Computer equipment (optional)	1,200	1,200	1,200	1,200
Total	**$12,512**	**$10,400**	**$26,041**	**$22,554**
	Public Colleges		**Private Colleges**	
	Resident	**Commuter**	**Resident**	**Commuter**
Two-Year Colleges				
Tuition & fees	NA	$1,766	$7,931	$8,085
Books & supplies	NA	675	731	735
Room & board	NA	2,205	5,144	2,384
Transportation	NA	970	620	961
Personal expenses	NA	1,266	1,100	1,281
Computer equipment (optional)	NA	1,200	1,200	1,200
Total	**NA**	**$8,082**	**$16,726**	**$14,642**

NA = Not Applicable

Remember that these are only estimated figures. Check specific institutions for exact costs.

Fewer than 10 percent pay list price at private colleges

Providing discounts on tuition and living costs is another way of saying "institutionally funded financial aid offered to students to help defer the cost of an education." It means gift money (scholarships and grants), not self-help aid (loans and jobs).

A nationwide study among 232 members of the National Association of College and University Business Officers (NACUBO), a nonprofit professional organization, reveals that *fewer than 10 percent of students in those schools actually pay the published tuition price.* This statistic may surprise you — it did us.

The practice of discounting rates is growing faster at small colleges with tuitions below $15,700 than at small colleges with higher tuition and at large colleges and universities.

Once You're Hooked, You're History

The NACUBO study, described in the sidebar "Fewer than 10 percent pay list price at private colleges," confirms what many students and parents have long suspected: *Gift money is far more generous coming in than going on.* After generous financial aid lures you inside the college's door, don't expect the same juicy awards the following years.

Colleges and universities today are run as businesses, not as what one writer describes as "bastions of high-minded collegiality." Colleges everywhere are paring down operating costs, from hiring fewer faculty to slotting in more graduate teaching assistants. In addition, the higher education marketing strategy at many schools presumes that after you're established on a campus, you'll hang around without being fed the substantial discount that induced you to enroll.

That's why all types of private colleges and universities discount the rate for first-year students substantially more than for all undergraduates. The shift as you move through the education pipeline may be from gifts to self-help, or from gifts to nothing. Ask your college if the awards are renewed at substantially the same rate, assuming family resources remain static!

 To avoid the ghastly surprise of having your aid award sink under your feet, make a four-year financial aid plan (see Chapter 1) and religiously revisit your plan every semester. Check in with the financial aid counselor at your school well in advance of each new school year.

If you prove to be the exception and the money keeps on coming year after year, thank your lucky stars. Your vigilance paid off!

Student daily cash needs are higher than you think

Don't forget to add $1,200 or more for a computer, a requirement at many schools. The 1998 Amendments to the Higher Education Act of 1965 now enable colleges to include the cost of a computer in the institution budget.

And how much walking-around money will you need? That depends on too many things to dip the answer in bronze and display it, not the least of which is whether your campus is rural or urban. Bear in mind that estimates by colleges tend to be conservative. If you're a party animal, increase your school's estimate of spending for food, dorm-room necessities, clothing, and recreation by 50 percent. If you're prone to ski weekends or hosting great parties and haven't budgeted adequately, you may have to take in laundry to survive.

Putting on the Brakes

Private colleges aren't alone in trying to make do with less reliance on runaway tuitions. State educators are planning a variety of actions to chop costs. Among the most discussed are the following:

- ✔ **Prepaid tuition plans:** These plans, usually operated statewide, enable families to lock into a tuition rate years in advance and set aside money in a state account. See Chapters 8 and 15.

- ✔ **Lowering costs by speeding academic progress:** Students are taking too long to graduate. Statistics show that fewer than a third of students finish in four years. A sprinkling of state schools across the nation are guaranteeing incoming freshmen that they'll be done in four years by ensuring that seats are available in required classes and that prerequisites are offered in the correct order. If more time is needed and it's not the student's fault for failing to take a class, taking too few credits, or taking off a term, the school picks up the bill.

    Ideas of how to move things along range all over the map: Encourage students to take more college-level courses in high school; improve academic counseling to help students more effectively choose a major and sequence their courses; advise high school juniors of courses they need during their senior year to better prepare for college-level work; improve high school education to eliminate need for remedial courses.

- ✔ **More proposals:** States can make policy decisions to freeze tuition, shifting funds from other programs (like prisons and Medicaid) to pay the difference. Some states tie tuition increases to the cost-of-living index.

The list of proposed fixes for exorbitant college costs is lengthy. Some may take root soon enough to benefit you. At least the unremitting upward spiral of tuition increases seems to have found the brakes.

Part II
How to Find the Aid You Need

The 5th Wave   By Rich Tennant

©RICHTENNANT

"It's part of my employer tuition assistance agreement with the 'Pizza Bob' corporation."

In this part . . .

Some people have such talent that they can replay a Mozart composition after hearing it once. The exceptionally bright bulbs don't even need sheet music. Most of us, though, need months of practice and reams of sheet music to manage the same feat.

Finding financial aid isn't that much different. These chapters reveal the techniques of one hard-working scholarship winner who his the jackpot. You also uncover ways to access federal, institutional, and private aid, whatever your merits.

But you won't necessarily have to settle for what you're awarded — you also pick up little-known facts about negotiating finaid packages, even when you're broke and school starts in 30 days. And don't skip the chapters on the hidden financial aid market and other frequently asked questions.

Chapter 6

Tapping the School's Own Aid

● ●

In This Chapter

▶ Meeting your secret money allies

▶ Finding your school's hidden aid sources

▶ Making an "early decision" can be a bad aid deal

▶ Discovering rich schools that have a big aid allowance

● ●

*I*f the College Money Hunt was a board game, square one would be campus doors. Figuratively speaking, go knock on them at all the schools you'd like to attend. Ask financial aid counselors how wide they're willing to open the *institutional aid* wallet.

When you start the student financial aid process, the staff at a school's financial aid office processes your application for the normal federal, state, and institutional awards. Institutional aid, as you may know, is the school's own money that it can do with as it pleases.

This hide-and-seek chapter takes you behind the scenes. We go beyond the normal, routine aid resources to find money — call it a big campus treasure hunt. We start where you start: the admissions office.

Calling All Allies: Find Me Funds

You have secret allies on campus: in general, the people in the admissions office and, in particular, the college recruiter who's responsible for your file.

The expense of recruiting you and others like you costs out at more than $2,400 a head. After you're recruited and admitted, admissions personnel want to hang on to you, especially at institutions that are in danger of opening a semester with empty seats. The recruiter in charge of your file can do two kinds of things to help fatten your wallet:

　　✔ Double-check that all the required documentation you need to receive financial aid is on file in the financial aid office.

✓ Recommend you for any special scholarships that are used to entice students and lock up their enrollments. In the workplace, a comparable practice is called a sign-on bonus — you're rewarded for committing to join the company or enroll at a specific college. Be sure your name is in the hat for these scholarships that are budgeted by the admissions staff.

Your advocate in the admissions office has a stake in your staying committed to the school and may also convey helpful information about new scholarships from the campus grapevine. A graceful way to establish your relationship is to ask the admissions recruiter to describe how other students have financed their way through your school-to-be.

If you find that your admissions recruiter at College A is more dedicated to your success than your admissions recruiter at College B, you may want to weigh this disparity of service as yet another factor in your final choice of schools.

Previously, you could expect to hear from financial aid personnel if you failed to include all the required supporting forms and data with your application. No longer can you count on getting a telephone call or e-mail asking you to supply missing documents. That's because financial aid offices are like Santa's Workshop on December 23 — busy! To be sure you aren't screened out because of missing documents, take the initiative. Two weeks after sending your application, e-mail (perhaps followed by a telephone call) the financial aid office to confirm that your file is complete. *Be proactive!*

The college's athletic office is a sure stop if you have athletic ability; ask your high school coach to assist. A good resource if you're athletically inclined is *How to Win a Sports Scholarship,* by Penny Hastings and Todd D. Caven (published by First Base Sports; 1999). You can order this book from Hastings Communications, P.O. Box 14927, Santa Rosa, CA 95402; 707-579-3479. Cost is $22.95 by mail.

Still another place to prospect for financial aid is the department where you'll major or at least spend a lot of time.

Don't overlook matching grants

More than 375 four-year colleges have a policy that matches outside grants with institutional awards. Lafayette College in Pennsylvania gives matching grants up to $5,000 if you can drag in a comparable outside scholarship. The University of Kentucky matches up to $3,400. Hood College in Maryland and Marymount College in New York match up to $3,000. Nationwide, the average matching grant is $1,000 per student, with a range from $100 to full tuition. Your college's financial aid or business office keeps the matching-grant books; ask for chapter and verse.

Try for Departmental Scholarships

Some scholarships are controlled by specific college departments. Contact heads of those departments directly; you can get their names and contact information from your admissions office ally.

Look over Table 6-1, which lists a sampling of merit-based scholarship opportunities offered by college departments of art, drama, music, and various other academic disciplines. You don't have to demonstrate need to qualify for these awards.

Table 6-1	Dr. Davis's Sampling of Departmental Scholarships			
Institution	*Art*	*Drama*	*Music*	*Merit/ Academic*
ALABAMA				
Alabama State University	X	X	X	X
Tuskegee University		X	X	X
ALASKA				
University of Alaska	X	X	X	X
ARIZONA				
Arizona State University	X	X	X	X
Arizona Western College	X	X	X	X
CALIFORNIA				
Pepperdine University	X	X	X	X
San Diego State University	X	X	X	X
University of California, Berkeley	X	X	X	X
University of California, Santa Barbara	X	X	X	X
Pitzer College	X	X	X	X
COLORADO				
University of Colorado, Boulder	X	X	X	X
CONNECTICUT				
University of Connecticut	X	X	X	
DELAWARE				
University of Delaware		X	X	X

(continued)

Table 6-1 *(continued)*

Institution	Art	Drama	Music	Merit/Academic
DISTRICT OF COLUMBIA				
Catholic University		X	X	X
George Washington University	X	X	X	X
FLORIDA				
Jacksonville University	X	X	X	X
University of Miami		X	X	X
GEORGIA				
Mercer University		X	X	X
Morehouse College		X		X
HAWAII				
Brigham Young University-Hawaii	X	X	X	X
ILLINOIS				
Bradley University	X	X	X	X
DePaul University	X	X	X	X
Knox College	X	X	X	X
Northwestern University		X	X	
INDIANA				
Earlham College				X
Indiana State University	X	X	X	X
Indiana University	X	X	X	X
KENTUCKY				
Kentucky Wesleyan College	X	X	X	X
University of Louisville	X	X	X	X
LOUISIANA				
Tulane University				X
Xavier University of Louisiana	X	X	X	X
MARYLAND				
Johns Hopkins University		X	X	X
University of Maryland	X	X	X	X

Institution	Art	Drama	Music	Merit/Academic
MASSACHUSETTS				
Boston University	X	X	X	X
University of Massachusetts	X	X	X	X
MICHIGAN				
University of Michigan	X	X	X	X
MINNESOTA				
Mankato State University	X	X	X	X
University of Minnesota	X	X	X	X
MISSISSIPPI				
Mississippi State University		X	X	X
MISSOURI				
University of Missouri	X	X	X	X
Washington University	X			X
NEW HAMPSHIRE				
Colby-Sawyer College	X	X	X	X
NEW YORK				
Fordham University	X	X	X	X
Ithaca College		X	X	X
New York University		X	X	X
Parsons School of Design	X			
St. John's University	X	X	X	X
St. Thomas Aquinas College	X	X	X	X
NORTH CAROLINA				
Duke University	X	X	X	X
East Carolina University	X	X	X	X
Elon College		X	X	X
North Carolina A & T State University	X	X	X	X
University of North Carolina		X	X	X
Wake Forest University	X	X	X	X

(continued)

Table 6-1 *(continued)*

Institution	Art	Drama	Music	Merit/Academic
OHIO				
Denison University	X	X	X	X
Miami University	X	X	X	X
Oberlin College		X	X	X
OKLAHOMA				
University of Tulsa	X	X	X	X
OREGON				
Lewis and Clark College		X	X	X
Pacific University	X	X	X	X
PENNSYLVANIA				
Drexel University	X	X	X	X
Duquesne University		X	X	X
Gettysburg College				X
Wilkes University	X	X	X	X
RHODE ISLAND				
Rhode Island School of Design	X			X
SOUTH CAROLINA				
Clemson University		X	X	X
Furman University	X	X	X	X
TENNESSEE				
Fisk University				X
Vanderbilt University				X
TEXAS				
Rice University		X	X	X
Southern Methodist University	X	X	X	X
UTAH				
Brigham Young University	X	X	X	X
VERMONT				
Bennington College	X	X	X	X

Institution	Art	Drama	Music	Merit/ Academic
VIRGINIA				
James Madison University	X	X	X	X
University of Richmond		X	X	X
WASHINGTON				
Gonzaga University		X	X	X
Seattle University	X	X	X	X
Whitman College	X	X	X	X
WEST VIRGINIA				
University of Charleston	X	X	X	X
West Virginia Wesleyan College	X	X	X	X
WISCONSIN				
Beloit College		X	X	X
Marquette University		X		X

Discover Colleges with Deep Pockets

Harvard, the University of Texas, and a few others among America's wealthiest colleges can admit any student they want without worrying about how much financial aid the student needs. They can welcome anyone they wish because these institutions have a big enough private endowment to make up the difference between tuition cost and ability to pay.

The schools that are rolling in endowment money spend it to lure students who really soar, such as the top 1 or 2 percent of high school classes. They may base full rides totally on merit and not demonstrated need. Table 6-2 lists American colleges and universities with the best endowments.

Table 6-2	America's Best-Endowed Colleges	
Rank	**Institution**	**Dollars (thousands)**
1	Harvard University	$13,019,736
2	University of Texas System	7,647,309
3	Yale University	6,624,449

(continued)

Table 6-2 *(continued)*

Rank	Institution	Dollars (thousands)
4	Princeton University	5,582,800
5	Emory University	5,104,801
6	Stanford University	4,559,066
7	California, University of	3,787,884
8	Massachusetts Institute of Technology	3,678,127
9	Texas A & M University System	3,531,517
10	Washington University (Mo.)	3,445,743
11	Columbia University	3,425,992
12	Pennsylvania, University of	3,059,401
13	Rice University	2,790,627
14	Cornell University	2,527,871
15	Northwestern University	2,397,715
16	Chicago, University of	2,359,358
17	Michigan, University of	2,303,054
18	Notre Dame, University of	1,766,176
19	Vanderbilt University	1,539,242
20	Dartmouth College	1,519,708
21	Southern California, University of	1,432,786
22	Johns Hopkins University	1,373,155
23	Duke University	1,359,992
24	Case Western Reserve University	1,328,800
25	Virginia, University of	1,227,880
26	California Institute of Technology	1,164,183
27	Minnesota and Foundation, University of	1,143,083
28	Brown University	1,111,760
29	Rochester, University of	1,069,641
30	Purdue University	1,052,614
31	Grinnell College	1,019,048
32	New York University	950,900
33	Ohio State University & Foundation	928,530
34	Rockefeller University	911,100

Rank	Institution	Dollars (thousands)
35	Saint Louis University	868,534
36	UNC at Chapel Hill & Foundation	847,420
37	Swarthmore College	833,659
38	Cincinnati, University of	807,965
39	Smith College	793,214
40	Texas Christian University	786,461
41	Boston College	784,500
42	Wellesley College	780,872
43	Pittsburgh, University of	772,525
44	Southern Methodist University	770,681
45	Washington & Lee University	768,376
46	Richmond, University of	752,309
47	Delaware, University of	749,613
48	Wake Forest University	747,989
49	Kansas University Endowment Association	724,668
50	Wake Forest University	499,798

(Source: National Association of College and University Business Officers)

The size of an institution's endowment is certainly not the most important consideration in your planning, but it can be one of your considerations. Think about including rich colleges on your enrollment wish list, as the following guidance tips explain:

- ✔ **Old conventional wisdom:** A free education is not worthwhile if it's not the education you want. Identify schools you want to go to, and then look for financial aid.

- ✔ **New conventional wisdom:** Factor in a school's endowment-driven generosity in selecting a college. Or don't choose your school for money, but go where money is and fall madly in love.

Making Early Decisions May Shrink Aid

Colleges in droves are rushing to offer *early decision enrollments,* meaning that you apply in the fall (usually by mid-November) and, if the school accepts you (usually by mid-December), you immediately agree to enroll.

Most of the issues involved in this controversial topic are beyond the purpose of this book, but the problem with early-decision enrollment from the financial aid viewpoint is that the school may offer you a downsized financial aid package because you're already hooked.

You may think that the early bird would get more financial aid worm, but what more likely happens is that you're considered a "sure thing," so why not save money for others who need enticement to enroll?

An admissions director of a liberal arts college in the Midwest once told a major newsmagazine this: "I am going to be pretty tempted to give you a larger loan [rather than gift money] or gap you [award an aid package that falls short of meeting documented need] if I've already got you under contract."

If obtaining merit-based financial aid is a determining factor for which school you'll attend, don't apply under "binding" early-decision timelines. If the school only offers need-based aid (such as the Ivy League schools), you can make your decision as early as you want to. Early decision will not affect your ability to obtain aid.

What bad thing happens to you if you do enroll under early-decision timelines and you later find out that you've been stiffed on financial aid? Can you change your mind and go to another school where they're less sure of signing you up and therefore treat you better? Maybe nothing happens. The early decision you make is supposedly binding — the schools consider the contractual agreement an ethical issue and request that you withdraw your application from other places. Even so, we found no evidence that you will be sued or banished from higher education if you change schools. You may be 'uninvited' from your early-decision school, though.

Jobs on campus

Your college's financial aid office coordinates the need-based Federal Work-Study Program (FWSP), but most college employment offices handle all part-time jobs on campus: cafeteria, janitorial, groundskeeping, library, parking attendant, and security guard, to name a few. These jobs often pay more than the FWSP jobs, and you can work more hours because they aren't restricted by FWSP regulations.

You may be in great demand if you have a skill certification or experience, such as computer skills, campus daycare, lifeguarding, or tutoring for individuals with disabilities. Campus offices that are responsible for supportive services offer financial assistance to students who have such certification or experience (lifesaving certificate, special instructor license, sign language, or any other documentation of your special skill or experience) qualifying them to handle specialized jobs.

Chapter 7

What Uncle Sam and Aunt Feddie Are Willing to Fork Over

- -

In This Chapter

▶ Federal grant programs

▶ Federal loan programs

▶ Federal work-study programs

- -

*T*he U.S. government is the Michael Jordan of the financial aid world —
number one, by leaps and bounds. The feds score with about 75 percent
of all available financial aid in the United States, a commitment that far
outstrips that of any other major country. That leadership role means that
you have to pay close attention to changes in financial aid, such as the
recent alterations made by the 1998 Amendments to the Higher Education
Act of 1965 (see Chapter 1).

For your reading pleasure, this chapter gives you the skinny on the major
federal financial aid programs.

Federal Grant Programs

The federal government offers the following grant programs to assist in
funding your higher education.

Federal Pell Grant Program

The 800-pound gorilla in the need-based programs, the Federal Pell Grant
Program awards gift money to nearly 4 million students in amounts ranging
from $400 to $3,525 yearly (2000–2001 school year).

Pell grants are off-limits to graduate students, as well as to students who
have already received a bachelor's degree.

The amount you get depends on the following factors:

- Your demonstrated need
- The costs of education at the particular college you want to attend
- The length of the program in which you're enrolled
- Whether your enrollment is full- or part-time
- The amount of money Congress approves divided by the number of qualifying students

You apply by filling out the FAFSA (see Chapter 3).

Federal Supplemental Educational Opportunity Grant Program (FSEOG)

Do you have exceptional demonstrated need? For instance, you can't make oatmeal or corndogs stretch to the end of the month? The Federal Supplemental Educational Opportunity Grant Program, fondly known as FSEOG (pronounced *eff-SEE-og*) is for you. To qualify, you must be enrolled at least half-time in an undergraduate program at an accredited institution. Grants in the neighborhood of $4,000 are possible on the basis of pure, unadulterated need (poverty). However, most colleges don't receive enough FSEOG funds to pay out maximum eligibility, and $1,000 to $1,500 is considered a good award. Roughly 1 million students receive this desperately needed funding that's designed to equalize college opportunity.

This program is *campus-based,* which means that, although the money comes from the federal government, the colleges hand it out to students who show exceptional need. (Typically, you're eligible for an FSEOG if you're eligible for a Pell grant.) If you think you qualify for the FSEOG, ask your school's financial aid counselor to put you down for one.

Federal Loan Programs

We report the information that you positively, absolutely must know about *private loans* in Chapter 16. The *federal loans* here are awarded directly or guaranteed by Uncle Sam and Aunt Feddie.

Federal Perkins Loan

The Federal Perkins Loan is the best federal loan program in the business, offering 5 percent interest! Perkins targets the neediest students — typically those who receive Pell grants. Given to both undergraduate ($20,000 total allowed) and graduate students ($40,000 total allowed), the loans come through a college's financial aid office. Here are a few key details:

- $4,000 annual limit for undergraduate study
- $6,000 annual limit for graduate school
- Interest free while in college
- Ten years to pay off the loan
- Loan forgiveness for some teachers (see Chapter 22)

Payments and interest start nine months after college ends if you're at least a half-time student; if your school load drops below half-time, or six credits, the nine-month countdown to payment begins.

Federal Direct Student Loan Program and Federal Stafford Loan Program

These two programs are for student borrowers. The difference is where the money comes from. Funds from the Federal Ford Direct Student Loan Program are federal money disbursed through your college. Funds from the Federal Stafford Loan Program come from private sources, such as banks, credit unions, savings and loan associations, and educational organizations.

Either program — Direct or Stafford — can be subsidized or unsubsidized. Here's what we mean:

- If you have demonstrated need, the loan is *subsidized,* meaning that the government pays the interest while you're in school.
- If you don't have demonstrated need, you pay interest from the time you get the loan until it's paid in full (although you may elect to defer interest payments until after you graduate). This loan is *unsubsidized.*

You can't borrow more money than the amount needed to study for a year. First-year students can borrow up to $2,625; sophomores can borrow some $3,500. Limits during the third, fourth, and fifth years rise to $5,500. Graduate students can borrow $18,500 per year ($8,500 subsidized and $10,000 unsubsidized). Interest rate is 91-day T-bill plus 2.1 percent in school and 2.5 percent in repayment.

The costs of the Federal Direct or Federal Stafford student loans can't rise above an 8.25 percent interest rate, plus an origination fee of 3 percent and sometimes an insurance premium of 1 percent. These fees are deducted from the amount of your loan before you receive payment. Look for lenders that waive the insurance fee and offer repayment breaks.

FAFSA (see Chapter 3) starts the sequence of action that enables you to borrow a Federal Direct loan or Federal Stafford loan, subsidized or unsubsidized. Lots of niggling details attend these two loans. Ask your high school guidance counselor or college financial aid counselor to help you understand these loan packages if you're having trouble.

FPLUS (Federal Parent Loans for Undergraduate Students)

FPLUS loans and Direct FPLUS loans are for parent borrowers. The difference is where the money comes from. Direct FPLUS loans are federal funds disbursed by your college's financial aid office. FPLUS loans come from private sources, such as banks, credit unions, savings and loan associations, and educational organizations. The maximum that parents can borrow under either of these loan programs depends upon the cost of the college and the amount of financial aid that the student receives.

Here's the formula for maximum eligibility for an FPLUS loan:

Cost of education (for example)	**$28,000**
(Minus) Student aid awarded (for example)	**$14,000**
(Equals) Amount of FPLUS eligibility	**$14,000**

The interest rate for FPLUS loans is figured annually by adding 3.1 percent to the rate of the 52-week U.S. Treasury bill. The rate is capped at 9 percent for the life of the loan. A one-time origination fee of 3 percent is paid to the federal government to help offset program costs, and a one-time, 1-percent insurance fee is paid to the state guarantee agency. (**Note:** Most guarantee angencies now waive the 1-percent insurance fee.)

Credit checks

FPLUS loans require a credit check, but student loans do not. The credit check doesn't use the formula applied to commercial credit, which consists of an income-to-debt ratio. The FPLUS credit check is less rigid, requiring only that the lender investigate to see if the parents pay their credit accounts within a reasonable period of time.

Will a bankruptcy experience by itself prevent a parent from receiving an eligibility rating for an FPLUS loan? No, but you do need a healthy credit history.

Several services complete an early credit check for pre-approval for an FPLUS loan. The Independence Federal Savings Bank offers a free pre-approval credit check. Ask someone at your financial aid office to call them toll-free at 800-733-0473, or check out the bank's Web site (www.ifsb.com).

If you're turned down for an FPLUS loan, call the lender and ask why. Often the reason is that the credit bureau provider hasn't updated its files on your family. Call a loan officer at the lending institution to help you resolve any error. If nothing works, call American Express (1-800-814-4595); they have a high success rate in getting a rejected FPLUS reversed and approved.

Silver linings

When parents are rejected for an FPLUS loan, it may actually be good news for the student who wants to enroll in a lower-cost college. Students get loans at lower interest rates than parents do, and repayment doesn't begin as quickly even though the interest is being capitalized.

So even if the family credit is poor and you anticipate an FPLUS or Direct FPLUS loan rejection, go ahead, Mom and/or Dad, and apply for an FPLUS or Direct FPLUS loan. If your loan is rejected, make a copy of the rejection letter and have the student send it to the college's financial aid counselor.

To make up for the turndown of an FPLUS or Direct FPLUS loan, college students can borrow an additional *unsubsidized* Federal Stafford or Direct loan as long as the parents' rejection letter is submitted. Through this process:

- ✔ As the student, you can borrow $4,000 for each of the first two years and $5,000 for each of the last two or three years of college.

- ✔ Although a parent's interest rate can rise to 9 percent, yours is capped at 8.25 percent.

- ✔ Your repayment on principal begins after graduation or when you're no longer attending college at least half time. By contrast, your parents' repayment on principal begins 60 days after receiving the disbursement.

In short, FPLUS or Direct FPLUS loan rejection may be great for your cash flow.

Federal Work-Study Programs (FWS)

The campus-based Federal Work-Study Program distributes federal dollars through colleges to pay for student employment. The jobs are almost always on campus, although some may also be arranged off campus in community service programs. To qualify for FWS, you must have demonstrated need and be enrolled for at least half-time study at either the undergraduate or graduate level.

In the past, colleges could not apply Federal Work-Study funds directly to a student's account. The 1998 amendments corrected the problem. Upon your request, colleges can credit your work-study earnings directly to your account to pay for tuition, fees, room, board, and other institutional services. Tell your financial aid counselor to credit your account.

The pay is at least the current federal minimum wage and may be higher. Compensation for off-campus jobs is left to the discretion of the employer and may be greater than pay for campus jobs.

More Federal Educational Support

The military offers a cornucopia of financial aid opportunities, which we describe in Chapter 17. Additionally, Uncle Sam and Auntie Feddie offer an assortment of other resources, ranging from medical and nursing scholarships to scholarships from the Bureau of Indian Affairs.

The federal government tries hard to help you make sure that your education money numbers add up to affordable years of college.

Additional reading

The Student Guide (annual) by the U.S. Department of Education: Order it from Federal Student Aid Programs, P.O. Box 84, Washington, D.C. 20044, or call 800-433-3243.

Chapter 8

States Make the "A" Grade

● ●

In This Chapter

▶ Guidelines for finding aid in your own state

▶ A 50-state guide to residency requirements

▶ A 50-state guide to financial aid agencies

▶ A 43-state guide to the new college savings plans

● ●

*Y*our state is coming up in the world of student aid. Not only do many states offer the best new college savings programs ever because they come with tax breaks, but all states help you hike off to college in two basic ways:

✔ **Your state delivers de facto financial aid in the form of an affordable college education in state schools.** In the best state schools, the quality of the education is as good as that offered by the best private colleges. The terms used to describe these elite public colleges and universities include *public ivies* and *flagship universities.*

✔ **Your state provide grants and loans to qualifying students who enroll at either public or private colleges and universities within their own state.** All states offer need-based awards, and about half of the states deliver merit-based aid. A handful of states don't cut off the money at the state line. They maintain reciprocity arrangements with other states that allow you to spend your state education dollars in reciprocating states. You stand to gain thousands of dollars, particularly in big states such as California, Florida, Wisconsin, Minnesota, Maine, Ohio, and Pennsylvania.

When Feds Say No, States May Say Yes

Hailing all middle- and upper-middle-income families: Don't forget to apply to your state for a hand even if your federal government financial aid foray was a dismal flop.

Some states are more generous than the federal government in figuring whether you qualify for financial aid. Federal awards are based on your adjusted gross income, which includes some notice of your assets. By contrast, in some states, aid is based solely on taxable income without notice of your assets.

In some states, you can own a posh estate, a stable of race horses, and several fast sports cars and theoretically still qualify for thousands of dollars in aid so long as your taxable income falls within state limits.

States like to do their own things. A number of states award a full ride, including room and board, to in-state students who participate in the federal free lunch program. In others, programs such as the Hope Scholarships in Georgia require students to maintain a 3.0 academic grade point average.

The rules are all over the map. Don't overlook inquiring about possible aid awards at your state's student financial aid agency.

Applying for State Aid

If the forms you need to apply for student aid aren't available at your high school or college financial aid office, contact your state financial aid agency at the address listed in the directory in the following section. States vary in the amount of information they need to decide if you're award-eligible; some use the data from the FAFSA, while others require a supplemental aid form that is processed by the state's agency for higher education financial aid.

Look to your home state to play a substantial role in supporting your education. Tuition at state schools is always much less costly when you are a resident of a state than when you live outside that state (because your taxes haven't been filling the state's coffers), unless you're looking at a school in a state that has reciprocity with your own. *The difference between being an in-state student and an out-of-state student can be as much as $10,000 per year.*

As an example, in the reciprocity issue, District of Columbia high school graduates who have resided in D.C. for at least one year have a good deal. Because of the sparse educational facilities within the district, they are entitled to in-state tuition rates at public universities in any state. The federal government pays the differential costs.

Although establishing residency in a state used to be fairly simple, rules are tighter today. Many states now insist that parents pay taxes within their borders and have the state as a primary residence. Even so, if you have your eye on another state's public university, morphing your way in from outsider to resident may be worthwhile. You may have to drop out of college for at least a year, work in that state, and pay taxes to establish residency and meet all the rules.

Residency requirements not only vary from state to state, but sometimes *from school to school within a state.*

Don't count on backing into education during the year that you're establishing your residency. Community colleges, usually operated by a county, add another tier of residency. You not only have to live in the state, you have to live in the school's county — or pay higher tuition rates.

A Directory of State Requirements and Financial Aid Agencies

To review what your state and others offer, here is a directory of state residency requirements that you must meet to qualify for in-state student status and state scholarships. The state's financial aid agency contact information follows each residency statement.

When you contact a state's college financial aid agency, don't expect the agency to know details about state residency requirements, which may change from year to year — and from college to college. What the financial aid agencies know about are the financial aid programs sponsored within the state.

But these agencies may know whom to contact to verify residency requirements. When you call a state financial aid agency's telephone number in the following directory and wish to verify residency requirements, ask these two questions:

   ✔ Whom should I call to verify eligibility for state residency?

   ✔ Whom should I call at (name of college) to verify residency eligibility?

For colleges, the most common answer will be the institution's financial aid office, but it never hurts to ask. *Without fail, verify residency requirements with the college you hope to attend.*

Key to listing

Following is a key to the terms that appear in the following state listings:

Student aid eligibility: The listing also includes the length of time that you must reside in the state to be eligible for college financial aid.

Requirements: Residency requirement, how long you must live in the state to attend state colleges and universities and pay in-state tuition (always much less than out-of-state tuition). Certain institutions in a state require more or fewer years to establish residency.

Military waiver: Some states grant instant resident status to members of the military and their families.

Documents required to prove residency: States vary in number and type of documents required.

Reciprocity: Some states have reciprocity agreements with other states to give each other's citizens the lower in-resident rate for tuition.

V: Voice telephone number
I: Internet URL (Web address)

WICHE/WUE: Western Interstate Commission Higher for Education/ Western Undergraduate Exchange. States that participate in WICHE are allowed to have students who qualify to entoll in certain majors at participating institutions and receive reduced rates. States that participate include the following: Alaska, Colorado, Hawaii, Montana, Nevada, New Mexico, North Dakota, Oregon, South Dakota, Utah, and Wyoming.

Academic Common Market (Southern Region Education Board — SREB). A consortium of 14 southern states that allow nonresident students to enroll in specific degree programs at in-state tuition rates if the academic programs are not offered in the student's home state. Participating states are Alabama, Arkansas, Florida (graduate level only), Georgia, Kentucky, Louisiana, Maryland, Mississippi, Oklahoma, South Carolina, Tennessee, Texas (graduate level only), Virginia, and West Virginia.

Alabama

Student aid eligibility requirements: 1 yr. residency, driver's license or voting card, bank account, state tax return
Reciprocity: No
Military waiver: Yes
Agency: Alabama Commission on Higher Education
100 N. Union St. P.O. Box 30200
Montgomery, AL 36130-2000
V: 334-242-1998
I: www.ache.state.al.us

Alaska

Student aid eligibility requirements: 1 yr. residency, driver's license or voting card, postal service verification
Reciprocity: No
Military waiver: Yes

Agency: AK Commission on Postsecondary Education and Alaska Student Loan Corp.
3030 Vintage Blvd.
Juneau, AK 99801-7109
V: 907-465-2962
V: 800-441-2962 (Alaska only)
I: www.state.ak.us/acpe

Arizona

Student aid eligibility requirements: 1 yr. residency, driver's license, vehicle registration, voting card, state tax return
Reciprocity: Yes, WICHE (Western Interstate Commission for Higher Education) states: AK, AZ, CA, CO, HI, ID, MT, NV, NM, ND, OR, SD, UT, WA, WY
Military waiver: No

Agency: AZ Commission for Post-secondary
Education
2020 North Central Avenue, Suite 275
Phoenix, AZ 85004-4503
V: 602-229-2591
I: www.acpe.asu.edu

Arkansas

Student aid eligibility requirements: Driver's
license, vehicle registration, state tax return,
residency requirement varies
Reciprocity: Yes, varies by institution
Military waiver: No
Agency: AR Department of Higher Education
114 East Capitol
Little Rock, AR 72201-3818
V: 501-371-2000; 800-54-STUDY
I: www.adhe.arknet.edu

California

Student aid eligibility requirements: 1 yr. residency
for state grant; each state institution determines
residency
University of California: 3 yrs.; driver's license, voting
card, vehicle registration, state tax return; considers
all documents
Reciprocity: No
Military waiver: Yes
Agency: CA Student Aid Commission
P.O. Box 419027
Rancho Cordova, CA 95741-9027
V: 916-526-7590 (Students only)
I: www.csac.ca.gov

Colorado

Student aid eligibility requirements: 1 yr. residency
immediately preceding the first day of classes;
driver's license, vehicle registration, voting card,
state tax return
Reciprocity: Yes, New Mexico
Military waiver: Yes
Agency: CO Commission on Higher Education
Colorado Heritage Center
1300 Broadway, Second Floor
Denver, CO 80203
V: 303-866-2723
I: www.state.co.us/cche_dir/hecche.html

Connecticut

Student aid eligibility requirements: 1 yr. resi-
dency; driver's license, vehicle registration
Reciprocity: Yes, DEL, DC, ME, MA, NH, PA, RI, VT
Military waiver: Yes
Agency: CT Department of Higher Education
Attn: Financial Aid
61 Woodland St.
Hartford, CT 06105-2391
V: 860-947-1855
V: 800-842-0229 (In state only)
V: 800-4-FED-AID
I: www.ctdhe.commnet.edu

Delaware

Student aid eligibility requirements: 1 yr. resi-
dency; driver's license, voting card, state tax return
Reciprocity: Yes, PA
Military waiver: No
Agency: DE Higher Education Commission
Carvel State Office Building
820 North French Street, 4th
Wilmington, DE 19801
V: 302-577-3240
I: www.doe.state.de.us/high-ed

District of Columbia

Student aid eligibility requirements: 15 consecu-
tive months residency; voting card, state tax return,
lease, deed, or real estate tax bill
Reciprocity: No
Military waiver: Must pay D.C. taxes
Agency: Office of Postsecondary Education,
Research and Assistance
2100 Martin Luther King Jr. Avenue, Suite 401, SE
Washington, DC 20020
V: 202-727-3685
I: www.ci.washington.dc.us

Florida

Student aid eligibility requirements: 1 yr. residency
before the first day of classes; proofs of residency
determined by institution
Reciprocity: No
Military waiver: Yes
Agency: FL Department of Education
Office of Student Financial Assistance
325 W. Gaines St.
Tallahassee, FL 32399-0400
V: 850-487-0049
I: www.bor.state.fl.us

Georgia

Student aid eligibility requirements: 1 yr. residency immediately preceding; driver's license, vehicle registration, voting card, state tax return
Reciprocity: No
Military waiver: Yes
Agency: Georgia Student Finance Commission
State Loans and Grants Division
2082 East Exchange Place, Suite 200
Tucker, GA 30084
V: 800-546-HOPE (4673) (Georgia only)
V: 800-776-6878
I: www.gsfc.org

Hawaii

Student aid eligibility requirements: 1 yr. residency; voting card, state tax return
Reciprocity: Yes, Pacific Islands
Military waiver: Yes
Agency: Hawaii State Postsecondary Education Commission
University of Hawaii
2444 Dole St., Room 202
Honolulu, HI 96822-2394
V: 808-956-6624
I: www.hern.hawaii.edu/hern

Idaho

Student aid eligibility requirements: 1 yr. residency; determined by institution
Reciprocity: WA, UT
Military waiver: Yes
Agency: Idaho State Board of Education
650 West State St.
P.O. Box 83720
Boise, ID 83720-0037
V: 208-334-2270
I: www.sde.state.id.us

Illinois

Student aid eligibility requirements: 1 yr. residency; driver's license, vehicle registration, voting card, state tax return
Reciprocity: No
Military waiver: Yes
Agency: Illinois Student Assistance Commission
1755 Lake Cook Road
Deerfield, IL 60015-5209
V: 847-948-8550 or 847-948-8500
800-899-4722 (IL, IA, IN, MO, WI only)
I: www.isacl.org

Indiana

Student aid eligibility requirements: 1 yr. residency on or before Dec. 31 of the year preceding application for award; must be a resident of Indiana
Reciprocity: No
Military waiver: No
Agency: State Student Assistance Commission of Indiana
150 West Market Street, Suite 500
Indianapolis, IN 46204-2811
V: 317-232-2350
V: 888-528-4719 (Toll Free; Indiana only)
I: www.ai.org/ssaci

Iowa

Student aid eligibility requirements: Established by the Iowa Board of Regents
Reciprocity: No
Military waiver: No
Agency: IA College Student Aid Commission
200 Tenth Street, 4th Floor
Des Moines, IA 50309-3609
V: 515-281-3501 or 515-281-4890
I: www.state.ia.us/government/icsac

Kansas

Student aid eligibility requirements: 1 yr. residency prior to first time college attendance; driver's license, vehicle registration, voting card, state tax return
Reciprocity: MO, with limitations
Military waiver: Yes
Agency: Kansas Board of Regents
700 SW Harrison, Suite 1410
Topeka, KS 66603-3760
V: 785-296-3517
I: www.ukans.edu/~kbor

Kentucky

Student aid eligibility requirements: Determined by each school
Reciprocity: Contact agency
Military waiver: Yes
Agency: KY Higher Education Assistance Authority
1050 U.S. 127 South, Suite 102
Frankfort, KY 40601-4323
V: 502- 696-7200 or 800-928-8926
I: www.kheaa.state.ky.us

Louisiana

Student aid eligibility requirements: 1 yr. residency; driver's license, vehicle registration, voter registration, document of employment in-state for one year
Reciprocity: No
Military waiver: Yes
Agency: LA Student Financial Assistance Commission
LA Office of Student Financial Assistance
P.O. Box 91202
Baton Rouge, LA 70821-9202
V: 800-259-5626; 504-922-1012
I: www.doe.state.la.us

Maine

Student aid eligibility requirements: 1 yr. residency; state tax return; the burden shall be on the student to prove that he/she has established a Maine domicile for other than educational purposes
Reciprocity: CT, MA, NH, RI, VT, MD, DE, DC, AK, PA
Military waiver: No
Agency: Finance Authority of Maine (FAME)
119 State House Station
Augusta, ME 04333-0949
V: 800-228-3734
I: www.famemaine.com

Maryland

Student aid eligibility requirements: 3 months to 1 yr. residency; driver's license, vehicle registration, voter card, state tax
Reciprocity: No
Military waiver: Yes
Agency: MD Higher Education Commission
Jeffrey Building
16 Frances Street
Annapolis, MD 21401-1781
V: 410-974-5370; 410-974-2971
I: www.mhec.state.md.us

Massachusetts

Student aid eligibility requirements: 1 yr. residency; driver's license, vehicle registration, voter card, state tax return
Reciprocity: Yes, New England states, PA, DC
Military waiver: Yes
Agency: MA Board of Higher Education
330 Stuart Street, Suite 304
Boston, MA 02116
V: 617-727-9420
I: www.mefa.org

Michigan

Student aid eligibility requirement: Residency determined by each institution; driver's license, vehicle registration and insurance in-state, voter card, state tax return, other documents as required
Reciprocity: Determined by institution
Military waiver: Yes
Agency: MI Higher Education Assistance Authority
Office of Scholarships and Grants
P.O. Box 30462
Lansing, MI 48909-7962
V: 517-373-3394
V: 888-447-2687
I: www.mde.state.mi.us

Minnesota

Student aid eligibility requirements: Residency determined by institution; state tax returns, auto insurance in-state, other documents as needed
Reciprocity: Yes, ND, SD, WI, IA, Manitoba Midwest Student Exchange Program
Military waiver: No
Agency: MN Higher Education Services Office
1450 Energy Park Drive
Suite 350
St. Paul, MN 55108-5227
V: 651-642-0567
V: 800-657-3866
I: www.mheso.state.mn.us

Mississippi

Student aid eligibility requirements: 1 yr. residency; state tax returns, driver's license
Reciprocity: Yes, AL, AR, FL, GA, KY, MD, SC, TN, TX, VA, WV
Military waiver: Yes
Agency: MS State Institutions of Higher Learning
Financial Assistance Board
Office of Student Financial Aid
3825 Ridgewood Rd.
Jackson, MS 39211-6453
V: 601-982-6663
V: 800-327-2980 (In state only)
I: www.ihl.state.ms.us

Missouri

Student aid eligibility requirements: 1 yr. residency; driver's license, vehicle registration, voting card, state tax return, personal and property taxes
Reciprocity: Yes, some state schools have agreements with selected members of the Midwestern Higher Education Commission
Military waiver: Yes, military personnel assigned to MO institutions pay non-resident fees; if stationed for other purposes, personnel and their dependents pay resident fees
Agency: MO Coordinating Board for Higher Education
3515 Amazonas Drive
Jefferson City, MO 65109-5717
V: 573-751-2361
I: www.mocbhe.gov

Montana

Student aid eligibility requirements: 1 yr. residency; driver's license, vehicle registration, voting card, state tax return
Reciprocity: No
Military waiver: Yes
Agency: MT University System
2500 Broadway
Helena, MT 59620-3103
V: 406-444-0078
I: www.montana.edu

Nebraska

Student aid eligibility requirements: 1 yr. residency; driver's license, vehicle registration, voting card, state tax return
Reciprocity: Yes, at certain institutions in specific areas of study
Military waiver: No
Agency: NE Coordinating Commission for Postsecondary Education
140 N. Eighth Street, Suite 300
P.O. Box 95005
Lincoln, NE 68509-5005
V: 402-471-2847
I: www.nol.org/NEpostsecondaryed

Nevada

Student aid eligibility requirements: 6 months residency prior to application, 1 year residency after; driver's license, voting card, state tax return
Reciprocity: Yes, WICHE, WWE, Good Neighbor
Military waiver: Yes

Agency: University of Nevada-Reno
Office of Admissions Administration Records, MS120
Reno, NV 89557
V: 775-784-6181
I: www.unr.edu

New Hampshire

Student aid eligibility requirements: 1 yr. residency; driver's license, vehicle registration, voting card, state tax return
Reciprocity: New England states
Military waiver: Yes
Agency: New Hampshire Postsecondary Education Commission
2 Industrial Park Drive
Concord, NH 03301-8512
V: 603-271-2555
I: www.state.nh.us/postsecondary

New Jersey

Student aid eligibility requirements: 1 yr. residency; driver's license, vehicle registration, voting card, state tax
Reciprocity: No
Military waiver: No
Agency: NJ Higher Education Student Assistance Authority
4 Quakerbridge Plaza, P.O. Box 540
Trenton, NJ 08625
V: 800-792-8670 x64350
I: www.state.nj.us/treasury/osa

New Mexico

Student aid eligibility requirements: 1 yr. immediately preceding the term for which the resident classification is requested; driver's license, vehicle registration, voting card, state tax return, evidence of employment. Exceptions exist: marriage, Navajo Nation, etc. (contact state agency)
Reciprocity: Yes, TX, CO, AZ
Military waiver: Yes
Agency: New Mexico Commission on Higher Education
1068 Cerrillos Rd.
Santa Fe, NM 87501-4925
V: 505-827-7383 or 800-279-9777
I: www.nmche.org

New York

Student aid eligibility requirements: 1 yr. residency prior to attending a postsecondary institution, regardless of receipt of financial aid; driver's license, vehicle registration, voting card, state tax return
Reciprocity: No
Military waiver: Yes
Agency: New York State Higher Education Services Corporation
One Commerce Plaza
Albany, NY 12255
V: 518-473-7087
TAP Inquiry 888-NYS-HESC
I: www.hesc.state.ny.us

North Carolina

Student aid eligibility requirements: 1 yr. residency; driver's license, vehicle registration, voting card, state tax return
Reciprocity: No
Military waiver: Yes
Agency: NC State Education Assistance Authority
P.O. Box 13663
Research Triangle Park, NC 27709-3663
V: 919-549-8614 or 800-700-1775
I: www.ncseaa.edu

North Dakota

Student aid eligibility requirements: 1 yr. residency; driver's license, voting card, vehicle registration, state tax return
Reciprocity: Yes, MN
Military waiver: Yes
Agency: ND University System
ND Student Financial Assistance Program
600 East Boulevard Ave.
Bismarck, ND 58505-0230
V: 701-328-2960
I: www.nodak.edu

Ohio

Student aid eligibility requirements: 1 yr. residency immediately preceding enrollment; driver's license, vehicle registration, voting card, state tax return, parent or employer statement evidencing residency
Reciprocity: Yes, PA
Military waiver: Yes

Agency: Ohio Board of Regents, State Grants and Scholarships
P.O. Box 182452
309 South Fourth St.
Columbus, OH 43218-2452
V: 614- 466-7420 or 888-833-1133
I: www.bor.ohio.gov

Oklahoma

Student aid eligibility requirements: 1 yr. residency; each case judged on its own merit by the appropriate institutional official consistent with State Regents' Policy
Reciprocity: WICHE, call 405- 858-4356
Military waiver: Yes
Agency: Oklahoma Tuition Aid Grant Program
500 Education Building State Capitol Complex
Oklahoma City, OK 73105-4503
V: 405-858-4356
I: www.okhighered.org

Oregon

Student aid eligibility requirements: 1 yr. residency; driver's license, vehicle registration, voting card, state tax return
Reciprocity: No
Military waiver: Yes
Agency: Oregon State Scholarship Commission
1500 Valley River Drive, Suite 100
Eugene, OR 97401
V: 541-687-7400
I: www.osshe.edu

Pennsylvania

Student aid eligibility requirements: 1 yr. residency; driver's license, vehicle registration, voting card, state tax return, lease, deed or real estate tax bill, employer letter stating full time employment
Reciprocity: Yes, except NY, NJ, MD
Military waiver: No
Agency: Pennsylvania Higher Education Assistance Agency (PHEAA)
200 N. Seventh St.
Harrisburg, PA 17102-1444
V: 800-692-7435 (In state only)
V: 717-720-2800
I: www.pheaa.org

Rhode Island

Student aid eligibility requirements: 1 yr. residency immediately preceding January 1 of the academic year for which the student is applying for aid; driver's license, state tax return, rent receipts
Reciprocity: Yes, U.S., Canada, and Mexico
Military waiver: No
Agency: Rhode Island Higher Education Assistance Authority
560 Jefferson Blvd.
Warwick, RI 02886
V: 401-736-1100; 800-922-9855
I: www.uri.edu/ribog

South Carolina

Student aid eligibility requirements: 1 yr. residency; driver's license, vehicle registration, voting card
Reciprocity: No
Military waiver: Yes, stationed in SC no later than September 1st of preceding year
Agency: SC Higher Education Tuition Grants Commission
1310 Lady St., Suite 811
Columbia, SC 29201
V: 803-734-1200
I: www.state.sc.us/tuitiongrants

South Dakota

Student aid eligibility requirements: 1 yr. residency immediately preceding the first scheduled day of classes; driver's license, vehicle registration, voting card, state tax return, income of student, residence of student's parents, marriage to SD resident, ownership of property, institution's required documents
Reciprocity: MN Western Interstate Commission on Higher Education, Western Undergraduate Exchange (WICHE)
Military waiver: Yes
Agency: SD Department of Education and Cultural Affairs
700 Governors Dr.
Pierre, SD 57501-2291
V: 605-773-3134
I: www.ris.sdbor.edu

Tennessee

Student aid eligibility requirements: Residency determined by institution; driver's license, vehicle registration, voting card, state tax return

Reciprocity: Within 30 miles of Austin Peay State University
Military waiver: Yes
Agency: TN Higher Education Commission
404 James Robertson Pkwy, Suite 1950
Nashville, TN 37243-0820
V: 615-741-1346
V: 800-447-1523 (Tennessee only)
V: 800-257-6526
I: www.state.tn.us/thec

Texas

Student aid eligibility requirements: 1 yr. residency; driver's license, vehicle registration, voting card, employment records
Reciprocity: States adjacent to TX
Military waiver: Yes
Agency: TX Higher Education Coordinating Board
P.O. Box 12788, Capitol Station
Austin, TX 78711-2788
V: 512-427-6340 or 800-242-3062
I: www.thecb.state.tx.us

Utah

Student aid eligibility requirements: 1 yr. residency; driver's license, vehicle registration, voting card, state tax return, institution may require additional documents
Reciprocity: Some graduate programs, WICHE states; WVE with ID, WY, NV
Military waiver: Yes
Agency: Utah Education Assistance Authority
355 W. North Temple, #3 Triad, Ste. 550
Salt Lake City, UT 84180-1205
V: 801-321-7200 or 800-418-8757
I: www.utahsbr.edu

Vermont

Student aid eligibility requirements: 1yr. residency prior to enrollment in postsecondary institution; driver's license, vehicle registration, voting card, state tax return, ownership of residential property
Reciprocity: Certain majors, New England Regional Student Program
Military waiver: No
Agency: VT Student Assistance Corporation
Champlain Mill
P.O. Box 2000
Winooski, VT 05404-2601
V: 802-655-9602
I: www.vsac.org

Virginia

Student aid eligibility requirements: 1 yr. residency; application for in-state tuition plus any documents required by the institution
Reciprocity: AL, AR, FL, GA, KY, LA, MD, MS, SC, TN, TX, WV (Academic Common Market)
Military waiver: Yes
Agency: State Council of Higher Education for Virginia
James Monroe Building, Ninth & Tenth Floors
101 N. Fourteenth St.
Richmond, VA 23219
V: 804-225-2137
I: www.schev.edu

Washington

Student aid eligibility requirements: 1 yr. residency; driver's license, vehicle registration, voting card, state tax return
Reciprocity: OR, ID, British Columbia
Military waiver: Yes
Agency: WA State Higher Education Coordinating Board
P.O. Box 43430, 917 Lakeridge Way, SW
Olympia, WA 98504-3430
V: 360-753-7850
I: www.HECB.wa.gov

West Virginia

Student aid eligibility requirements: 1 yr. residency, and not primarily for the purpose of attendance at a WV institution; driver's license, vehicle registration, voting card, state tax return
Reciprocity: PA
Military waiver: No
Agency: WV State College and University Systems
1018 Kanawha Blvd., East, Suite 700
Charleston, WV 25301
V: 304-558-4614
I: www.scusco.wvnet.edu

Wisconsin

Student aid eligibility requirements: 1 yr. residency, not primarily than to obtain an education; driver's license, vehicle registration, voting card, state tax return
Reciprocity: MN
Military wavier: Yes

Agency: Higher Educational Aids Board
P.O. Box 7885
Madison, WI 53707-7885
V: 608-267-2206
I: www.heab.state.wi.us

Wyoming

Student aid eligibility requirements: 1 yr. residency; driver's license, vehicle registration, other documents required are determined by the institution
Reciprocity: CA, OR, WA, AZ, NV, ID, MT, CO, AK, NM, NE, HI, UT, ND, SD
Military waiver: Yes
Agency: Wyoming Community College Commission
2020 Carey Avenue, Eighth Floor
Cheyenne, WY 82002-0110
V: 307-777-7763
I: www.k12.wy.us/higher_ed.html

American Samoa

Board of Higher Education
American Samoa Community College
P.O. Box 2609
Pago Pago, AS 96799-2609
V: 684-699-9155

Guam

University of Guam Education Council
303 University Dr.
Mangilao, Guam 96923
V: 671-735-2287

Trust Territory of the Pacific Islands

Federated State of Micronesia
College of Micronesia-FSM
P.O. Box 159 Kolonia
Pohnpei, FM 96941
V: 011-691-320-2480
I: www.interwork.sdsu.edu/com

Puerto Rico

Council on Higher Education of Puerto Rico
P.O. Box 23305-UPR Station
Rio Piedras, PR 00931
V: 809-758-3350

Virgin Islands

VI Joint Boards of Education
Charlotte Amalie, P.O. Box 11900
St. Thomas, VI 00801
V: 809-774-4546

Federated States of Micronesia

1725 N. St., NW
Washington D.C. 20036
V: 202-223-4383

Republic of the Marshall Islands

RMI Scholarship Grant and Loan Board
P.O. Box 1436
3 Lagoon Road
Majuro, RMI 96960
V: 692-625-3108

Republic of Palau

Ministry of Education Bureau
P.O. Box 9
Koror, Republic of Palau, TT96940
V: 680-488-2470

Saver-Friendly Changes in State Tuition Programs

For parents who look at their paychecks and suspect that the government has legalized mugging, you may be having nicer days soon, thanks to the new college savings plans.

State-sponsored prepaid college tuition plans that enable you to save to cover tuition, fees, supplies, and books have been around for a dozen years; a big attraction is the tax breaks that come with them. We don't go

Every scholar's a winner in lottery scholarships

State lotteries are beginning to draw scholar- as well as customer-winners. After Florida in 1997 launched the idea of assigning some pro- ceeds from its state lottery to students who earn a B average or better, West Virginia and Kentucky signed on with a lottery-funded schol- arship. Kentucky offers $2,500 maximum for four years if your GPA meets state standards. You must attend a state school, whether it's a col- lege or a vocational-technical institute.

In Florida, you can collect $1,500 a year for college, plus some money for books. This is about 75 percent of tuition and fees at a state university, community college, or vocational- technical school.

If you do better academically, earning a GPA of 3.5 or higher, Florida rewards you with about $2,000 annually, or 100 percent of tuition and fees, plus $600 a year for books at state schools.

Other states are said to be thinking about lot- tery scholarships. If your state has a lottery (Mississippi, Nevada, North Carolina, Okla- homa, and Tennessee are among those that do not), ask your department of education if a lottery scholarship is in the works, or if a state scholarship funded from any source and tied to academics is available.

into detail about the original plans because information about them abounds. Instead, we concentrate on the new, enhanced state-sponsored college savings plans.

Today's big news reflects the changes in the 1996 and 1997 tax laws that, in effect, double the tax advantages of the original prepaid state plans. Why? Because you can use the new state-sponsored college savings plans to cover room and board expenses, which easily can cost as much as tuition and books.

The original plans are often called the *original prepaid tuition plans,* while the recent versions are termed the *new college savings plans.* Prepaid tuition plans are guaranteed to keep pace with tuition inflation but return no additional monies. Savings plans pay with returns based on investment performance. Taken together, both are called *qualified state tuition programs.*

Some 43 states, plus the District of Columbia, offer a state-sponsored college savings plan. Each state plan is designed to meet the needs of its residents, but certain benefits span all state plans. Every state program allows you to use the savings for either a public or private institution, either in state or out of state, so that a student has total freedom of college choice.

In both types of programs, federal taxes on state-sponsored plans are deferred until your child actually begins college and then the funds are taxed at your child's lower income level rather than your potentially higher rate. This federal tax relief is defined in Internal Revenue code 529 (*529 Plans*) and nearly all states exempt the plans from state taxes as well.

All states that have state income taxes offer either a deductiion or an exemption on earnings, or both.

Both the original and the enhanced programs now pay the costs of attending out-of-state public colleges, a benefit for students who choose not to attend school in their home states.

Parents across America are starting to find out about the new college savings plans, already adopted by about half the states. The appeal of the new college savings plans is that your money for college grows tax-deferred and qualifies for a hefty state income tax exemption as well.

Don't confuse the two types of plans. It's easy to mistake the new savings plans with the original prepaid-tuition plans that guarantee returns, ensuring that a set payment today will cover tuition at certain schools when their child enrolls. By contrast, the new plans are more like a normal investment plan except that the funds are invested by state officials.

The original prepaid plans cap annual returns at the rate of inflation in college tuition, often 6 percent to 7.5 percent. The new plans put more money into stocks in the hope of boosting returns, but they offer no guarantees; if the market sags, so does your fund.

Like the original plans, the newcomers offer generous tax breaks to parents, grandparents, and anyone else who wants to invest in a student's education. More importantly, the newcomers permit savers to put aside bigger piles of money. Most states cap the new plans' savings nest egg at $100,000.

The original prepaid plans hold the money in the student's name, which makes it more difficult to get financial aid. In the new genre of plans, the money is held in the parent's name, where it counts less in student-aid formulas. Although the impact of savings plans on the overall financial aid picture is unclear, in aid formulas that are not based on the FAFSA, your savings could be counted as an asset, compromising aid eligibility.

To avoid paying federal gift tax, savers should limit contributions to $10,000 per year or up to a lump sum of $50,000, prorated over five years on tax returns.

Another plus factor for the new plans on the block: Funds can be transferred to siblings or other relatives. Although the original plans don't limit students to home state schools, some pay out less to benefactors of students who don't choose home public colleges.

The new savings plans aren't just for kids. Say you're a single adult who wants to save for graduate study. You can claim deductions on your state income tax. If you don't go back to school but instead start a family, you can name your child as beneficiary.

What if your state doesn't offer the new genre of plans? You can still participate through an out-of-state plan. You won't get the state tax deduction in another state, but you will get tax-deferred investment growth. When you do have to pay taxes, the growth will be taxed at the student's rate, usually 15 percent. That's better than the parent's 20 percent capital gains tax on profits. Many states already exempt savings plans from state tax, and the Congress may do away with federal taxes on plan earnings.

A Directory of Qualified State Tuition Programs

The states actively promote both the new savings plans and the original prepaid tuition plans for an obvious reason: They hope that if enough people sock away adequate money in an education chest, the state's economic development will flourish with better educated citizens who attend college or vocational school. Only a handful of states offers both types of plans, which we identify in the directory in this section.

State savings plans: Right for you?

Pros

- ✔ Taxes are deferred and then paid at the child's lower rate.

- ✔ Families are eligible regardless of income or state of residence. (Roth IRAs cut off at $100,000 income.)

- ✔ Tax deductions from state income taxes are attractive.

- ✔ You can use them at private and out-or-state schools and transfer them to other family members.

- ✔ States can match contributions.

Cons

- ✔ Savings plans can't be counted as an asset in the FAFSA formula. We don't know yet how the CSS Profile or institutional aid formulas will treat money produced by savings plans. If counted as assets, college savings plans would compromise eligibility for financial aid. If resolved favorably — not counted as assets — state savings plans will be hard to beat.

- ✔ Results are not guaranteed. (Earnings could dip.)

- ✔ States levy penalties on investment gains when money is not used for school, but the penalty is only 10 percent.

Some 73 percent of parents told national survey takers for the College Savings Plans Network (CSPN) that they are putting away part of their income for their children's college education. That could mean anything from saving $1 a week to a fund that will pay all costs, but two-thirds have savings goals of more than $10,000.

Only 4 percent of savers are using qualified state tuition plans, presumably because they haven't figured in the full impact of tax savings available through the plans. Only 30 percent said they were aware of special tax benefits with college savings plans, while 80 percent said they would be interested in such tax-favored plans.

A bill before the U.S. Senate, backed by 21 cosigners and thought to be poised for approval, will grant federal tax exemption on the plans' earnings. If the plans indeed do become both federal and state tax-favored, look for explosive growth in qualified state tuition plans. **One more if:** If college financial aid policies do not overly penalize the new savers, these plans will become a prime financial aid vehicle for millions of middle-income families. The College Savings Plans Network, an association of state college savings programs, maintains both a national toll-free number (877-CSPN4YOU) and a Web site (www.collegesavings.org) to keep you updated on qualified state tuition programs.

We give Web addresses for most states in Table 8-1, but if you have trouble accessing your state's page, zip into the College Savings Plan Network (see preceding paragraph) and click your state on the U.S. map. Clicking that link speeds you to your state's tuition plan.

Table 8-1 presents a listing of current state tuition plans.

Key to Listing

#1 Refund for nonattendance.

#2 Refund without interest, just contributions.

#3 Guarantees program will cover future tuition costs for in-state public colleges.

#4 Guarantees program will cover future tuition costs for in-state public or private colleges.

#5 Does not guarantee that contributions will cover tuition costs in the future.

#6 Allows for funds to be used for out-of- state colleges.

#7 Forfeiture costs.

#8 Will cover costs above in-state tuition.

Table 8-1   **Qualified State Tuition Plans**

State	Plan	Program	Enrollment	Key Notes	Details
Alabama 800-252-7228	Prepaid	Prepaid Affordable College Tuition (PACT)	9th grade or younger	#1, #2, #3, #6	
Alaska 800-478-0003 (Alaska Only)	Prepaid	Univ. of Alaska Advanced College Tuition Payment Plan		1#, 2#, #3, #6, #8	Guarantees tuition at Univ. of Alaska
Arizona 602-229-2592 www.acpe.asu.edu	Savings	Family College Savings Program		#6	
California 916-526-3027 www.csac.ca.gov/scholar/scholar.htm	Savings	Golden State Scholarshare Trust			
Colorado 800-478-5651 www.prepaidtuition.org	Prepaid	Colorado Prepaid Tuition Fund	Open	#3,#4,#6	State exempts earnings from plan
Connecticut 888-799-2438 www.aboutchet.com	Savings	Connecticut Higher Education Trust			Investment plan only
Delaware 800-544-1655 www.doe.state.de.us/high-ed Click Delaware	Savings	Delaware College Investment Plan	Open enrollment		Invest funds for family; Maximum investment is $112,950
District of Columbia 202-727-6055	Savings	National Capital College Savings Trust			
Florida 800-552-4723 www.fsba.state.fl.us/prepaid/	Prepaid	Florida Prepaid College Program	Grade 11 or less younger	#2,#3, #4,#6	Earnings are capped at 5% if student attends out-of-state

(continued)

Table 8-1 (continued)

State	Plan	Program	Enrollment	Key Notes	Details
Illinois 877-877-3724	Prepaid	College Illinois (Illinois Prepaid Tuition Program)	October–January	#3, #6, #7	Earnings exempt from state taxes
Indiana 888-814-6800 www.che.state.in.us/ifcsp	Savings	Indiana Family College Savings Plan	Open		
Iowa 888-446-6696 www.treasurer.state.ia.us	Savings	Iowa Educational Savings Plan Trust	Up to age 17		Can invest a state-tax deductible up to $2,000/year/child; earnings free of state taxes
Kentucky 800-338-0318 www.kheaa.com/about.Html	Savings	Kentucky Educational Savings Plan Trust	Up to age 15	#1, minimum return of 4%	Contributions free from state income taxes
Louisiana 800-259-5626 ext.0523 www.osfa.state.la.us	Savings	Louisiana Student Assistance and Revenue Trust			
Maine 207-623-3263 www.collegesavings.org Click map	Prepaid	Maine College Prepaid Tuition Program		#1, #3	
	Savings	Maine College Savings Program			
Maryland 888-463-4723 www.prepaid.usmd.edu	Prepaid	Maryland Prepaid College Trust	February–June 9th grade or younger	#3, #6, #8	State and federal tax benefits

State	Plan	Program	Enrollment	Key Notes	Details
Massachusetts 800-449-6332 www.mefa.org 1-800-544-2776 www.fidelity.com/ufund	Prepaid	U-Plan – The Mass. College Savings/Pre-Paid Tuition Program	April-May; 10th grade or younger	#1, #4	Contributions free from state tax and maybe federal tax
	Savings	U-Fund – The Mass. College Savings Program		#4, #9, #10	Flexible investing schedule; no income limits, no residency requirements
Michigan 800-638-4543 www.treas.state.mi.us	Prepaid	Michigan Education Trust	December-January; 8th grade or younger	#3, #5, #6	Contributions are state-tax deductible
Minnesota 800-657-3866 ext.3201 www.mheso.state.mn.us	Savings	Minnesota EDVEST			
Mississippi 800-987-4450 www.treasury.state.ms.us/	Prepaid	Mississippi Prepaid Affordable College Tuition Program (MPACT)	September-November; under age 18	#1, #3, #6, and private in-state colleges	Contributions are state-tax deductible; earnings are state-tax free
Missouri 573-751-0779 www.sto.state.mo.us	Savings	Missouri Family Higher Education Savings Plan			
Montana 800-888-2723 montana.edu/wwwbor/docs/borpage.html	Savings	Family Education Savings Program	Open		Residents can deduct contributions of up to $3,000/year
Nevada 888-477-2667 www.treasurer.state.nv.us	Prepaid	Nevada Prepaid College Tuition Program	October-November; 9th grade or younger	#1, #3, #5, and private in-state colleges	
New Hampshire 800-544-1722 www.collegesavings.org Click map	Savings	Unique College Investing Plan	Open		Tax-free earnings

(continued)

Table 8-1 (continued)

State	Plan	Program	Enrollment	Key Notes	Details
New Jersey 877-465-2378 www.state.nj.us/ treasury/osa/ njbest.	Savings	Better Educational Savings Trust (BEST)	Open		Eligible for one-time $500 scholarship, if in-state
New Mexico 800-279-9777 www.collegesavings.org Click map	Savings	New Mexico College Savings Program			
New York 877-697-2837 www.nysaves.org	Savings	College Choice Tuition Savings Program	Open; account must be open 3 years before 1st; penalty-free withdrawal		Earnings state-tax exempt; cap on contributions for tax deductions
North Carolina 800-600-3453 www.college visionfund.org	Savings	College Vision Fund	Open; 10th grade or younger		
Ohio 800-233-6734 www.prepaid-tuition.state.oh.us	Prepaid	Ohio Tuition Trust Authority	October–February	#1, #3	
Oklahoma 405-858-4422 www.state.ok.us/ ~sto/college.html	Savings	Oklahoma College Savings Plan			
Pennsylvania 800-440-4000 www.patap.org	Prepaid	Pennsylvania Tuition Account Program	Open	#3, #6	Earnings are state-tax-free for residents

State	Plan	Program	Enrollment	Key Notes	Details
Rhode Island 877-474-4378 www.rihest.com	Savings	R.I. Higher Education Savings Trust	Open		No limit on contributions
South Carolina 888-772-4723 www.state.sc.us/tpp/	Prepaid	South Carolina Tuition Prepayment Program	September-December; 10th grade or younger	#1, #3, #5 penalty of up to $100	State-tax-free earnings
Tennessee 888-486-2378 www.treasury.state.tn.us/best.html	Prepaid	Tennessee Baccalaureate Education System Trust (BEST)	August-October	#3	Can invest up to $42,000
Texas 800-445-4723 www.texastomorrowfund.com	Prepaid	Texas Prepaid Higher Education Tuition Program (TOMORROW)	October-February	#2, #3, only if before high school graduation	
Utah 800-418-2551 www.utah-student-assist.org/uesp.htm	Savings	Utah Educational Savings Plan Trust	Open, under age 17	#1, no more than $50; penalty after 2 years	Earnings are state-tax-free
Vermont 800-642-3177 www.vsac.org	Savings	Vermont Higher Education Savings Plan	Must be resident		Earnings are state-tax-free
Virginia 888-567-0540 www.vpep.state.va.us	Prepaid	Virginia Prepaid Education Program (VPEP)	October-January; 9th grade or younger	#3	State-tax-free earnings; contributions are state-tax deductible up to $2,000/year
Virginia	Savings	Virginia Education Savings Trust (VEST)	Can enroll anytime all year; no age limits; no residency requirements	#1,#5, #6, #9, #10	No income restrictions; state and federal tax advantages; low initial contributions; flexible contributions

(continued)

Table 8-1 (continued)

State	Plan	Program	Enrollment	Key Notes	Details
Washington 877-438-8848 www.get.wa.gov	Prepaid	Guaranteed Education Tuition Program (GET)	September-January	#1, #3, #6,#9	
West Virginia 800-307-4701 wvtreasury.com	Prepaid	West Virginia Prepaid College Plan	October-December; 9th grade or younger	#1, #3 lose no more than $150	
Wisconsin 888-338-3789 http://edvest.state.wi.us	Savings	EdVest Wisconsin (Wisconsin Education Investment Program)	Open		State-tax-free earnings
Wyoming 307-766-5766 www.collegesavings.org Click map	Prepaid	Advanced Payment for Higher Education Cost		#3	

Make a Date with Your State

In the search for money to pay for college, the federal government is target number one. Target number two is your state government, whether you want to receive scholarships and grants, borrow money or — can you imagine? — *save* money? For many middle-income families, the state is the place.

Chapter 9

Negotiating: Get Ready to Bargain

*I*t's the last spring before you enter college. You know you're embarking on some of the best years of your life, but the next couple of months are pure torture, waiting for answers from the half dozen colleges you applied to, requesting aid from each. You live from one mailbox visit to the next, ready for good news or — perish the thought — bad news.

Finally, the envelopes come straggling in. At first glance, you're happy to see that they're all thick acceptances, not thin little notes of rejection. But wait a minute . . . what's this on the bottom line of your number one college choice? Good grief, your financial aid award is $4,000 short of the amount you need to make it through the year. Bummer!

Isn't it strange how the college you love above all others is the one that either turns you down or doesn't give you enough money? "It's like everyone but the person you like best asks you to the prom," says Geraldine J., a student in Des Moines.

Don't give up. The unfortunate shortfall — in this example, $4,000 — doesn't spell doom for your chances of attending your first choice. If you strategize correctly, you may be able to negotiate your way through that $4,000 gap. This chapter shows you how to do it.

A Backgrounder on Bargaining

Parents of young students, more often than students themselves, conduct financial aid negotiations because they usually are the ones who pay the bills. Nevertheless, on the theory that life is one big negotiation, we address most of our suggestions to students — of any age — who probably need practice in the dynamics of bargaining. *Remember:* Thousands of dollars are at stake.

Before earnestly considering ways to upgrade your financial aid award, don't bother looking for negotiating partners in all the wrong places: Certain schools do not negotiate. You don't have to guess which schools will bargain and which ones won't. Colleges usually state their appeal policies early on in an acceptance or award letter. When you're in doubt about the negotiation policy, anonymously call the financial aid office and ask if award appeals are accepted.

The colleges that say *take our offer or leave it* tend to be elite institutions in the top tier of schools. (The number of top-tier colleges ranges between 30 and 65, depending upon who's counting.) These selective and elite schools take a rigid stance because they can. Esteemed institutions like Harvard enjoy a surplus of academically qualified applicants whose parents are able to pay cash without a quibble.

Fortunately for you and most people, colleges that refuse to reconsider award offers are relatively few. The great majority of colleges in the United States are so pressured to enroll students that they discount tuitions by accommodating financial needs whenever possible.

Most colleges will negotiate their financial aid award offers if you provide a good enough reason to do so or make a sincere plea for guidance. Basing your negotiation on facts — presenting new information or calling attention to factors the financial aid counselor may have overlooked — is the surest way to win an appeal.

But when a "new fact" can't be found for miles around, make an emotional appeal to the college's financial aid counselor. Admit that you have a power failure in your financial circuits and ask the counselor's help in finding more aid switches to turn on. Try to make your appeal face-to-face. If that's not possible, write your appeal in a letter and follow up with a telephone call.

Make your appeal for more aid within two weeks after you receive your award letter. Do it before all the money's gone. If you procrastinate, you have one more window of opportunity — approximately the last week in October through the first week in November. That's when the college will know how much money it has in the kitty generated by students who had accepted admission and financial aid and then went somewhere else or took fewer classes, thereby quaifying for less aid. To be certain of your timing in the fall, look in the college catalog (in print and online) and determine when students will no longer receive funds if they drop a class. When the refund period is over, be first in line with your hand out at the financial aid office.

Why threats and ultimatums won't work

Some parents make a big mistake by irately threatening to educate their child elsewhere if a college doesn't cough up more funding. The selection of another college indeed may be the logical answer, and you may have to say so — but *say it nicely*. The point here is not what is said but the way in which it is said.

As an East-coast aid counselor in a public college candidly admits:

> *You [the authors] asked how I feel about parents who demand more funding — or else! Well, I don't react well to huffy ultimatums from people in ski masks. What a contentious parent doesn't realize is that whether a particular student enrolls or goes elsewhere may affect admission office personnel, but it doesn't affect my job. When a parent threatens to pull a potential student away from here, I pleasantly agree that decision is the parent's right and give the appeal no more thought.*

> *My reaction is different when the parent or student has exhausted all their known possibilities and there doesn't seem to be any recourse except to study at a less expensive college. That's when I try very hard to help.*

> *I can't speak for my colleagues in the field, particularly in student-starved, nonelite, regional private schools, but that's my reaction to families that demand more just because they think they're entitled to more.*

Now that's negotiating!

The Baroness von Trapp (the real life heroine in *The Sound of Music*) was a charming negotiator. When producer Leland Hayward offered her 5 percent of the stage musical, the Baroness said she'd have to think about it a bit. Returning a few hours later, the Baroness said, "Whenever I have a puzzle in my head, or a decision to make, I always pray to the Holy Ghost. And I prayed to the Holy Ghost, and the Holy Ghost says 10 percent."

Fat cat schools: Follow the money

Colleges with large endowments have greater flexibility than do their poorer cousins in awarding their own funds. They can afford to recruit students who best meet their institutional objectives. This largesse can work to your advantage with a well-crafted negotiation. Chapter 6 contains a list of endowment-favored colleges and universities.

Hold back one fact for the appeal

As we say earlier in this chapter, initiating an award appeal that pays off is easier when you can bring up new or overlooked information.

Consider omitting a minor (never a major) special circumstance as a negotiating strategy to keep the door open for an appeal. What could be considered a minor special circumstance? Child care expenses or health insurance for students no longer covered by parental health plans, to name two. (We describe other special circumstances in the family-based tips given later in this chapter.)

The special circumstance you forget to mention in your original aid request need not be earth-shattering in importance, just true and logical enough to give you a graceful entry into an appeal process.

The Dynamics of Issue-Based Appeals

Everyone who has tried to get more of anything knows that background information is needed to unravel the basic dynamics of friendly persuasion.

The following analysis looks at the underlying factors, marketing issues, and family complexities that can affect the aid process.

To make the issues easier to use, we split the negotiating tips into two camps — issues that are *college-based* and issues that are *family-based:*

✔ **College-based issues:** We give you the issue's framework, noting why the factor may sway aid decision makers to act in your favor. We follow that with a strategy to cinch the increased funding you need. You usually need not document with paperwork the college-based issues in your aid appeal.

✔ **Family-based issues:** These are special circumstances. We give you only a reminder list of conditions that you can use to expand your aid, assuming any of them fit your family circumstance. We omit the depth of detail found in the college-based issues because you already know how the circumstance affects your family, and the strategy does not vary from issue to issue. You simply relate the issue and prove it with paper documents.

The documentation is essential to back your claims of family-based issues that qualify you for an increase in financial aid.

Negotiating tips for college-based issues

The information you need to effectively implement the negotiating strategies presented in the following sections is available from four sources:

✔ **Printed information:** The college's catalog or letters to you are the first stops on your research trail.

✔ **Personal inquiries:** Ask an admissions counselor at the college's admissions office; for example, if you can't find out what percentage of demonstrated need the college has historically granted, call an admissions counselor and ask. (Admissions office personnel tend to be very cooperative because this staff must "meet its numbers" of expected enrollments or jobs will roll.)

Query the college's representatives who attend college fairs.

Check, too, with other fountains of information, such as your high school guidance counselors and the college's alumni.

✔ **Software and college Web sites:** The College Board's software *ExPAN* (see Chapter 12) contains specific information about institutions' diversity, financial aid history, and typical aid package mix. Each college's Web site may also contain the information you need.

✔ **Networks of friends:** Reaching out for information from your friends and their friends who attend or have graduated from the college may provide the data you need to pull the financial aid system's levers.

First, the issue that may be particularly effective with a specific college (because the college is vulnerable), followed by comments and a suggested strategy. You may be able to combine several of these tips in your appeal.

Issue 1 — How badly does the college need students?

Discover trends in the college's enrollment figures. Is the enrollment down?

When a college is experiencing a smaller-than-usual application pool, its management team may be frantic to add students, advertising such enticements as sushi and waffle bars in the student unions and prime cable service in the dorms. You can bet its institutional ears are open to student pleas for more aid.

Strategy: After making your appeal, ask if it isn't better to have a student paying at a reduced level than having an empty seat in the classroom or an empty bed in the dorm. You need not mention an anemic enrollment — school managers are well aware of the problem. This strategy is useless, of course, at MIT and other high flyers, and at state schools that are swamped with applicants.

Issue 2 — How do costs compare with those of other institutions?

With the exception of the top-tier schools that would sooner allow their students to saunter naked across campus than negotiate price, colleges that punch a high cost ticket have room to discount tuition rates.

Strategy: Incorporate research into your appeal, noting that the college is whatever percent more expensive than the average annual tuition at four-year private schools, which is approximately $15,700. Ask if the cost structure possibly has enough margin to offer you more consideration? By researching tuition at somewhat similar colleges, you can refine the over-and-above comparison even more by citing "comparable private schools."

Issue 3 — Geographic diversity: Does the college value it?

Most Ivy and near-Ivy League schools believe all types of diversity enhance the education of all students because diversity provides a window on the real world. One example is geographic diversity. Consider these examples:

- ✔ Indiana University, located in southern Indiana, intentionally recruits students from outside the Hoosier state to enrich its population with students from other parts of the nation and the world. Even though this school is located outside of major metro areas, it has reached out to recruit a large Jewish population of more than 2,500 students, has developed a major Jewish studies option, and maintains an active Hillel program.
- ✔ Some eastern colleges cast nets for students hailing from Wyoming, Idaho, and the Dakotas.
- ✔ Some southern schools recruit students from northern states.

Your first step is to identify the region that provides most of the school's student body — if you're not living in that region, you have ammo to use in your appeal.

Strategy: Whether you offer new facts or make a personal plea, when your research shows that your intended alma mater is blessed with endowment money, emphasize your geographical desirability as an enrichment of perspectives on campus.

Liberally use the word *diversity* in your appeal. Say you can contribute to the cultural richness of the student body but that you need help with the level of your financial aid. Ask how you can help the financial aid counselor help you cover the last $4,000 you need to enroll without incurring more loans.

Issue 4 — Cultural diversity: Does the school need more minorities?

Colleges are pressured by the feds, states, alumni, faculties, and even student bodies to increase minority student representation on campus. Even in California, where minority enrollments in public higher education fell after voters tossed out affirmative action, various activities are aimed at getting the numbers back up. Overall in the United States, one-fourth of college students come from minority groups.

If you're a minority student, you're a hot commodity at top schools seeking diversity if your grade point average is high — above 3.5 out of 4.0.

Many minority students grow up in big cities and select urban campuses over those in less populated areas, providing another clue about where to use this negotiation — at colleges located in small towns with a relatively uniform population. For this diversity tip, minority includes religion and heritage, as well as race and color.

At colleges where 90 percent of applicants from all racial and ethnic groups are admitted, minority group status has little or no negotiating muscle. Florida International University, for instance, has stopped awarding Hispanic students minority-based scholarships because half of its students are Hispanic.

Strategy: If you are a member of a minority group and are negotiating with a school where your group is in short supply, remind them of your status. You can say something like the following:

> *According to your catalog, you appear to be underrepresented in Hispanic students, of which I am one, although I may have overlooked indicating that fact on my admissions application. In fact, I may have overlooked several things that would count in my favor — I'm the first one in my family to go to college and my high school counselor has been pretty busy so I haven't had much expert advice. My goal is to attend (name of college), but the numbers in my award letter are going to keep me out of this wonderful school. What additional information would you need to increase my award (or scholarship aid), making it possible for me to enroll?*

The bottom line: At institutions that value and recruit for cultural diversity, the odds weigh heavily in the direction of the minority student who has a well-prepared appeal for any credible reason.

Issue 5 — What is the college's track record on financial aid?

This tip calls for super sleuthing on your part. You must discover the college's *going rate* for aid awards by ferreting out two pieces of information:

✔ What is the typical mix (self-help and gift) of aid the college has historically awarded?

✔ What percentage of demonstrated need has the college traditionally met?

(For hints on gathering this "intel," review the section a few pages back titled "Negotiating tips for college-based issues.")

Without comparative reports, you lack a basis for comparison with how the school has dealt with other students. You can't be certain you haven't already received the school's best offer.

A well-kept secret within the collegiate financial aid industry is one you should know.

The college financial aid process doesn't always result in the best deal for every student. Often what the industry terms the *initial offer* comes first, which means the opening bid is less than you need and less than the college can deliver. The rationale is that the offer can always be raised if that's what it takes to get you enrolled. When you bite and accept the initial offer without trying for more, the college is richer and you are poorer.

Strategy: Even when a college's aid policy is straightforward — their first offer is their last offer — it pays to determine the school's norms in aid awards before you launch an appeal. A computer probably ground out your award letter with programming based on specific parameters. Financial aid counselors routinely modify your award if the parameters are unreasonable after you submit new information.

You can frame your comments with these thoughts in mind:

> *As I understand it, the normal gift aid mix for a student with my EFC is (20 percent to 50 percent). I didn't understand why my letter specified so little gift aid until I realized you may not have figured in (bit of new information, such as parent lost a job or the high cost of medical care for a family member). Does this fact mean I'm eligible for more gift funding? How much more? How soon can you make it happen?*

Or

*My research indicates the university usually meets 100 percent of demon-
strated need. My award seems to be only 75 percent of my demonstrated
need. I think I'm dead here. That missing $4,000 may make it impossible
for me to enroll. Did I get something wrong somewhere? I am not sure
that I let you know that (bit of new information). What else must I do to
help you close the gap to 100 percent so that I can become one of your
students?*

Issue 6 — Why has the college decreased your Year 2 award?

In this situation, you are no longer a freshman. The college has given you
enough money for your first year. But now for the next year, you are advised
that (1) your actual dollars have been cut or that (2) your aid package has
been reworked — you are now expected to come up with more funding in
self-help aid (loans and jobs) as you receive less in gift aid (scholarships
and grants).

When the shock wears off, you wonder what happened. Chances are high
that you've received an initial award to test the water. The college's slash-
and-churn tactics are designed to find out if you'll hang in as an educational
customer if they cut off big chunks of your aid. Race to the financial aid
office and find out exactly why your aid went down, not up.

Strategy: No single strategy is inclusive but, in general, anticipate your
talking points:

- ✔ Did your grades slip? Note that you had to study twice as hard for a
  difficult semester.

- ✔ Are you a low-income student? Remind them that you depend almost
  entirely on financial aid for the basic necessities, including the food on
  your table.

- ✔ Are you a middle-income student? Point out that your family already
  faces sacrifice, debt, and hard choices. You aren't even sure that you
  can stay in school if more, not less, help isn't forthcoming. Everyone
  knows that for the past two decades college costs have risen much
  faster than inflation.

Issue 7— Does the college seek National Merit finalists?

Academic excellence enhances future student recruitment as well as
fundraising efforts. A great way for colleges to give their academic standards
a shot in the arm is to populate their campuses with National Merit finalists.
Some colleges, such as Macalester College in Minnesota, even set aside
financial aid funds for students who are National Merit finalists.

Approximately 7,300 National Merit Scholars attend nearly 400 different
colleges and universities. These attendees normally have some of their
costs paid for by the National Merit Scholarship Corporation or other

corporate sponsors. Whereas, those merit scholars who attend public colleges are sponsored primarily by the college's own institutional funds. The top five colleges selected by merit winners are (1) Harvard University (370), (2) University of Texas at Austin (202), (3) Stanford University (201), (4) University of California at Berkeley (184), and (5) Rice University (169).

Strategy: Lace your language with comments about excellence and achievement. You are establishing an environment to deliver your true agenda:

> *As I am a National Merit finalist, I believe I can meet your academic standards and bring value to the student body at (name of college). What's stopping me is the high ratio of debt in the financial aid package you offer. It's towering. I'll be paying it off until the 22nd century. Or at least until my own future children are old enough for college. Can you possibly restructure the offer with more scholarship or grant funding? Is there something else I can do? I really need your help.*

Issue 8 — Is the college seeking special talent?

Students who can tutor in computer labs, handle art materials, catalog library books, work the cafeteria cash register, stock supplies in a bookstore, handle school intramural programs, or fill any school need are in demand.

Your appeal should embrace all of your accomplishments and skills — in high school you were a newspaper editor, musician, theater performer, or whatever.

Strategy: Admit that your family is staggering under a burden of loans. Even though America enjoys a peak job market, downsizing and job instability rage. As recently reported in *Fortune* magazine's Finished at Forty article, career experts contend that a year or two may pass before comparable income is achieved for a parent over 40 who loses a job. This makes parental loans very difficult to repay on schedule. Whatever words you use, express yourself in human terms, like this:

> *I am experienced at sports equipment management — I did it for the high school football team and the softball team. I'm glad to work as much as I can and still keep my grades up, but are any scholarships or grants available that we missed out on? What can you advise at this point other than sinking into a mountain of debt? Should we conclude that the cost of college has risen above the average person's ability to pay?*

Issue 9 — What's the ratio of financial aid recipients to total enrollment?

Does your research reveal that a large proportion of the college's student population is receiving financial aid, chiefly gift aid? If so, the college's financial aid professionals are sensitive to the college's high costs and the students' needs. This college is student-oriented, rather than research-oriented, and is investing in its potential alumni. This college is receptive to aid appeals.

Strategy: Pull out all the stops with a factual or emotional appeal. Here's an example.

> *Your offer, while greatly appreciated, leaves a void of $4,000, which I can't handle. Is it true that 67 percent of your student population receives aid and that much of it doesn't have to be repaid? There must be some factor in my background that can help you find another $4,000 in scholarships. Did I tell you that my mother just changed jobs and she earns less than she did at her old job? Did I mention that my computer was stolen and I didn't have replacement insurance? Isn't there something you can do to help me work this out?*

Issue 10 — Does the college respond to competing offers?

Although some prestigious colleges now actually invite haggling for better awards, the managers of most institutions of higher education don't like to admit that they're as affected by market forces as anyone else. When dealing with financial aid counselors, who are professionals and proud of it, be sensitive in how you leverage one financial aid offer to increase another. Take a low-key, diplomatic approach. Financial aid professionals wince and tell you to take the other offer and run when your appeal style is insincere.

Strategy: Share the competitive letter with the counselor you hope will raise the amount or quality of your award. State that you had your sights set on attending your first-choice college but without more aid, you'll be forced to attend the college with the better offer because (give a reason — no money, your family can't or won't support the higher price, or any true justification). Ask the counselor to match the award. You may not get an equivalent offer, but you'll get something more.

> *I have a difficult problem that I hope you can help me with. Indiana University is my number one choice by far. But ABC College has offered me more liberal aid — as you can see on this offer letter — and my parents are insisting that I enroll there because college costs so much. Is there any possible way that you can even out this gap?*

Negotiating points for family-based issues

Although the amount of financial aid awarded is based on standard formulas, your family may be far from standard issue. Each factor increases your award and reduces the amount of expected family contribution.

We said it before but because so many people forget, we beat the drums again.

Prove every claim for nonroutine, diminished family income with such documents as expense charts, canceled checks, medical bills, divorce papers, employment termination notices, and Social Security notifications.

The following points provide legitimate reasons for the college's financial aid counselor to enlarge your award.

Your budget is not standard issue

Financial aid is based on a standard student budget. You must prove that your expenses will be greater than the standard. The areas of health, diet, disability, transportation, and even special tutorial expense if you need remedial work justify an appeal.

Education costs escalate for other family members

Do other members of your family have uncommon costs that take away from your family's ability to pay the assessed expected family contribution? For example, perhaps a brother or sister is required to attend a private school because of learning disabilities or other disabilities. The FAFSA or CSS Profile has no place to put this information. You have to focus on it in your appeal.

Family obligations drain money from your family's income

Many parents are caught in the "sandwich" generation. They provide for children and for their own aged parents. Costs of providing care in a home, a nursing facility, or a residence on another continent can be overwhelming.

Income cuts mean more aid

Social Security benefits for children are reduced at age 18 or on the last day of high school attendance, whichever date comes last. Usually, this occurs after the FAFSA documents are filed, which means the college's financial aid counselor has no way of knowing that your SS benefits are lower and your family will have fewer dollars for college.

Another income cut that your counselor won't know about unless you announce it in an appeal occurs in families where parents are split apart. Most noncustodial divorced or separated parents are not obligated to contribute child support after your 18th birthday.

In a related issue, when a divorce or separation of parents actually occurs after the financial aid forms have been submitted, inform your counselor how much child support and/or home maintenance support your custodial parent expects to receive from the other. Your expected family contribution is likely to be lower under the new arrangement.

Illness or death in the family is reason to appeal

Similar to divorce, if the parent who was a wage earner during the base year of income is no longer able to contribute, your income drops and aid rises.

Educational transportation may qualify for funds

When you are required to complete an internship, co-op education assignment, or another program that requires an automobile for transportation, ask for additional aid funding to cover the related expenses.

Required study abroad requires another look at aid

If you are enrolled in college for credit and must complete a study-abroad program to fulfill curriculum requirements, you may be able to get more money for transportation and living expenses.

A parent is out of work

Because your demonstrated need is assessed on income earned by your parent(s) in the previous calendar year (base year), if a parent's job is lost, you have a ready-made aid appeal.

Bad credit ratings make good aid awards

When you and your parents are tapped out, have a bad credit history, owe the IRS, are overextended on credit cards, or for any other reason can't borrow more college money, share that fact with your financial aid counselor. The counselor may be sympathetic and award you more gift funds.

Family size increases

Is a new sibling on the scene? A central element in calculating your eligibility for aid is the number of household members. For aid in the 2000–2001 school year, count all your family's *children who will receive more than half their support from your parents* between July 1, 2000, and June 30, 2001. As an example, your appeal is based on your mother being pregnant and expecting birth in the spring of 2000, which adds another mouth to feed during your school year.

Parents retire

The college financial aid counselor has no way of knowing that your mother or father is planning to retire during your school year. Explain the retirement benefits, presumably lower than employment earnings, and ask the counselor to calculate a new base year.

New academic statistics may increase dollars for scholars

Many colleges give discounts related to class rank or SAT/ACT scores, sometimes as much as 50 percent for high achievers. If your SAT/ACT scores have increased or your high school rank has risen, you may qualify for favored status.

Family obligations force aid layaway

When you've already received your award letter and suddenly find that family responsibilities will keep you out of school until the second semester, negotiate with your counselor to hold your second semester funding for you and not give the money away to someone else.

Writing a Winning Aid Appeal

Many avenues for appeal are open after you begin to think through the college's issues and your family's fiscal fitness. Learn to write a good appeal letter. Even when you plan a face-to-face encounter in the financial aid office, bring a letter stating the facts with you. The following three letters show you how to construct an effective appeal.

Parent Letter

July 10, 2000

Jeremy Greatperson
Director of Student Financial Services
Bluffton College
280 W. College Ave., Box 788
Bluffton, OH 45817-1196

Subject: (1) Self-Employment Business Statement and (2) Special Circumstances

Re: Rebecca Heart, SSN 000-00-0000

Dear Mr. Greatperson:

As per your office's instructions, we enclose information documenting our self-employment and special circumstances. We have no tangible assets except for the file cabinets and computer we use to provide our services. My husband is a private counselor and I am a writer.

Because of these circumstances, we have not completed the business form. We declared the business income as $98,010 on our federal income tax form 1040, and enclose copies of related documents.

We understand that our application and request for aid missed the established deadline. When our daughter, Rebecca, applied for early decision acceptance, we assumed that because we have only one child and, in light of our combined income, we could not qualify for financial assistance.

However, we recently consulted a general financial advisor regarding our need for self-employed retirement coverage, and a college financial aid advisor regarding our financial planning. Both advisors agree that without better planning, we will face tremendous difficulties in funding both our retirement and Rebecca's education. These advisors gave us the following reasons to apply for college financial aid:
1. Our relatively low net worth
2. Our highly variable income
3. Our current medical expense burden: In addition to paying $1,200 per month to Blue Cross Blue Shield, we must pay significant medical fees for a serious, chronic mental health condition, which is only partly covered by our medical insurance. This treatment will not decrease in the next five years. We have also learned that we will require $10,000 in dental, nonelective, noncosmetic work over the next six months. We have no dental insurance and our dentist can only allow three monthly payments. We can provide documentation to verify such facts.

In conclusion, we expect a shortfall of at least $6,000 after considering Rebecca's unsubsidized Stafford and the PLUS program. We would greatly appreciate any advice from your office as we struggle to meet our financial obligations and keep Rebecca in college.

Most sincerely yours,

Maria Heart

Maria Heart
(Mother)

enc: 10 documents

Parent Letter

March 25, 2000

Ms. Jenna Savy
Office of Student Financial Aid
Adelphi University
Garden City, New York 11530

Subject: Letter of Appeal, Loss of Income

Re: John Scholar, SSN 000-00-0000

Dear Ms. Savy:

I write to you to inform you of my loss of income for the current year 2000. I understand that students' financial aid is based on their demonstrated need, which involves the parents' and student's income and assets for the 1999 calendar base year.

My income has reduced significantly; I have enclosed a copy of a letter from the International Medical Group that confirms that my service agreement with them will not be renewed. On my 1999 income tax, I listed the income from the contract, $21,300. My income for 2000, however, will consist only of my full-time job, which pays me a salary of $58,358. This is a tremendous decrease from the original $79,658.

I hope you can consider this new and disheartening information in a reevaluation of my son's financial need. John and I would greatly appreciate it.

Most sincerely yours,

Jane Scholar

Jane Scholar
(Mother)

enc: 1 document

Student Letter

March 10, 2000

Dr. John Moneypenny
Director of Financial Aid
5000 Forbes Ave.
Carnegie Mellon University
Pittsburgh, PA 15231

Subject: Financial Aid Appeal Letter
Ref: William Wilneed (SSN 000-00-000)
Telephone: #555-555-1355

Dear Dr. Moneypenny:

I have signed and enclosed the award notification from your institution, but I ask for your guidance.

My parents and I have reviewed our family's plan for paying for college. As you are aware, I have two brothers who will apply for college in the next three years. You may recall that my brother Thomas is a junior with a 3.9 GPA and SAT scores of 1480. My sophomore brother, Timothy, has similar academic achievements.

I am the brother with a less awesome academic record — 3.6 GPA and combined SAT score of 1300. Even so, I am troubled because I was not found eligible for more that a $2,625 Stafford Loan from Carnegie Mellon.

My parents are concerned that they will not have the funds to support me for the next four years without some help from CMU. I have taken the liberty of describing our budget plan, which shows a gap of $7,875. Can you assist me in identifying resources to fill the gap in our unmet need?

COA at Carnegie Mellon including living on campus for 2000-01 will be.................... $33,000.

Student's contribution from savings.................................. $3,500
Student's contribution from summer work............................. $2,000
Student's contribution from Stafford Loan............................ $2,625
Parent's contribution from savings & wages........................... $9,000
Parent's contribution from PLUS... $8,000

Total.. $25,125

Shortfall (GAP)... $7,875

As you can see, we are short only about $8,000 in our budget. Your assistance in identifying additional financial aid would be appreciated.

Sincerely yours,

William Wilneed

William Wilneed
Class of 2004

Fine-Tuning Your Bargaining Skills

Negotiating is a skill you should learn. Because a college financial aid counselor has the authority to use *professional judgment* on a case-by-case basis, fine-tuning your bargaining skills really pays. Third-party (outside) scholarships prove the point.

The average award package is made up of 60 percent self-help funds (loans and/or jobs) and 40 percent gift funds. When you receive an outside scholarship, some colleges want to take back their gift aid in like proportion, leaving you with the same amount of debt. Ugh. Good negotiation may modify that disappointment by persuading the college to reduce each type of assistance in the award letter by 50 percent of the outside award.

Example: Suppose you win an outside scholarship of $2,000, and your award letter specifies a $3,500 loan and a $2,000 grant. You want your loan reduced by $1,000 and your grant reduced by $1,000. You don't want your grant reduced by $2,000, leaving you with $3,500 to pay off.

If you don't really understand the financial aid formulas and don't really know what's going on, you're going to pay many thousands of dollars more than you really must. In any industry — and education is an industry — business managers try to get you to pay as much as possible, while you try to pay as little as possible.

Chapter 10

Merit Scholarships for the Talented

Damon Darnell Williams of Washington, D.C., is on the A-Team of scholarship winners.

Damon made it his business to know so much about the financial aid system that he racked up an astonishing $542,681 in college scholarship offers, including full-ride prizes from seven highly regarded colleges and universities. He won so many awards that the excess pays for books and other school expenses. Damon knows that having too much money is better than having too little and so he went all out in his search.

Ultimately, Damon chose George Washington University because he wanted to complete his education, at least through his undergraduate college years, within Washington, D.C. boundaries.

A hospitality (hotel and restaurant management) major, Damon began learning the financial aid system during the summer after his sophomore year at H. D. Woodson High School. He read books and watched videos, but placed heavy emphasis on the personal touch. Damon spent time with his high school guidance counselor and called financial aid counselors at colleges. He asked for advice. "I wanted people who could affect my future to perceive me as a person, not just as a name on a piece of paper," Damon says.

We asked Damon for suggestions on becoming a big scholarship winner.

"First, learn how the financial aid system works. Learn to work within the system and how to work around it," Damon advises.

Work around the system?

"Find a connection! Getting student aid is a form of networking. When you can't find a person who knows a student aid director or counselor at a college, call the director cold. In my experience, some directors mentioned new scholarships that might fit me. I always tried to tailor my approach to scholarships that I really wanted by showing I'm a serious-minded individual who goes after what he wants."

Other tips from Damon:

- ✔ Start early and be persistent. Don't wait until you're a high school senior to suddenly realize college is just around the corner. And no matter how tired you are, make time to complete your applications and turn them in by the deadlines.

- ✔ Write sincere letters to presidents of colleges and universities. (Usually they're passed to the financial aid office.) Use the name and precise title of the president and spell everything correctly. You want to project the image of a student with great promise of being a mature person who will contribute to society. Your letters show purpose and that you care enough to make an all-out effort worthy of reward. The letters also show you're worth helping and that a helping hand extended to you now will be returned to society many times over.

- ✔ Prepare an essay pool of perhaps four or five core essays, on topics such as what you hope to be doing in 20 years, why you want to go to a specific college, and so on. Adapt your core essays quickly to scholarship programs or to college financial aid offices. Having a starting point on essays keeps your momentum going — you then have no excuse to delay sending in the application because you don't know what to say in a required essay.

- ✔ Go in person to local colleges and universities, or call the institution if it is out of town. If you, for example, live in Washington, D.C., you may be able to travel to a college in Philadelphia but you would telephone a college in Chicago. Give financial aid counselors the details of your financial history so that they can understand your circumstances. Try to establish a relationship with financial aid counselors.

Don't think that Damon spent all his time grinding out financial aid applications — his academic record was superb. Valedictorian of his class, Damon graduated from high school with a 4.29 in his school's 4.0 system. (He received extra points for college-level and honors courses.)

Damon's leadership record was also impressive. Among a raft of activities, he served in two citywide positions: as president of Future Business Leaders of America and as a member of the student government executive committee.

Damon's scholarship resume, which is a compilation of all his financial aid awards, stretches over four pages and misses nothing. It cites distinctions in education, honors and awards, vocational leadership, other leadership, community service, work experience, affiliations, public speaking experience, television and radio appearances, and newspaper clips about him.

His scholarship resume also includes Damon's career objective to be an entrepreneur specializing in hotel and restaurant management, and his hobbies of chess, miniature golf, reading, and watching films and sports.

Few students can hope to match Dynamo Damon's record-breaking performance, but it's a goal worth eyeing.

Good Prospects Even If You're Not a Budding Einstein

You may not be a world-class competitor like Damon, but are you an above-average student in academics, sports, music, art, or another ability? Colleges and universities pant for your presence. They, being competitive creatures, have school reputations to keep up and need to brag that they're the place to be.

That's why virtually all colleges and universities put their money where their mouths are by awarding a combination of merit and need-based scholarships.

That's why nine out of ten four-year colleges give no-need scholarships. That's why all schools want the best talent they can attract.

The very students that the schools are trying to attract may not be fully cooperating. The biggest problem in lining up free money for college is understanding how the system works, from the point of discovery to the point of receiving the awards.

Much like you have to buy a ticket to win the lottery, you have to heavily invest yourself in the system if you hope to reap substantial scholarship rewards. Many students and their parents don't get the message. They have a feeling that what they're doing is so monumentally valuable that scholarships will seek them out.

That's not how the big-scholarship-money printing presses roll. To receive major private scholarships, you have to do more than distinguish yourself academically, athletically, in the arts, or in community service. Throwing in your status as an all-around great kid isn't enough either. *You have to work the system before all of these virtues pay off.*

Need is in the eye of the beholder

You may have little idea whether or not you're a financially needy student when you apply for a scholarship. Most students don't.

Many private scholarship organizations have their own definition of demonstrated need, and they don't adhere — and may not even be close — to the Federal Methodology (a calculator formula based on the FAFSA) that colleges use to determine a student's eligibility:

✔ Always assume that you have demonstrated need and allow the scholarship sponsor to determine its level.

✔ Never disqualify yourself based on the level of need specified by the government or your college.

Nine Rules of the Scholarship Hunt

When it comes to scholarship money, you can't afford to let opportunity go knocking. But as someone once observed, the trouble with opportunity is that it always comes disguised as hard work. That's certainly the case with the scholarship hunt. We wish we could say the hunt is like a walk on the beach, but really no shortcuts exist if you want to end your treasure hunt with at least two fists full of college money — enough to pay for four years of college.

With that goal in mind, here are nine rules for a winning scholarship hunt.

Shed the lead, think ahead

When should you start smartening up about scholarships? Sit down for startling news: Don't wait until your junior year — start in your first year of high school.

Even though you may already be pushing yourself so hard to get into a "good" college that you have little time to sleep or have fun, the burdens of debt for years after college are so debilitating that the sooner you plan, the easier you land.

In your first year, you can begin participating in high school governance, newspaper journalism, Girl Scouting or Boy Scouting, community service, school club activities, and any other activity that shows you're developing skills and making labor contributions to worthy causes. This early start can develop into a strong visible credential to use in your scholarship search by the time you graduate.

Find sponsors and causes dear to your future

Many service organizations — Kiwanis Clubs, Lions, Eagles, Elks, and Moose — raise scholarship funds to sponsor college students. These same organizations usually have a national project, such as eye banks, food and shelter for the homeless, and children's hospitals. If, by chance, you plan to major in a career field related to the areas of interest to an organization's national project, track down the local scholarship chairman of the organization, share your goals, and ask for sponsorship.

During your first year, begin collecting information on scholarships. Get everyone in the family to help you clip news of scholarships to add to your collection. At this stage, don't limit the type of scholarship information you collect because you're unsure of your college major or career pathway. Save information on any type of scholarship.

Reviewing your scholarship collection at this early stage can save you time in the long run. You quickly see what is important and what is not important to win a particular scholarship.

You must learn the answer to this question: *How is a student evaluated for a specific scholarship?*

If you have no demonstrated need, you'd be wasting your time to apply for the $2 million Elks National Foundation's "Most Valuable Student" scholarship award, for example. For this award, the selection committee assesses applicants on leadership and activities, but the final decision tilts toward demonstrated need.

True scholarships do not have a financial need criteria. Many students who spend time looking for private scholarships do not have need. Students who have need try for aid from their colleges.

Become an awards detective

Arguably, the most important part of the scholarship hunt is research. Most parents and students don't know where to begin. A good place to start is the career center at your high school. Most centers have software you can use to make a computerized search.

If you attend a high school that refuses to let you get your hands on the scholarship computers until you're a senior, turn to the Internet and do a free scholarship search online. See Chapter 12 for the best sources of online help.

Does searching free online databases have drawbacks? Yes!

✔ The free search is advertising-driven, designed to collect your name and address for marketing efforts. Be prepared to compromise your privacy and to be flooded with "spam" and junk mail.

✔ The database may not be frequently updated or validated. Value in a database is based on accuracy and currency. Do you want to spend hours and wasted postage applying for scholarships you'll never receive?

✔ The free online scholarship tips may come from entrepreneurs who either do not have your best interests at heart or who don't know what they're talking about.

Nevertheless, the free online searches can help you discover where scholarships are located.

Alternative computerized searches are available:

✔ The National College Scholarship Foundation provides a computer scholarship search and literature, *College Aid Resources for Education,* for $24.

✔ The American Legion offers a booklet, *Need a Lift,* and a computerized search for $20.

Scholarship research is not a one-time exercise. It starts in the early years of high school and continues through graduate school. Your motto should be "Start early, stay late." Make collecting snippets and chunks about scholarships a family affair as brothers, sisters, aunts, uncles, grandparents, and friends join your parents and you in forming a *scholarship research team.* Devote a file drawer or a bedroom corner for your scholarship library.

Despite the part you, the student, should play in financing your own education, the reality is that Mom and Dad become the true scholarship team leaders. The sad fact is that most students see a college education as an entitlement and are not concerned about who pays the bill. Isn't it true that you value more highly the things in which you personally invest? You'll never be tempted to ditch classes if you're busting your chops to pay by winning scholarships or by working.

Research includes not only finding hidden scholarship funds but being able to get the applications to apply for the money. One reason so many students fail to receive scholarships is that they don't get the applications in time to compete for the awards, a topic we discuss later in this chapter.

Stockpile marketing ammo

Give your research team ammunition to win your battle for money. Prepare a Personal Financial Aid Inventory by photocopying and filling out the form shown as Figure 10-1.

Using your Personal Financial Aid Inventory, look for connections with all organizations, agencies, clubs, and the like that may have scholarships available. Don't overlook such local groups as parent-teacher associations, professional organizations, and veterans groups. Include corporations. Parents should check with employers and unions to see if aid for offspring is offered. Ethnic heritage groups like the Alliance of Poles or the German-American Club also provide financial aid.

Your scholarship team will benefit from your personal aid inventory. They need to know about all of your characteristics, skills, and experiences. Consider these awards:

- ✔ **St. John Fisher College** in New York awards more than $150,000, without regard to demonstrated need or GPA requirement, to students who've contributed to community service activities.

- ✔ **Juniata College** in Pennsylvania gives scholarships to people who are left-handed.

- ✔ **Lyon College** in Batesville, Arkansas, pays students who play the bagpipes between $1,000 and $6,000 without regard to need or merit.

- ✔ At **North Carolina State University,** students who are named Gatlin or Gatling can receive up to $6,000 with no requirements for academic excellence or need.

- ✔ The **University of Rochester in New York** passes out $5,000 to any student who is a New York resident when enrolling.

Save every scrap of accomplishment

The scholarship hunt is the perfect reason for comprehensive, systematic record-keeping.

You and your parents should retain copies of any significant happening during your high school years — special award for scouting, 4-H, music, community service, or any kudos.

Keep your records by activity, separating your high school activities from your community activities.

Personal Financial Aid Inventory

ACADEMIC INFORMATION

High school grades _____ Rank in class _____

Special aptitudes,
abilities, and hobbies _____

Special awards and
recognition _____

School and community
activities _____

College major(s) _____

Career plans _____

STUDENT INFORMATION

Citizenship _____

Ethnic heritage _____

Age _____ Gender _____

Clubs _____

Physical traits _____

Religious affiliations _____

PARENT INFORMATION

Occupations Mother _____ Father _____

Veteran status Mother _____ Father _____

Professional
organizations/unions Mother _____ Father _____

Figure 10-1: Review your financial aid inventory.

Although your high school transcript will be sent to scholarship sponsors to verify grades and how they've improved or worsened from year to year, the transcript doesn't tell your entire story.

The transcript doesn't describe your award for the honor roll or an award for most-improved student. The transcript says nothing about how your research paper in a particular class received special recognition.

Special notes and special awards catch the eye of the scholarship readers who review and evaluate your application.

Keep careful records, too, each time you put your name in the ring for a specific scholarship. Save a list of the forms required by the scholarship sponsor, and keep dates when the documents were mailed to the sponsor. Note for each sponsor that although you have sent an unofficial (high school or transfer) transcript, your school must mail an official copy of your transcript before the scholarship committee can act on your file.

Record-keeping focuses your attention on each potential scholarship application and whether you need to follow up your initial effort.

Follow the money trail

Imagine this scene: A room filled with civic-minded, good-hearted, unpaid women and men sitting at tables sorting through gazillions of scholarship applications, getting a little punchy in the process because scholarship selection is just one more assignment they've unselfishly taken on to help others. We call these people *volunteers*, bless 'em all.

Many volunteers today have full-time jobs or kids to look after, and the time they spend wading through pounds of the aspirations and dreams of college hopefuls isn't their number one priority in life.

The reading and clerical load of processing scholarship applications can become overwhelming, causing some volunteers to put aside work for the "next time" or to take student mail home to finish their assignments. Let's face it: Day-in-day-out continuity of tasking can be missing in many volunteer organizations.

If you've been a member of a volunteer organization, you know first-hand how easily inefficiencies occur — inefficiencies that can leave the scholarship seeker out in the cold in one or both of the two stages of scholarship solicitation, as the following disqualifying scenarios illustrate:

✔ **Stage 1: You ask for an application.**

But you don't receive the application and you're automatically disqualified.

So what happened to your request for an application, assuming it wasn't lost in the mail? In a volunteer environment, your request may be stuck in someone's desk drawer or hiding in a stack of unopened mail or locked in a car trunk beside the reader's bowling shoes that won't be worn for the next ten days.

✔ **Stage 2: You complete and mail an application and enclose documents.**

But you forget to enclose one or more required documents. No one gets back to you with that oversight. You are automatically disqualified because of lack of information.

So why didn't someone notify you that your scholarship application is incomplete? Maybe a reader thought that if you are unable to follow directions, you're not college material. Who knows? Who cares? The answer could be any number of reasons, none of them important in the sense that you're out of the running if you don't fix the problem.

The willingness to follow-up on every single application request is vital. If you don't receive a requested application form after two or three weeks, pick up the telephone and call the scholarship sponsor. (Yes, we agree that long-distance telephoning is expensive, but ask yourself which is more expensive — telephone calls or paying for college?)

Never assume that one request should suffice and drop the scholarship when you don't get the application:

✔ After you get the form and return your comprehensive scholarship application package, telephone to ask if the sponsor received it, and confirm that all your supporting documents are present and accounted for.

✔ When you speak to a sponsor's employee or volunteer, be certain to get the person's name and job title.

✔ Record pertinent facts of your conversations in your records. If, at a later time, a sponsor says your application was not received on time, you can nail that misstatement on the spot by tactfully quoting dates, chapter and verse.

When you receive an award, you've got one more follow-up job to handle: Write to the sponsor with your acceptance and thanks for the award.

Keep a close watch on each scholarship application as it moves through the system and follow up relentlessly.

Get thee to financial aid on time

Pay attention to your scholarship calendar (see Chapter 4) in general and to an October deadline in particular in making sure you have received virtually all scholarship application forms. This gives you time to prepare a powerful application package complete with endorsements, letters of recommendation, notices of honors, 500-word essays when required, and other self-marketing materials.

Throughout the scholarship application process, don't fail to meet all deadlines. As Duke University financial aid director Jim Belvin says, "It wouldn't matter if the student were the son of the president of the university, if he did not meet the deadline he would not be considered for financial aid."

Are there no extenuating circumstances that would justify an extension if you miss a deadline? We can think of one — being shipwrecked at sea.

There are usually more applicants for aid than there is aid to distribute. Most financial aid staffs are looking for ways to rule you out. Don't give them the opportunity by neglecting to completely fill out your application and mail it in on time.

Tailor your application to win the prize

When you whip out a generic (one-size-fits-all) application for every scholarship you come across, what you prove is that you have access to a working photocopy machine.

But when you design your scholarship application package to maximize your appeal in a specific scholarship award environment, you prove you have access to a working mind.

Cut to the chase: Get the rules

Find out what really matters in each scholarship award. Request a copy of the scholarship's rules. You want to know how many points are given for need, for the essay, for leadership, for scholarship, for part-time work while in college, for participation in extra-curricular activities, for volunteer work, and the like. Aim your application where the points are.

Develop a core application and then tailor it to fit specific scholarships. You are trying to get the scholarship selection readers to see that your qualifications match the award's criteria.

In addition to your core scholarship application, select appropriate items from the following list that show how well you match the kind of student the scholarship sponsor says it seeks:

- ✔ Unofficial high school transcript (college transcript for returning adults). Official transcripts must be mailed by originating schools so there's no chance that you could alter them. But scholarship sponsors accept even photocopies as unofficial transcripts until they receive official versions.

- ✔ Recommendation letters from teachers, community leaders, business and professional people, members of the clergy.

- ✔ A 500-word essay on a national theme (scholarship watchers say half of all students who apply for scholarships will not complete an application if the scholarship requires an essay).

- ✔ A list of all awards, such as those bestowed for scouting, debating, poster design, and so forth.

- ✔ A list of references who can comment on your skills and work experience.

- ✔ A list of volunteer or community service activities in which you have participated.

- ✔ A list of positions held in school that show leadership and responsibility.

- ✔ A list of work experiences that show you can manage your time between school, work, and extracurricular activities.

- ✔ Copies of documents and newspaper clippings verifying your awards, honors, commendations.

Go all out to gain an edge against your competitors. Present scholarship decision-makers with a superb, self-marketing application package that shows you as a strong match for the award's requirements, who should be among the top tier of candidates. Show them why they should give you the money. An outstanding and targeted presentation package is the secret weapon that wins you the big prizes. But even if you don't have the greatest qualifications, gift money may be available.

Find your strong suits: Money's out there for average people, too

Maybe you're no great shakes as a scholar, your SAT or ACT wasn't cheering material, and your athletic abilities don't rival Michael Jordan's. If you've got a talent, it's wrapped away in tissue paper and hasn't been seen for 17 years. Even so, you'd be surprised at how much money is available that has little to do with academics, but relies on

- ✔ Ethnic or racial heritage
- ✔ Membership in clubs
- ✔ Community activities

✔ Career plans or field of study

✔ Hobbies and special interests

✔ Physical traits (very tall, short) or disabilities (asthmatic)

✔ Religious affiliation

✔ Parents' employers or their unions

Scholarships based on some of these aspects are profiled in the Resource Guide at the back of the book.

Set your hounds on student aid

Maintain a resolute determination to win and don't take "no" for an answer. After following up on the receipt of your application package and confirming that it's in order with no pieces missing, you may not hear a word back for months and months:

✔ If you have not heard from a sponsor in three months, call and find out the status of your application.

✔ If you have received notice that you're not in the final cut for a scholarship award, call and find out why. Maybe the scholarship committee didn't receive all your material although it all arrived at the sponsoring organization. Student records are frequently misfiled, and applicant documents disappear from the scholarship folders. If you detect an irregularity, ask that your application be reinstated with all the required documents present.

✔ If you have been awarded a scholarship but haven't received the funds by July 15, ask the person who signed your award letter when you can expect to receive your scholarship money.

Once in a while an unusual situation develops: You're notified that you were a finalist but, unfortunately, the money ran out. If this happens to you, wait until college starts in the fall and, about mid-term, call the person who signed the bad-news letter to find out if any of the finalists failed to attend college or have dropped out; if so, ask if you can have funds returned by the college where the no-show or drop-out enrolled. Scholarship committees generally don't want to have to report to their organizations that funds raised for scholarships are sitting idle.

Lock that scholarship dream in steel jaws and hang on. Cease only if you are told by someone important to "Stop calling us, you bowser." Until that happens, continue with the determination of Hannibal the elephant-riding conqueror, who, as he sought a way to cross the forbidding Alps, clenched his teeth and announced, "We will either find a way, or make one."

Mother is right: Say thanks

Although you aggressively pursue the scholarship prize, after you've made yourself known, stand down and allow the system to work and stop kissing up.

In addition to the acceptance and thank-you letters you write when you do win, make yourself available for the scholarship luncheon or similar event. Not only is it gracious behavior, but you want to make sure that when your name comes up for renewal awards for the next three years, they know who you are.

Fighting for Scholars

Schools give the largest number of no-need awards for academic achievement. Why? Colleges need bright students who in turn attract good faculty who in turn generate research funds. And bright students who graduate remember their colleges fondly and make alumni gifts.

Now you know why colleges treat finalists in the annual National Merit Scholars, the nation's most prestigious high school academic-talent competition, like uncrowned royalty.

In Louisville, Kentucky, Garet Thomas — who scored 33 out of a possible 36 on the American College Test (ACT) and 1,510 out of a possible 1,600 on the Scholastic Assessment Test (SAT) — was wooed by three or four colleges a day, finally including at least one from every state.

Thomas, according to news reports, chose the University of Kentucky. His prize was spectacular — a full ride with money left over. Because that school and others, such as the University of Oklahoma, have determined to upgrade their academic standing, they are aggressive about recruiting National Merit Scholars and give excellent awards.

To National Merit finalists who list the University of Kentucky as their first choice, the school offers the following: free tuition, free room and board, and $450 per year for books for the freshman year. For the sophomore, junior, and senior years, these students can attend at the in-state tuition rate plus $2,500.

Finalists who name the University of Oklahoma as their first choice get free or heavily discounted tuition, an additional $2,750 a semester, and the right to register for classes before other students. In 1984, academic scholarships cost the school $100,000; this year, awards by the merit-aid office topped $8 million, and academic scholarships university-wide totaled nearly $13 million.

She did her homework and won

LaNesha NeGale McCoy of Saginaw, Michigan, won 27 scholarships worth more than $97,000. Now a student at Kalamazoo College majoring in history and secondary education, LaNesha says that smart time management is everything if you want to financially secure your college education. The busy high school student with a 3.94 GPA juggled several activities, held two part-time jobs, and still reserved time for student aid research and "countless" applications.

But the National Merit finalists don't find similar blandishments of automatic financial aid at highly selective schools like Princeton and Duke. These schools choose instead to emphasize need-based aid.

The trick is to apply to schools that especially want what you have to offer (athletics, drama, art, for example) or to schools where your grades and test scores place you in the upper 25 percent of the applicant pool. Your upper-level status influences the attractiveness of your aid package.

How can you tell if you're in the top 25 percent? Look at the college's _selectivity score range._ Nearly half of four-year colleges report selectivity by average or median selectivity figures in terms of the middle 50 percent of entering students, such as 60 to 75. If your selectivity rating is above 75, you're in the top 25 percent. Your high school guidance counselor can expand on this concept, or you can look in the College Board's reference, _The College Handbook,_ or study its software, _ExPAN_, both of which are cited at the end of this chapter.

Alternatives to Scholarships

Suppose the unthinkable happens and you receive no scholarship money to speak of. Apart from loans, you can consider other ways to pay for college, such as participating in work-study and co-op programs, participating in the ROTC, and working for an employer with a tuition assistance plan — all of which we discuss in this book.

Remember, too, that some career-oriented programs only kick in with financial aid after you become a sophomore, so be alert when reapplying for your second year.

Additional resources

The following resources can help you in your search for merit aid:

✔ *College Costs and Financial Aid Handbook;* The College Entrance Examination Board; annual; available from booksellers or from College Board Publications, Two College Way, Forrester Center, WV, 25438; www.collegeboard.org.

✔ *ExPAN software;* from The College Entrance Examination Board; priced for institutional use — check your school or library.

✔ *Free Money for College,* Laurie Blum, Facts on File, 1999. Available at booksellers or order from the publisher, www.factsonfile.com

✔ *College Aid Resources for Education;* available for $29.95 from the National College Scholarship Foundation, 16728 Frontenac Terrace, Rockville, MD 20855; 800-220-3919.

✔ *The Scholarship Book 2000;* Daniel J. Cassidy, Prentice Hall, 1999. Available from booksellers or the National Scholarship Research Service, Santa Rosa, CA; 800-HEADSTART; www.800 headstart.com.

Chapter 11

Keep Up the Good Work

. . . .

In This Chapter

▶ The truth about getting aid when you work

▶ Student jobs as a bridge to adult careers

▶ What every dollar earned really costs in student aid

. . . .

Mia Mendez (not her real name) attends a prestigious and pricey college. She pays for classes in political theory and international policy by serving drinks at a popular lunchtime bar. To cover the costs of practical needs like rent, food, and clothing, Mia scrubs hospital rooms at a local hospital. To make time for studies, she works weekends, nights, and holidays.

What does Mia do for fun? She laughs and rolls her eyes, admitting, "Fun is a theoretical concept to me. Everybody keeps asking me how I do it — I just tell them I give up having a life."

Mia and nearly half of U.S. college students work while in college. About 25 percent work 20 or more hours a week; 6 percent work 35 or more hours.

"Last year I worked an average of 56 hours a week, and the people in financial aid basically told me I'd have to work less to prove I need money to qualify for financial aid. They won't give me all I need to survive; it's like they're saying I should plunge into debt rather than try to work my way through," says Mia.

Like this hard-working young woman, many dedicated college students must put their shoulders to the work-wheel long before they enter the field they're studying.

What the cost of today's college comes down to for most people is this: You can work, you can borrow, or you can try to do a bit of both.

Job Experience Is Essential for New Grads

Need a job? Get experience. Need experience? Get a job. The old beginner's dilemma is getting harder to solve, not easier. Today's competitive job market demands that new graduates have some sort of workplace experience, whether you gain that experience in jobs or internships, paid or unpaid.

No longer can you graduate, go into the job market experience-naked, and expect to be hired on the basis of your fine education. Few organizations are looking for blank canvases to paint on. Employers want skills validated by work experience. Summer jobs are one means to more than extra money. Whether you spend your summer developing software or selling shoes, you can make your experience pay off on your resume.

Get the experience that employers want and avoid becoming one of those students who have loans sticking out their ears when they graduate — about $16,000 for public school graduates and $23,000 for private school graduates. If you're not a workforce newbie, but an adult returning to school, you already know how important work experience defined by skills has become.

Finding Jobs in Your Major

If you decide to work while you're in college, try to maximize benefits to your future by finding employment in career areas of interest to you as reflected in your potential major. Stop in at your college's career services center and ask a counselor for suggestions. In the meantime, the following Web sites will give you some general ideas. They answer the question, "What can I do with a major in — ?"

✔ **University of North Carolina, Wilmington**

www.uncwil.edu/stuaff/career (click on What Can I Do?)

✔ **University of Buffalo**

www.ub-careers.buffalo.edu/career/jobchoice.html

Won't I Lose Student Aid by Working?

Perhaps you've heard that the greedy financial aid monster gobbles 50 cents in aid eligibility for every $1 earned above $2,200, and if you save the money you earn, you lose an additional 35 cents. So when you try to avoid overdosing on debt as well as try to put muscle into your resume, you come out ahead by only 15 cents on the dollar. Have you heard that? Don't believe it hook, line, and sinker.

The work-and-lose-money story does contain a kernel of fact. But the truth is that the financial aid consequences of your student job depend on how much you earn, your tax bracket, your assets, and your family status. Moreover, the financial aid counselor has the power to make a *professional judgment*, which can modify the consequences if it looks as though the system is unfairly knocking you down for having the ambition to go out and earn money to pay a few bills.

Suppose, for instance, that you take a year off school to work, making an income of $15,000. When you go back to school, your FAFSA results shown on your SAR say that you're obligated to pay an ESC (expected student contribution) of $6,154. Your financial aid counselor knows that's a crazy tab to expect you to pay — you won't be working and making that much money while attending college. The counselor has the authority to reduce that amount to much less. How much less depends on a number of considerations, but your ESC could even go down to zero.

When you hear that working during college is a stupid idea because you lose money in financial aid, remember the divisions of financial aid — gifts (scholarships and grants) and self-help (jobs and loans). The aid you lose by virtue of a larger expected student contribution could well fall into the loan column. The less money you need to borrow while in school, the less encumbered your future as a new worker will be.

If you earn more than $2,200 per year as a student, other than reductions possible by a counselor's professional judgment, you can't avoid being penalized 50 cents on the dollar in financial aid awards. But you can avoid being dinged another 35 cents on the dollar by not depositing any excess funds (joke) in a savings account where your stash will be considered an asset. Find other ways to spend that money. (See the discussion of asset shifting in Chapter 1.)

How Your Paycheck Shapes Your Share of Tuition

Table 11-1 shows how much financial aid eligibility you give up in return for a paycheck. Subtract your taxes, and you'll have an idea of how many cents on the dollar you may forfeit for each dollar you earn. Here are some examples:

✔ You can earn $2,000 and lose nothing. But if you earn $5,000 and are a single, dependent student, you're expected to kick in $1,258.

✔ If you earn $15,000 as a single, dependent student, you lose $6,154; if you are a single, independent student, you lose $4,692; if you're a single parent with one child, you lose nothing; if you're married, you lose $2,126.

Table 11-1	Expected Student Contribution (ESC) from Student's Annual Earnings			
Earnings	*Single (Dependent)*	*Single (Independent)*	*Single (One Child)*	*Married*
$1,650	$0	$0	$0	$0
$2,000	$0	$0	$0	$0
$2,500	$29	$0	$0	$0
$3,000	$274	$0	$0	$0
$3,500	$519	$0	$0	$0
$4,000	$764	$0	$0	$0
$4,500	$1,009	$0	$0	$0
$5,000	$1,258	$0	$0	$0
$5,500	$1,499	$37	$0	$0
$6,000	$1,744	$28	$0	$0
$7,500	$2,479	$1,017	$0	$0
$10,000	$3,704	$2,242	$0	$0
$15,000	$6,154	$4,692	$0	$2,126
$17,500	$7,379	$5,917	$764	$4,854
$20,000	$8,604	$7,142	$1,292	$6,079
$22,500	$9,829	$8,367	$1,820	$7,304
$25,000	$11,054	$9,592	$2,348	$8,529

Note: *This table shows pretax income and does not reflect assets. Pretax income and assets vary by student. Dr. Davis created this table using calculations based on data from the College Scholarship Service Fund Finder (Federal Expected Student Contribution).*

Chapter 12

Use This Hotlist and Get Wired for Financial Aid

In This Chapter

▶ Nearly 50 awesome Internet places to ferret out financial aid

▶ More than 100 dynamite telephone contacts for quick answers

*H*ere comes a practical listing of electronic tools to ease your financial aid search. Whether you're a techno-buff or you've just unpacked your first computer and your first Net phone, these lists have something for everyone: Internet Web sites and telephone resources. They're right on the money — and waiting for you.

Internet Resources

When first we practice to retrieve, oh what tangled Webs we weave. Not anymore. We help you become aid-astute with this selective online guide to beating down those pricey financial aid stickers.

Access America for Students

www.students.gov

This is a U.S.-government initiative to provide electronic services from government agencies and organizations to postsecondary students. The site includes a number of hot links to government agencies dealing with student loans and financial aid, as well as information on planning and paying for your education.

ACT

www.act.org/cc/index.html

This site, called College Connector/College NET, includes college search, college applications, and a financial aid need estimator.

Adventures in Education, Financial Aid Office

www.tgslc.org/adventur/fao.htm

The Texas Guaranteed Student Loan Corporation's Financial Aid Office has a large collection of links to scholarships, grants, and fellowships. The site also includes a reference that gives you facts and a beginner's guide to financial aid. Click on paying for school.

Chinook College Funding Service

www.chinook.com/

This site contains a broad spectrum of information about the financial aid process, meeting deadlines, and sample financial aid sources. Chinook is an award-winning, high-scoring search service, so we figured you should check it out, even if its service isn't free.

Chronicle of Higher Education

www.chronicle.merit.edu

This is a good place to find information on changes in the financial aid process.

Citibank Student Loan Corporation

www.citibank.com/student/CSLC.html

Citibank provides practical advice for planning and financing college along with a smorgasbord of financial aid loans and financing plans.

College Board Online

www.collegeboard.org

This site offers information about colleges, financial aid, admission, entrance exams, and FAQs.

CollegeEdge

www.CollegeEdge.com

CollegeEdge offers a scholarship search of financial aid at more than 3,400 educational institutions and approximately 4,000 scholarship sponsors. Involving a short questionnaire, CollegeEdge enables you to explore specific schools, ferreting out info on tuition and fees, financial aid application procedures, payment plans, and statistics. The site also contains relevant articles and an "Ask CollegeEdge" question-and-answer forum.

College Fund Finder

www.apollo.co.uk/a/cff

This site is a financial search service.

College Saving Plans Network

www.collegesavings.org

This state-orientated financial aid page is focused on qualified tuition aid programs.

CollegeSelect

www.cyber-u.com

CollegeSelect provides financial aid and registration information for four-year U.S. colleges. You must register to use the search engine and EFC calculator.

College Xpress

www.collegexpress.com/index.html

Providing information on college admission and financial aid for every level of student, this site includes financial aid databases and hot links.

DirectHit

www.Directhit.com

This search engine serves you the most-accessed Web sites on a topic. Clicking on "List of Colleges" brings up ten popular sites which can lead you to demon research on colleges and universities.

EASI — Easy Access for Students and Institutions

www.easi.ed.gov

EASI neatly organizes all the major federal loans and grants into a concise list with links to their respective sites. The site exposes you to details that financial aid seekers commonly overlook. EASI covers what to do after college when you start paying back loan money.

Ecola Directories College Locator

www.ecola.com/college

This site contains more than 2,500 links to colleges and universities, including their libraries and alumni pages.

Educaid

www.educaid.com

This site guides you on loans and gives behind-the-scenes info on financial aid resources and loan programs.

eduPASS

www.edupass.com

This site caters to international students, with information on a variety of topics, including choosing a college in the U.S., the cost of a U.S. college education, sources of financial aid, and testing on English as a second language.

Elm Resources

www.elmresources.com

This site offers access to loan information, providing numbers for loan amounts and disbursements. You don't need to submit personal financial data.

ExPAN Scholarship Search

www.collegeboard.org/fundfinder/html/ssrchtop.html

ExPAN is an online version of the College Board's FUND FINDER scholarship database. After you enter information about yourself, the search returns scholarships that you're eligible for. This free service includes thousands of colleges.

FAFSA (Free Application for Federal Student Aid)

www.fafsa.ed.gov

Apply on the Web and find federal school codes.

FASTaiD

www.800headstart.com

This site is operated by Dan Cassidy's National Scholarship research Service, a well-established leader in the financial aid field. Its multiple attractions include a scholarship search feature.

fastWEB

www.fastweb.com

fastWEB has a huge database of scholarships, fellowships, grants, and loans. You can set up a personalized mailbox by supplying gobs of information about yourself (things like ethnicity, religion, desired major, age, veteran status, and so forth); for your efforts, fastWEB mails you contact info and requirements for scholarships that best match your information.

Federal Student Financial Aid Page

www.Ed.gov/studentaid

This government site discusses electronic aid application, federal school codes, the student guide, loan consolidation, defaulted loans, and more.

FinAid — The Financial Aid Information Page

www.finaid.org

This site is a major financial aid information page on the Net. On this page, you can use financial aid calculators, look up laws and lenders, find specialized scholarships, or browse links to other sites.

Financial Aid Professional Associations

www.finaid.org/finaid/faa/assocs.html

This site links you to professional associations for financial aid administrators and related disciplines. Here's a good place to give your financial aid administrator's practices the once-over.

Independence Federal Savings Bank

www.ifsb.com

This site offers comprehensive information on bank loans and answers important FAQs about financial aid.

International Education (College Board)

www.collegeboard.org/ie/student/html/links.html

This page helps students outside of the United States who are interested in educational opportuniities in the U.S.

KapLoan

www.kaploan.com

KapLoan presents well-organized information about loans for parents or students and an online form to request more information about specific financial aid. Free software calculates your expected family contribution. (See the software section later in this chapter.)

Mapping Your Future

www.mapping-your-future.org

This site is sponsored by a group of guaranty agencies that participate in the Federal Family Education Loan Program. It covers selecting a school and paying for it.

LookSmart

www.Looksmart.com; click on Reference and Education, then on Higher & Continuing Education

This comprehensive link page sends you to a raft of education pages useful in finding and financing college. Includes some sites you may not find elsewhere, such as the University Film & Video Association and Canada School Finder, a database of Canadian college resources including financial information.

MOLIS Scholarship Search

www.fie.com/molis/scholar.htm

Designed especially to help major minority groups find and get scholarships, MOLIS has a straightforward search engine to find all the scholarships that match your race, gender, age, and location.

NACAC — National Association of College Admissions Counselors

www.nacac.com

This site provides useful, behind-the-scenes info on financial aid issues and developments in the field.

Peterson's Education Center

www.petersons.com
www.collegequest.com

Peterson's has two of the best sites on the Web with extensive financial aid info for beginners and experts alike. This site also provides an admissions calendar so you can synchronize with the rest of the financial aid world.

PHEAA (Pennsylvania Higher Education Assistance Agency)

www.pheaa.org

At this site, find financial resources, advice on mapping your future, and info on institutions.

The Princeton Review

www.review.com/College/Find/index.html

This site provides a very basic, step-by-step explanation of procedures and forms you must complete to get financial aid. The site has a tutorial on the many types of loans and how to get them.

RSP Funding Focus

America Online: keyword **RSP**

This America Online area has a searchable database of financial aid sources; in its Money Trail Message Center, chatters discuss nonprofit fundraising, business ventures, and so forth.

Sallie Mae

www.salliemae.com

This site offers a hard-core look at the ins and outs of loans, lenders, and repayment.You can calculate loan repayments and more.

Scholarship Resource Network Express

www.rams.com/srn

This site offers a free scholarship search service and information for students; it also links to a loan forgiveness directory.

ScholarStuff.Webring

www.Scholarstuff.com/webring.htm

This is a meta-list of college pages with a large number of financial aid resources.

Special Operations, The Warrior Foundation

www.specialops.org

This site advertises the foundation's own heavy-duty financial aid and offers thorough advice on financing and entering college.

The Student Guide

www.ed.gov/prog_info/SFA/StudentGuide/

This yearly service provided by the U.S. Department of Education tells you all about eligibility, deadlines, and mounds of information on government grants and loans. All of the information is current and accurate.

StudentLoan.com

www.EStudentLoan.com

A "marketplace" site that delivers information, servicer links, and an interactive tool (LoanFinder) to help families find and compare various private and altenative loans for specific colleges.

Student Services

www.studentservices.com/search

This site offers an impressive, searchable database of more than 180,000 financial aid sources, concentrated in private sector funding for U.S. college students. It requires on-site registration.

The Colleges, College Scholarships and Financial Aid Page

college-scholarships.com

This site contains a directory of admissions office e-mail addresses and telephone numbers plus a free scholarship search service.

Think College

ed.gov/thinkcollege

This government site encourages college attendance for people of all ages. It contains links for middle-school students, high school students, and returning adults.

U.S. Bank

www.usbank.com/studentloans/index.html

This site helps answer serious questions about attending college and taking and applying for loans. It also offers a list of hot links on related topics.

U.S. News.Edu

www.usnews.com/usnews/edu

This *U.S. News and World Report* site gives the latest stats and rankings of fields and schools, helping you make serious choices about them.

Yahoo!'s Financial Aid Search

www.yahoo.com/Education/Financial_Aid

This site allows you to locate online financial aid and provides a long linklist of college financial aid offices listed alphabetically by college.

Key Financial Aid Phone Numbers

Telephone these agencies for a variety of financial aid services.

Financial aid applications

Call these offices for information about applying for aid:

- ✔ **California Student Aid Commission (Cal Grants)** 916-445-0880
- ✔ **College Scholarship Service (CSS)** 800-778-6888
- ✔ **Questions about Financial Aid PROFILE** 800-778-6888

- **Federal Student Aid Information Center (U.S. Department of Education)**
  - Federal Financial Aid 800-433-3243
    The government provides this toll-free number to provide you information about federally subsidized loans, grants, and scholarships. Operators are on hand to answer questions about your FAFSA or a particular school's loan interest rates.
  - U.S. Department of Education Inspector General Hotline. Fraud/Waste/Abuse of Federal Student Aid Funds 800-647-8733 (press 3)
  - Immigration and Naturalization Services (INS) 800-870-3676
  - Internal Revenue Service (IRS) 800-829-1040
  - Duplicate/ Missing Student Aid Report (SAR) 800-433-3243. You can find out your SAR's status or request a copy of your Student Aid Report (SAR).
- **National and Community Service Program (AmeriCorps)** 800-942-2677
- **Selective Service** 847-688-6888
- **Social Security Administration** 800-772-1213
- **State Student Assistance Commission of Indiana (SSACI)** 317-232-2350
- **National Council of Education Opportunity Association** 202-347-7430

  Included here are TRIO Programs — Upward Bound, Student Support, Talent Search, Educational Opportunities, and Ronald E. McNair Post-baccalaureate Achievement. Representatives can direct you to colleges and programs in your state.

Information hotlines

Call these numbers for the hottest financial aid information around:

- **College Answer Service (Sallie Mae)** 800-222-7182 or 800-239-4211

  You can call this hotline to receive brochures about how to pay and borrow for college.
- **College Savings Bank** 800-888-2723
- **College Scholarship Service** 609-771-7725 or for **PROFILE** 800-778-6888
- **Educaid — The Student Loan Specialists** 800-776-2344
- **FAFSA Express Questions** 800-801-0576
- **Federal Student Aid Hotline** (U.S. Department of Education) 800-433-3243
- **Kaplan Student Loan Information Program** 888-527-5626

Direct loans

Direct Loans are serviced by the U.S. Department of Education:

- ✔ **Direct Loan Origination Center** (Applicant Services) 800-557-7394
- ✔ **Direct Loan Origination Center** (Consolidation) 800-557-7392
- ✔ **Direct Loan Servicing Center** 800-848-0979
- ✔ **Direct Loan Servicing Center Consolidation Department** 800-848-0979
- ✔ **Direct Loan Servicing Center** (Collections) 800-848-0981
- ✔ **Direct Loan Servicing Center** (Debt Collection Service) 800-621-3115
- ✔ **Direct Loan School Relations** (Origination & Servicing) 800-848-0978

Loan programs

Loan programs are available from the following banks and other institutions (those marked with an * also offer consolidation programs):

- ✔ **Access Group** 800-282-1550*
- ✔ **American Express College Loan Program** 800-814-4595
- ✔ **Bank of America***
  - • Bank of America National Student Lending 800-344-8382
  - • Bank of America (Texas Student Loan Center) 800-442-0567
  - • Bank of America (loans in Idaho, Seattle, and Washington) 800-535-4671
- ✔ **BankBoston** 800-226-7866
- ✔ **Bank One Education Finance Group** 800-487-4404*
- ✔ **Chase Manhattan Bank Educational Loans (Education First)** 800-242-7339
- ✔ **Citibank Student Loan Corporation** 800-692-8200*
- ✔ **Commerce Bank** 800-666-3910
- ✔ **Connecticut Student Loan Foundation (CSLF)** 860-257-4001, ext. 470
- ✔ **Crestar Bank's Student Lending Department** 800-552-3006
- ✔ **Educaid: A First Union Company** 800-EDUCAID
- ✔ **Extra Credit Extra Time** 800-874-9390
- ✔ **First Union Education Loan Services** 800-955-8805
- ✔ **Fleet Education Finance** 800-235-3385

- ✔ **GATE Student Loan Program** 800-895-4283
- ✔ **Independence Federal Savings Bank** 800-733-0473
- ✔ **KeyBank USA** 800-539-5363
- ✔ **Law-Access Group** 800-282-1550
- ✔ **Massachusetts Educational Financing Authority** 800-842-1531
- ✔ **MBA Loans** (Graduate students) 888-440-4622
- ✔ **MED Loans** 800-858-5050; Customer Assistance
- ✔ **Mellon Bank EduCheck** 800-366-7011
- ✔ **Nellie Mae** (Excel Loan Program) 800-634-9308
- ✔ **Norwest Wells Fargo Student Loan Center** 800-658-3567
- ✔ **PHEAA** (Graduate Loan Center, division of Pennsylvania Higher Education Assistance Agency) 800-446-8210
- ✔ **Sandy Spring National Bank** 301-774-8488
- ✔ **Sallie Mae** (College Answer Service) 800-239-4211
- ✔ **TERI Supplemental** (The Educational Resources Institute) 800-255-8374

Loan processing centers

These agencies clear the loans for disbursements. If you want to know what's happened to your loan application, these agencies can tell you:

- ✔ **American Student Assistance** 800-999-9080
- ✔ **New York State Higher Education Services Corporation (HESC)** 800-642-6234
- ✔ **PHEAA (Pennsylvania Higher Education Assistance Agency)** 800-692-7392
- ✔ **Texas Guaranteed Student Loan Corporation (TGSLC)** 800-845-6267
- ✔ **United Student Aid Funds** 800-824-7044

Loan consolidation

In addition to the agencies astricked under "Loan Programs," you can use the following numbers to consolidate your loans into one manageable monthly payment:

✔ **Nellie Mae** 800-634-9308

✔ **PHEAA (Pennsylvania Higher Education Assistance Agency)** 800-692-7392

✔ **Sallie Mae Educational Loan Center** 800-524-9100

Loan forgiveness program

Call the **National College Scholarship Foundation** at 301-548-9423 for information regarding their loan forgiveness database and directory.

Tuition payment plans

Tuition payment plans are available through the following organizations:

✔ **Academic Management Services (AMS)** 800-635-0120

✔ **FACTS Tuition Management System** 800-624-7092

✔ **Key Education Resources and Knight College Resources Group** 800-225-6783

✔ **Tuition Management Systems, Inc. (TMS)** 800-722-4867

Miscellaneous

These groups can provide information about more financial aid opportunities:

✔ **Academic Common Market (South Regional Education Board)** 404-875-9211

✔ **American Association of University Women Educational Foundation** 319-337-1716

✔ **Americorps Information Hotline** 800-942-2677

✔ **Council of Better Business Bureaus** 703-276-0100

✔ **Institute of International Education** 212-883-8200

✔ **National Association for College Admissions Counseling** 703-836-2222

✔ **U.S. Department of Education, Inspector General Hotline** 800-647-8733

✔ **USA Group** 800-562-6872

✔ **Western Interstate Commission for Higher Education (Student Exchange Program)** 303-541-0210

Keeping Ahead of the Information Age

We've grown spatula hands checking and rechecking these resources but things electronic change quickly. A television interviewer doing a news segment on financial aid asked Dr. Davis if, in view of the notoriously volatile electronic listings, he'd, again, list these types of resources in the next revision of this book. "Sure," Dr. Davis replied, "But not the same ones."

Additional reading

Internet Guide for College-Bound Students by Kenneth E. Hartment; the College Entrance Examination Board; 1998; available from booksellers or for $14.95 from College Board Publications, Box 886, New York, NY 10101-0886; 800-323-7155, www.collegeboard.com

Last Minute College Financing, Daniel J. Cassidy, Career Press, 1999. Available at booksellers or order from National Scholarship Research Service, Santa Rosa, CA; 800-HEADSTART; www.800 headstart.com.

Chapter 13

Just the FAQs: Dr. Davis Answers Your Questions

*F*amilies with college-bound students have turned to Dr. Herm Davis for guidance for 30 years. Students and parents have asked questions and received answers about virtually every aspect of the financial aid system. Here are *FAQs* (frequently asked questions) from Dr. Davis's vast data bank that answer many of your nagging, unsolved mysteries:

✔ The first FAQ group addresses an assortment of nitty-gritty concerns, including panic-buttons for all students when it's time to pay tuition and you don't have dollar one.

✔ The second FAQ group deals with emergency funding.

✔ The third FAQ group discusses independent student status.

✔ The fourth FAQ group covers transfer students' problems.

Nitty-Gritty FAQs

Among the thousands of questions he has fielded, these are evergreens. They turn up again and again.

How long do I have to wait for a response from the financial aid office? What should I do if I sent my FAFSA and have no response after six weeks?

First, call the FAFSA information center at 1-800-433-3243.

The odds are that your FAFSA has been processed and for one reason or another your SAR (see Chapter 3) was lost in the mail. Second, call your college's financial aid office to see if they have received the results of your FAFSA. Let your financial aid counselor know that you did file on time and that, even though you don't have your copy of the SAR, you are on the ball and taking the responsibility for your documentation.

Now go the extra mile. Tell your financial aid counselor that you are sending a copy of your FAFSA, federal tax Form 1040 for parents and yourself, and W-2 forms for parents and yourself to the financial aid office by certified mail. In essence, you are doing the financial aid counselor's job for him or her. This approach wins you friends where they count.

Send your refiled FAFSA by regular mail. Don't send your refiled FAFSA by certified mail because it goes to a post office box, where no one signs for it. (Don't get confused by the certified mail issue. Do send certified mail to your financial aid counselor because there's someone there who can sign for it. Don't send certified mail to the FAFSA Central Processing Center because there isn't.)

If the FAFSA information center personnel ask you when you filed your FAFSA and you say "nine weeks ago," they'll say it must have been lost in the mail and you should refile. Do so.

Will half-time status lessen my chances of winning financial aid?

Many private and school-awarded scholarships are for full-time students only. Of those that are not, you are likely to receive the amount proportional to being a half-time or three-quarters-time student.

If I submit my FAFSA with the wrong Social Security number, how can I correct my mistake?

If you identified this error early in the processing year (January or February), complete a new FAFSA and resubmit it with the correct Social Security number. You'll then get a control number that matches your Social Security number.

But if you found your goof late in the process, you should correct your SAR and mail it in with your correct Social Security number. Unfortunately, the control number on your SAR will remain that of the wrong Social Security number. The good news is that the correct Social Security number will be read at college financial aid offices even though the control number is not changed.

Why shouldn't you submit a new SAR with the right number so that everything is neat and orderly? Some state scholarship boards and some colleges award funds based on the date that the FAFSA was submitted. Your original FAFSA has seniority and also confirms that you met all deadlines for all awards.

If my family qualifies for the simplified needs test, should I still fill out Questions 49-52 and 72-75 on the FAFSA?

These questions refer to student and parental assets. If a parent can file a 1040A or EZ tax form and earns less than $50,000 annually, the parent need not fill out these asset questions to qualify for maximum aid.

But some states and most private colleges require the asset information questions so they can estimate their own financial aid awards. This information won't affect your eligibility for federal financial aid. In general, include the information even if none of your schools of choice request it.

In short, completing these questions does not hurt your chances. Be sure to answer question 63 as yes, which tells the system to consider you for the simplified needs test.

If my parents are divorced or separated, who fills out the FAFSA?

The *custodial parent* (the parent with whom you've lived with the most for the past 12 months) fills out the FAFSA. If you haven't received support from either parent during the past 12 months, use the most recent calendar year for which you received some support from a parent or lived with a parent.

When determining household size, list those who live with the parent who continually provides more than half of your support. Oddly enough, even if the custodial parent provides less than half of your financial support, she or he can also list you as a member of his or her household.

Note that the child support must be included on the FAFSA on line 70.

Am I sunk if my divorced mother cannot get her ex-husband (my natural father) to complete a non-custodial statement that is required by a high-cost private college?

You could be. Some private colleges are adamant about receiving information on both of the natural parents before they consider your file complete. In essence, these colleges want to financially remarry the natural parents to see if, as a family unit, they can support your college expenses.

If your father has remarried and has started a new family, colleges may be more lenient on this requirement. When you can document that the couple has been separated or divorced for a relatively long period of time, the college is probably going to be less demanding. If the natural father has been making reasonable child support payments and has indicated that he is willing to pass those payments through to the college while you're enrolled, the college becomes downright agreeable.

The bottom line is that high-cost colleges expect natural parents to help support your college education.

Bear in mind that this problem applies only to private colleges and does not affect your FAFSA for federal funds.

What if I have been awarded financial aid but the college tuition bill arrives before the aid shows up on my student account at college?

At most colleges you must pay bills when they are due or risk losing your classes. You may request a deferment if you have proof of your financial aid award (for example, an award letter).

Contact the college financial aid office to ask if your award letter has been processed. Request a faxed copy of that letter for your records. If your tuition bill doesn't show your financial aid award, return the bill to the student accounts office with a copy of your award letter. Include a check for the difference and a note that asks the student accounts office staff to credit your award money toward the bill. Follow up this mailing with a call to the student accounts office asking if your action is all that is required.

If you must ask for a deferment, realize that even deferments are temporary. A loan from a relative, friend, or institution may keep you in good standing while you await the award or loan. Most colleges accept credit cards.

If I temporarily leave school, does loan repayment begin immediately? What happens to my financial aid if I withdraw?

Most loans provide a grace period before repayment begins. Some even wait to bill borrowers (for the principal, interest, or both) until they have an income if a *forbearance* has been arranged in advance (see Chapter 23).

If you plan to return to school, many loans stall repayment or only require that you pay the interest. Consult your loan agreement or lender for specific limitations, as some loans defer for limited time periods, while others require documents from you or your college verifying your intent to return to school.

You'll probably need to fill out some forms for the school's financial aid or registrar's office that formalize your withdrawal. Most schools have their own policies for refunding tuition and reimbursing financial aid funds. Typically, colleges do not refund money to students after the established refund period — the first three or four weeks — has passed.

Are my parents responsible for loans in my name?

The Federal Perkins, Federal Stafford, and Direct Student loans do not require a co-signer or endorsement from parents. Your parents are responsible only for Federal PLUS loans and other loans taken out in their name(s). If your parents want to help pay off your loan, they can ask your lender to automatically deduct monthly payments from their bank accounts. But if they forget a payment, the problem is yours.

If I were awarded aid as an early-decision student and I change my mind about attending the school, what happens?

The early-decision process normally only affects elite colleges, and their policies vary. Only school-based rules cover early-decision changes. If it happens to you, you'll have to deal with it on an individual-case basis. Best advice: Get in touch with the admissions counselor or the financial aid counselor at the school as quickly as possible to find out what you must do to receive aid at the new school. The aid from the early-decision college does not transfer to the new college.

Must I report outside scholarships to my school's financial aid office?

Yes, you are supposed to report all sources of aid. Scholarship checks usually are written to the college you designate; if a strange award turns up in your name, you lose credibility. Although financial aid administrators must adjust your award accordingly, some universities use outside scholarships to reduce the amount of self-help or loan aid they award.

You can negotiate the issue of having your school aid reduced by the amount you win in an outside scholarship. Some colleges encourage students to bring in outside awards, and may match the funds rather than take money away. For negotiating hints, see Chapter 9.

What if my family didn't earn enough to pay the expected contribution?

Contact your school financial aid counselor. Inform the counselor of the special circumstances that kept your family from earning what you anticipated. Your loan or other financial aid may increase due to the cutback; many offices require that your family document the shortfall in writing.

My family bought a prepaid tuition plan for me. Must the plan be reported as an asset on my FAFSA?

No. Prepaid tuition plans are excluded from being reported as an asset on the FAFSA, as discussed in Chapter 8.

I have a trust fund split between my mother and myself. Do I have to report this as an asset on my FAFSA?

Yes. A trust fund in the name of a specific person should be reported as that person's asset on applications for aid. When the trust is owned jointly, the value is split for reporting purposes unless the terms of the trust specify another method of dividing the money.

An exception is when you have a large savings account or trust because of a car accident. A court probably restricted the trust to pay for future medical bills. When a trust is restricted by court order, do not report it as an asset, but be prepared to document this if asked.

Panic-Button FAQs

These questions focus on urgent and immediate needs for cash to pay for college.

School opens next month. What should I do if I have no financial aid and the semester is about to begin? What if I miss the application deadline?

If you haven't yet applied for financial aid, contact your college's financial aid counselor instantly to find out what you must do to apply. Some offices may accept a copy of your FAFSA and do some preliminary calculations while they await the official copy.

If you qualify, you probably still have a shot at the Federal Pell grant and/or the Federal Stafford Student Loan. Financial aid officials normally will extend credit up to the amount of the unsubsidized student loan.

All parents who have good credit are eligible to participate in the Federal PLUS loans, which are not based on demonstrated need.

Some colleges offer low-interest *bridge loans* to cover student emergency needs. These 90-day loans bridge your financial gap until other funds can be rounded up.

You've probably missed deadlines for state aid, college scholarships, and private gift programs. You may have to ask for a 30-day extension to pay your account.

Here's a neat move: Charge your tuition, especially at high-cost colleges, to a credit card that rewards plastic spending with free airline mileage. Then quickly switch the high-interest credit card tab with a lower-cost, long-term loan.

Loan and credit applications take about five to ten working days to process; add delays related to enrollment verification and miscellaneous information processing, and even the fastest loan application may take up to 20 days.

If you win no financial aid, you'd probably need a loan anyway; if you do win financial aid, you may be able to reshuffle your budget and pay off loans pronto.

Better luck next semester when you meet deadlines.

If you've already applied but received no response, ask at your financial aid office for a status report on your application. Financial aid offices are so busy that they rarely have the time to call applicants who may have omitted crucial information or documents. If your award has come through, ask when it will be *reconciled* (posted) to your student account.

Q **The school won't take credit cards, and the bill isn't paid. What now?**

Register for the minimum hours of enrollment to be eligible for financial aid, which is half-time or six semester hours, and add credit hours when funds are forthcoming.

Q **What other payment options are available in an emergency?**

Most colleges offer a tuition installment plan through which you can pay off your student bill with a number of payments within a specific time period, typically the semester.

The tuition installment plans require a maximum of three or four installment payments at no interest or market-rate interest. Colleges charge a small administrative fee for handling the paperwork, but such a plan may buy time for getting your financial aid award cleared up.

Another variation: tuition payment plans. These plans are sponsored by your college or by a third-party agency (contractor) that has been authorized by the college to administer the program on its behalf. Repayment schedules for these plans vary, ranging from ten months to years to pay off four years of a college education.

Independent Student FAQs

Students on their own — not supported by families — have a smaller income and thus qualify for higher amounts of financial aid.

Q **What are the requirements to become an independent student?**

You are considered independent if you are 24 years old. Otherwise, you must meet one of the following criteria:

- ✔ You are a veteran of the U.S. Armed Forces.
- ✔ You are an orphan or ward of the court.
- ✔ You have legal dependents (children) other than a spouse.
- ✔ You are married.
- ✔ You are a graduate or professional student (your parents may be able to claim you as a U.S. tax exemption for the years you are in graduate or professional school if you qualify under IRS guidelines).

My parents want me to pay my own way, but their income kept me from qualifying for adequate financial aid. Am I out of luck?

Just about. Financial aid administrators generally don't award aid or declare students independent simply because their parents won't foot the tuition bill. They usually measure your family's ability to pay for college, not its willingness. The ugly truth is that if your parents don't cooperate, you will have to pay your own way. If you have good grades, seek merit-based financial aid and consider working part-time while attending school half-time.

Call or write to your financial aid office explaining your situation. Ask your financial aid counselor for suggestions. The school may accept a notarized statement of parent nonsupport as proof that you are independent, if you can show that you have reasonable income and expense receipts that prove you have been supporting yourself.

A financial aid counselor can override students' dependency status, case by case, using his or her *professional judgment*. If your parents are incarcerated, or you can document an adversarial relationship (letters from your counselor or social worker, a protection-from-abuse order, or a restraining order, for example), the financial aid counselor may declare you independent.

Two more ideas: Apply for a job at the college human resource office; at some colleges, employees get free or reduced tuition. Or attend night school, which may be less expensive than day school.

Transfer Student FAQs

A *transfer student* ends enrollment in one institution and subsequently enrolls in another, usually with *advanced standing credit* (meaning credits earned at one college transfer to another so that the student doesn't have to start over from scratch).

The term is sometimes applied to students who transfer from one college to another within an institution. A popular transfer is from a two-year community college to a four-year institution. But as an undergraduate, a transfer from one college to another is possible at any time before the senior year of college.

Transfer students make their moves either in the fall at the beginning of the academic year, or by mid-year, at the beginning a new semester or quarter.

Can transfer students get financial aid?

Yes. Students must reapply annually for aid, which levels the playing field every year for everyone. Financial aid counselors see little difference between a transfer student's application for aid and a continuing student's.

Must I have a financial aid transcript?

Maybe not. Not all schools require the Financial Aid Transcript (FAT). The federal database information is now all that is required in many cases unless you are transferring mid-year.

What should I do if I'm transferring, have never applied for financial aid, and don't know the routine. What do I need?

Collect your and your parents' tax forms and W-2s. Some colleges also require the FAT (financial aid transcript), even if you've never applied for financial aid. Obtain the FAFSA form at your new or old school, complete it, and ask the financial aid office at the new college if special documentation is required.

What paperwork should I do to apply for financial aid if I'm transferring?

If you've already completed your FAFSA and SAR for your present college, call the FAFSA information center at 800-433-3243 and ask them to send the SAR to your new college. You'll need the PIN number on the SAR to make this request. Otherwise, correct Part II of your SAR (naming colleges you plan to attend) and add your transfer school. Some colleges to which you're transferring take the initiative by using the Federal Electronic Data Exchange to instantly update your record.

Whom should I notify if I transfer?

Notify the student billing office at both the old and the new college and your lender(s), and scholarship providers. Advise your new financial aid office, as well.

If I transfer mid-semester and apply for last-minute aid, what help can I expect?

If you're applying mid-year, you're probably too late to receive priority for institutional aid because college funds are committed early in the awarding season. You may win a combination of federal grants and loans plus state and outside private scholarships. If you already receive outside private aid through your original college, you may be able to transfer that aid; your new college financial aid office can evaluate this possibility. (A good book on this topic is *Last Minute College Financing* by Daniel J. Cassidy, published by Career Press, 1999, available through 1-800-HEADSTART or www.800.headstart.com)

Is it better to apply for financial aid at the end of the academic year?

No. You should apply as early in the financial aid season as possible, right after January 1.

Transfer students applying at the beginning of the academic year usually receive the same privileges as other returning students and have the same shot at federal and state funds as anyone else. Some colleges entice transfer students with generous financial aid.

Part III
Financial Aid Planning for the Long Haul

The 5th Wave   By Rich Tennant

Dr. H. Robb
Plastic Surgeon

"My daughter's college education is costing me an arm and a leg and over 60 noses a year."

In this part . . .

You wouldn't try rock climbing unless you were in the best of shape. For that matter, you probably wouldn't try a mountain hike without conditioning your body. You spent a lot of time preparing for college, hoisting loads of homework and power-lifting paper late into the night for exams. So what makes you think you can enter the college financial aid championships without stretching a financial muscle or two?

You understand that financing higher education takes preparation, or you wouldn't be reading this book. This part moves you closer to financial fitness with detailed examinations of savings and borrowing strategies, and helps you warm up for the next four years and beyond.

Chapter 14

Choosing a College Financial Aid Planner

In This Chapter

▶ Locating a new kind of professional

▶ Distinguishing experts from hustlers

▶ Deciding if a planner can really help

*M*eet a new arrival on the college scene: the *college financial aid planner*, an expert who leads families through the Byzantine aid process, designs strategies on how to fill out forms to attract the maximum gift aid, and teaches poker-playing techniques for handling your financial aid hand of cards. In this chapter, we give you the essentials on how much a planner should charge you, how to avoid hustlers, and deciding whether you really need a planner.

What's the Market Rate for Planners?

College financial aid planners cost money but save more. At least, that's how their service is supposed to work. Over a four-year period, expert planners can save you thousands of dollars.

Payment ranges from hourly charges, often $125 to $150 per hour, to package prices of more than $750 for a year's service. The size of a reasonable fee depends on the level of service you need.

Suppose you only want your FAFSA completed. Are your financial affairs simple or complex? If your money matters are uncomplicated and you hired a tax preparer to complete a short form 1040A or 1040EZ, you probably paid about $75 to $100. Expect to pay approximately the same amount for your rudimentary FAFSA.

If, however, your fiscal situation is complex enough to require a 1040 long form, you probably paid a tax preparer up to $400 to fill it out. Expect to pay a college financial aid planner roughly the same for a comparable task.

Should a college financial aid planner's charges ever be higher? Yes, when you are middle-income and need to learn about alternative loans, state residency requirements, institutional policies on award packaging, financial aid appeal processes, or future financial aid award structuring. In this situation, investing as much as $300 to $750 per year with a college financial aid planner may be well worth the price.

Still higher? Probably not.

Avoid planners who hit the high C-notes, charging up to $1,500 per year. The more you pay for services *does not* mean the more you save in financial aid.

Choosing Experts, Not Hustlers

Anyone can hang out a financial aid expert shingle. No certification, degree, or license requirement exists for an individual to open a financial aid service and charge a fee for consulting.

Like many other consultants, financial aid professionals come in three basic groups: *experts, incompetents,* and *hustlers.*

Financial aid planners: What's in a name?

Private financial aid experts are also called

✔ College specialists

✔ Financial aid consultants

✔ CPAs

✔ Financial planners

✔ Financial aid brokers

Their services are often called

✔ College aid advising

✔ College-bound financial planning services

✔ College financial services

✔ Education credit company

✔ Independent college counseling

✔ Educational consulting

✔ Financial aid and admissions consulting

✔ College funding

✔ Financial services

Experts have special knowledge derived from training or experience. Many, perhaps most, financial aid experts have worked as financial aid counselors on a college campus. Sometimes, they were later hired by banks or loan agencies and delivered education loans to college students and their families. A few who have professional counseling degrees worked first for foundations or private financial aid family services.

Experts have been in the field and know the process inside out:

- ✔ They know which regulations are changing and whom the changes affect.

- ✔ They have returning clients from across the United States who consistently feed them with information from the financial aid trenches.

- ✔ They place themselves on call throughout the financial aid process to keep their clients from freaking out with worry.

- ✔ They know which appeal letters work with which colleges.

- ✔ They know which out-of-state public universities award only loans and jobs and no gift aid.

- ✔ They're willing to certify on the FAFSA that they assisted in preparing the FAFSA as required by federal regulation.

In one way or the other, the real experts are deep inside the financial aid system.

Incompetents may have exhaustive knowledge of taxes or other financial planning strategies but lack detailed, up-to-date knowledge of local state educational grants, specific scholarships, or effective ways to deal with the financial aid structure at various institutions. They crunch numbers and crush hopes.

Hustlers are entrepreneurs who usually have superficial, if any, knowledge, recommend unethical strategies, guarantee results, overcharge, or do a number of other numbers on you. Stay clear of these folks. It's all pain and no gain for you.

To protect yourself, use the guidelines in the following sections.

Get recommendations

Referrals from satisfied clients work best. Also, call your high school guidance counselor and college's financial aid counselor. They'll recommend an expert, not an incompetent or a hustler.

Hustlers and incompetents know they're recommendation-free, so they use smoke and mirrors to look reputable. They claim that they belong to a local Better Business Bureau, a state professional financial aid association, or even the National Association of Student Financial Aid Administrators. They may, in fact, be members. Anyone can become a member of these organizations by paying membership dues.

Seek emphasis on four-year planning

The expert cares enough about your four-year financial aid plan to develop long-range designs that accommodate the multitude of documents, regulations, and college inquiries. The expert does all this work without compromising ethics or breaking rules or regulations.

The incompetent focuses on paying for a single year and rarely focuses on a comprehensive plan.

The hustler calls you nightly with a sales pitch about how cleverly the hustler can fill out the FAFSA (which, you may notice, warns that lies can bring $10,000 fines and/or a jail sentence).

Hustlers have been known to direct parents to keep two sets of forms, one for the IRS and the other for the completion of the FAFSA. This duplicity may be discovered if a college asks for a signed waiver to obtain tax records from the IRS.

Another hustler scam is the so-called "Granny Loan." Home equity was discarded as a factor on the FAFSA in 1993, lessening the expected family contribution (EFC) for middle-income families. Although some top schools (for example, Yale, Princeton, and Stanford) are downgrading home equity, too, this asset is still taken into account on the CSS Profile form used by many of the perhaps 50 select colleges in the United States. Hustlers frequently tell families to claim that the family home has been sold to grandparents for $50 or so with certain stipulations. And presto! — no family asset to run up the EFC! This subterfuge doesn't fool college officials.

Still another hustler scam directs married parents to file separate tax forms and then choose for FAFSA reporting whichever parent's 1040 shows the lesser amount of income.

Expect a place of business

The expert asks you to come to his or her office, which may be a residence, because that's where the expert has professional resources to assist in setting up a financial aid plan. The incompetent may also invite you to an office, but he probably won't have all the professional resources needed to set up your financial aid plan. The hustler comes to your house with a three-ring binder promising you great results no matter what college you pursue. Be especially wary of hustlers who stage lecture meetings at hotels where they pressure you to contract for sizable fees.

Anticipate issues to be discussed

The expert discusses the following topics:

- ✔ **Family structure:** The parental legal status: married, separated, thinking about separation, divorced, single, or widowed (Some colleges require a separated or divorced statement.)

- ✔ **Home equity:** The family's equity in its primary home (Equity may affect the CSS Profile and other forms required by a college.)

- ✔ **Retirement accounts:** The history of retirement accounts (These funds must be reported on some college applications.)

- ✔ **Employment history:** The parents' job record and similar subjects (Some colleges require business and farm supplemental documents.)

The incompetent or hustler probably won't know about these issues and is unlikely to bring them up or answer a question intelligently.

Avoid influence peddling

The expert never promises to slip in a college's side door to intercede with the financial aid office on behalf of a client. The expert knows that the college's financial aid counselor has high legal liability if student confidentiality is breached. Influence peddling doesn't happen among reputable professionals, including incompetent planners.

The hustler, by contrast, pretends to have connections with college financial aid counselors that make a gift award "a sure thing."

Pay only for services rendered

The expert charges either by the hour or by the year. Ditto the incompetent but honest planner.

The hustler wants to be paid up-front for four years. If you quit school before graduation, don't expect a refund. The hustler never gives money back.

Expert Planners Put Money in Your Bank

Question: Can you do everything for yourself for free that a college financial aid planner does for a fee?

Answer: Yes.

Better question: Can you do so as cheaply?

Answer: Probably not.

From Dr. Davis's files, here are three case histories that show how a financial aid planner can win you more than his or her fee while your do-it-yourself approach may cost you a modest fortune:

- ✔ **$50,000 savings:** Paul wanted to become an aeronautical engineer to launch a career as a commercial airline pilot. Dr. Davis advised Paul to price the program at the University of North Dakota (UND), where the cost was less than half that of Embry-Riddle Aeronautical University in Florida. Plus, UND offered more financial aid. The net savings to the student and his family exceeded $50,000.

- ✔ **$30,000 savings:** Harry, a Maryland resident, narrowed his choice of engineering schools to Virginia Polytechnic Institute, which offered out-of-state students only self-help (loans and work).

  Upon Dr. Davis's recommendation, Harry then applied to Texas A&M, where an in-state student pays $38 per credit hour versus an out-of-state student's cost of $275. But the college's rate card has an interesting twist: When an out-of-state student wins a scholarship of $1,000 or more from any source, state residency status for tuition purposes is conferred. Harry did even better: He was accepted into Texas A&M's Cadet Corps, which resulted in a full scholarship at in-state tuition prices. Over four years, Harry's family saved more than $30,000.

- ✔ **$8,000 savings:** Terry received an immediate $2,000 increase in financial aid on the telephone (even before the documentation was submitted) when Dr. Davis helped her document her appeal to Syracuse University. This single act saves Terry $8,000 over the next four years of school.

An expert college financial aid planner looks around financial corners, anticipating problems and solving them before they explode into major obstacles that prevent you from getting the best values in financial aid.

Chapter 15

Grading Ways to Save for College

●●●

In This Chapter

▶ Saving: What's in it for parents?

▶ Choosing an education-savvy financial planner

▶ Analyzing savings programs, tuition freezes, and education IRAs

▶ Investing well: Bonds and stocks

●●●

*T*his chapter is for parents and grandparents. Frankly, we wish we didn't have to write it, but few of us go to the head of the class when it comes to saving for education. Considering the northern direction of school prices, however, unless you're about to be evicted or suffer long-term unemployment, bite the bullet and put money away for your child's future.

Saving for college takes many forms, as this chapter outlines. We give you the critical news but don't pretend to cover every form of investment (such as real estate, which can be golden. As one grandfather told us, "I'd love to unload that condo I've had for 12 years because it's a real headache keeping it rented and repaired, but it's paid for and that's my granddaughter's college education".)

Are You a Sucker for Saving?

You may have heard horror stories about prudent, dutiful parents who worked hard and sacrificed to save for their children's college and lost out on financial aid to people who didn't save a dime. Such things have happened; that's why, in Chapter 1, we emphasize that you can and should legitimately shift assets during the two years before college.

Here's the drill: When your student applies for financial aid, not only does the financial need analysis system ignore the first $40,000 in parents' assets, but the parental contribution rate is pegged at 5 percent or less for assets over $40,000 (the asset allowance). Suppose that you have squirreled away

$90,000 in assets, of which $50,000 is in savings. The system will want 5 percent of that $50,000, or about $2,500, from you. If you are earning a 5 percent return on your investment, you can give the school the $2,500 and still keep your savings at $50,000.

What are you buying for that $2,500? You're buying your child a wider range of colleges to choose from at a time when rising costs are forcing colleges to become less "need-blind" in their admissions policies. More and more colleges are admitting students who can afford to pay ahead of students who can't.

At the same time, demographic changes are allowing colleges to become more selective than in the recent past. The admissions curve is shooting up again, an echo of the years when the baby-boom generation crowded the nation's institutions. Now the boomers' kids are college age and competing for those seats. This trend means that the familiar education buyer's market is morphing into a seller's market. Saving for education gives your child more choices and removes worry about money at the same time you're coping with admissions challenges.

Not convinced? You're still wondering why you shouldn't spend your children's "school inheritance"? Here's one more reason: Be nice to your kids. They'll choose your nursing home.

Long-Term Planning Pays Handsomely

Like most college-minded families, perhaps you're asking yourself these questions:

- ✔ What will college cost when my child's ready for college?
- ✔ How much should I start saving?
- ✔ When should I start saving?
- ✔ Where's the money going to come from?

Table 15-1 projects the cost of college way down the road, which gives you a general idea of what you're facing and how much you should target as a savings goal. Perhaps you've seen similar projections and wonder why they vary. Briefly, investment companies tend to come in on the high end, wanting you to cover all bases by saving huge amounts, from which they draw commissions. Educators project lower future costs, perhaps because they don't want to scare you away from higher education. Who's right? Your call. College-cost increases have "stabilized" at a lower rate (about 4 to 5 percent each year) in the past several years after a wild ride (8 to 9 percent annually) in the years before that. Dr. Davis chose a middle scenario when calculating the figures in Table 15-1, charting annual increases for public colleges at 5 percent and private colleges at 6 percent.

Table 15-1	Projected College Costs	
Year	*Public, 4-year*	*Private, 4-year*
2000–2001	$12,512	$26,041
2001–2002	$13,138	$27,603
2002–2003	$13,795	$29,259
2003–2004	$14.485	$31,015
2004–2005	$15,209	$32,876
2005–2006	$15,970	$34,848
2006–2007	$16,768	$36,939
2007–2008	$17,606	$39,155
2008–2009	$18,487	$41,505
2009–2010	$19,411	$43,995

How much should you save? Pick a number. We could name a percentage of your income but some authority would stop payment on our reality check. Seriously, we don't know your specific situation, and savings goals can vary widely. You have to pencil out a personal savings schedule, perhaps with the help of a reputable financial planner. If holding onto money hasn't been your thing, you may be surprised at the impressive growth of even a relatively small amount of dollars regularly tucked away, thanks to the magic of time and the power of compounding.

When should you start saving? The earlier the better — when your child is a baby isn't too soon. Some experts recommend that, if you haven't started earlier, you should begin to save when junior is 12 to 10 years from college. This gives you a number of years to build up contributions, and the interest earned will add a sizeable chunk to your education account.

Can you miss a month of saving now and then without disabling your plan? Yes, but the financial wizards recommend using regular payroll deduction. They figure if you don't see it, you can't spend it.

Find an Expert in Financial Aid

Where's the money to come from? Managing your money toward wealth is the area where financial self-help books, such as *Personal Finance For Dummies* and *Investing For Dummies,* written by Eric Tyson and published by IDG Books Worldwide, Inc., are invaluable.

After you begin checking around, you'll be amazed by the variety of software programs, slick newsletters, newspaper and business sections, mutual funds, and brokerage houses — all giving advice on turning spare change into serious money.

Even if you're a sharp investor, you may want to consider consulting a financial planner who can help you set reasonable goals and develop an education plan that works well with your individual circumstances. *The trick is to find a great financial planner who has a sophisticated grasp of how the college financial aid process works.*

The problem is that financial aid issues may be inexpertly commented on by those financial planners who don't comprehensively track the financial aid system and its nuances. As a result, their poor advice (which might be good advice if financial aid needs weren't complicating the picture) can cost your child many thousands of dollars in financial aid.

An unintelligent example: Some financial planners advise that, for tax reasons, parental savings be kept in a student's name. Wrong. In need analysis systems, the contribution rate on parents' savings is 5 percent, compared to 35 percent for student savings, meaning it will cost you 30 cents more on each financial aid dollar if the money is listed in the student's name.

An ethically challenged example: The new or sweetened college tax breaks created by the Taxpayer Relief Act of 1997 have spawned a new feeding frenzy by financial planners espousing gamesmanship without scruples. One adviser recommends that you "make sure that your child is no longer dependent." The idea is that a parent may have too much income to qualify for the education tax credits, but the child who is set up as an independent student may not. To accomplish a status makeover, the financial planner recommends an incredibly complex round of financial shenanigans, but they then admit that the IRS can and often does challenge the phony independent status.

A *financial planner* is not the same professional as a *college financial aid planner* (described in Chapter 14). In the student aid arena, a financial planner is a generalist, while the college financial aid planner is a specialist. Both types of professionals can help you send your children to college, but they have different areas of expertise.

Five questions to ask a financial planner

How can you judge which financial planners know their stuff about student aid? Here's a list of questions to ask in your initial consultation. These questions aren't fail-safe, but you'll get a good inkling of financial aid prowess:

1. **What are the costs for attending a four-year, private/public college?**

   Are the planner's figures up-to-date?

2. **Does it cost the same to go to a four-year, public college out of state as it would a four-year, private college out of state?**

   If the planner says attending an out-of-state public college is cheaper than attending an out-of-state private college because of the tuition difference, watch out. Many out-of-state public colleges do not award out-of-state students gift aid; instead, they give only work and loan funds. By contrast, private colleges typically meet maximum need with an equity package that includes gift aid as well as work and loan aid.

3. **Is it better to save in my name or in my child's name?**

   That's your call, but here are factors to consider. Financial planners and tax preparers typically recommend that, for tax purposes, the savings be kept in the child's name. But remember, students are expected to contribute 35 percent of their assets in the expected family contribution (compared to only 5 percent for parental assets). The 35 percent from a student could easily cause the student to miss out on free financial aid money.

4. **What form(s) does my child need to fill out to receive financial aid?**

   If the planner discusses only the Free Application for Federal Student Aid (FAFSA) and not the CSS Profile, he or she doesn't have a very deep understanding of how financial aid works, especially at high-cost, private colleges and some not-so-high-cost.

5. **Can I combine an Education IRA, a college savings plan, and a Hope Scholarship tax break all in the same year?**

   No. Only one of the three may be used in any given year. A good planner should know which is best for you.

Organizing Your Financial Plan: The Ingredients

After you decide that saving is a good idea, how much to save, and when to begin, you can turn your attention to the kinds of money-growing labs that can make your hopes and dreams for your child come true.

College savings plans

In addition to commercial college savings plans (such as CollegeSure CD, 800-888-2723), you can choose from two kinds of college savings plans: the qualified state tuition programs (meaning both the original state-sponsored prepaid plans and the new state-sponsored college savings plans discussed in Chapter 8) and colleges' own tuition-freeze programs.

Qualified state tuition programs

Although the earlier state-sponsored prepaid tuition plans (you pay now and attend later) certainly are classified as a savings vehicle, much interest today is focused on the enhanced version — the new college savings plans.

Money that you stash in the new state-sponsored or private college savings plans described in Chapter 8 grows tax-deferred and may earn a fat state income tax exemption as well. Federal tax exemptions may come soon.

The money is held in a parent's name — or both parents' names — where it counts less (5 percent) than if it were in the student's name (35 percent) in student aid formulas. You can set aside as much as $100,000 for expenses at any U.S. college.

Plans vary from state to state. Approximately half offer the new plans, but the trend is growing fast — check out the College Savings Plans Network Web site (www.collegesavings.org) for up-to-the-minute details.

A number of states (see Chapter 8) continue to offer the original prepaid tuition plans, which also allow savings for college with returns guaranteed to cover tuition when the child is ready for school. Although some of the original plans have been revised to permit greater flexibility and to qualify for tax breaks, financial planners suggest that you check very carefully before storing funds in the original prepaids.

Colleges' own tuition-freeze plans

More than 500 colleges have adopted tuition-discount programs; a *tuition freeze* allows you to prepay four years of college at the tuition price current when you enroll in the program, not the increased fee you'd pay later when your child attends college. Inquire at the admissions office of your college of interest.

As a single example, Washington University in St. Louis offers a tuition-freeze plan. Parents pay for four years of college at the time the student enrolls. The university even offers loans for parents to prepay the four years of tuition.

Student savings and investment accounts

Although savings in the student's name typically subtract from financial aid eligibility, some tax breaks and earned interest plans *may* make up for the loss. For example, if the parent or grandparent zaps money into a custodial account for the student under the UGMA (Uniform Gifts to Minors Act) or the UTMA (Uniform Transfers to Minors Act), the IRS provides some tax breaks on the earned interest.

Although the student remains custodian of the account until the age of majority (meaning your child can't arbitrarily opt to buy a jet ski instead of the first semester of tuition), you can't take back the money to cover a vacation or add a new room to the family home. These limitations can be helpful or harmful depending on your situation.

Advantages of student accounts

Here are the advantages of student accounts:

- ✔ First $700 in earned interest is exempt from federal income tax.

- ✔ Second $700 of earned interest gets taxed at the child's tax rate, which could be next to nothing if junior earns nearly zilch.

- ✔ Earned interest above $1,400 gets taxed at your rate until Junior turns age 14.

- ✔ Funds can only be withdrawn for education and other specific reasons until Junior reaches an age between 18 and 21 (varies with the state). Funds can be withdrawn for costs parents would normally not antici- pate paying, such as private summer school, emergency medical costs, and college tuition while in high school.

Disadvantages of student accounts

Here are the disadvantages of student accounts:

- ✔ Funds in these accounts cannot be used, in most states, for anything deemed to be normal parental expense while your child is under the age of majority.

- ✔ Your child may decide not to attend college or may need less money than the amount saved. Junior gets the cash — a frightening possibility if your child's greatest aspiration is to sleep on the beach and live on berries and saltwater.

- ✔ The funds saved in your child's name do subtract heavily — to the tune of 35 percent of the amount saved annually — from Junior's financial aid eligibility.

Education IRAs

Parents and grandparents together can put away as much as $500 a year for any child younger than 18 (that's a total of $500 from all sources — if gramps sets aside $300, parents can only set aside $200). You pay into these accounts with after-tax dollars, meaning you get no tax deduction. As long as you spend the money on education, you can withdraw the interest gain tax-free.

Most parents and gramps qualify. You can make the full contribution if you're single with an adjusted income no higher than $95,000 or married with an adjusted income up to $150,000. The benefit phases out at higher incomes: $110,000 for singles and $160,000 for marrieds.

Analysts say the Educational Savings Account (ESA) option is not necessarily a good deal *by itself*. For example, if your kid receives 15 years' savings at $500 a pop, with interest, you may wind up with $15,000 — way short of what you'll need.

Note: A child can't get both a college savings plan and an Education IRA deduction in the same year, even if different people contribute. Because the annual limit for an education IRA is $500, a state plan is usually better.

Bonds

Bonds are basically IOUs from corporations or a city, local public agency, state, or the federal government to you, the buyer. Bonds carry varying degrees of risk.

High-risk bonds offer no guarantees that they'll grow or survive. All bonds normally pay more in returns than bank savings or money-market mutual funds, but high-risk bonds are bigger gambles.

Low-risk bonds are far less speculative, and those issued by government entities earn you tax-exempt interest; examples are municipal (munis), state, and U.S. government (*Treasury bonds*) bonds.

With that introduction, consider the following college savings options to decide which may be right for you.

U.S. Series EE and I savings bonds

If you have little to invest, these bonds may be your best strategy because they can cost as little as $50 or as much as $10,000 each. The most you can buy in any one year is the face value (what the bond is worth when you cash it in) of $30,000 or $15,000 (purchase price) if single. The maximum if married is $60,000 face or $30,000 price paid. For more information, call 202-377-7715 or check out these Web sites: www.savingsbonds.gov or www.publicdebt.treas.gov.

U.S. bonds guarantee earnings with their fixed interest rate, but on the downside, they may return less than other savings tools. Nevertheless, U.S. savings bonds that qualify for education and tax benefits do have some advantages over other types of long-range saving: A qualified U. S. savings bond is a Series EE bond or Series I bond issued after 1989 and includes the following characteristics:

- You purchase Series EE bonds for half their worth — for example, if you want to buy a $30,000 savings bond, you pay $15,000 for it.

- You purchase Series I bonds at face value.

- You can redeem bonds after six months in return for the exact purchase price plus any interest earned; however, you get hit with a three-month interest penalty.

- The *coupon rate* (interest due at a given time) is reset every six months, resulting in little risk of losing interest and no risk of losing the capital investment. The original purchase price (or capital outlay) never goes down, and its interest will always be a plus — not high, but not zero. For current recorded rate information, call 800-487-2663.

- Series EE bonds are Treasury securities that earn interest at market-based rates for up to 30 years.

- Taxes on the interest earned are deferred until the bond is cashed, as long as the bond is held for a minimum of five years.

- The savings bond education tax exclusion permits qualified taxpayers to exclude from their gross income all or a portion of the interest earned on the redemption of eligible Series EE savings bonds issued after 1989 in the name of a taxpayer age 24 or older.

- Taxes on the interest earned are forgiven if you cash in the bonds to pay for college fees and tuition. (***Note:*** These bonds depend upon the parents' income; as this book goes to press, a combined parents' income when redeeming a bond can't exceed $78,350 up to $108,350 if filing joint and $52,250 up to $67,250 if single. This level adjusts annually according to inflation. The Technical and Miscellaneous Revenue Act of 1988 — P.L. 100-647 — mandates that no interest be charged on earnings from EE bonds purchased after 1990 if they're withdrawn to pay for college.)

- Bonds purchased in the name of a minor child aren't eligible for the education tax exclusion. Bonds must be issued in the name of a parent to qualify.

- You can name any person as a beneficiary without affecting the eligibility of the bond for exclusion including a child. However, a child may not be a co-owner of such a bond.

✔ You can purchase savings bonds through more than 40,000 financial institutions nationwide or through employers offering the U.S. Payroll Savings Plan.

✔ No limit exists on the amount of bonds that you can accumulate for educational expenses over time as long as these bonds do not exceed the annual purchase limitations set by the feds.

U.S. Treasury bonds (T-bills or T-notes)

Just as secure as savings bonds, T-bills require you to accept the fed's IOU for a longer period of time. But the longer you sit on T-bills, the more they're worth.

Don't buy Treasury bonds that exceed five years because other investments will probably earn you more over a longer period.

To purchase Treasury bonds, contact your nearest Federal Reserve Bank branch. Although Treasury bonds may not be your lifelong best buddies, they have redeeming qualities worth considering for college financing:

✔ T-bill earnings are exempt from state and local taxes.

✔ T-bills have virtually no credit risk (as long as the U.S. government is sound, these bills are sound).

✔ T-bills are more liquid than some other investments, such as CDs, meaning that you can quickly convert them to cash when needed.

✔ T-bills can be cashed in any time subject to market fluctuation without penalty — after the maturity date.

✔ T-bills can be purchased at maturity dates that coincide with college bills.

✔ T-bills can be withdrawn at any time (before maturity) to pay for college without penalty fees. However, if interest rates rise, you get less money back if you sell before maturity

On the downside, T-bills normally have lower returns than other investments, and limits exists as to how much you can purchase at any one action. Financial planners do not consider government bonds appropriate for long-term goals because they don't grow large in value.

Municipal bonds (munis)

Many organizations issue municipal bonds, including city, county, and state governments; and agencies with a public purpose, such as electric utility companies, hospitals, and universities. Municipal bonds have the following features:

✔ Interest rates are lower than interest rates on other comparable taxable bonds because you don't have to pay taxes on the interest you pull on your investment.

✔ Munis generally help parents in tax brackets higher than 31 percent to cover college expenses far better than bonds that require taxable interest.

✔ Interest is exempt from federal and state taxes.

✔ Munis are low risk so long as the credit rating on bond is good.

✔ Munis are redeemable before date of maturity; however, values may fluctuate depending on interest rates.

State college tuition bonds

More than 20 states sponsor programs to finance higher education. Parents can buy state-sponsored college bonds (state versions of U.S. Series EE bonds) at extremely high discounts. Because the bonds serve as a college savings vehicle, they are sometimes referred to as *baccalaureate bonds*.

States issue these bonds as a way for families to save for future education expenses. In the bond worlds, these instruments are known as *zero-coupon bonds* because they enable you to buy a bond with a high interest rate at a price highly discounted from face value; you receive no interest (the zero coupon), however, until interest the bond reaches maturity (at which time the interest is paid in full).

Like U.S. savings bonds, baccalaureate bonds sell for less than their face value and pay no interest until maturity. States use the proceeds from college savings bonds to meet the cost of building projects targeted by the state. State college savings bonds cost about $1,000 to $5,000, with maturities between 5 and 20 years. For college planning, the bond should mature the same year in which your child goes to college.

Following are some features of tuition bonds:

✔ The minimum bond amount is $1,000.

✔ You can purchase them at high discount.

✔ These bonds have a low credit risk.

✔ Interest earned is tax-exempt (federal and state — for residents of the issuing state).

✔ These bonds pay no interest until maturity.

✔ You can use them for any college — even out of state.

✔ You can purchase them anytime.

In some states, tuition bonds can't be included in the college financial aid assessment. Although marketed as a means for saving for college, no requirements obligate you to use them for college tuition (although Illinois and other states pay a bonus if you use the bonds to pay for college). You don't even have to designate a beneficiary, such as a college.

Money-market mutual funds

These setups allow short-term investments while holding onto the cash you'll need for college. Money-market mutual funds slot money into government and corporate bonds. You can collect a fair amount of interest off these shortest of short-term bonds. Although not insured by FDIC, these funds provide low-risk investments with fairly high returns. Consider the following:

- ✔ The best money-market mutual funds provide higher yields than bank savings accounts.

- ✔ Money-market mutual investments tend to involve little risk. They typically plug your investment money into low-risk, government securities, commercial certificates from well-established corporations, and bank certificates.

If all this money talk has made you a bit woozy, remember that there are three kinds of people: those who can count, and those who can't.

Additional reading

Personal Finance For Dummies, 2nd Edition, and *Investing For Dummies,* both books by best-selling Eric Tyson and published by IDG Books Worldwide, Inc. Order by calling 800-762-2974 or through your bookseller.

The Unofficial Guide to Investing, by Lynn O'Shaughnessy, Macmillan, 1999. Order by calling 800-428-5331 or through your local bookseller.

Chapter 16

Becoming an Educated Borrower

● ●

In This Chapter

▶ Loans: Cull the best, don't futz with the rest

▶ Rooting out low-cost private loans

▶ Looking at some of the best commercial lenders

● ●

So you filled out every form in the financial aid office and wore rags hoping to demonstrate financial need, but somehow the financial aid administrator couldn't find enough money to fill the gaping holes in your pockets.

That's not surprising. The amount of free money available to college students has climbed over the last 20 years, but it hasn't been enough to keep up with escalating tuition costs.

The cost of a college education has quadrupled over the past two decades, growing nearly twice as fast as inflation. Because of an earlier round of double-digit growth, tuition at public four-year colleges in the last decade has risen 50 percent, adjusted for inflation. Family income during that time rose just 1.5 percent, also adjusted for inflation.

As a result, borrowing has become stylish. So much so that the Congress closed out the millennium by pushing down student loan interest rates on federal direct and guaranteed loans by about half a percent, which would save a typical student borrower with a $13,000 debt about $700 over a standard ten-year repayment period.

After you've used the tips in Chapter 9 to negotiate, you and your family may want to get government or private loans. The trick is to become an educated borrower. In fact, maybe you should read Chapter 23 about paying back what you owe before you read this chapter about racking up debt.

Hold borrowing to a college yell

When you attend a formal loan entrance interview, you'll likely get a long lecture on the evils of unpaid debt — you may even have to watch a video about making calls when you need deferment or forbearance. Though such warnings may seem ritualistic and arcane, they're not to be ignored.

Loan default or a poor payment record gets on your credit report, and scars it so deeply (for up to seven years) that you may not be able to get other loans, credit cards, mortgages, or even an apartment lease. In addition, your wages or income tax returns may be garnished, your assets may be attached, your professional licenses may not be renewed or granted, or you may end up in court. Increased interest, late fees, and court and attorney fees may be added to your unpaid total.

Choosing the Best Loan

Many lenders offer carefully designed programs that enable you to pay less when you earn less. Many programs even defer those payments for several years if the payments pose undue hardship. Some employers offer loan repayment assistance as one of their benefits. The possibilities that lending institutions offer have made many students' education possible.

Choosing the right loan (or combination of loans) makes all the difference. Factor in the following as you examine educational loans:

- ✔ Who must repay the bulk of the loan (student or parents)?

- ✔ How *little* can the family afford to borrow?

- ✔ How *much* can the family afford to repay (estimate monthly payments)?

- ✔ How much can the graduate expect to earn upon graduation?

Before you sign on the dotted line and split to the bank with the check, don't hesitate to bug lenders with questions about every nook and cranny of repayment. So what if you drive them around the bend — you've got to get it straight. All lenders — banks, loan servicers such as Sallie Mae, United Student Aid Funds, PHEAA, credit bureaus, organizations, and educational institutions — provide information both in hard copy and on the Web describing the many options that you have to pay back loans.

Review the rules for repaying your loan with a magnifying glass. For instance, ask these questions:

- What happens to the debt if you become permanently disabled or die?
- In what circumstances and how should you apply for deferment or forbearance?
- If both parents assume a joint loan, who pays how much if they divorce?
- Can you begin repaying even before interest accrues?

Loans usually require payment of such charges as loan, origination, and insurance fees — all this in addition to interest. Students are given options to stretch out payments over 30 years. But remember, the longer you stretch out loan repayment, the more you have to pay in interest. A better idea: Get three jobs if necessary and limit your repayment to ten years.

Don't know where to start? The following sections describe types of loans to help you decide which is the least painful method of going into debt.

The first group of resources in "Primary Wellsprings of Loan Money" revisits two kinds of federally guaranteed loans and offers two examples of direct state loans. This group also looks at borrowing on family equity and at borrowing to pay for four tuition-frozen years of college.

Keep those cards and calls coming

However distant a relationship may seem between you and an organization to which you owe major money, forge a close relationship immediately and constantly. Don't be shy. Organizations indeed may be lending money strictly for altruistic reasons, but commercial lenders earn profits, and colleges want to ensure that they have the means to keep attracting top students.

Make a habit of communicating with your college loan lender just like you would a credit card company — call them to inform them of these changes:

- Changes in your finances
- Changes in name, address, employment
- Withdrawal from school, failure to enroll in the specified period, or less than half-time attendance

Primary Wellsprings of Loan Money

If you're not eligible for subsidized Federal Stafford loans, then start by looking at the Unsubsidized Federal Stafford loans and the Federal PLUS loans (see Chapter 7), because they're the biggest loan programs. Ordinarily, these two classes of loans are the cheapest, but some private and commercial loans have a lower interest rate than the government's loans (which we identify later in this chapter). First, an instant replay of the federal offerings:

Unsubsidized Federal Stafford Loans
U.S. Department of Education
Federal Student Aid Information Center
P.O. Box 84
Washington, DC 20044-0084
800-433-3243

✔ **Loan limits:**

- *Dependent students*

  $2,625 (first year), $3,500 (second year), $5,500 (third, fourth, or fifth year). Aggregate for undergraduate school is $23,000.

- *Independent students*

  $6,625 (first year), $7,500 (second year), $10,500 (third, fourth, or fifth year). $18,500 (each year of graduate school). Aggregate for independent undergraduate student loans is $46,000.

  Exception: Graduate students attending institutions that participate in HEAL Loans and are majoring in medicine, dentistry, or veterinarian science may borrow up to $38,500 per year.

- *Graduate or professional students*

  The graduate debt limit including undergraduate Federal Stafford Loans may not exceed $138,500.

  Exception: Graduate students majoring in medicine, dentistry, or veterinarian science may borrow up to $189,125.

✔ **Interest rate:**

- *Continuing students:* Variable rate based on ten-year T-bill +2.5 percent while the student is in school. Variable rate based on 91-day T-bill +3.1 percent when in repayment period. Loan is capped at 8.25 percent with rate being adjusted annually. These rates apply to new loans made after July 1, 1995.

- *New students:* The interest rate on new student loans has been changed to reduce the rate while in college to 1.7 percentage points above the rate on three-month Treasury bills, and to 2.3 percentage points above the Treasury-bill rate after the borrowers are in repayment.

✔ **Fees:** 3 percent origination fee and a 1 percent guarantor insurance fee for Federal Stafford Loans; 4 percent origination fee for Federal Direct Loans.

✔ **Deadline:** Apply at least 60 days before school starts to allow the college and the lender time to process the application.

✔ **Features:** Unsubsidized Stafford/Direct loans are available to students who do not qualify for need-based loans. *Unsubsidized* means that the federal government doesn't pay the interest while you are in college — you pay the interest. Payments can be deferred under some conditions. Repayment of principal follows a six-month grace period after the student is no longer enrolled half-time. Loans may be repaid early with no penalty. Loans do not require a credit test and do not require need.

This loan is available to you as long as you are in school at least half-time. You get better loan terms than your parents, and you can let your poor ol' folks off the hook and repay the loans yourself after you graduate. You can put off repayments until six months after graduation and take up to ten years to pay under the Standard Repayment Plan.

Most loan service groups and lenders will reduce your interest rate by up to two percentage points if you pay the first 48 payments on time, plus a whiff of a discount for using electronic banking transfer (usually up to $1/4$ percent.

Federal Stafford loans come from financial institutions, such as banks and credit unions under the Federal Family Education Loan Program or the Department of Education under the Federal Direct Loan Program.

Federal PLUS Loans
U.S. Department of Education
Federal Student Aid Information Center
P.O. Box 84
Washington, DC 20044-0084
800-433-3243

✔ **Loan limits:** Up to cost of education minus any student financial aid.

✔ **Interest rate:** Parent Loans for Undergraduate Students, or PLUS loans, have been changed to 3.1 percentage points above the rate on three-month Treasury bills with a cap of 9 percent.

✔ **Fees:** 3 percent origination and 1 percent guarantor fees for Federal PLUS loans; 4 percent origination fee for Federal Direct loans.

✔ **Deadline:** Submit your application at least 60 days prior to the start of the academic year to allow for school and lender processing.

✔ **Features:** Parent(s)/guardian of the student may apply. The FPLUS requires a credit check.

A parent cannot be turned down for having no credit history — only for having an adverse one. If the parent(s) doesn't pass the credit check, the parent may still be able to receive a loan if someone, such as a relative or friend who is able to pass the credit check, agrees to cosign the loan. The parent does not have to complete a FAFSA to qualify for this loan (unless the school requires a completed FAFSA). Eligibility does not depend on demonstrated need. Checks are made payable to the school, and disbursements are made two or more times during the year. Parents do not make payments on the loan until 60 days after the final disbursement of the loan. Interest begins to accrue on the day the loan is disbursed. Parents have up to ten years to repay the loan.

Your parents can borrow all your education costs, minus any other financial aid. If your total college costs are $10,000 and you have already borrowed $4,000 on a Federal Stafford or Federal Direct loan, your folks can borrow another $6,000 on an FPLUS. Banks, colleges, and other financial institutions usually furnish the cash. Your folks have to repay, without any grace period, almost as soon as school starts and normally take ten years to retire the loan. However, parents may consolidate loans and receive a longer repayment period option.

MEFA Loan

Massachusetts Educational Financing Authority
125 Summer St., 14th Floor
Boston, MA 02110-9740
800-449-6332
www.mefa.org

✔ **Loan limits:** $2,000 up to cost of education less any student financial aid.

✔ **Interest rate:** Fixed interest rate at 4.89 percent (or) variable interest rate at 6.57 percent, interest reset annually.

✔ **Fees:** 3.75 percent origination fee.

✔ **Deadline:** Open.

✔ **Features:** The MEFA Loan allows the borrower 15 years to repay the loan. You have no prepayment penalty and no application fees. The borrower, usually the parent or guardian, must be creditworthy and the student must sign the loan. Repayment begins a month after the loan is made. Loans are available to Massachusetts residents and out-of-state residents pursuing an education at any participating institution of higher education in Massachusetts.

MEFA also provides the MEFA Loan for graduate education: a low-cost, fixed-interest-rate loan, assisting graduate students attending a Massachusetts college or university.

At the request of Massachusetts colleges and universities, the Massachusetts Educational Financing Authority was established in 1982 under Massachusetts general law to assist families, colleges, and universities in financing the cost of higher education.

Keystone Rewards Stafford Loan (state loan)
Pennsylvania Higher Education Assistance Agency (FA)
1200 N. Seventh St.
Harrisburg, PA 17102-1444
800-692-7392

- ✔ **Loan limits:** $2,625 for the first year, $3,500 for the second, and $5,500 for the third and fourth years.

- ✔ **Fees:**

    Guarantee fees: 0 percent vs. 1 percent for all other Stafford and Direct loans.

    Origination fees: 2 percent vs. 3 percent for all other Stafford and Direct loans.

- ✔ **Interest rate:** May not exceed 8.25 percent.

    Fee savings on $16,000: $320 on subsidized loans; $160 on unsubsidized loans.

    Interest savings: 2 percent interest rate reduction after 48 consecutive on-time monthly payments; .25 percent interest rate reduction for electronic debit.

    Total interest rate savings on $16,000 would be $1,255.

- ✔ **Restrictions:** Program is available for all Pennsylvania residents who attend any U.S. Department of Education-approved school and nonresidents attending a U.S. Department of Education-approved school in Pennsylvania.

Home-equity line of credit or loan

The next stop on your loan shopping list should be a home-equity line of credit or loan. You can deduct on your federal tax return the interest on a home-equity loan of as much as $100,000. For middle- and upper-middle income families, the after-tax cost of home equities is attractive.

Both an equity loan and an equity line of credit win you tax deductions, but differences exist between the two. An *equity loan* requires you to pay interest on the full amount; you must repay it within a negotiated period, at a fixed or variable rate. You may end up paying higher interest on money that you don't need immediately — for example, if you borrow $100,000, you'll pay interest on that entire amount even if you only use $25,000 in the first year. Look at an equity loan as a second mortgage.

An *equity line of credit* allows you to negotiate for the maximum line of credit possible based on the equity in your home. But you only make payments on the funds you withdraw on that line of credit. If you're only using the funds for college tuition, this option may be smarter and less expensive than the equity loan.

Either program of credit obligations can negatively affect your credit report, because most credit institutions estimate your eligibility by examining your debt-to-income ratio. An $80,000 debt, for example, may disfigure an other-wise attractive, middle-income profile.

Features of these loans include the following:

✔ Equity lines are less expensive because you won't immediately pay interest on entire college cost.

✔ If you itemize your tax deductions, both types of credit are tax deductible.

✔ Equity loans are established at a fixed interest rate.

✔ Equity lines are often established at a variable interest rate.

Contact your bank or mortgage company for more information.

401 (k), 403 (b), and other retirement accounts

Should your parent(s) borrow from themselves by dipping into their retire-ment account? They can, and under new IRS rules, they no longer pay a penalty for early withdrawl. They will owe taxes on the proceeds, however. If they don't repay in five years they're in tax-deep guacamole. If a parent changes jobs or gets fired, the money could be due right now. Another problem: The missing money slows down a retirement fund. Overall: Not such a hot idea.

Tuition-freeze programs

Next on the borrowing billet: Should your folks take a loan to buy a guaran-teed tuition price for four years?

Hundreds of colleges have adopted tuition discount programs, a tuition freeze that enables you to prepay four years of college. In return, you pay the present tuition price, not the increased fee you'd pay later when college rolls around.

Colleges can even loan you the money if you don't have an extra $60,000 or more sitting around. If your college of choice offers such a program and its tuition is skyrocketing, maybe you should jump on this opportunity to save big bucks. Or maybe not, depending upon tuition inflation rates compared to your family's financial status. In a negative example: If tuition is only increasing at 4 percent and the usual interest charge on the loan is increasing to 8 percent, prepayment will cost you 4 percent overall.

If you have $20,000 in bank savings paying 3.5 percent interest and take an unsubsidized loan that charges 8 percent interest, you'll come out ahead by 5 percent. But, if you have $20,000 in mutual funds earning 12 percent return — well, you do that math!

Features of the tuition-freeze program include the following:

- ✔ Your family is spared tuition increases while you're in college.

- ✔ If you take a loan approved as an equity line of credit, your federal and state tax bills will be reduced (but you have no guarantee that you'll profit from the program).

- ✔ Interest on loans may cost more than the discount you get for paying early.

For more information, contact the financial aid office at your colleges of choice.

Loans From and For Specific Groups

These loans are from private-sector educational, service, professional, or membership organizations and loans from philanthropic foundations, many of which are targeted at specific groups.

Albert Baker Fund
5 Third St. #717
San Francisco, CA 94103
415-543-7028

- ✔ **Loan limit:** $1,600–$2,500
- ✔ **Interest rate:** None
- ✔ **Deadline:** July 1

> ✔ **Eligibility:** Students must be active Christian Scientists and members of the Mother Church (First Church of Christ Scientist in Boston). Foreign students must have a U.S. resident as a co-signer. The fund places no restrictions as to field of study.

American Society of Mechanical Engineers (ASME)
3 Park Ave.
New York , NY 10016
212-591-8131

> ✔ **Loan limit:** Up to $3,000

> ✔ **Interest rate:** 1 percent below the Stafford Loan rate

> ✔ **Deadline:** April 15 (for summer and fall); October 15 (for winter and spring)

> ✔ **Eligibility:** Graduate or undergraduate students majoring in mechanical engineering or engineering technology who are members of ASME may apply. Graduate students must have a 3.2 GPA; undergraduates must have a minimum of 2.2 GPA. U.S. citizenship is a prerequisite.

Delaware Academy of Medicine
1925 Lovering Ave.
Wilmington, DE 19806
302-656-1629

> ✔ **Loan limit:** $1,000–$3,000

> ✔ **Interest rate:** Noninterest bearing while in college

> ✔ **Deadline:** May 15

> ✔ **Eligibility:** Graduate and professional students must be majoring in allied health fields, medicine, or dentistry and be residents of Delaware who are enrolled in full-time study and have financial need. U.S. residency or permanent residency is a prerequisite.

Emanuel Sternberger Educational Fund
P.O. Box 1735
Greensboro, NC 27402
910-275-6316

> ✔ **Loan limit:** $1,000 (first year); $2,000 (succeeding years)

> ✔ **Interest rate:** None

> ✔ **Deadline:** March 31

> ✔ **Eligibility:** Residents of North Carolina who are juniors, seniors, or graduate students may apply. Loans may be used at any accredited institution. Eligibility is determined by grades, need, references, credit rating, and personal interview.

The Engineering Society of Baltimore
ESB Memorial Scholarship Fund
The Garret Jacobs Mansion
11 W. Mt. Vernon Pl.
Baltimore, MD 21201
410-539-6914 (voice)
410-783-9372 (fax)

✔ **Loan limit:** Varies

✔ **Interest rate:** Noninterest bearing while in college

✔ **Deadline:** April 15

✔ **Eligibility:** Student must be majoring in Engineering and have good academic record. No demonstrated need required. Must live in greater metropolitan area of Baltimore.

Field Co-Operative Association
P.O. Box 5054
Jackson, MS 39296-5054
601-713-2312
601-713-2314 (FAX)

✔ **Loan limit:** $3,000

✔ **Interest rate:** 6 percent

✔ **Deadline:** Open

✔ **Eligibility:** Only third-year undergraduate or graduate students who are Mississippi residents may apply for this loan. Students must have demonstrated need. U.S. citizenship or permanent residency is a prerequisite.

Franklin Lindsay Student Aid Fund
c/o Chase Manhattan Bank
P.O. Box 550
Austin, TX 78789
512-479-2634
512-479-2656 (Fax)

✔ **Loan limit:** Up to $3,000 per year (aggregate of $12,000)

✔ **Interest rate:** Noninterest-bearing while in college; 6 percent after nonattendance

✔ **Deadline:** July 1

✔ **Eligibility:** Students who have completed one year of college with a 2.0 GPA may apply for this loan. Proceeds of the loan disbursement must be used to attend an accredited postsecondary institution in Texas.

Hattie M. Strong Foundation
1620 Eye St. NW, Rm. 700
Washington, DC 20006
202-331-1619

- ✔ **Loan limit:** Up to $3,000

- ✔ **Interest rates:** None

- ✔ **Deadline:** January 1–March 31

- ✔ **Eligibility:** Students must be U.S. citizens attending undergraduate or graduate school. Eligibility is based on merit. This loan is only for the final year of college for students pursuing a baccalaureate degree or higher.

Jewish Family and Children's Services
2245 Post St.
San Francisco, CA 94115
415-449-3726

- ✔ **Loan limit:** $5,000 aggregate

- ✔ **Interest rate:** 80 percent of prime

- ✔ **Deadline:** Open

- ✔ **Eligibility:** Available to college students of the Jewish faith who are U.S. citizens living in the San Francisco Bay area.

Knights Templar Educational Foundation
5097 N. Elston, Suite 101
Chicago, IL 60630-2460
733-777-3300

- ✔ **Loan limit:** $6,000 aggregate

- ✔ **Interest rate:** 5 percent

- ✔ **Deadline:** Open

- ✔ **Eligibility:** Payments and interest are deferred until student is no longer enrolled in college. Students who are in their junior, senior, or graduate year may apply, as well as vocational-technical student enrollees. U.S. citizenship or permanent residency is a prerequisite.

Lemberg Scholarship Loan Fund
60 E. 42nd St., Suite 17
New York, NY 10165

- ✔ **Loan limit:** Varies

- ✔ **Interest rate:** None

- ✔ **Deadline:** April 1

- ✔ **Eligibility:** Loans are available to Jewish men and women for under-graduate, graduate, or professional study. Loan repayments commence after graduation with a ten-year repayment period.

Pickett & Hatcher Educational Fund, Inc.
1800 Buena Vista Rd.
P.O. Box 8169
Columbus, GA 31908-8169
407-327-6586
www.pickettandhatcher.org

- ✔ **Loan limit:** Maximum of $5,500 per year

- ✔ **Interest rate:** 6 percent after leaving college; 27 percent while in school

- ✔ **Deadline:** May 15 (funds awarded first-come, first-served)

- ✔ **Eligibility:** Applicants must be residents of and attend colleges in one of the following states: Alabama, Florida, Georgia, Kentucky, Missis-sippi, North Carolina, South Carolina, Tennessee, or Virginia. Students majoring in law, ministry, or medicine are not eligible.

Six good commercial loan providers

Here are Dr. Davis's picks for top-tier private commercial loans.

Bank of America Student Maximizer
Student Banking Services
275 S. Valencia Avenue, Third Floor
Brea, CA 92823
800-442-0567
www.bankamerica.com/studentunion

- ✔ **Loan limit:** Up to the cost of education per annum; $45,000 cumulative total for undergraduate years; $95,000 cumulative all years

- ✔ **Interest rate:** 52 week T-bill + 2.5 percent in school (6.96 percent as of January 1, 1999)

- ✔ **Fees:** This loan allows you to finance modest origination fees of 5 percent as part of the loan. There are no application fees.

✔ **Deadline:** Open

✔ **Features:** Payments may be deferred while in college and there is a six-month grace period following graduation. There is no penalty for repayment and borrowers have up to 20 years to repay. Interest is capitalized only once at repayment thereby saving borrowers significant interest costs. Multiple repayment options are available as well as forebearance options in cases of temporary financial hardship. Additional savings are available of .25 percent reduced interest for having payments automatically deducted from checking or savings.

Excel Program
Nellie Mae
50 Braintree Hill Park, Suite 300
Braintree, MA 81753
800-634-9308
www.nelliemae.com

✔ **Loan limit:** $5,000 for freshmen/sophomores; $7,500 for juniors/seniors, up to cost of education less any student financial aid

✔ **Interest rate:** Prime + .5 percent for first year of college, prime + 1 percent thereafter; 7 percent guarantee fee

✔ **Deadline:** Open

✔ **Features:** A credit test is required to be eligible for the loan. This loan is not based on demonstrated need. The student has 20 years to repay the loan with no penalty for early repayment. The loan program allows the student to defer the loan payments while in college, but the interest is capitalizing.

Signature Loan
Sallie Mae
P.O. Box 9500
Wilkes Barre, PA 18773-9500
888-888-3461
www.salliemae.com

✔ **Loan limit:** Cost of attendance less the amount of the financial aid acccepted at the college

✔ **Interest rate:** Prime + .5 percent

✔ **Fees:** No fees with co-signer; 3 percent fees at point of repayment

✔ **Deadline:** Open

> ✔ **Features:** First-year student must have a co-signer. Payments are deferred until six months after graduation. Interest on loans accrues while loans are in deferment. During repayment period, if you make 48 payments on time, the interest rate on the loan is reduced by .5 percent. If you make direct repay (having each payment automatically deducted from your checking account), your loan interest is further reduced by .25 percent.

Achiever Loan

Key Education Resources
745 Atlantic Avenue
Boston, MA 02111
800-KEY-LEND
www.Key.com/educate

> ✔ **Loan limit:** $2,000 up to the total cost of education, less financial aid received.
>
> ✔ **Interest rate options:**
>
> - **Annual option:** Interest rate varies quarterly, set to the 13-week T-bill rate plus 4.50 percent loan fee
>
> - **Multiple-year option:** Interest rate varies quarterly, set to the 13-week T-bill rate plus 2 percent loan fee
>
> - **Interest-only option:** Interest rate varies quarterly, set to the 13-week T-bill rate plus 4.50 percent loan fee
>
> ✔ **Fees:** Annual option: 3 percent loan fee; multiple-year option; 2 percent; interest-only option: 4 percent loan fee
>
> ✔ **Deadline:** Open
>
> ✔ **Features:** Loans are not based on establishing demonstrated need. No application or processing fees are charged. Conditional approval is guaranteed within 24 hours. Options available to meet specific family needs.

TERI Loan

The Education Resources Institute
P.O. Box 312
330 Stuart St., Suite 500
Boston, MA 02117-9123
800-255-8374
www.teri.com

> ✔ **Loan limit:** $2,000 up to cost of education less financial aid; unlimited aggregate
>
> ✔ **Interest rate:** Variable not to exceed prime +2 percent
>
> ✔ **Fees:** 5 percent guarantee fee
>
> ✔ **Deadlines:** Open

✔ **Features:** The Teri loan requires a credit check but no demonstrated needs test. Loan deferment is available while the student is in college, but the interest on the loan is capitalizing. The loan has a 45-day grace period after the student is no longer enrolled in college. The loan requires a minimum payments of $50 or payments as established by the payment schedule with 25 years allowed to repay the loan. There is no penalty for early repayment.

CitiAssist Undergraduate
Citibank Student Loan Corporation
Citibank (New York State)
P.O. Box 22945
Rochester, N.Y. 14692-6805
716-248-7672
800-692-8200
www.citibank.com/student/assist.htm

✔ **Loan limit:** $10,000 per year with an aggregate of $50,000

✔ **Interest rate:** Prime + 1 percent

✔ **Fees:** None

✔ **Deadlines:** Open

✔ **Features:** Student borrowers may defer the loan while in college. Interest capitalizes only once at the start of repayment. Loan allows for a six-month grace period after separation from the institution. Students are allowed up to ten years to repay the loan with $50 minimum monthly payments. Loans are available for full, half-time, or part-time study. Loans may be available for international students with a U.S. citizen's co-signature. For four-year institutions and graduate schools only.

Commercial lenders offer varying policies. Simplify your life by sticking with one lender whenever possible. This policy, of course, doesn't apply to direct loans made only by the federal government or loans from nonprofit organizations and foundations.

All in a loan officer's day

A frog goes into a bank and walks up to a loan officer. He sees from her nameplate that the loan officer's name is Patricia Whack. So the frog says, "Ms. Whack, I need a college loan to pay for my tuition and living expenses."

Patti looks at the frog in disbelief and asks how much he wants to borrow. The frog says $30,000. The teller asks his name and the frog replies that his name is Kermit Jagger and that it's okay — he knows the bank manager.

Patti remarks that $30,000 is a lot of money and asks for collateral against the loan. Sure, the frog says, "I have this," and produces a tiny pink porcelain elephant, about half an inch tall.

Confused, Patti explains that she'll have to consult with the manager. When she finds the manager, Patti reports; "There's a frog called Kermit Jagger out there that claims to know you and he wants to borrow $30,000. And he wants to use this as collateral."

She holds up the tiny pink elephant. "I mean, what the heck is this?"

The bank manager smiles back at her and says:

"It's a knickknack, Patti Whack. Give the frog a loan. His old man's a Rolling Stone!"

—*Author unknown*. This shaggy frog story hopped around on the Internet before landing on Joyce's desk, courtesy of Bruce Gittleman of Click4Kids. If the author reads this page, please raise your hand (JLK@sunfeatures.com).

Chapter 17

Can You Smile and Salute?

"*H*ello, sailor, buy you an education?" That question could be asked of anyone serving in any branch of the U.S. Armed Forces. If you say "yes," you'll be surprised at how much in financial aid resources is related to serving in the U.S. armed forces and how widely college study is supported via several channels of funding.

Four populations of people get dollars for school when a family member serves in a military service. These populations are the following:

🗸 College student on active duty

🗸 College student who is a veteran

🗸 College student who is a veteran's dependent

🗸 College student who will become a veteran

Four funding sources service these four populations. These funding sources are the following:

🗸 Federal government

🗸 State governments

🗸 Colleges

🗸 Private organizations and agencies

This chapter examines each student population and itemizes funding sources that service it.

College Student on Active Duty

Who says you can't suit up in uniform and bolster your education at the same time? The possibilities are nearly endless.

As an active military member, you can attend college on a part- or full-time basis:

- ✔ **What the military wants.** The Department of Defense (DOD) pays the tuition to upgrade your skills in your military occupational specialty. On your military employer's time — on-duty hours — you probably won't be able to select the education or training you prefer but will be assigned to learn skills that your service needs.

- ✔ **What you want.** On your own time — off-duty hours — the U.S. Department of Veterans Affairs (VA), under the Montgomery GI Bill, pays for you to learn subjects of your choosing. For example, more than 20,000 military personnel around the world study everything from American history to economics in courses taught by the University of Maryland, the largest provider of higher education to the armed forces. The University of Maryland's yearly catalog list hundreds of courses offered at military sites. Just about every subject taught domestically is also taught somewhere overseas.

A U.S. Department of Veterans Affairs publication, *Summary of Educational Benefits, VA Pamphlet 22-90-2,* describes details of higher education that you choose. If you want a copy, or have questions, contact a VA office at the addresses listed in Table 17-1.

Table 17-1	Regional Veterans Administration Offices
Region Address	*States in Region*
EASTERN REGION VA Regional Office P.O. Box 4616 Buffalo, NY 14240-4616 800-827-1000	Connecticut, Delaware, Maine, Massachusetts, New Hampshire, New Jersey, New York, Ohio, Pennsylvania, Rhode Island, Vermont, West Virginia
SOUTHERN REGION VA Regional Office P.O. Box 54346 Atlanta, GA 30308-0346 800-827-1000	Alabama, Arkansas, District of Columbia, Florida, Georgia, Louisiana, Maryland, Mississippi, North Carolina, Puerto Rico, South Carolina, Tennessee, Virginia, Foreign Schools

Region Address	States in Region
CENTRAL REGION VA Regional Office P.O. Box 66830 St. Louis, MO 63166-6830 800-827-1000	Colorado, Illinois, Indiana, Iowa, Kansas, Kentucky, Michigan, Minnesota, Missouri, Montana, Nebraska, North Dakota, South Dakota, Wisconsin, Wyoming
WESTERN REGION VA Regional Office P.O. Box 8888 Muskogee, OK 74402-8888 800-827-1000	Alaska, Arizona, California, Hawaii, Idaho, New Mexico, Nevada, Oklahoma, Oregon, Philippines, Texas, Utah, Washington

You are considered to be on active duty if you attend one of the federal military academies. For more information, contact the academy admission offices listed in Table 17-2 or your Congressional Representative or Senator.

Table 17-2	U.S. Military Academy Program Directory			
U.S. Air Force	**U.S. Army**	**U.S. Coast Guard**	**U.S. Merchant Marine**	**U.S. Navy/ Marines**
ADMISSIONS DIRECTOR HQ USAFA/RRS	ADMISSIONS DIRECTOR U.S. MILITARY ACADEMY	ADMISSIONS DIRECTOR U.S.C.G. ACADEMY	ADMISSIONS DIRECTOR U.S.M.M. ACADEMY	ADMISSIONS DIRECTOR U.S.N. ACADEMY
2304 Cadet Drive Ste. 200 USAF Academy, CO 80840-5025 719-333-2520 800-443-9266	2304 Cadet Drive Ste. 200 West Point, N.Y. 10996-1797 914-938-4041 800-822-USMA	606 Thayer Rd. New London, CT 06320-4195 860-444-8503 800-883-8724	15 Mohegan Ave. Wiley Hall Kings Point, NY 11024 516-773-5392 800-732-6267	117 Decatur Rd. Annapolis, MD 21402-5018 410-293-1858 800-638-9156

Academy dropouts have safety net

Suppose you campaign for and win a seat in one of the military academies, a seat that some observers say is worth $250,000 including its full-ride tuition and monthly pay.

Then suppose you discover that the military life just isn't for you. If you withdraw under honorable conditions, you're still ahead in the financial aid process. That's because you automatically become an *independent student*, which generally results in maximum eligibility for federal student aid. Your pay as a former cadet is not counted and neither is your parents' income.

College Student Who Is a Veteran

Now that you're out of uniform and into the civilian higher education scene, check out ways you can wind up with money to pay your way through school.

Federal

Uncle Sam and Aunt Feddie channel your scholarly benefits through the U.S. Department of Veterans Affairs. Most veterans attending college are funded under the *Montgomery GI-Bill*, also known as *Chapter 30* by regulations of the U.S. Department of Veterans Affairs.

The Montgomery GI-Bill applies to those who enter active duty for the first time after June 30, 1985. Active duty for benefit purposes includes full-time National Guard duty performed after Nov. 29, 1989. An honorable discharge is required. To receive maximum benefits, you must serve continuously on active duty for three years — or two years' active duty plus four years in the Selected Reserve or National Guard. The top dollars are $528.00 a month for 36 months, with annual adjustments for inflation as of October 1, 1998.

What if you don't finish your stretch? Those who enlist and serve for less than three years receive $429 per month.

Questions? Check with your VA Regional Office listed back in Table 17-1.

State

Most states give qualified veterans free or reduced tuition at any state four-year public institution. Details? Ask your state scholarship administration, which is listed in a directory included in Chapter 8.

Colleges

Most colleges have an Office of Veterans Affairs whose employees have responsibility for coordinating the paperwork for the federal VA office. Additionally, this office helps you with loans and study programs, including providing extra tutoring money if you need it. In essence, Veterans Affairs staffers are supposed to smooth your pathway through college and keep you from blowing your great educational opportunity.

Student Who Is a Veteran's Dependent

A grateful nation provides for the children and spouse of veterans who have paid a heavy price to serve their country.

Federal

VA educational assistance benefits are available to the children and spouses of

- Veterans who died or are permanently and totally disabled as the result of a disability arising from active service in the Armed Forces
- Veterans who died from any cause while rated permanently and totally disabled from a service-connected disability
- Veterans who are missing in action or captured in the line of duty by a hostile force
- Veterans who are presently detained or interned in the line of duty by a foreign government or power

Monthly benefits are paid at the rate of $485 per person for up to 45 months. You usually must be between the ages of 18 and 26. Benefits to a spouse end ten years from the date the VA notifies the spouse of eligibility. In addition, a spouse can apply for VA education loans.

State

Most states honor with education benefits their former residents who joined the Armed Forces and paid a stiff price in the course of duty. The service members honored are those who became prisoners of war (POW), were classified as missing in action (MIA), died, or became disabled.

The states award education benefits to the veterans themselves or to their dependents in varying degrees. Some states, for example, do not include benefits for the spouse, while others generously reward the entire family. Table 17-3 offers a sampling of key benefits, whether they are administered by a Veterans Affairs or higher education agency. To get the entire scope of veterans' education benefits for your state, consult the relevant state office.

	Table 17-3	Veterans' Benefits for Dependents and Spouses of MIA/POW/Disabled/Deceased Veterans				
State & Address		**Tuition**	**Fees**	**Books**	**Stipend**	**Comments**
ALABAMA State Dept. of VA P.O. Box 1509 Montgomery, AL 36102I 334-242-5077		Free	Free	Free	No	
ARKANSAS Contact college's financial aid office		Free	Free	No	No	
CALIFORNIA State Dept of VA Div. of Veterans Svcs. P.O. Box 942895 1227 O St., Rm. 101 Sacramento, CA 95813 916-653-2573		Free	Free	No	No	Cal. State Univ. System, U. of California, Cal. Comm. Colleges
COLORADO CO Commission on Higher Education 1300 Broadway, 2nd Fl. Denver, CO 80203 303-866-2723		Free	No	No	No	
CONNECTICUT CN Dept. of Higher Ed. Ed. Employ. Information Ct. 61 Woodland St. 3rd Fl Hartford, CT 06105-2391 800-842-0229		$400;	No	No	No	Dependents only
DELAWARE DE Higher Ed. Comm. 820 North French St. Carvel State Bldg. 4th Fl Wilmington, DE 19801 302-577-3240		Free	Yes	No	No	Dependents only; spouse excluded
FLORIDA Contact college's financial aid office		Free	Free	No	No	
GEORGIA		Pending	Pending	Pending	Pending	

State & Address	Tuition	Fees	Books	Stipend	Comments
ILLINOIS IL Dept. of VA P.O. Box 19432 833 So. Spring St. Springfield, IL 62794 800-827-1000	Free; also for Veteran	Certain fees	No	No	
INDIANA IN Dept. of VA Attn: Education Div. 302 West Washington St. Room E-120 Indianapolis, IN 46204 317-232-3910	Free or Partial related to cost of the college	Partial fees	No	No	Up to 4 years at any postsecondary institution
IOWA IA Comm. of VA Camp Dodge Office 7700 NW Beaver Dr. Bldg. A6A Johnston, IA 50131-1902 515-242-5331	$600 up to $3,000	No	No	No	Dependents only; spouse excluded. War orphans=$600 IA Vets Foundation= $500
KANSAS KS Comm. of VA Jayhawk Towers, 700 SW Jackson Rm 701 Topeka, KS 66603-3150 785-296-3976	Free	No	No	No	Dependents only; spouse excluded
KENTUCKY KY Vet. Dependents Ed. Assistance KY Ctr for VA 545 So. 3rd St., Rm 123 Louisville, KY 40202 502-595-4447	Free	No	No	No	Up to 36 months or until age 23
LOUISIANA Dept. of VA Affairs Local Parish Vet. Svcs. P.O. Box 94095 Capitol Station Baton Rouge, LA 70804-9095 225-922-0500	Free	Free	No	No	

(continued)

Table 17-3 *(continued)*

State & Address	Tuition	Fees	Books	Stipend	Comments
MAINE ME Vet. Benefits Ofc. State Ofc. Bldg., Stn 117 Augusta, ME 04333 207-626-4464	Free	No	No	No	Dependants only; tuition benefits may be used at any state of Maine supported college or university
MARYLAND MD State Scholarship Board 16 Francis St. Annapolis, MD 21401 410-974-5370	Free	No	No	No	Tuition benefits may be used at any college in-state, not to exceed tuition at Univ. Maryland
MASSACHUSETTS MA State Scholarship Office 330 Stuart St. Boston, MA 02116 617-727-9420	Free; Dependents only	No	No	No	Tuition benefits may be used at any college in state, not to exceed tuition at a public college
MICHIGAN MI Vet. Trust Fund 611 West Ottawa Lansing, MI 48913 517-373-3130	Free	Free	No	No	Dependents only; spouse excluded
MINNESOTA Dept. of Vet. Affairs Veterans Svc. Bldg., 2nd Floor 20 West 12th St St. Paul, MN 55155 651-296-2562	Free except for the U. of MN	See Note	See Note	See Note	*NOTE:* Eligible students may receive up to $350 in any one year to be used for expenses
NEBRASKA Dept. of VA 301 Centennial Mall, So. P.O. Box 95083 Lincoln, NE 68509-5083 402-471-2458	Free	No	No	No	Includes state colleges, U of NE, and technical colleges
NEVADA Contact the College Admissions Office	No	No	No	No	Out-of-state tuition is waived for all veterans

State & Address	Tuition	Fees	Books	Stipend	Comments
NEW HAMPSHIRE *To attend: 4 yr. College* Contact U. System of NH Durham, NH 03824 603-862-1502 *To attend: 2 yr. college* Contact: NH Dept. of Ed. Concord, NH 03301 603-271-2555	Free	No	No	No	Dependents only; spouse excluded Not to exceed $1,000 per year
NEW JERSEY Dept. of Mil. & Vet. Affairs P.O. Box 340 Tenton, NJ 08625-0340 609-562-0668	Free	No	No	No	Dependents of MIA/POWs from Southeast Asia conflict only
NEW MEXICO NM Vet. Svc. Comm. P.O. Box 2324 Santa Fe, NM 87504 505-827-6300	Free	Up to $600	No	No	Dependents of deceased parents only
NEW YORK NY State Higher Ed. Washington Ave., Albany, NY 12255 518-474-8615	No	No	No	No	Award is $450 per year regardless of income, tuition, or costs
NORTH CAROLINA NC Div. of VA Albemarle Bldg. Ste 1065 325 No. Salisbury St. Raleigh, NC 27603 919-733-3851	Free *$1,200 to $3,000	Free	Free	Free	*Students attending 2-yr. colleges or private colleges may receive this benefit
NORTH DAKOTA ND Dept. of VA P.O. Box 9003 Fargo, ND 58106-9003 701-239-7165	Free	Free	No	No	Dependents and spouse
OHIO Ohio Board of Regents 88 E. Broad St. Ste. 350 Columbus, OH 43218-2452 888-833-1133	Free	No	No	No	Dependents only; spouse excluded

(continued)

Table 17-3 *(continued)*

State & Address	Tuition	Fees	Books	Stipend	Comments
OKLAHOMA Contact college's financial aid office	Free	No	No	No	Dependents of POWs or MIAs only; spouse excluded
PENNSYLVANIA (1)PHEAA 1200 No. 7th. St. Harrisburg, PA 17102 800-692-7435 (PA Only) 717-720-2850	(1)Up to $2,600 or $800 out of state	No	No	No	Veteran benefit for bona fide PA residents
(2)PA Dept. of Military and VA Affairs Fort Indiantown Gap Bldg 5-0-0-47 Annville, PA 17003-5002 717-861-8901 800-54PAVET	(2) Up to $500	No	No	No	Dependents only; spouse excluded
TEXAS TX Veterans Comm. P.O. Box 12277 Austin, TX 78711 512-463-5538	Free	No	No	No	Includes Texas Nat'l/Air Nat'l Guard
VIRGINIA Commonwealth of VA Dept. of VA 270 Franklin Rd. SW Poff Fed. Bldg. Rm 503 Roanoke, VA 24011 540-857-7101	Free	No	No	No	Dependents only; must meet certain residence requirements
WEST VIRGINIA WV Div. of VA 1321 Plaza East, Ste. 101 Charleston, WV 25301 304-558-3661	Free	Up to $500	Up to $500	Up to $500	Dependents only; spouse excluded
WISCONSIN WI Dept. of VA P.O. Box 7843 30 West Mifflin St. Madison, WI 53707-7843 608-266-1311	Up to 50% reimbursal	50%	Free		Tuition exemption for nonresident veterans; education loans up to $10,000; up to 50% reimbursement

State & Address	Tuition	Fees	Books	Stipend	Comments
WYOMING WY Dept. of VA 2360 E. Pershing Blvd Cheyenne, WY 82001 307-778-7396	No	No	No	No	Monthly stipends only

Private organizations and agencies

Need more help in finding scholar dollars generated by military service for yourself, child or spouse? The following organizations can provide or help you track down the information you need. With the exception of the American Legion, which covers a wide range of benefits for former members of all military services, you can guess from the organization's name the type of assistance it provides.

American Legion
P.O. Box 1055
Indianapolis, IN 46206
www.legion.org

Air Force Sergeants Association Scholarship Program
P.O. Box 50
Temple Hills, MD 20757
800-638-0594

Disabled American Veterans' Scholarship Program
P.O. Box 14301
Cincinnati, OH 45250-0301
www.dav.org

Non-Commissioned Officers Association Scholarship Program
NCOA Scholarship Foundation
P.O. Box 33610
San Antonio, TX 78265
www.ncoausa.org

Retired Officers Association Scholarship Foundation
Scholarship Loan Program
201 North Washington Street
Alexandria, VA 22314
www.troa.org

Student Who Will Be a Veteran

Study now, pay your dues later! The money's good while you're in school, and you pay up in labor (yours) after graduation.

The U.S. government operates several scholarship programs for students who are willing to serve their nation in return for the scholarship funds, such as the Navy's Armed Forces Health Professions Scholarship Program for medical school and the Army's Health Professions Scholarship Program for dental education.

Reserve Officer's Training Corps (ROTC) offers scholarships that cover as much as 100 percent of tuition, fees, textbooks, plus a $100 monthly stipend for four years of college. If you wait to join until you're in the upper-division ROTC program (junior and senior years of college), you'll receive less aid — only a $100 monthly stipend, but your service obligation is also less. Each branch of the military operates ROTC offices. For information, contact the branch of your choice:

- ✔ **U.S. Air Force ROTC,** HQ AFROTC/RROO, 551 East Maxwell Blvd., Maxwell AFB, Al 36112; 334-953-2091

- ✔ **U.S. Army ROTC,** Gold Quest Center, PO Box 3279, Warminster, PA 18974; 800-USA-ROTC

- ✔ **U.S. Marines ROTC,** Command General Recruiting Command, Code ON, 3280 Russell Rd. 2nd floor Quantico, Va 22134-5103 ; 703-784-9448

- ✔ **U.S. Navy ROTC,** Navy Opportunity, Information Center, PO Box 9406, Gaithersburg, MD 20898; 800-327-NAVY.

In addition, each state maintains a National Guard for the Army and Air Force, providing a little known avenue of educational funding. Some state National Guard units pay 50 percent to 100 percent of members' tuitions at state colleges. Each state decides how much to reimburse. You'd have to serve one weekend a month and two weeks a year for three years or more. Here are the particulars:

- ✔ **Montgomery GI Bill:** You can use the GI Bill to pursue an undergraduate or a graduate college degree as a member of the Army National Guard. If you attend a school approved by the U.S Department of Veterans Affairs, you'll receive a check each month you're in school. As a full-time student (12 or more hours), you'll receive $251 per month for 36 months; as a three-quarter-time student (9 to 11 hours), $188 per month for 48 months; and as a 1/2-time student, $125 per month for 72 months or for less than 1/2 time, $62.75 per month for 144 months. After graduation, you must have served, or agree to commit yourself, for six years of service in the Selective Reserve.

✔ **Enlistment Bonus:** If you have a skill the Army National Guard wants, you can get an enlistment bonus of $2,500 for choosing a designated military occupational specialty (MOS). See your Army National Guard recruiter for more information.

✔ **Student Loan Repayment Program:** If you qualify when you join the Army National Guard, you can get a big assist in paying back your college federally insured or guaranteed loans of up to $10,000. See your Army National Guard recruiter for more information.

✔ **Tuition Assistance (TAP) — Army Continuing Education System (ACES):** This program that pays for part-time undergraduate or graduate study is available to all members of the Army National Guard. The rules limit payment to 75 percent of tuition charges for a maximum of $1,000 per semester. Books or other fees are not reimbursed. Undergraduate studies are limited to 12 semester hours per fiscal year; graduate studies are limited to six semester hours per fiscal year. Payment for undergraduate studies at a four-year college is limited to a semester-hour cap of $85.00; payment for graduate studies is restricted to a semester-hour cap of $150.

Because the National Guard passage to college financial aid is unfamiliar to most students, Table 17-4 lists a 50-state National Guard Directory with financial aid contact information, scholarship programs, and tuition waivers.

Table 17-4	State National Guard Directory	
State National Guard/ Education Offices	*State Tuition Waiver*	*Scholarship Programs*
ALABAMA Education Services Office Military Dept. P.O. Box 3711 Montgomery, AL 36109-0711 334-271-7580	TAP-ACES only	None
ALASKA Education Services Office Education Officer P.O. Box 5800 FT. Richardson AK 99505-5800 907-428-6844	TAP-ACES	None
ARIZONA Education Services Office 5636 East McDowell Road Phoenix , AZ 85008-3495 602-267-2885	TAP-ACES AZ reimburses up to $250 per year	None

(continued)

Table 17-4 *(continued)*

State National Guard/ Education Offices	State Tuition Waiver	Scholarship Programs
ARKANSAS Education Services Office N. Little Rock, AR 72118-2200 501-212-4021	TAP-ACES only	None
CALIFORNIA California Army National Guard 9800 Goethe Rd. Sacramento, CA 95827-3561 916-854-3227	TAP-ACES CA reimburses up to 75% of tuition	None
COLORADO Education Services Office Public Affairs Officer 6848 So. Revere Parkway Englewood, CO 80112-6709 303-397-3159 800-762-4503 (x-3159)	TAP-ACES CO reimburses up to 75% of tuition	Not to exceed $100 per credit hour for undergraduate school and $170 per credit hour for graduate school; state tuition assistance for public schools up to 75% in Colorado
CONNECTICUT Education Services Office National Guard Armory 360 Broad Street Hartford, CT 06105-3795 860-524-4953	TAP-ACES CN tuition waiver pays up to 100% of tuition at any state-supported college, university, or community college	None
DELAWARE Education Services Office First Regiment Road Wilmington, DE 19808-2191 302-326-7001	TAP-ACES DE pays up to $1,300 per year for any state-supported institution	None
DISTRICT OF COLUMBIA Education Services Office National Guard Armory 2001 East Capitol St. Washington, DC 20003-1719 202-433-4960	TAP-ACES DC pays up to 75% of tuition not to exceed $1,000; 15 sem. hrs. maximum per year	$1,000 per semester

State National Guard/ Education Offices	State Tuition Waiver	Scholarship Programs
FLORIDA Education Services Office P.O. Box 1008 St. Augustine, FL 32085-1008 904-823-0350	TAP-ACES FL	N.G. Officers Association Scholarships; N.G. Enlistee Association Scholarships
GEORGIA Education Services Office GA Dept. of Defense 1519 Highway 42 South Ellenwood, GA 30294 404-675-5371	TAP-ACES only	Svc. Cancellable Educational Loan (SCEL). Pays tuition up to cost of U. of GA tuition.
GUAM Education Services Office 622 E. Harmon Industrial Park Rd. Fort Juan Muna Tamuning, GU 96911-4421 011-671-475-0803	TAP-ACES	None
HAWAII Education Services Office 3949 Diamond Head Rd. Honolulu, HI 96816-4495 808-733-4133	TAP-ACES HI state program varies based on funding	None
IDAHO Education Services Office 4040 W. Guard Street Boise, ID 83705-5004 208-422-3761	TAP-ACES only	None
ILLINOIS Education Services Office 1301 N. MacArthur Blvd. Springfield, IL 62702-2399 217-761-3782	TAP-ACES IL provides 100% tuition for any IL state-supported institution	Illinois National Guard Scholarship
INDIANA Education Services Office Adjutant General of IN ATTN: MDI-AG, 2002 South Holt Road Indianapolis, IN 46241-4839 317-247-3502	TAP-ACES IN provides 75% tuition at any state-supported college or univ. in Indiana	None

(continued)

Table 17-4 *(continued)*

State National Guard/ Education Offices	State Tuition Waiver	Scholarship Programs
IOWA Education Services Office 7700 N.W. Beaver Drive Camp Dodge Johnston, IA 50131-1902 515-252-4414	TAP-ACES only; state program provides 50% tuition at any Iowa college or university	10-15 $500 NG scholarships are awarded annually
KANSAS Education Services Office 2800 S.W. Topeka Blvd. Topeka, KS 66611-1287 785-274-1081	TAP-ACES KS provides 100% tuition for any new enlistment or reenlistment	ROTC scholarship is available up to four years in return for four years' service to KSNG
KENTUCKY Education Services Office Bldg 112-100 Minuteman Pkwy Frankfort, KY 40601-6168 502-607-1550	TAP-ACES KY provides 100% tuition at any state-supported postsecondary institution	None
LOUISIANA Education Services Office Headquarters Building Jackson Barracks New Orleans, LA 70146-0330 800-899-6355	TAP-ACES LA provides 100% tuition at any state-supported postsecondary institution	None
MAINE Education Services Office Military Bureau Hdqtrs. Maine National Guard Camp Keyes Augusta, ME 04333-0033 207-626-4370	TAP-ACES pays tuition for four seats per campus at seven Maine Technical Colleges	None
MARYLAND Education Services Office 5th Regiment Armory Baltimore, MD 21201-2288 410-576-1499	TAP provides 25-50% and ACES MD provides up to 75% tuition at any public institution	None

State National Guard/ Education Offices	State Tuition Waiver	Scholarship Programs
MASSACHUSETTS Education Services Office MA National Guard 50 Maple Street Milford, MA 01757 508-233-6552 617-944-0500 Ext. 2254	TAP-ACES MA provides 100% tuition at any state-supported institution in MA	Adjutant Scholarship Program at Norwich U(3 @ $1,000); Nat'l. Guard Asc. of MA Scholarship
MICHIGAN Education Services Office 2500 So. Washington Ave Lansing, MI 48913-5101 517-483-5519	TAP-ACES only	National Guard
MINNESOTA Education Services Office Dept., Military Affairs 1st Fl. Veterans Services Bldg. 20 West 12th Street St. Paul, MN 55155-2098 651-282-4591	TAP-ACES MN provides 50% tuition at any state-supported institution in MN; or at private or out-of-state colleges not to exceed 50% cost at U of MN	Minnesota National Guard Scholarship
MISSISSIPPI Education Services Office P.O. Box 5027 Jackson, MS 39296-5027 601-313-6300	TAP-ACES only	None
MISSOURI Education Services Office 2302 Militia Drive #DPP-I Jefferson City, MO 65101-1203 573-526-9537	TAP-ACES only	Missouri National Guard State Sponsored Scholarship
MONTANA Education Services Office 2475 Broadway St. Helena, MT 59604-4789 406-444-2260	TAP-ACES bill proposed; pending approval for state benefits	None
NEBRASKA Tuition Assistance Office 1300 Military Road Lincoln, NE 68508-1090 402-471-7170	TAP-ACES NE provides for 50% tuition assistance at any state-supported school in NE	None

(continued)

Table 17-4 *(continued)*

State National Guard/ Education Offices	State Tuition Waiver	Scholarship Programs
NEVADA Nevada Air National Guard State Headquarters Education Services Office 2525 South Carson St. Carson City, NV 89701-5502 775-887-7288	TAP-ACES NV provides up to 50% reimbursement at any state-supported college in Nebraska	None
NEW HAMPSHIRE Education Services Office #4 Pembroke Concord, NH 03301-5652 603-227-1550	TAP-ACES NH provides 100% tuition at any state-supported institution of higher education in NH	All applicants receive up to $500 annually
NEW JERSEY Education Services Office New Jersey Department of Military and Veterans' Affairs Eggert Crossing Rd., CN 340 Trenton, NJ 08625-0340 Education Services Officer 609-562-0668	TAP-ACES provides 100% tuition at state-supported institutions of higher education in NJ	None
NEW MEXICO Education Services Office 47 Bataan Boulevard Santa Fe, NM 87505 505-474-1245	TAP-ACES NM provides 100% tuition at state-supported institutions of higher education, 75% federal tuition assistance	None
NEW YORK Education Services Office 330 Old Niskayuna Road Latham, NY 12110-2224 518-786-4937	TAP-ACES NY recruitment/ retention incentive program provides for 100% tuition only, not to exceed cost of attending SUNY	YES

State National Guard/ Education Offices	State Tuition Waiver	Scholarship Programs
NORTH CAROLINA Education Services Office 4105 Reedy Creek Road Raleigh, NC 27607-6410 919-664-6194 or 800-621-4136	TAP-ACES NC provides up to $1,000 per state fiscal year toward tuition and fees; $4,000 over Guard career	North Carolina National Guard Association Scholarship
NORTH DAKOTA Education Services Office P.O. Box 5511 Bismarck, ND 58506-5511 701-224-5903	TAP-ACES ND provides 100% tuition at any state-supported institution in ND	None
OHIO Education Services Office Tuition Grant Program 2825 West Dublin-Granville Rd Columbus, OH 43235-2789 614-274-8003	TAP-ACES OH provides 60% tuition at any state-supported institution; private schools receive an avg. grant based on OU's tuition	None
OKLAHOMA Education Services Office 3501 Military Circle Oklahoma City, OK 73111-4398 405-425-8207	TAP-ACES OK provides 100% tuition at state-supported institution up to Bachelor's degree	None
OREGON Education Services Office Oregon Military Dept. P.O. Box 14350 Salem, OR 97309-5047 503-945-3816	TAP-ACES	None
PENNSYLVANIA Education Services Office Tuition Assistance Office Fort Indiantown Gap Annville, PA 17003-5002 717-861-8536	TAP-ACES provides from $1,200 to $2,400 per school year	None

(continued)

Table 17-4 *(continued)*

State National Guard/ Education Offices	State Tuition Waiver	Scholarship Programs
PUERTO RICO Education Services Office P.O. Box 3786 San Juan, PR 00904-3786 787-289-1400	TAP-ACES TAG-PR provides 100% tuition not to exceed $75 per credit for maximum of 6 credit hours for postgraduate and doctorate courses, or 9 credits at U of PR	Military dependents; program defrays tuition costs up to 100% for 12 credits or less, not to exceed $20 per college credit for undergraduate school; or 50% for up to 6 credits, not to exceed $25 at master's level
RHODE ISLAND Education Services Office 645 New London Cranston, RI 02920-3097 401-457-4309	TAP-ACES	None
SOUTH CAROLINA Education Services Office #1 National Guard Road Columbia, SC 29201-4766 803-806-4200	TAP-ACES legislation pending regarding additional tuition benefits; estimated to be $1,000 per year	None
SOUTH DAKOTA Education Services Office 2823 West Main Rapid City, SD 57702 605-399-6729	TAP-ACES only	Partial state tuition and textbook reimbursement
TENNESSEE Education Services Office Houston Barracks P.O. Box 41502 Nashville, TN 37204-1502 615-313-0594	TAP-ACES only	Yes; scholarships available through enlisted and officers' associations
TEXAS Education Services Office ATTN: AGTX-PAE P.O. Box 5218, Camp Mabry Austin, TX 78763-5218 512-465-5515	ACES only	RSVP Scholarship plus GI provides nearly $5,000/year

State National Guard/ Education Offices	State Tuition Waiver	Scholarship Programs
UTAH Education Services Office 12953 S. Minuteman Dr. AOPCA-ESO Draper, UT 84020-1776 801-576-3614	TAP-ACES only Up to $1,000 annually 1. 24 courses awarded annually at St. Michaels College. 2. $3000 Adjutant General scholarship at Norwich (1 annually); 25% tuition discount for part-time students at several private colleges	None
VERMONT Education Services Office Green Mountain Armory Camp Johnson Colchester, VT 05446-3004 802-654-0348	TAP-ACES only	None
VIRGINIA Education Services Office Education Services BLDG-316 Ft. Pickett Blackstone, VA 23824-6316 804-298-6155	ACES-Federal TA VANGTAP provides 50% tuition not to exceed $500 per semester and $1,000 per year	Scholarships available through enlisted and officers associations
VIRGIN ISLANDS Education Services Office 4031 La Grande Princess Lot 1B Christiansted, VI 00820-4353 340-692-9244	TAP-ACES	None
WASHINGTON Education Services Office Camp Murray, Building 15 Tacoma, WA 98430-5073 253-512-8899	TAP-ACES WA provides 75% tuition, based on space availability at selected colleges	WANG-Washington Army National Guard Scholarship Program
WEST VIRGINIA Education Services Office 1703 Coonskin Drive Charleston, WV 25311-1085 304-341-6335	TAP-ACES	None

(continued)

Table 17-4 *(continued)*

State National Guard/ Education Offices	State Tuition Waiver	Scholarship Programs
WISCONSIN Education Services Office P.O. Box 8111 Madison, WI 53708-8111 608-242-3448	TAP-ACES provides 100% tuition based on undergraduate admissions at UW-Madison	None
WYOMING Education Services Office 5500 Bishop Boulevard Cheyenne, WY 82009-3320 307-772-5262	TAP-ACES provides $3,000 per year credit for nonresidents attending University of Wyoming	None

Be Glad You Wear Army Boots

You don't need a drill sergeant to scream that no matter which branch of the military you select, going to school in or out of uniform is a lot cheaper than hoofing it on your own.

Additional reading

Need A Lift? The American Legion's annual college scholarship and financial aid guide for veterans and their families is a true public service. Send $3 to: Need A Lift, P.O. Box 1050, Indianapolis, IN 46206.

Chapter 18

Planning for Graduate and Professional Study

• •

In This Chapter

▶ Understanding graduate and professional financial aid

▶ Anticipating your ability to pay back loans

▶ Explaining why you can borrow more for certain fields

▶ Comparing private loan programs

▶ Considering advanced study where others pay the tab

▶ Playing all your aces to come up with the money

• •

*F*ewer than half of all graduate students receive financial aid, but in the humanities, about six out of ten graduate students are on their own, and in the social sciences, seven out of ten graduate students receive no financial aid dollars.

Graduate student support is more abundant in the science and engineering precincts, but even there some graduate and professional students are financially flying solo.

Other than jobs and gifts from Aunt Sue, what resources are left? In a word, loans. In fact, *loans are the chief source of funding* for most students who pursue graduate and professional study.

Graduate students acquire loans and grants from many of the same places that undergraduate students do. In addition, institutions award money to graduate students for fellowships and teaching assistantships, which carry teaching or research responsibilities.

Climbing a Mountain of Debt

Rosa and her husband, Dan, recently graduated together from a private law school. If you hyperventilate easily when you think about big numbers, catch your breath before you read the next paragraph.

Because they'd financed most of their entire education with borrowed money, the newly minted professional couple now owes $220,000 in education loans, and it's payback time. Dan and Rosa can expect to keep sending fat checks to loan providers long after the dust settles on their law degrees. Payments will be roughly $2,000 monthly for both. That's a gloomy $24,000 a year.

Rosa and Dan's mix of madness and money are hardly rare. As tuition for advanced education climbs and the government and private lenders pass out loans by the fistful, futurologists predict that the $3.3 billion increase in graduate/professional loans in the last four years will continue to rise rapidly. For example, the government's Federal Stafford loan (see Chapter 7), which covers most medical studies, raised its annual limit to $18,500 per student, not to exceed an aggregate of $138,500 for all years of college.

The exception to this is related to eligible medical, dentist, and veterinarian professional students. The total unsubsidized Stafford loan limit for these health profession students is $189,125 less the total amount of the subsidized loans made to each student.

Terrifying, isn't it? Especially when you consider the entry-level salary you can expect in the first few years after you graduate.

The race to gain an advanced education and pay for it is like trying to run a marathon wearing leg irons. If you decide to enter the race, you have to take the attitude that the odds are merely formidable, not insurmountable.

Then again, some debt burdens do seem insurmountable, such as a newsmagazine report of a husband and wife who graduated from medical school recently owing almost $500,000 in student loans. (Quick! Pass the life support system!)

The insanity of borrowing a debt load that may have you looking over your shoulder for bill collectors most of your life is not going to go away. A frightening career uncertainty has slithered into the work world, and smart first-time and returning students alike are in the educational trenches, taming the serpentine beast by earning imposing professional degrees.

BASICS

A question of degree: Terms for advanced education

The term *advanced study* describes both graduate and professional study.

Graduate study means study that follows a bachelor's degree in a given academic field, such as history, chemistry, or literature. The Ph.D. is a graduate degree, as is the Master of Arts.

Professional study describes the practical application of knowledge and skills, such as in

business, law, architecture, and medicine. J.D. (for *juris doctor*) is a first professional law degree, not a doctorate in law.

In everyday usage, the term graduate degree is often substituted for the correct term of advanced degree when referring to both graduate and professional degrees.

Whether you're a dedicated scientist in the making or a hard-core numbers-cruncher, your future's far more alluring when you have a competitively edged degree in hand. You know that! What you may not have focused on so clearly is the financial aid planning and sacrifice needed to cushion your landing when you must repay all those loans.

As you consider borrowing for graduate education, anticipate what the monthly cost to repay the loans will be, especially if you have a spouse, kids, pets, a mortgage, two autos, and a boat to support. Table 18-1 shows a ten-year monthly repayment schedule that gives you clues to what debt burdens you can face for jumbo loans of amounts up to a quarter of a million dollars at 8, 9, or 10 percent interest.

Table 18-1	Ten-Year Monthly Repayment Plan		
Amount Borrowed	*8%*	*9%*	*10%*
$75,000	$910.50	$950.25	$991.50
$100,000	$1,214.00	$1,267.00	$1,322.00
$125,000	$1,517.50	$1,583.75	$1,652.50
$150,000	$1,821.00	$1,900.50	$1,983.00
$175,000	$2,124.50	$2,217.25	$2,313.50
$200,000	$2,428.00	$2,534.00	$2,644.00
$225,000	$2,731.50	$2,850.75	$2,974.50
$250,000	$3,035.00	$3,167.50	$3,305.00

Source: Sandy Springs National Bank of Maryland

When you weigh the cost of graduate or professional study, give your imagination something positive to play with: The U.S. Census Bureau finds that over a lifetime, those with professional degrees earn $3 million on average; those who have a baccalaureate earn $1.4 million.

The payoff for professional degrees is especially high in technology, law, medicine, and business. Janice, for example, a new biomedical Ph.D., landed a plummy job at a biomedical firm in San Diego. The job pays enough to cover a new car payment, rent, a comfortable lifestyle, and her $850 monthly education-loan payments.

Graduate Loans for Fields with High Earnings Potential

Students who pursue professional degrees are granted larger loans than those who go after graduate degrees in academic fields such as biology or English. That's because lenders expect doctors, lawyers, and M.B.A.s to outearn lab workers and English teachers, placing them in a better position to pay off their loans. When you borrow for graduate study, realistically research and assess your future earnings potential in making your borrowing decisions.

A Sampling of Graduate/Professional Private Loans

The following loan sampling highlights qualifying fields of study to give you an idea of what's available in your discipline. They represent but a handful of the many popular loans for graduate and professional students. Remember that the loan industry is dynamic. Always recheck the particulars — including the fine print — of any loan program in which you're interested. After looking over this listing, turn to the directory that follows for a compilation of lenders to graduate and professional students.

Federal Stafford and Direct Student Loans
(for graduate students in any discipline)
U.S. Department of Education
Federal Student Aid Information Center
P.O. Box 84
Washington, DC 20044-0084
800-433-3243
www.ed.gov

Signature Health Loan
(for allopathic medicine, dental, optometry, osteopathic medicine, pharmacy, podiatry, and veterinary medicine only)
Sallie Mae
P.O. Box 59011
Panama City, FL 32412-9011
888-888-3461 or 800-695-3317
www.salliemae.com

MEDLOANS and Alternative Loan Program (ALP)
(for medical students only)
Association of American Medical Colleges
2450 N. Street, NW
Washington, DC 20037
202-828-0400

Medical Access Loans
Dental Access Loans
(for medical and dental students only)
Access Group
P.O. Box 7430
Wilmington, DE 19803-0430
800-282-1550
www.accessgroup.org

MEDSHARE
(for medical and dental students only)
The New England Loan Marketing Association
Nellie Mae
50 Braintree Hill Park, Suite 300
Braintree, MA 02184
800-634-9308
www.nelliemae.com

LawLoans
(for law students only)
Sallie Mae
P.O. Box 59011
Panama City, FL 32412-9011
800-984-0190
www.salliemae.com

Law Access Loan
(for law students only)
Access Group
P.O. Box 7430
Wilmington, DE 19803-0430
800-282-1550
www.accessgroup.org

LawEXCEL
(for law students only)
The New England Loan Marketing Association
Nellie Mae
50 Braintree Hill Park, Suite 300
Braintree, MA 02184
800-634-9308
www.nelliemae.com

MBAEXCEL
(for business students only)
The New England Loan Marketing Association
Nellie Mae
50 Braintree Hill Park, Suite 300
Braintree, MA 02184
800-634-9308
www.nelliemae.com

Business Access Loans
(for business graduate students only)
Access Group
P.O. Box 7430
Wilmington, DE 19803-0430
800-282-1550
www.accessgroup.org

Professional Education Plan (PEP)
(for graduate and professional students including but not limited to chiropractic, osteopathic, optometric, veterinary, physical therapy, physician's assistant, nursing, or occupational therapy fields)
The Education Resources Institute (TERI)
330 Stuart St., Suite 500
Boston, MA 02116-5237
800-255-8374
www.teri.org

Graduate Access Loans
(for graduate students in any discipline)
Access Group
P.O. Box 7430
Wilmington, DE 19803-0430
800-282-1550
www.accessgroup.org

GradEXCEL
(for graduate students in any discipline)
The New England Loan Marketing
Association
Nellie Mae
50 Braintree Hill Park, Suite 300
Braintree, MA 02184
800-634-9308
www.nelliemae.com

Option 4 Loan Program
(for graduate students in any discipline)
USA Funds
P.O. Box 6198
Indianapolis, IN 46206-6198
800-635-3785
www.usagroup.com

Achiever Loan
Key Education Resources
17 Corporate Woods Blvd.
Albany, NY 12211
800-540-1855

CitiAssist
(for graduate students in any discipline)
Citibank Student Loan Corporation
99 Garnsey Rd.
Pittsford, N.Y. 14534
800-946-4019
TDD 800-846-1298
studentloan.citibank.com

Teri Alternative Loan
330 Stuart St., Suite 500
Boston, MA 02116-5237
800-255-8374
www.teri.org

A Directory of Lenders That Offer Private Loans to Graduate and Professional Students

Like the mortgage industry, private education has become a shop-it-yourself process, complete with eye-popping graphics, silky admonitions to ease your money-money worries, and even online interactive loan comparison features showing why Lender A beats out Lenders B, C, and D.

With this list of lenders in hand, we bet you can hardly wait to fire up your computer, visit the lenders' Web sites, and discover how much you should borrow and how to spell rate relief with the plethora of special price breaks that each lender advertises. Hang on to these Web addresses for dear updated life: the education loan industry is "in play." At press time, Sallie Mae bought Nellie Mae — and that "mae" mean a new round of changes.

Association of American Medical Colleges
2450 N. Street. NW
Washington, DC 20037
202-828-0400
Loan programs (for medical students only):
MEDLOANS
Alternative Loan Program (ALP)

Access Group
P.O. Box 7430
Wilmington, DE 19803-0430
800-282-1550
www.accessgroup.org
Loan programs:
Business Access Loan
Bar Examination Loan
Dental Access Loan

Dental Residency/Board Exam Loan
Graduate Access Loan
Law Access Loan
Medical Access Loan
Medical Residency Loan

Bank of America
Student Banking Service
275 S. Valencia Ave. Third Floor
Brea, CA 92823
800-442-0567
www.bankamerica.com/studentunion
Loan programs:
Grad Maximizer
Student Maximizer

Citibank Student Loan Corporation
Citibank
99 Garnsey Road
Pittsford, NY 14534
800-946-4019
studentloan.citibank.com
Loan programs:
CitiAssist Loan (all areas of graduate school)
CitiAssist Loan for Medical Students (Allopathic or Osteopathic)

International Education Finance Corporation (IEFC)
International Student Loan Program (ISLP)
424 Adams Street
Milton, MA 02186
USA
888-296-IEFC (4332)
617-696-7840
www.iefc.com
Loan programs:
ISLP/CanHELP (Canadian Higher Education Loan Program)
Graduate Loans for study in foreign countries
ISLP Foreign Enrolled
ISLP International
ISLP Study Abroad

Key Education Resources
Key Bank USA
745 Atlantic Avenue
Boston, MA 02111
800-KEY-LEND
www.key.com
Loan programs:
Alternative DEAL (dental school)
Best Bet (fourth-year dental students only;dental boards and travel)
GradAchiever (graduate school)
LawAchiever Loan
Law Achiever Bar Loan
MBAchiever (business school)
MedAchiever Loan (medical school)
MedAchiever Loan (for medical student's residential, travel, and relocation)

Massachusetts Educational Financing Authority (MEFA)
125 Summer Street, Suite 1450
Boston, MA 02110
800-449-MEFA (6332)
617-261-9760
www.mefa.org
Loan program:
MEFA Graduate Loan (All graduate majors)

MedFunds
A Division of Ohio College of Podiatric Medicine
10515 Carnegie Avenue
Cleveland, OH 44106
800-665-1016 (for MedFunds information)
800-665-6750 (for A+ Funds information)
www.medfunds.com
Loan programs:
A+ Funds (all non specified majors)
Alternative Graduate Loan (for health related majors: Allopathic, Dentistry, Medicine, Nursing, Nursing Nutrition, Nurse Practitioner, Nutrition, Occupational Therapy, Optometry, Osteopathy, Pathologist Assistant, Pharmacy, Physical Therapy, Physician Assistant, Podiatry, Public Health, and Veterinary)

Missouri Higher Education Loan Authority
Mohela
14528 South Outer Forty Drive, Suite 300
Chesterfield, MO 63017-5705
1-800-6MOHELA
www.mohela.com
Loan programs:
BARCASH
EDCASH
GRADCASH
LAWCASH
MBACASH
MEDCASH
MEDCASH+

New England Loan Marketing Association, The
Nellie Mae
50 Braintree Hill Park, Suite 300
Braintree, MA 02184
800-634-9308 (or) 800-FOR-TUITION (367-8848)
www.nelliemae.com
Loan programs:
EXCEL GRADLOAN
Dental-EXCEL
LawEXCEL
MBA-EXCEL
Medical -EXCEL

Norwest Corporation
Norwest Student Loan Center
P.O. Box 5115
Sioux Falls. SD 57117-5115
800-658-3567
www.norwest.com
Loan programs:
LAWLOANS (SM)
MBA Loans (SM)
MedCAP Alternative Loan for Health Professionals
MedCAP Allternative Loan for Allied Health
Norwest Collegiate Loan Program (NCLP) for Graduate Students

Student Loan Marketing Association
Sallie Mae
PO Box 59023
Panama City, FL 32402-9023
888-888-3461
800-695-3317 (Signature Loan)
888-774-3142 (Signature Loan)
800-984-0190 (LAWLOANS Program)
www.salliemae.com
Loan programs:
LAWLOANS (LSI)
MEDLOANS
MEDEX
MBALOANS
Executive MBA Loan
Signature Health Rewards
Signature Health Loan

The Education Resources Institute (TERI)
c/o TERI
330 Stuart St., Suite 500
Boston, MA 02116-5237
800-255-TERI (8374)
www.teri.org
Loan programs:
Business
Dentistry
Engineering
Law
Loans for graduate-professional programs
MedChoice Loan
Osteopathic Medicine
Professional Education Plan (PEP) (any graduate majors)
Pharmacy (Ph.D. degree)
Physical Sciences

Comparing Your Loans

You may want to do online comparisons on a lender's Web site, or you may want to use eStudentLoan (www.eStudentLoan.com), a terrific one-stop-shopping resource that offers a loan finding and instant comparison feature, as well as a digital application option.

Even when you prefer to work online, you may find that old-fashioned scribbling on paper helps reinforce the magnitude of what you're letting yourself in for at payback time.

Jot down the data about the most promising loans on Dr. Davis's Graduate/Professional Loan Comparison Form (see Table 18-2). Then compare each category of one loan with its equivalent in other loans. Putting it in buzzwords, compare "apples to apples."

Table 18-2	Dr. Davis's Graduate/Professional Loan Comparison Form		
Loan Program	_____	_____	_____
Annual Loan Amount	_____	_____	_____
Maximum Loan Limit	_____	_____	_____
Interest Rate	_____	_____	_____
Fees (Guarantee, Origination, Insurance)	_____	_____	_____
Deferment	_____	_____	_____
Grace Period	_____	_____	_____
Repayment Calendar	_____	_____	_____
Minimum Monthly Payment	_____	_____	_____

Other Resources for Graduate School

The GEM Ph. D. Science Consortium
(National Consortium for Graduate Degrees for Minorities in Engineering and Science)
P.O. Box 537
Notre Dame, IN 46556
219-631-7771
www.nd.edu/~gem

National Health Service Corps Scholarship
2070 Chain Bridge Rd.
Vienna, VA 22182
800-221-9393
aspe.os.dhhs.gov/cfda/
p93288.htm

National Science Foundation
Oak Ridge Assoc. of Universities
4201 Wilson Blvd.
Arlington, VA 22230
703-306-1234
www.nsf.gov

National College Scholarship Foundation
(national loan forgiveness database)
16728 Frontenac Terrace
Rockville, MD 20855
800-220-3919
ncsf@aol.com

Fellowships and Assistantships: Financial Aid for Advanced Study

Only advanced study offers the form of financial aid known as fellowships and assistantships.

Fellowships

Most fellowships are outright awards that require no service in return. Fellowships often provide the cost of tuition and fees, plus a stipend to cover bare-necessity living expenses. They may be based primarily on demonstrated need, on academic merit, or on a combination of need and merit.

Both university and foundations provide fellowships. Most often the fellowships sponsored by universities are merit-based because the schools want students whose accomplishments add to their institutional prestige.

The awards often must be renewed annually. Fellowships attract graduate to post-doctoral students with sterling academic records; the competition is fierce, but the rewards are tremendous and prestigious.

Assistantships

First-year graduate students often become teaching assistants (TAs), research assistants (RAs), or administrative assistants (AAs). Some universities provide financial support in the form of a project assistantship (PAship). Most schools reduce or waive tuition fees for assistants.

TAs pursuing an advanced degree in a subject taught at the undergraduate level (arts and sciences, for example) typically work 20 hours a week as a teacher-in-training. You may give lectures, grade papers, correct classwork, and advise students. TAs receive salaries. This type of financial aid comes from academic departments, not the university's financial aid office.

RAs assist a faculty member in research. These positions go to the most promising students, but usually not before the second year of advanced study. Hours vary. The appointment pays a salary.

AAs toil 10 to 20 hours each week in an administrative office of the university. Some administrative assistantships pay a salary, others provide a tuition waiver, and still others provide both.

By riding the coattails of a faculty member as an assistant, you earn not only money and maybe tuition, but you also gain crucial experience for your first after-graduation job.

Conditional trades

Designed to recruit good people for understaffed areas, some scholarships and grants are really loans in that recipients agree to return the value of the education in work, usually with a specific employer or in a specific career or geographic area.

A student physician, for instance, in return for a medical education may agree to work at a medically underserved rural area for four years; a nurse whose training costs were paid by the federal government may agree to serve in a military service for four years.

If a recipient chooses not to make good on the promise, the award generally must be repaid in full.

Employer-Aided Study in Selected Fields

Employers are another alternative to loans (see Chapter 2). A number of current and future employers give special financial assistance to students in specific fields. The examples of business and engineering follow.

Business administration

Employers often help cover the expenses of students pursuing an M.B.A. (Master's in Business Administration) degree. For example, a prospective employer may cover the costs of a second-year business school student who looks like a hot hire. Another popular approach is for employers to help pay the costs for current employees enrolled in part-time M.B.A. programs.

An M.B.A. who has consulting capabilities and a degree from a top school can look forward to a starting salary of more than $78,000 — an income that more than compensates for pregraduation expenses. Management consulting (especially the type that helps trim overstretched companies), finance, marketing, and management information systems are promising employment spots in the new millennium.

Engineering

The National Research Council says that only four out of ten engineering students who receive a Ph.D. are in debt at graduation — meaning that the majority of engineering doctoral candidates obtain enough grants and fellowships to stay virtually debt-free. At private universities, annual costs often exceed $30,000 per year; at public universities, about $18,000.

Engineering and scientific fields are generally big on grants because the government has set up several funds to encourage technological growth. Current grants come especially easy to females and minority group members who are currently underrepresented in the technical and engineering fields.

After receiving their advanced degree, graduates can look forward to eager employers. Computer science and engineering Ph.D.s are rewarded with an average starting salary of more than $56,000.

When compared to repaying jumbo loans, employer-paid alternatives are appealing alternatives.

The tax man biteth

Graduate-level tuition reimbursement from employers used to be tax-free, but it is currently treated as taxable income. Because graduate-level education is increasingly seen as important for mid-career professionals who want to change jobs or be promoted, as well as for younger graduate students, lawmakers will be urged by many voters to reconsider the issue. Maybe in the next Congress, the tax man goeth. Watch the news.

In the meantime, anticipate a bite out of your paycheck when you create your educational financial plan.

As a rule, you can find out what free money is available in a profession by quizzing the relevant professional organizations, which you can find online by using the organization's name in a keyword search or by looking in such references as the *Encyclopedia of Associations.*

With effort, most students can scarf up some form of aid besides loans. If you choose the right field, your feverish financial aid quest will pay off later when you have a fast-track future. But only if you complete the degree.

Too many graduate students leave school with what amounts to a partial degree, which can be a liability. Some employers interpret unfinished education as evidence of an inability to stick with a project to completion or a lack of passion for the work.

Don't let money worries bog down your education; apply your study skills and energy to finding the financial aid that can help you complete that degree.

Additional resources

The College Blue Book — Scholarships, Fellowships, Grants and Loans, 26th Edition; Huber William Hurt, Harriet-Jean Hurt, and Christian E. Burckel, Macmillan Publishing Company, 1998.

Dan Cassidy's Worldwide Graduate Scholarship Directory, 5th Edition; National Scholarship Research Service, Santa Rosa, CA; order by calling 1-800-HEADSTART.

Foundation Grants to Individuals, 11th Edition, Mills, Carlotta, R., ed. New York: The Foundation Center, 1999.

The Graduate Student's Complete Scholarship Book, Inc. Staff Student Services. Sourcebooks Trade, 1998.

Peterson's Grants for Graduate & Post Doctoral Study, 5th Edition; Petersons Guides, 1998.

Real Life Guide to Graduate and Professional School: How to Choose, Apply for, and Finance Your Advanced Degree! Cindy Rold, Pipeline Press, 1998.

Scholarships, Fellowships and Loans, Gale Research Inc., Detroit, 1999.

Yale Daily News Guide to Fellowships and Grants 2000, Ali Mohamadi, Kaplan Educational Center, 1999.

Part IV

Filling Out Forms and Other Fine Print

The 5th Wave   By Rich Tennant

"I really can't have a relationship now – I'm afraid it might impact my 'needs analysis form'."

In this part . . .

The innocuous statement "Read instructions and complete this form" may seem simple. The hundreds of blanks in the typical aid application may even seem harmless. But one false move and your chances for financial aid could crash down on hard earth. This part helps you jack up your aid by correctly filling out need analysis forms. You also get the plain English version of how to understand your award letters and when you should expect your first check. These chapters give line-by-line tips on every blank, from the no-brainers to the brain-buster questions.

Chapter 19

Blooper-Proof These Lines

● ●

In This Chapter

▶ The fumbles are in the details

▶ Knowing who answers what

▶ Confusion-proofing your applications

▶ Best Blooper Award nominees

● ●

Chapter 18 discussed serious pitfalls to avoid on financial aid application forms. This chapter focuses on what should be no-brainers.

Don't Let These FAFSA Questions Fool You

Many of the questions on the Free Application for Federal Student Aid (FAFSA) seem easy — too easy. Just because the form asks for information you can recite in your sleep doesn't mean you can't be information-wise and form-foolish. You, the student, should fill out the FAFSA. But most often, college students who are put off by the tangles of blanks and lines and requests for numbers freak out and pass the work on to Mom or Dad.

Anxious applicants all over the country are blemishing their applications at this very moment due to pure carelessness. Don't join the bumbling, fumbling throngs. As you, or your folks, gingerly print in your information, tend to the tips that follow.

Line 8: What's Your Number?

When well-meaning moms or dads fill out the FAFSA, sometimes they get so intense that they give their own Social Security number when the form asks for the student's.

The same dear parents can be so consistent that they give their own dates of birth as well. The joke's on the student when the application reviewer looks at the age listed and classifies the student as an independent student.

Line 16: Are you married?

This question asks if the student is married; parents filling out this form may mistakenly answer Yes, which means the typically single student is instantly married in the financial aid reviewer's eyes — an amusing misconception, but not really so funny, because the rest of the answers on the form won't make sense and will confuse the federal processor. This puzzler can cause the form to be questioned, delayed, and even rejected before it is finally processed.

Line 33: A diploma is not a degree

This question asks if students will have a first bachelor's degree by July 1 before entering college in September. Students have been known to confuse a diploma with a degree and answer Yes. Oops.

With this slip of the pen, students become seriously ineligible for the major federal grant programs (Pell, FSEOG) and most state scholarship programs The bulk of grant programs assist students toward their first degree. Graduate aid usually comes from loans or work-study. See Chapter 18 if you need graduate assistance.

Lines 49-52: No student assets

This question asks the value of the student's assets. Many parents continue to build up this account thinking that it will get the student more money. Wrong way to go. Students are penalized 35 cents on the dollar, or 35 percent, for their assets. Parents who leave money in their own asset accounts always do their children's finances a full-on favor.

Line 59: Dependents

This question asks for the number of dependents for which the student pays childcare. The parent who is dutifully completing this FAFSA is likely to list the number of children (including the student) in the entire family. However, newly sprung college hopefuls are usually without dependents.

Line 63: Use the short form

This question asks for U.S. income tax figures reported on the parents' income tax form. Historically, parents and tax preparers in this situation use the long form 1040. But if parents make less than $50,000, they are always more eligible for aid if they file the short forms 1040A or 1040EZ. If they use the short form or were eligible to use the short form and net less than $50,000, they will be given special consideration in having their family asset values reduced.

Line 76: Apart is separate

This question asks the parents' current marital status. Students normally get more aid if the parent is single, separated, or divorced. However, many parents don't consider themselves separated because they're not "legally" separated. In other words, faced with a formal form, they get overly particular for their own good. Legal separation isn't required for this question. If the parents are living apart for the purpose of eventually becoming divorced, answer the question "separated." Complete the rest of the form using the information about the parent with whom the student chiefly lives or, if custody is split, who provided the most financial support during the last 12 months.

Line 78: Anybody else in school?

This question asks for the number of people in the family who will be attending an eligible college program at least half-time while the student attends college. The more people in college, the more eligible the student is for financial aid. Parents are no longer considered in the count, but graduate students and family members attending at least half-time can be considered. (Although parents who are serious, full-time students can't list themselves on the FAFSA, they may be considered in the count if a college financial aid counselor, exercising the authority of *professional judgment,* agrees and lists them on the FAFSA.)

Nominees for Best Blooper Award

The SAR (Student Aid Report) is where the rubber meets the road in the race for financial aid. That's when blundering students discover they goofed in filling out their FAFSA. The SAR goes to the student and the information on the SAR goes to the colleges that the student designates.

As discussed in Chapter 3, colleges receive the SAR information via electronic transmission. However, students are supposed to either update, correct, or submit unamended copies of their SARs in hard-copy form to the college's financial aid office, if required by the institution.

In the process that starts with filling out the FAFSA and ends with receipt of the SAR, lots of room for calamity is present. Dr. Davis knows this well because he has counseled thousands of aid-seeking students in his private practice — sometimes after the fact, when the student needs help to straighten out a financial aid disaster.

From Dr. Davis's file of best blunders, here are true stories of train wrecks that could have been avoided with an information infusion. To protect the formerly unaware, we don't use real names.

The case of too many zeros

When Roger received his SAR, he was surprised to see that he and his family had an EFC (expected family contribution) of 00000. Roger often received grades of F in school, which was probably the reason Roger thought the string of zeros meant he had failed and wasn't eligible for aid of any kind. Roger thought about those zeros. He decided that he could never attend college because he wasn't eligible for financial aid, and he joined the Navy. In fact, however, the zeroes meant that his family needed to contribute nothing to his education as he was eligible for the total amount of aid.

They jumped to the wrong conclusion

Jonathan had his heart set on attending the college where all his friends were going — good old State U. When Jonathan's SAR came back, it reflected the fact that his family's expected contribution was too high to make him eligible for a Federal Pell grant, a grant reserved for low-income families. Jonathan's SAR included this specific message: "Based on the information given us, you are not eligible for a Federal Pell grant."

Jonathan's family misinterpreted the message to mean he was ineligible for any financial aid and stopped applying for it. Good old State U. was out the window. Too bad. Jonathan was eligible for institutional aid, state aid, and private aid; he would have received enough funding to cover tuition, fees, and room and board, although none of the money would have come from the Federal Pell grant program.

The moral to this story: Never assume, always ask.

Efficiency to the fourth power

In today's News of What Passes for Weird in Financial Aid Land, here's Laura's story. The high school senior believes in doing a thing right the first time so she'll only have to do it once. Knowing that she'd require four years of student financial aid, Laura took the time to fill out four identical but original (no photocopies) FAFSAs, one for each year she requested aid. What the hay, she reasoned, I may as well take care of everything going in. Then, following her game plan, Laura sent off all four of her FAFSAs at the same time.

You probably know that only one FAFSA is accepted each year by the federal processing center. The lesson: An applicant and her leisure time are soon parted. Laura's loss of hours could have been productively spent filling out apps for scholarships.

All forms are not created equal

Laura had too many forms; Chris had too few. Chris filled out a College Scholarship Service Profile form and sent it to all the colleges he wanted to attend. Chris assumed, incorrectly, that the Profile was the only one needed. He failed to fill out the mother of all financial aid forms, the FAFSA, from which needs-analysis figures are calculated.

The two private colleges on his list called Chris to ask "Where's your FAFSA?" By contrast, his preferred institution, the University of Maryland, never contacted him about money. Why? Because its financial aid office uses only the FAFSA, not the Profile, and thus the University of Maryland never knew Chris wanted aid.

You can bet Chris won't lose out next year. He's marked his calendar on January 1: "Remember the FAFSA! Or leave the country."

Wiser but poorer by $3,500

Maryann's parents were married when she submitted her original FAFSA. They separated in December. Her mother, a stay-at-home mom, didn't have an income to report.

The bungle: Maryann's mom didn't bother to correct her SAR because she thought they'd have to wait until the next school year. If only mom had refiled, Maryann would have been eligible for a Pell grant retroactive to the beginning of the school year, which, with the other aid the refiling would trigger, would have saved the family $3,500.

Two cannot pay as cheaply as one

Sonny's parents had been separated for more than three years, although they continued to file joint income taxes. Sonny lived with his mother — the custodial parent. Only the custodial parent has to include his or her taxable and untaxable (child support) income and assets on the FAFSA.

Unaware of that fact, Sonny's parents reported both parents' income and resources. This miscalculation was an expensive one: Sonny lost $4,200 in financial aid funding. That's one mistake they won't make again.

Dollars short and days late

Rebecca missed the aid boat because she missed the deadline for filing for aid from her state and her college. She wasn't forgetful; she just thought she had to be accepted by a college before asking for financial aid. No, no, no. Not so.

She did manage to apply in time for a Pell grant and Federal Stafford Loan, which she received, but Rebecca's loss of free money was $5,000. Ouch.

The next year she knew better than to wait — she made all her deadlines and is decidedly richer for her promptness.

Twins who made the same mistake twice

Allison and Emily are twin sisters in a family of six, none of whom had ever attended college. The family income is under $45,000. When Allison filled out her FAFSA for the fall semester, she was the only one who was college-bound. Her request for a Pell grant was a near-miss but she did receive state aid and a subsidized student loan.

Emily, seeing how well Allison was doing in school, decided to enroll as a full-time student in the nearby community college.

Allison didn't think to refile her SAR with the new information (two in college), a failing that denied her a full Pell grant, which would have canceled out her student loans.

Even worse, Emily never applied for aid for the second semester, causing the proud parents to take out an equity loan to help pay Emily's tuition. Emily would have been eligible for a full Pell grant for the second semester.

Because each twin failed to let their college financial aid teams know both sisters were in college, the twins lost more than $5,000.

Lined Up and Ready to Go

Knowing the right ways to fill out your forms, as discussed in Chapter 20, and the wrong ways that are discussed in this chapter, you're all set to move ahead. Figure 19-1 is a handy checklist that you can photocopy to keep track of your forms and applications.

Dr. Davis's Checklist for Forms and Applications

Key: #1 = Date institution must have forms				#2 = Date you sent forms			
Name of College A		B		C		D	
Date #1	#2	#1	#2	#1	#2	#1	#2
Admission							
H.S. Transcript College Transcripts Recommendation Letters Other 1. 2. 3.							
Financial Aid							
Application FAFSA PROFILE Divorced / separated statement Business / farm statement Parent's 1040 Parent's W-2 Student's 1040 Student's W-2							

Figure 19-1: Lasso those forms and applications on your newly created paper ranch by keeping good records of deadlines, when you meet them, and what you send.

Chapter 20

Storm the Aid Storehouse Line by Line

● ●

In This Chapter

▶ Figuring your family contribution

▶ Questions you can't afford to answer wrong

▶ The art of recording unusual facts

● ●

*I*n thinking about how to make the point that little things mean a lot on your FAFSA, we came across this story:

> *A grandfather gardener was building a stone wall around his yard when a neighbor wandered by and asked why gramps used so many small stones along with the big ones "The stones are like people," gramps replied." Many small people like me are needed to keep the big ones in place. If I leave the small stones out, the big ones will shift out of place and the wall will fall."*

Chapter 20 dwells on little lines that, metaphorically speaking, can cause your FAFSA to come crashing down! While this chapter isn't exactly a page-turner, the time you spend with us here could turn out to be some of your best-paid work.

We repeat for emphasis: This chapter dwells on little lines that can trip you up big time.

If you don't feed financial aid processors the correct information in the correct form, they become befuddled and you lose all the chances at free money and loans.

Calculating Your Need

The formula for calculating your need is as follows:

Total college cost budget for example:	$26,175
(–) Expected family contribution (EFC) for example:	$ 2,432
(=) Demonstrated financial need:	$26,175

The college financial aid need (level of eligibility) in this model is $26,175 and, the award letter from the college may include self-help funds — loan and/or work and some gift money (grant and/or scholarship).

If you're not a numbers-cruncher, determining your own financial need may seem absolutely alien. But you can easily estimate your Estimated Family Contribution ahead of time on the Web at www.collegeboard.com. (Click the Tools listing on that Web page.) After you know how much colleges will expect you to shell out, you can start scrimping — or not scrimping. Simply enter your financial data next to the mathematical symbols in each box. Using the symbols, calculate figures until you reach the final boxes, which estimate the student's and parents' contributions (divided by the number of family members in college).

Understanding and reading your SAR

Eligibility for all federal grants, work-study, and subsidized loans is based on a need analysis system: the *Federal Methodology Need Analysis* system. To get the best results, use the advice in this chapter as you fill out the FAFSA. When you send your FAFSA to your designated federal processor, the agency will use the Federal Methodology to determine the Expected Family Contribution (EFC) and then mail you a Student Aid Report (SAR).

The SAR forms (usually, blue, pink, green, or some other pastel color) contain the official EFC, which appears on Part I below the date of processing and will look like the following example:

EFC: 03535

It resembles a serial number. But if you exchange the first zero for a dollar sign, it will have greater meaning:

EFC: $3535

The College Scholarship Service (CSS) provides another need analysis system required by some colleges. Students must complete a CSS Need Analysis Application referred to as a CSS Profile. After submitting a CSS Profile to the CSS processing center, you will receive a CSS Profile Acknowledgement. Although you won't see your own EFC anywhere on the Acknowledgement, CSS sends your need analysis information to colleges that will in turn decide how to treat the results. This practice is known as *Institutional Need Analysis Methodology*. After you've estimated your family contribution, call your financial aid administrator and ask how the financial aid office plans to treat the results of the Profile.

Use the following advice to complete each blank of the FAFSA and effort-lessly turn the base metal of your financial information into educational gold.

Instructions for Completing the FAFSA

If you don't file either the FAFSA or the Renewal FAFSA, you won't get any federal or state financial aid. Most state institutions and all two-year colleges and trade schools use only this form. Some colleges require additional documentation. Check with each college to which you apply.

Locate these records

Locate the following records to simplify the process:

- ✔ 1999 federal income tax form for both the student and parent(s)

- ✔ 1998 federal income tax forms — to estimate 1999 income in lieu of a 1999 federal income tax form

- ✔ W-2 Forms and other records of money earned in 1999

- ✔ Copy of last payroll stub that may give an indication of the year-to-date earnings for estimating annual income in lieu of the 1999 federal income tax form

- ✔ Records of untaxed income such as welfare, Social Security, AFDC, ADC, voluntary contributions to tax-deferred income programs such as annuity programs, IRA, KEOGH, 401(k), and the like, and housing allowances

- ✔ Business and farm records

- ✔ Records of stocks, bonds, and other investments for parents and student

- ✔ Student's Social Security and driver's license numbers

Remember these guidelines

Use a black or dark ink pen or a #2 pencil. Blue ink will not scan the informa-tion as well:

- ✔ Print carefully — others need to be able to read your writing.

- ✔ When marking the ovals, keep the ink inside the ovals. (Scanners get confused when the markings are outside of the ovals.)

✔ Do not use a special handling mail service if you're preparing your forms late. Special mailing only delays the process because this form goes to a P.O. Box and no one can sign for delivery.

✔ Do not enclose, attach, or staple any documents with the FAFSA. They will only be thrown away and will slow down forms processing.

✔ For all but questions 1 to 37, use numbers or a zero to respond to questions. Do not use responses such as N/A — or leave a question blank.

✔ Round off all figures to the nearest dollar.

✔ Use numbers to reflect dates (for example, 02-15-99).

✔ The term *school* relates to the postsecondary institution (college, university, two-year college, career school, or trade school) that you plan to attend.

✔ Make copies of all documents that you prepare.

Start Form-Filling!

The following sections explain what you need to know to fill the FAFSA completely and correctly. An error in this form could sink your chances of qualifying for needed aid. Check the boxes at left as you fill them out in the form.

Step One: Questions 1 through 37 — personal background

This section pertains only to the student applicant.

❑ **Lines 1–3:** Use your proper name — no nicknames.

❑ **Lines 4–7:** Use a permanent mailing address; processors use this address to communicate with you.

❑ **Line 8:** A Social Security number is required for this form to be processed. If you do not have one, apply for one as soon as possible. This form won't be processed without one. (The SSN question has one of the most frequent error rates and is among the main reasons students lose eligibility.) To order a new or replacement Social Security card, call 1-800-772-1213. (Service is offered in English and Spanish).

❑ **Line 10:** List your permanent telephone number. Do not list your school or a temporary apartment telephone number.

❑ **Lines 12–13:** List your driver's license number. If you don't have one, write **none.** Abbreviate State of Issuance.

❑ **Lines 14–15:** Mark the appropriate box for citizenship status.

❑ **Line 16:** Respond to marital status questions as appropriate.

❑ **Line 17:** Write date of marriage, separation, divorce, or widowhood.

❑ **Lines 18–22:** Complete the FAFSA questionnaire as requested.

❑ **Lines 23–24:** Fill in the oval that represents the highest educational level or grade level your father and mother completed. Highest level is defined to mean at what educational level did your parent complete. (That is, 10th grade of high school would reflect "High School." One semester of college would reflect "College or beyond.")

❑ **Line 25:** State abbreviation: Use the state of permanent residence — not the state of college residence. (If you're planning on living in the state after graduation, find out how to become a state resident and qualify for lower tuition fees and state scholarships.)

❑ **Line 26:** Complete the FAFSA questionnaire as requested.

❑ **Line 27:** Date of legal resident status. If you were born in the state, use your date of birth. If you move to the state of residence, give the month and year.

❑ **Lines 28–31:** Complete the FAFSA questionnaire as requested.

❑ **Line 32:** ○ Yes ○ No

If you will receive a high school diploma or a GED before the first date of your enrollment, ink in the correct response. *Note:* If you have been attending college as a special student or on a part-time basis without having a high school diploma or GED, you should know that. A college transcript that reflects two years of college credit towards a baccalaureate degree is equivalent to a high school diploma. If you have one of these, respond with a yes.

❑ **Line 33:** Bubble in the No oval if you don't have a bachelor's degree and/or won't have one by July 1, 2000. Fill in Yes if you already have a bachelor's degree or will have one by July 1, 2000.

If you have a degree from another country equal to a bachelor's degree, bubble in the Yes oval.

If you already hold a bachelor's degree, you won't qualify for a Pell grant (free money), a Federal Supplemental Educational Opportunity grant (free money), or some state grant and scholarship programs.

❑ **Lines 34–37:** Complete the FAFSA questionnaire as requested.

Questions 38 through 52 — income, earnings, and benefits

Questions 38–52: These questions refer to taxable and untaxable income for you and/or your spouse. If you are now married (even if you were not married in the previous tax year), report both the income for you and/or your spouse. If you are not married, ignore the term spouse. Answer all questions with "0" if they do not apply to you.

❑ **Line 38–39:** Respond to these questions reflecting the status of your tax filing at the time you submit this document. (**Note:** *Will file but have not yet filed* means you are filing using estimated income for the 1999 tax year.)

❑ **Line 40:** You normally get special consideration for lowering the assessment on your parents' assets if your parents' income is less than $50,000, and your parents can file an income tax Form 1040A or 1040EZ. *Note:* Even if your parents filed or will file an IRS Form 1040, if they were eligible to file the 1040A or 1040EZ, check the box for 1040A or 1040EZ. Why? Because if your parents can file tax returns by using either of these forms, the parents' and student's assets will be disregarded.

❑ **Lines 41–46:** Taxable income:

1999 Adjusted Gross Income (AGI)	41. [$_____]
1999 U.S. income tax paid	42. [$_____]
1999 Total number of exemptions	43. [$_____]
1999 Earned Income Credit	44. [$_____]
1999 Income earned from work (You)	45. [$_____]
1999 Income earned from work (Your spouse)	46. [$_____]

❑ **Line 47:** 1999 Untaxed income

(See Worksheet A)   47. [$_____]

Untaxed income sources are listed in the following chart, which is Worksheet A.

WORKSHEET A

(Your Untaxed Income)		*(Your Parents' Untaxed Income)*
[$_____]	Payment to tax-deferred pension and savings plans (paid directly or withheld from earnings) as reported on the W-2 Form. Include untaxed portions of 401(k) and 403(b)plans. Welfare benefits (except AFDC or ADC reported on Line 59 or 71).	[$_____]
[$_____]	Deductible IRA and/or Koegh payments. (See IRS Form 1040-total of lines 23 and 29, or 1040A-line 15.)	[$_____]

(Your Untaxed Income)   **(Your Parents' Untaxed Income)**

[$ _____]	Child support received for all children. Don't include foster care or adoption payments.	[$ _____]
[$ _____]	Welfare benefits, including temporary Assistance for Needy Families (ANF). Don't include food stamps.	[$ _____]
[$ _____]	Tax exempt interest income from IRS Form 2555.	[$ _____]
[$ _____]	Foreign income exclusion from IRS Form 2555 or 2555EZ.	[$ _____]
[$ _____]	Untaxed portions of pensions from IRS Form 1040 excluding rollovers.	[$ _____]
[$ _____]	Credit for Federal tax on special fuels from IRS Form 4136-Part III- nonfarmers only.	[$ _____]
[$ _____]	Social Security payments that were received and not taxed.**	[$ _____]
[$ _____]	Housing, food, and other living allowances (excluding rent subsidies for low-income housing) paid to members of the military, clergy, and others, including cash payments and cash value of benefits).	[$ _____]
[$ _____]	Workers' Compensation.	[$ _____]
[$ _____]	Veterans' noneducation benefits such as Death, Pension, Dependency and Indemnity Compensation (DIC).	[$ _____]
[$ _____]	Any other untaxed income and benefits, such as Black Lung Benefits, Refugee Assistance, or untaxed portions of Railroad Retirement Benefits. (Don't include student aid, JTPA benefits, or benefits from flexible spending arrangements, such as cafeteria plans.)	[$ _____]
[$ _____]	Cash or any money paid on your behalf, not reported elsewhere on this form.	[$ _____]

[$ _____]	**Student (and spouse) total**	You enter this amount in question 47. Your parents enter this amount in question 79.	**Parent(s) total** [$ _____]

*Support Payments (CSP) received in 1999 should be reported in terms of the annual amount. Most CSP stop when the applicant reaches age 18, which will be in 2000 for most students. You may wish to notify each school's financial aid office and appeal that your CSP be disregarded because those funds won't be available during the year you are applying for aid.

**Social Security Benefits (SSB) that parents collect on behalf of the student should be reported under parents' income. Most stop at age 18, which will normally come in the 2000 calendar year. Many college financial aid officers will disregard the applicant's SSB reported on Line 70 because they won't be continuing while the student attends college. You may wish to contact the financial aid office to discuss this concern.

❑ **Line 48:** 1999 Income exclusion   [$_____]

See the following Worksheet B to determine funds you can list that will reduce your taxable and untaxable income. (*Note:* This is important because the more excluded income you have, the more eligible you may be for financial aid.)

WORKSHEET B

(Your Excluded Income)		*(Your Parent's Excluded Income)*
[$_____]	Education Credits (Hope and Lifetime Learning Tax Credits).	[$_____]
[$_____]	Child support you or your spouse (or your parents) paid because of divorce or separation (not child support received).	[$_____]
[$_____]	Taxable earnings from Federal Work-Study or other need-based work programs.	[$_____]
[$_____]	Allowances and benefits received under the National and Community Service Trust Act of 1993 (AmeriCorps awards).	[$_____]
[$_____]	Student grant and scholarship aid in excess of the tuition, fees, books, and supplies that was reported in question 41 for students and 64 for parents.	[$_____]
[$_____]	Enter this amount in question 48.	[$_____]
[$_____]	**Student (and spouse) total** **Parent(s) total**	[$_____]
[$_____]	**Student (and spouse) total** Your parents enter this amount in question 71.	**Parent(s) total** [$_____]

Lines 49–52: Your available assets

❑ **Line 49:** Total current balance of cash, savings, and checking account.
[$_____]

❑ **Line 50:** Total current net worth of investments (worth minus debt).
[$_____]

Investments include real estate, trust funds, money market funds, mutual funds, certificates of deposit, stocks, bonds, other securities, installment and land sale contracts, commodities, and the like. (Trust funds are discussed in Chapter 13, in Q&A, but as a general rule, trust funds in the name of a specific individual are reported as that person's asset on the FAFSA. If you have a trust fund, you must report the present value of the trust as an asset.)

Investments do not include, for FAFSA purposes, the primary house in which the family lives, life insurance plans, prepaid tuition plans, retirement plans (pension funds, annuities, IRAs, Keogh plans).

❑ **Line 51:** Current net worth of business (business value minus business debt).   [$_____]

Business value includes the market value of land, buildings, machinery, equipment, and inventory. *Business debt* includes only those debts for which the business was used as collateral.

❑ **Line 52:** Current Net worth of investment farm.   [$_____]

Do not include a farm that you or your parents' live on and operate.

Step Two: Questions 53 through 58 — student status

The questions in this section determine your eligibility for aid as an independent or dependent student. An independent student can normally qualify for more aid. However, the main criterion for establishing independent status while attending undergraduate school is age. The magic age is 24. A student 24 years of age or born before January 1, 1977, automatically qualifies for independent status. However, some institutions may require further criteria for independent status before qualifying the student for institutional aid.

❑ **Line 53:** ○Yes ○ No

Were you born before January 1, 1977?

❑ **Line 54:** ○ Yes ○ No

Will you be enrolled in a graduate/professional program (beyond a bachelor's degree) in 2000-2001?

❑ **Line 55:** ○ Yes ○ No

Fill in Yes if you're married as of today or if you are separated. You're still considered married until officially divorced. If you're divorced and less than 24 years of age, you may be considered a dependent student and may have to list your parents' assets. Complete this FAFSA and submit it to your college financial aid officer to review your circumstances and certify you as an independent student (see Step Six). (School Use Only) is for the financial aid officer to determine your dependency status. D/O means *dependency override*. If this financial aid counselor agrees that you are independent, the counselor will certify you as such and submit your data as an independent student.

❑ **Line 56:** ○ Yes ○ No

Are you an orphan or a ward of the court, or were you a ward of the court until age 18? Answer Yes if

- You're currently a ward of the court or were until age 18.

   (or)

- Both of your parents are deceased and you do not have an adoptive parent or legal guardian. (Legal guardian is defined as a person appointed by a court to be your legal guardian in a legal relationship that will continue after June 30, 2001, and who is directed by a court to support you with his or her own financial resources.)

❑ **Line 57:** ○ Yes ○ No

Are you a veteran? Answer Yes if you have engaged in active service in the U.S. Army, Navy, Air Force, Marines, or Coast Guard or if you are not a veteran now but will be one by June 30, 2001.

Note: If you've attended any U.S. Military academy and were dismissed for any reason but dishonorable discharge, answer Yes and you qualify as an independent student.

❑ **Line 58:** ○ Yes ○ No

Do you have legal dependents (other than a spouse)? Answer Yes if

- You have children who receive more than half their support from you;

   (or)

- You have dependents (other than your children or your spouse) who live with you and receive more than half of their support from you and will continue to get that support, from you, now and through June 20, 2001.

- *Note:* This person does not necessarily have to be claimed on the IRS Form1040, but you must be able to document that you provide at least half of his or her support.

If you answered Yes to any of the questions in Step Two, respond to questions 59–60. If your answers are no, go directly to Step Four.

Note: Graduate health profession students applying for federal aid under the Public Health Service Act — Title VII programs must also complete all questions in Step Four on the form for your parent(s) as well as for yourself. Why? Because these funds are regulated under different federal authorization, which legislates that the parents' income and assets must be factored into the need analysis formula. Check with your financial aid office to verify the institution's policy. Otherwise, complete the *blue, gray,* and *white* areas.

Step Three: Questions 59 and 60 — students household information

This section pertains to student and spouse (independent students only).

❑ **Line 59:** Write in the number of your household.

The following persons may be included in the household size of independent students:

- Yourself.

- Your spouse; exclude a spouse if not living in the household as a result of death, separation, or divorce.

- Your dependent children, if they received or will receive more than half their support from you between July 1, 2000 and June 30, 2001.

- Your unborn child, if that child will be born before or during the award year and you will provide more than half the child's support from the projected date of birth to the end of the award year.

- Other persons, if they live with you and receive more than one half of their support from you at the time of application and will continue to receive that support for the entire 2000–2001 award year (July 1, 2000 through June 30, 2001).

❑ **Line 60:** Write the number of household members reported in Line 59 who'll be attending college at least half-time (6 credit hours) in 2000–2001. This response must always be at least one (1).

The following are the definitions that apply:

- **Enrollment Period:** July 1, 2000 to June 30, 2001

- **College:** Any accredited post-secondary institution

- **Enrollment:** Registered for at least half-time for one term in a degree or certificate program

- **Half-time:** Six semester hours or 12 clock hours per week

- **One-term:** One quarter, one semester, and so on

Step Four: Questions 61 through 82 — parents' income, earnings, benefits, and assets

Questions 61–71: These questions refer to taxable and untaxable income for your parent(s). If the answer is zero or the question does not apply, enter "0".

❑ **Lines 61–62:** Respond to these questions reflecting the status of your parents' tax filing at the time you submit this document. (*Note: Will file but have not yet filed* means your parent(s) are filing using estimated income for the 1999 tax year.)

❑ **Line 63:** You normally get special consideration for lowering the assessment on your parents' assets if your parents' income is less than $50,000, and your parents can file an income tax Form 1040A or 1040EZ. *Note:* Even if your parents filed or will file an IRS Form 1040, if they were eligible to file the 1040A or 1040EZ, check the box for 1040A or 1040EZ. Why? Because if your parents can file tax returns by using either of these forms, the parents' and student's assets will be disregarded.

❑ **Lines 64–69:** Taxable Income

1999 Adjusted Gross Income (AGI)	64. [$_____]
1999 U.S. income tax paid	65. [$_____]
1999 Total number of exemptions	66. [$_____]
1999 Earned Income Credit	67. [$_____]
1999 Income earned from work (Father /Stepfather)	68. [$_____]
1999 Income earned from work (Mother/Stepmother)	69. [$_____]

❑ **Line 70:** 1999 Untaxed Income   70. [$_____]
(See Worksheet A in Step 2)

❑ **Line 71:** 1999 Income Exclusion: 71. [$_____]
(See Worksheet B in Step 2)

Questions 72–75: Your parents' available assets

❑ **Line 72:** Total current balance of cash, savings,
and checking account   72. [$_____]

❑ **Line 73:** Total current net worth of investments
(worth minus debt)   73. [$_____]

Investments include real estate, trust funds, money market funds, mutual funds, certificates of deposit, stocks, bonds, other securities, installment and land sale contracts, commodities, and so forth. For FAFSA purposes, do not include investments related to the primary house in which the family lives, life insurance plans, prepaid tuition plans, retirement plans, pension funds, annuities, IRAs, Keogh plans, and the like.

❑ **Line 74:** Current net worth of business (business
value minus business debt)   74. [$_____]

Business value includes the market value of land, buildings, machinery, equipment, and inventory. Business debt includes only those debts for which the business was used as collateral.

❑ **Line 75:** Current net worth of investment farm   75. [$_____]

Do not include a farm that your parents' live on and operate.

Questions 76–82: Parental information

Note: The level of financial aid eligibility is largely determined on how you answer the next three questions.

❑ **Line 76:** Fill in your parents' marital status:

Married (○), Single (○), Divorced/Separated (○), Widowed (○)

Definition of Parent:

- **Adoptive Parent:** Considered same as natural parents.

- **Foster Parent:** Not considered a parent of the student.

- **Grandparent:** Not considered student's parent. Grandparents' income can't be reported on the FAFSA unless the grandparents are court-appointed legal guardians or have legally adopted the student. (When in doubt, contact the financial aid office.)

- **Legal Guardian:** Considered same as natural parents if the legal guardian is appointed by a court that will continue after June 30, 2001, and who is directed to support you with his or her own financial resources.

- **Stepparent:** Considered same as a natural parent. Stepparent's income and assets are treated same as natural parent's even if no adoption takes place. Prenuptial agreements are disregarded for FAFSA. (*Note:* If natural parent has died and stepparent survives, the student is independent unless stepparent legally adopts this student.)

- **Married:** Natural parents remain married (or) have remarried; in either case the answer is married.

- **Separated:** Parents are separated and getting an eventual divorce. Separation doesn't have to be "legal or formal," but it must be a reality even if it is a trial separation.

- **Divorced:** Natural parent that student lives with is divorced and a single head of household. If the parent is now remarried, respond to Question 76 as married.

❑ **Line 77:** Number of persons in your parents' household in 2000-2001. Include all persons who live in the household for whom your parent or guardian provides at least half their support and will continue to do so from July 1, 2000 to June 30, 2001.

Note: For the purpose of including children in household size, the *support test* is used rather than *residency test* due to divorce and separation situations. In such cases, the parent who provides more than half of the child's support may claim the child in household size even if this person does not live in the same domicile. The following persons may be included in the household size of the dependent student:

- The student.

- The student's parent(s), excluding a parent not living in the household as a result of death, separation, or divorce.

- The student's siblings, if they received or will receive more than half their support from the student's parent(s) between July 1, 2000 and June 30, 2001.

- The student's children, if they received or will receive more than half their support from the student's parent(s) between July 1, 2000 and June 30, 2001.

- The student's parents' unborn child and/or the student's unborn child, if that child will be born before or during the award year (July 1, 2000 through June 30, 2001) and the student's parent(s) will provide more than half the child's support from the projected date of birth until the end of the award year.

- Other persons, if they live with and receive more than one-half their support from the student's parent(s) at the time of application and will continue to receive that support for the entire 2000 – 2001 award year (July 1, 2000 through June 30, 2001).

Financial need is based on household size and not on the exemptions on the IRS Form 1040. The larger the size of the household, the more need can be demonstrated.

Question 77 is considered to be one of the most important questions on the FAFSA. Why? Because the Federal Methodology divides the parents' contribution by the number of family members attending college during the same academic year. For example, if this formula calculates that after looking at all of the responses, the parents' contribution is $12,000 for one family member in college, then the amount would be approximately $6,000 for two in college, $4,000 for three in college, and so on.

In cases where a parent has remarried and the new parent is paying at least 50 percent of support for a child living at the other residence, the parent should list the child living at another residence as part of the family size on Line 77. More importantly, if any of these children are attending college and meet the definition of enrollment, then they should be listed on Line 78 as college students.

If graduate students meet the definition of family members to be included in Line 77, include them in Line 78. However, a financial aid counselor may use "professional judgment" and disqualify the graduate student as a family member or member of the family attending college. Always include the graduate student as a family member in college and personally discuss the entry with the appropriate financial aid office.

❑ **Line 78:** Number of college students in household in 2000–2001.

(**Note:** Starting the 2000–2001 academic year, parents are no longer to be considered as family members in college unless approved by the financial aid office.)

From Line 77: Determine how many household members will attend college (any postsecondary institution) for at least 6 semester hours in one term or 12 clock hours per week and will be working towards a degree or certificate leading to a recognized education credential at a college that is eligible to participate in any of the federal student aid programs, even though they do not complete a term.

Remember that the answer to this question must be at least one; the applicant student is included.

Note: Applicants who are required to register for college credit to renew their professional certificates (for example: teachers' professional certificates or nurses' certificates) to be employed aren't required to be enrolled in certificate or degree-seeking programs.

❑ **Line 79:** Your parents' state of legal residence abbreviation. Parents may have dual residence, as in the case of military personnel or when parents pay state income tax in different states. The FAFSA document only allows for listing one state of residence. "Residence" is your parents' true, fixed, and permanent home.

❑ **Line 80:** Yes (○), No (○). Did your parents become legal residents of the state in question 79 before January 1, 1995?

❑ **Line 81:** Month and year when your parents became state residents if you said no to question 80. If they were born in the state of residence, give their date of birth. Use the older of the parent(s) information used to complete this form.

❑ **Line 82:** What is the age of your older parent? List the age of your parent as of the date that you are submitting your FAFSA document. The older the parent, the more protection allowance is allowed against your parent's asset. The older the parent, the more eligible you are for financial aid if the parent is declaring assets on the form.

Step Five: Questions 83 through 94 — college selection and housing indicator

In Step Five, be sure to fill in all college codes where you want this information sent. Don't overlook the housing options. If housing options are left unmarked, the processor will assume that you are living with your parents. This housing plan will result in the financial aid officer at your college using the lowest cost budget resulting in you receiving less aid.

Be especially careful in completing Step Five. If you use the wrong codes, list the wrong schools, or forget to sign and date the form, you subtract from your aid amount.

❑ **Lines 83–94:** The FAFSA results (shown on the Student Aid Report — these are pastel-blue-colored paper forms for 2000–2001) will be sent to up to eight colleges you list. Some state scholarship agencies consider the costs of the college you write on the first line (83) when determining their state aid awards. Doing so assures that they can use an institution-specified budget to assess your need.

Except for a few state scholarship programs, a student cannot use a state award for an in-state college outside of the student's state of residence. Ask your state scholarship agency if your state has reciprocity agreements with other states. State scholarship agencies are listed with contact information in Chapter 8.

Note: Housing codes are a big deal. A common mistake in this section is failure to complete the housing code column, Questions 84–90, on the right side of the form across from the corresponding school code. This code is very important because it tells the college financial aid counselor which budget to use. If you don't list a housing code, the college will most likely use the lowest budget, and you won't receive the maximum award. On-campus budget codes tend to result in more aid than off-campus or living-with-parent codes.

Special note: If you are applying to more than eight colleges, you may wish to prioritize the schools with the earliest deadlines.

Here's how to have information sent to more than eight colleges:

- Don't write the name of more than one college per line. Doing so only delays the process. You will receive a Student Aid Report (SAR) about four weeks after submitting the FAFSA to the processing center.

- When you receive your SAR (the colored-paper forms) you can deliver or send a photocopy of your SAR to a new college.

- You can write a letter to your assigned FAFSA processor requesting that information be sent to new colleges.

- You can add new colleges on Part II of the SAR and return Part II to the address provided on the SAR.

- Additional colleges can be added by telephone: Call the U.S. Department of Education at 1-800-4FED-AID (1-800-433-3243), have the DRN (Data Release Number) available (found on the blue SAR).

Step Six: Questions 95 through 100 — release and signature

Date and sign this document. (Be sure not to date this form before January 1. It will be rejected.) If you're a dependent student, fill out lines 97–100 as appropriate.

We mention these pointers in earlier chapters, but they bear repeating:

- ✔ Do not mail the FAFSA to the processor before January 1st.
- ✔ Do not attach or include other documents or paper with the FAFSA.
- ✔ Do not mail by special delivery — doing so slows up processing.

Student Aid Report (SAR)

The colored-paper forms that make up the Student Aid Report (SAR) are the secret to receiving financial aid — the end result of submitting the FAFSA. After the FAFSA is submitted to the federal central processor, the student receives the SAR about four to six weeks after submission. The SAR has two parts. Part I restates everything you submitted on the original FAFSA. Part II allows you to make revisions. Review all data for accuracy.

For example, the first time you submit the FAFSA, you provide estimated income to meet deadlines. Now that you have the SAR, hold onto it until you've completed all federal income tax forms. When the new income forms are complete and ready for submission, transfer the new information to the SAR, Part II. Resubmit Part II of the SAR to the federal central processor to update the original information. Each college listed on the SAR receives the new information. If you added schools in excess of the original maximum of eight schools, the new schools will be listed on your corrected SAR, but the original eight schools will still have access to your data as well.

The SAR's main purpose is to show the expected family contribution (EFC). The EFC is in the upper-right-hand corner of the SAR under the processed date. Remember, the mission for completing all documents is to arrive at a low EFC. The EFC appears as a five-digit number without the dollar sign (place a $ sign before the number to better understand what it means).

To restate, the cost of attendance (COA) at the college (minus the EFC) is your demonstrated need. To receive the maximum financial aid, you need a low EFC. By following all the preceding suggestions, you'll greatly improve your odds for earning college money.

New: Your Personal Electronic Access Code (EAC)

You millennium creature, are you wondering how you're going to go online with your renewal FAFSA and keep your financial affairs private from cyberspies? The U.S. Department of Education (DOE) has an answer — the *Electronic Access Code (EAC)*.

The EAC serves as your unique identifier to let you access your personal information in various DOE systems. It's like the personal identification number (PIN) that you get from your bank that enables you to access your account.

In addition to using your EAC to file your renewal FAFSA — using the FAFSA on the Web site (fafsa.ed.gov) — your EAC will access other aspects of your financials delivered by the feds, such as loan history, FAFSA processing information, eligibility for Pell grants, and the scoop about your Federal Direct Student Loan.

An EAC should simplify your life, at least the part you spend on federal financial aid issues. Start the process by hitting the Web (eac.ed.gov) and asking for your EAC. After you complete your request, the feds will mail your EAC to you via postal mail, which will take approximately 10 days to reach you.

Chapter 21

Figuring Out Your Best Deal

- -

In This Chapter

▶ Sample award letters

▶ Tips on comparing awards

▶ Your awards comparison chart

- -

*B*e happy when your award letters arrive. Then be critical. Analyze each letter and try to figure out its bottom line. How good is the deal you're being offered?

In this chapter, we tell you how to analyze your award letters and compare them to others that you get. And in case you've never seen an award letter, we reprint four letters (with student identities deleted).

What to Do When You Get an Award Letter

As we mention in Chapter 3, award letters are kicked out by computers programmed with specific criteria. College financial aid counselors may not have reviewed each one before mailing the letters, especially at large institutions where the reading task is formidable.

Because the letters come off an assembly line, you should go over yours with a fine-toothed mental comb. You're trying to find both your best deal among the various awards and reasons to appeal for even more gift aid.

 Immediately accept each part of each award. You're keeping your options open. Even if you end up turning down a particular school and its award later, you want to be sure that the school doesn't give your aid to someone else while you're making up your mind. You need a little time to sort things out, to compare competing offers.

After you finally decide which school and aid offer to accept, notify the financial aid offices of the rejected schools as quickly as possible. Your thoughtfulness allows the spurned schools to offer the vacated admission set to another student and to free up money for students on the award waiting list.

What if the offer you finally select contains a job or a college work-study position, and you don't want to be employed — at least, not during your first year when you're uncertain how much time you'll need for studies? You can turn down work opportunities and accept only the gift aid if you wish. But you may make a big mistake if you do so. As we comment in Chapter 11, employers hiring new graduates consistently favor applicants who gained work or internship experience during college years. Furthermore, working improves your time management skills, which will prove to be a blessing throughout your entire life.

If you're really a marginal student who needs every free hour to study, perhaps you shouldn't work during your undergraduate years. The conventional wisdom, however, says that a job won't interfere with your college education experience as long as you don't toil beyond 14 hours a week.

Another reason to turn down a work-study position or campus job is that you're already in the workplace as an adult student who has a job. If you decide to turn down the work portion of the award, however, the financial aid counselor may bounce the money-gap ball back to your court, leaving you on your own to solve the shortage of funds.

We detail four sample award letters on the pages that follow.

WASHINGTON·UNIVERSITY·IN·ST·LOUIS

Student Financial Services

Name   February 15, 1999
Address
City State Zip

Dear First Name,

We are delighted to learn of your admission into Washington University's Class of 2003, and we congratulate you on being named a Thomas H. Eliot Scholar. This is a scholarship in recognition of your record of outstanding academic achievement.

Thomas H. Eliot served as professor and chair of the Department of Political Science in the College of Arts and Sciences at Washington University from 1952 until 1960, when he was called upon to serve as the Dean of the College of Arts and Sciences. Dean Eliot became Vice-Chancellor and Dean of the Faculties the following year, and in 1962 he became the twelfth Chancellor of Washington University, serving in that capacity until his retirement in 1970.

Thomas H. Eliot's leadership was instrumental in developing a strong commitment by the University to undergraduate teaching. Chancellor Eliot held that the liberal arts stood at the core of an undergraduate education. This commitment, coupled with his example of public service and leadership in the community, still serves as a role model for students today.

Before coming to the University, Professor Eliot had been in government service as counsel for the committee on Economic Security, where he crafted the bill that became the Social Security Act of 1935. He went on to serve as Congressman from the State of Massachusetts, and then practiced law and taught in Boston before coming to St. Louis and placing his invaluable imprint on Washington University. It is an honor for a student in the College of Arts and Sciences to be named a Thomas H. Eliot Scholar.

Our award of this scholarship to you expresses our belief in the strong talents you bring to Washington University and the contributions you will make. We hope you will join our community, and we are pleased to offer you the following renewable financial assistance award for the 1999-2000 academic year:

Thomas H. Eliot Scholarship (full tuition) $23,400

YOUR TOTAL FINANCIAL ASSISTANCE AWARD $23,400

We congratulate you on your admission to Washington University and on your financial assistance award. My colleagues in the Student Financial Services Office join me in welcoming you to our community, and we look forward to meeting you in person.

                                        Sincerely,

                                        William H. Witbrodt
                                        Director of Student Financial Services

Washington University
Campus Box 1041
One Brookings Drive
St. Louis, Missouri 63130-4899
(314) 935-5900

Letter 1 — Washington University:

Washington University's full-tuition Eliot scholarship on behalf of its College of Arts and Sciences is princely, but you may have to go back and negotiate if you need help with room and board (Chapter 9 describes negotiation techniques). The liberal arts recipients of an Eliot apply for financial aid in general — not specifically for this scholarship. The award becomes firm after you sign and return the award letters to the school's Office of Student Financial Services.

THE STATE UNIVERSITY OF NEW JERSEY

RUTGERS

FINANCIAL AID AWARD OFFER
1999 – 2000

Carol Cook
P.O. Box 9999
New Brunswick, NJ 08901

Date: 03/05/1999
ID#: 222-22-2222
Sch: 11

Award Information:

Your award package is based on the information you supplied on your Free Application for Federal Student Aid. In the event of a change in your eligibility for financial aid and/or your receipt of additional aid from outside sources, Rutgers University reserves the right to adjust your award.

Enclosed you will find the Award Letter Guide which provides you with additional information on the types of aid awarded as well as the terms and conditions for receiving aid at Rutgers University. Please review these carefully. You will be responsible for understanding and complying with each item which relates to the financial aid you receive.

Awards:

We are pleased to offer you the following assistance for the 1999-2000 academic year. You must accept or decline each of the awards offered to you. To accept less than the amount shown, please write in the amount you wish in the space provided.

	Fall	Spring	Summer	Total	Accept? Yes	No	Amount
Federal PELL Grant	$ 1,500	$ 1,500	$ 0	$ 3,000	___	___	_____
NJ Tuition Aid Grant	$ 2,046	$ 2,046	$ 0	$ 4,092	___	___	_____
Educational Opport. Fund	$ 550	$ 550	$ 0	$ 1,100	___	___	_____
Edward J. Bloustein U.D.S.P.	$ 500	$ 500	$ 0	$ 1,000	___	___	_____
Federal Perkins Loan	$ 500	$ 500	$ 0	$ 1,000	___	___	_____
Federal College Work-Study	$ 500	$ 500	$ 0	$ 1,000	___	___	_____
Rutgers Univ. Loan Program	$ 250	$ 250	$ 0	$ 500	___	___	_____
Federal Direct Loan Subsidized	$ 1,154	$ 1,154	$ 0	$ 2,308	___	___	_____
Total	$ 7,000	$ 7,000	$ 0	$14,000			
Amount to be Credited to Bill	$ 6,454	$ 6,454	$ 0	$12,908			

Refer to the Award Letter Guide for an explanation of the difference between total aid and the amount credited to your term bill.

What To Do Next:
You must complete the reverse side, sign and return this award offer immediately, along with any requested documents.

Student copy-keep for your records

Letter 2 — Rutgers University:
The Rutger's award letter mentions an "Award Letter Guide" to which you must refer to understand differences (deductions) between your award and the funds that are actually credited to your student account. All schools make similar deductions — for example, loan origination fees and unearned funds in work-study programs.

UNIVERSITY OF COLORADO AT BOULDER
1999-2000 Planning Letter

Golden Buffalo
123 Campus Avenue
Boulder CO 00000

Date: March 2, 1999
SID: 000-00-0000

STEP 1: Estimate your total expenses for one entire academic year (9 months) for each college or university

	CU-BOULDER	Institution B	Institution C
Estimated Expenses			
Resident Tuition/Fees	3093		
Room/Board	5200		
Books/Supplies	695		
Expenses Dependent on Life Styles:			
Personal	1845		
Transportation	1170		
Medical	1170		
Total Estimated Expenses	$ 13173	$	$

STEP 2: Estimate the total amount of financial aid available to you from each college or university

	CU-BOULDER	Institution B	Institution C
Financial Aid			
Scholarships reported at this time:			
1st Generation	4000		
Grants:			
Pell	3000		
CU-Boulder Grant	1100		
Work-Study:			
Loans:			
Subsidized Direct Stafford	2620		
Parent PLUS Loan	2450		
Total Financial Aid	$ 13170	$	$

STEP 3: Subtract "Total Financial Aid" from "Total Expenses" to determine the cost to you for each college or university

	CU-BOULDER	Institution B	Institution C
Expenses minus Financial Aid	$ 3	$	$

Letter 3 — University of Colorado:

The award letter gives good consumer information. The expected family contribution in this case is $2,453. In this award document, the college is offering a PLUS loan of $2,450 to meet the EFC. This is a common practice and one that is very helpful to assist the family with its cash flow. The base award is well balanced, with the grant (gift aid) representing 76 percent of the award, compared to the student loan (self-help) representing only 20 percent of the award.

MACALESTER

Admissions Office   **MACALESTER COLLEGE**, 1600 Grand Avenue, Saint Paul, Minnesota 55105-1899   Telephone 651-696-6357

February 15, 1999

Dear Fred:

Congratulations! In addition to being offered admission to Macalester College, you have been selected as a recipient of the Catharine Lealtad Scholarship. You will receive a $5,000 scholarship for each of your four years at Macalester, a total of $20,000.

Dr. Catharine Lealtad '15 was Macalester's first African-American graduate. This scholarship exists to honor Dr. Lealtad for her lifetime of service to the medical profession and her community, which reflects Macalester's traditions of academic excellence and service to others. The multicultural population at Macalester has, of course, increased greatly since Dr. Lealtad graduated 84 years ago, as has the College's commitment to providing outstanding educational opportunity to students from all backgrounds.

You are being honored as a Lealtad Scholar for your achievements in high school, as demonstrated by your academic record and your contributions to school and community. The dedication to excellence which you have demonstrated by your past performance speaks well of what the Admissions Committee views as even greater potential. We feel that Macalester College, with its outstanding faculty, broad range of academic programs, excellent facilities, and global perspective, offers you the opportunity to realize that potential.

Once again, let me congratulate you on this honor. We look forward to seeing you on campus next fall, if not before.

Sincerely,

Lorne T. Robinson
Dean of Admissions & Financial Aid

P.S. If you have applied for additional need-based financial aid through Macalester's Financial Aid Office and all required aid forms have been received, you should receive a financial aid package within the next several days. Your Lealtad Scholarship will be incorporated into your financial aid award.

Letter 4 — Macalester College:

This letter is not a full-spectrum financial aid package award; instead, it's a notification of a handsome single award designed for African-American students. This award has been made prior to the financial aid awarding process. The financial aid office will package this scholarship into the award letter at a later date. Meanwhile, this early scholarship award letter acts as an enticement award to hold the student's interest until the total financial aid award letter is delivered to the student.

Comparing Your Awards

Jot down the data about each award on *Dr. Davis's Awards Comparison Chart*. (We give you your own blank copy later in this chapter.) Then compare each category of an award with its equivalent on other awards.

Study Table 21-1, which compares the awards of College USA versus Ivy Green, to quickly see the value of making standard comparisons.

Table 21-1	Dr. Davis's Awards Comparison	
Factors to Consider	**College USA (Example)**	**Ivy Green (Example)**
1. Total tuition, room, board, fees (hard costs)	$27,000.00	$29,000.00
2. Cost of Attendance (COA) Total costs (hard + soft costs — books, supplies, transportation, and so on)	30,130.00	32,000.00
2A. Expected family contribution	1,200.00	1,200.00
2B. Student's financial need	28,930.00	30,800.00
GIFT AID (free money)		
3. Scholarship (#1)	8,000.00	4,000.00
4. Scholarship (#2)	0.00	2,000.00
5. Federal Pell Grant	2,700.00	2,700.00
6. Federal SEOG Grant	800.00	400.00
7. State grant	1,000.00	00.00
8. Merit grant	0.00	00.00
9. Need grant	0.00	00.00
10. TOTAL AMOUNT OF FREE MONEY (gift awards)	12,500.00	9,100.00
11. Line 1 – line 10 = Best gift aid	14,500.00	15,900.00
SELF-HELP (loans and jobs)		
12. Federal Perkins Student Loan	1,500.00	1,000.00
13. Subsidized Stafford/Direct Student Loan	2,625.00	2,625.00
14. Other student loan	0.00	4,000.00
15. Campus job/ federal work-study	1,400.00	3,000.00
16. Other	00.00	00.00

(continued)

Table 21-1 *(continued)*

Factors to Consider	College USA (Example)	Ivy Green (Example)
17. TOTAL AMOUNT OF SELF-HELP (loans and jobs)	5,525.00	10,625.00
18. TOTAL FINANCIAL AID AWARDED (award package) (Line 10 + Line 17 = award offer)	18,025.00	19,725.00
Best awards can be assessed on one of the following factors:		
A. Ratio of gift aid to self-help	$12,500/5,525	$9,100/10,625
B. Gap between awards and demonstrated need	(gap) $10,905.00	(gap) $11,075.00
C. Money you need to pay for college after awards are made	$12,105.00	$12,275.00

Chart Source: Dr. Herm Davis

Comparing the gift aid awarded by each school, College USA offers this student $3,400 more free dollars than Ivy Green does. Assuming the college's awards remain constant over the next four years, College USA will fork over $13,600 more cash that doesn't have to be repaid than Ivy Green will.

In looking at loan awards, you see that College USA gives this student $4,125 the first year. Ivy Green awards $7,625. The net difference for one year is $3,500 more money that this student has to pay back. Assuming each college increases the Federal Stafford/Direct Student Loan to the maximum to make up the difference in the increased cost of education, Ivy Green saddles this student with $14,000 more in loans to repay than College USA does (see Table 21-2).

Table 21-2   Comparing Gift Aid

College	Year	Perkins	Stafford	Other	Total
USA	1	$ 1,500	$ 2,625	$ 0,000	$ 4,125
IVY	1	$ 1,000	$ 2,625	$ 4,000	$ 7,625
USA	2	$1,500	$3,500	$0,000	$5,000
IVY	2	$1,000	$3,500	$4,000	$8,500
USA	3	$1,500	$5,500	$0,000	$7,000
IVY	3	$1,000	$5,500	$4,000	$10,500
USA	4	$1,500	$5,500	$0,000	$7,000
IVY	4	$1,000	$5,500	$4,000	$10,500

College	Year	Perkins	Stafford	Other	Total
USA	Total	$6,000	$17,125	$0,000	$23,125
IVY	Total	$ 4,000	$ 17,125	$ 16,000	$ 37,125

[$37,125 - $23,125 = $14,000]

When adding up the difference in grants of $13,600, plus not having to pay back an additional $14,000 in loans, you see that one of the two colleges offers a clear financial advantage. By selecting College USA, this student will be ahead $27,600 in real money after graduation.

Additionally, when comparing money awarded from work, College USA asks this student to work an average of 10 hours per week, about one third of the 28 weekly hours programmed by Ivy Green.

As soon as your award letters come in, record them on your own copy of Dr. Davis's Awards Comparison Chart (see Table 21-3) and figure out your best deal!

Table 21-3	**Dr. Davis's Awards Comparison Chart**			
Factors to Consider	*(School Name)*	*(School Name)*	*(School Name)*	*(School Name)*
1. Total tuition, room, board, fees (hard costs)				
2. COA=Total costs (hard + soft costs – books, supplies, transportation, and so on)				
2A. Expected family contribution				
2B. Student's financial need				
GIFT AID (free money)				
3. Scholarship (#1)				
4. Scholarship (#2)				
5. Federal Pell Grant				
6. Federal SEOG Grant				
7. State grant				
8. Merit grant				
9. Need grant				

(continued)

Table 21-3 *(continued)*

Factors to Consider	(School Name)	(School Name)	(School Name)	(School Name)
10. TOTAL AMOUNT OF FREE MONEY (gift awards)				
11. Line 1 – line 10 = Best gift aid)				
SELF-HELP (loans and jobs)				
12. Federal Perkins Student Loan				
13. Subsidized Federal Stafford/ Direct Student Loan				
14. Other student loan				
15. Campus job/ federal work-study				
16. Other				
17. TOTAL AMOUNT OF SELF-HELP (loans and jobs)				
18. TOTAL FINANCIAL AID AWARDED (award package) (Line 10 + line 17 = award offer)				
Best awards can be assessed on one of the following factors:				
A. Ratio of gift aid to self-help				
B. Gap between awards and demonstrated need				
C. Money you need to pay for college after awards are made				

Chart Source: Dr. Herm Davis

The College Business Office and Your Account

After you've made your final selection of a college and an aid award, the college financial aid office notifies the business office of your awarded funds.

Don't worry about the colleges you initially accepted and later rejected; the paperwork on your account will be canceled.

The funds described in your award letter are credited to your account, which is also called *the student bill*.

When you receive your student bill, the financial aid funds show a credit against your expenses. You're responsible for paying any outstanding balance on your bill.

Table 21-4 is an example of how a student bill shows a financial aid credit.

Table 21-4	Example of Student Bill at New College		
(FOR FALL SEMESTER- 1999)			
07-01-99	*Debit*	*Credit*	*Balance*
Tuition	$5,850.00		
Fees-Student Activities	200.00		
Fees-Lab	125.00		
Housing	1,250.00		
Board-Plan II	1,400.00		
Advance Deposit		$ 300.00	
Fed. Stafford Loan-Sub.		1,650.00	
Fed. Perkins Loan		1,000.00	
Fed. Pell Grant		1,350.00	
Fed. Supplemental Grant		400.00	
State Incentive Grant		950.00	
P.T.A. Scholarship		1,200.00	
Fed. PLUS		2,500.00	
Balance	**$8,825.00**	**$9,350.00**	**+ $525.00**

(The balance of $525.00 will be refunded to you within 15 working days from the date of this invoice.)

The credit will be refunded to this student in about three or four weeks after school starts. At that time, the student can spend the excess funds on personal maintenance, off-campus housing, books, supplies, and other school-related costs. The student can also use the funds to repay bridge loans (those that keep you financially alive) made by parents or others when school first begins.

Affordability as a Value

In earlier generations, factors for choosing a college clustered around these kinds of values: intellectual challenge, a nurturing environment, geographic location, family tradition, good party school, and probability of acceptance. The cost of the school was usually "something to be worked out" — the equivalent of "we'll worry about that later — just get in."

Although these values are still intact, we observe that today's students are far more apt to enroll in a particular school for two reasons that are more closely aligned to a changing economy and a revalued cost/benefit ratio:

- ✔ The school's reputed ability — curriculum, prestige of degree, and contacts — to prepare its graduates for the best jobs
- ✔ The cost of the school

Affordability, while always of some concern, has now raced to the head of the values parade when students and families decide which institutions they'll attend.

Part V
It's Payback Time — Or Is It?

The 5th Wave By Rich Tennant

"Our plan is to buy the rest of it when we pay off our college loan."

In this part . . .

Years or months from now, you graduate. Big sigh of relief, you think you've just crossed your biggest hurdle — completing a degree. But one potentially high-priced milestone lies ahead if you're in debt: repayment. These chapters help you look around expensive corners to see the best ways to handle your student loan repayment, including jobs that bring loan forgiveness. Whether you're terrified of hefty debt now or later, read these essential tips to plan your financial survival.

Chapter 22

Can Your Loans Be Forgiven?

In This Chapter

▶ Volunteering and working to wipe out your loans

▶ Uncommon ways to cancel debt

▶ Loan escape for law and health care pros

Six out of ten college students go to school on borrowed money. Because loans often seem more like Monopoly paper money than real money, you may not take the certainty of repayment seriously when you borrow. And then comes the shock: As you begin or recharge your adult life, you owe a lot of money!

But nonprofit entities, including government agencies, have discovered that it pays to reward graduates for putting their education to use to serve society by granting partial-to-full loan forgiveness. This chapter illustrates the forgiveness principle.

Wipe Out Debt: Volunteering and Working

The following programs provide partial or complete loan forgiveness for people who volunteer to help others or who work under special circumstances.

AmeriCorps

AmeriCorps is a program of volunteer service in return for help with college tuition. Participating states have programs that reward 12 months' volunteer service with up to $7,400 in stipends plus $4,725 that can be used to pay educational loans. You can collect that $4,725 only twice, although volunteering is unlimited. Call AmeriCorps at 800-942-2677 or visit the AmeriCorps Web site, which contains details about loan repayment and positions available in every state, at www.americorps.org.

Myths about loan forgiveness

The following myths about lifestyle and professional issues relate to a specific health care forgiveness program in the state of Washington and are debunked by the Higher Education Coordinating Board in Olympia.

They do not apply across-the-board to all forgiveness programs but are useful as a guide to know what questions to ask about conditions in specific programs. The Web sites noted in this chapter may answer your questions.

Myth: Recruits cannot choose their sites.

Choices abound. Program participants are allowed to choose from among areas designated by the Washington Department of Health that have a broad range of options and great need. Vacancy lists are available.

Myth: All clinic conditions are terrible.

Not so. At a minimum, all sites must provide a system of care with referrals and backup procedures in place, as well as accept Medicaid and Medicare beneficiaries, and have the funds to pay the provider's (health care professional who is working out a loan) salary and benefits. Site visits are always recommended to prevent unwelcome surprises.

Myth: You'll be all by yourself.

Providers are seldom placed in solo practices. Group practices are the norm rather than the exception. Most practices are community based and employ two or more providers.

Myth: You won't have a life outside of work.

Even rural areas provide opportunities for community involvement from volunteer fire departments, churches, and schools, to recreational resources.

Myth: You work in rural areas — "out in the sticks."

Many sites are in rural areas; however, most are located within short driving distances of large cities or within proximity to scenic National Parks. And there are many openings in urban underserved areas.

The Perkins Loan

Established under the Eisenhower administration, the National Defense Student Loan (now called the Perkins Loan) encouraged students to become math, science, and foreign language teachers. The National Defense Education Act rewarded new teachers for arming the population's minds by forgiving their loans.

Today, the Perkins Loan may forgive all your loan if you teach full-time in an elementary or secondary school that serves students from low-income families. It forgives 15 percent of your loan for the first and second years of service, 20 percent for the third and fourth, and 30 percent for the fifth. Teachers should contact their personnel offices for the list of eligible schools in their district.

Federal Family Education Loan Program — LOAN

The 1998 Amendments to the Higher Education Act of 1965 instituted several loan-forgiveness provisions that can assist you in ridding yourself of payback loans in the future if you fit the following criteria:

- ✔ You may have your student loan forgiven if you enter and stay in the teaching profession for five years commencing after October 1, 1998. Forgiveness includes your subsidized and unsubsidized loans.

- ✔ You may have your loan forgiven if you teach in a secondary school in the the subject areas related to your academic major in college.

- ✔ You may have your loan forgiven if you are judged to be proficient in teaching of reading, writing, and mathematics by your school's chief administrator.

- ✔ You may have your loan forgiven if you obtain a degree in early childhood education and you are hired to teach in a low-income community in a child-care facility. (Funds for this program must be appropriated each year.)

Military service

See Chapter 17 for information about loan forgiveness available through Army Reserve and National Guard programs in each state.

Peace Corps

Volunteering in the Peace Corps as a student can cancel up to 70 percent of your loan and defer the remaining balance while you are in service. The Peace Corps offers a wide variety of positions, training, and overseas experiences, and the corps may pay you back with skills as well as loan cancellation. Contact the Peace Corps at 1990 K Street, NW, Washington, DC 20526; 800-424-8580.

VISTA (Volunteers in Service to America)

Volunteering for this part of AmeriCorps may cancel a good chunk of your loan. You can participate in private, nonprofit, community development, antipoverty, antihunger, antihomelessness, and health or literacy-related organizations at the local, state, or federal level in return for an allowance and a stipend at the end of service.

Members who volunteer for 1,700 hours can receive an education award of $4,725 for one year of service. A relocation allowance is also available. This award accompanies a living allowance, health coverage, and special non-competitive eligibility for other federal employment — some VISTA positions require some college education or a bachelor's degree. Contact VISTA at 800-942-2677.

Uncommon Ways to End Debt

The following are some special programs that reward achievement with loan forgiveness:

- ✔ **For good grades and teaching in Mississippi:** The William Winter Teacher Scholar Loan is for students who meet academic requirements and are education majors. After receiving this loan and teaching in Mississippi for one year, one year of loan will be forgiven. If you teach in a shortage area, you are eligible for two years of loan forgiveness for one year of service. Contact the Mississippi Office of State Student Financial Aid, 3825 Ridgewood Rd., Jackson, MS 39211-6453; 601-982-6663.

- ✔ **For graduation from Baker University:** Baker University provides a loan-forgiveness program for students who complete a bachelor's degree at Baker University's College of Arts and Sciences. Contact Baker University, P.O. Box 65, Baldwin City, KS 66006-0065; 785-594-6451.

- ✔ **For Alaska state troopers:** The Michael Murphy Loan Program allows students who receive this loan in college and major in law enforcement, law, probation and parole, penology, or other related fields to work it off, one-fifth per year, as full-time law enforcement (or related field) employees in Alaska. Contact Alaska State Troopers, Director's Office Scholarship Fund, 5700 E. Tudor Rd., Anchorage, AK 99507; 907-269-5511.

- ✔ **For Maryland state and local government employees:** If you work in Maryland and earn an annual gross salary that is less than $40,000, you may be eligible for this loan-repayment-assistance program for the fields of study of law, nursing, physical and occupational therapy, social work, and teachers of mathematics, science, and special education. Contact Maryland State Scholarship Administration, 16 Francis St., Annapolis, MD 21401; 410-974-2971 (ext. 146).

Law Students' Loan Forgiveness

Because law graduates often owe an excess of $80,000 (if they went to a public college) or $125,000 (if they went to a private college), we thought these resources would be especially helpful. The National Association for

Public Interest Law and the American Bar Association developed *An Action Manual for Loan Repayment Assistance* to encourage states, colleges, and private groups to support loan-forgiveness programs. Maryland offers such a program and gives lawyers priority.

More than 30 law schools forgive students' loans if they serve in public interest or in nonprofit positions. Among them are Loyola University, Stanford University, University of California, University of San Diego, University of Southern California, Georgetown University, American University, Chicago-Kent College of Law, Northwestern University, University of Chicago, University of Notre Dame, Valparaiso University, University of Minnesota, Brooklyn University, Cornell University, Fordham University, New York University, Hofstra University, Duke University, Temple University, Brown University, Southern Methodist University, University of Virginia, Washington and Lee University, and the University of Washington.

Contact the Director of Financial Aid or National Association for Public Interest Law, 1666 Connecticut Ave., Suite 424, Washington, DC 20009; 202-265-7546. Or check out the National Association for Public Interest Law's Web site at www.napil.org.

Health Care Students' Loan Forgiveness

Every medical student knows that the usual six years' study at an expensive program runs up quite a tuition tab. But not every future white-coat knows that alternatives to major repayment exist. If you take the maximum Federal Stafford loans for six years' medical education, you're looking at $111,000 in debt. If you attend a public school, add $50,000 in other loans. If you attend a private school, add a mega-debt of $120,000 in additional loans.

Medical school students

Several programs may take the bitterness out of med school debt. For example, The University of California at Irvine's College of Medicine offers a loan-forgiveness repayment program. Fully trained allopathic (MD) and osteopathic (DO) physicians with primary care specialties are eligible. Program participants agree to provide primary care services in a priority health professional shortage area for a minimum of two years. In return, qualified education loans (both public and private) are repaid at a maximun of $25,000 for each of the two required years.

For information on similar programs in California, contact the State Loan Repayment Program, Primary Care Resources and Community Development Division, Office of Statewide Health Planning and Development, 1600 Ninth St., Room 440, Sacramento, CA 95814; 916-654-1833; www.oshpd.cahwnet.gov.

Other states offer comparable programs sponsored by the National Health Service Corps or programs that recruit primary care physicians to practice in medically underserved areas. Award recipients get an annual salary plus payments for medical school loans and costs, but they must commit to a minimum number of years of practice, depending on the state (see Chapter 8).

Nursing students

Nursing school programs currently have a shortage of applicants to fill their needs. Contact the National League for Nursing at 61 Broadway St., New York, NY 10006 (800-669-1656) for help in hunting down employers with the best loan-forgiveness options.

Occupational and physical therapy students

Because licensed/certified occupational and physical therapists remain a rare species, many hospitals and private health-related organizations use student loan forgiveness fringe benefits as a recruitment tool. Wherever you apply in these fields, ask how the employer's loan forgiveness package compares to those of other employers.

For example, the Florida Department of Education pays up to $2,500 per year on undergraduate loans and up to $5,000 for graduate loans for licensed occupational and physical therapists. You're eligible for this tantalizing program if you're a licensed therapist (valid temporary permit is okay) who's worked full-time in Florida public schools for one year and you declare your intent to work for Florida public schools for at least three years. Contact the Florida Department of Education, Bureau of Education for Exceptional Students, 622 Florida Educational Center, Tallahassee, FL 32399-0400.

For general resources on loan forgiveness in the occupational or physical therapy biz, contact the following organizations:

✔ **American Physical Therapy Association**
1111 N. Fairfax St.
Alexandria, VA 22314-1488
800-999-2782

✔ **National Clearinghouse, Professionals Information Center Council for Exceptional Children**
1920 Association Dr.
Reston, VA 20191-1589
800-641-7824

✔ **American Occupational Therapy Association**
P.O. Box 31220
4720 Montgomery Ln.
Bethesda, MD 20814-1220
800-729-2682

Additional reading

For more about loan forgiveness, send for *The Student Loan Forgiveness Directory* by Dr. Herm Davis and the National College Scholarship Foundation; 1999. This resource is available only by mail for $25, postage included, from NCSF, 16728 Frontenac Terrace, Rockville, MD 20855; 800-220-3919.

Chapter 23

Drowning in a Sea of Debt

● ●

In This Chapter

▶ Sounding an SOS when you're in over your head

▶ Considering consolidation, deferment, and other lifeboats

● ●

*A*re you out of school and worried that you're about to go under in a sea of student loan debt? Here we present a composite story of two graduates who got in too deep. How will they survive? Read on and see what the future may hold.

Kenneth, who graduated with a degree in theater arts and a huge student loan debt five months ago, is still hunting for his first "real" job. As a rule, six months after graduation, borrowers are required to start repaying; Kenneth has one month to go. When he closes his eyes at night, Kenneth can almost feel the waves of loan repayment obligations washing over him, pushing him down . . . down . . . down. . . .

His thoughts keep flashing to Michelle, a woman Kenneth met in college and about whom he'd recently heard some unhappy news. Michelle graduated with a liberal arts degree last year and quickly became a travel agent. But she's already in trouble. Beginning travel agents don't always, as writer Dorothy Parker once quipped, earn enough to keep body and soul apart. Before Michelle could put her life on sound financial footing, she got caught up in a monthly student loan repayment of $206, a monthly car payment of $300, and rent and utilities payments of $1,200. Two months ago, Michelle defaulted on her loans, sinking her once-buoyant credit.

Michelle, the defaulting borrower, is hardly in a class by herself. Nearly 2 million student borrowers have defaulted during the 1990s (roughly 200,000 per year), for a total loan volume (through 1998) $199.4 billion. But most for defaulters enter repayment, and the net loss to the government during those same years was much less, $25.5 billion.

Michelle's mistakes, rarer but still too common among new grads, caused Kenneth to think about hitting bottom in a downward spiral. Default would be horrendous, he decided. Maybe his parents could help — no, they're tapped out and his father was just downsized. His parents can't lend him a dime. "Got to help myself," Kenneth realized and resolved to find out what it would take to solve his predicament.

Busted! Defaulted Loans Get Thousands in Hot Water

The thought is distressing but must be faced: Failing to pay your loan has serious consequences. Unlike the Middle Ages, you aren't thrown into debtors' prison, but your credit is tossed into a vat of red ink, making it nearly impossible for you to borrow money for a car or home, or rent an apartment. Even a history of delinquent payments punches holes in your credit rating. Sanctions from private lenders are bad enough, but federally backed loans carry even more penalties when you fail to pay up.

Here are some more things to think about when defaulting on a loan:

- ✔ Do leg-breakers come after you? No, but if your defaulted loan is passed to a guarantee agency for collection, you're saddled with collection fees, which may be as high as 50 percent. If you're hauled into court and lose (most likely), all legal costs, including lawyers fees for the servicer or loan servicer, are added to your bill.

- ✔ The federal government has the option of "calling the loan," demanding that you immediately pay the total unpaid balance and interest. (Calling the loan is not an arbitrary action but is done for a number of reasons, such as the fact that the borrower can afford to pay but keeps putting it off, or the government wants to eliminate the expense of litigating overdue loans.)

- ✔ More loans for more education? Without formal rehabilitation, forget it. More federal aid for anything? You may as well forget it. What's more, the federal government has the right to keep any tax refund and apply it to your debt.

- ✔ Your pay can be garnished, and in some states you won't be able to obtain or renew a professional license.

- ✔ Dunning letters will spoil your mail, and in hoping to avoid bill collectors, you'll find yourself pretending to be your cousin when you answer your telephone.

- ✔ On top of everything else that's ugly about defaulting on a student loan, employers increasingly use credit reports in evaluating job applicants. A loan default, which makes you look like a deadbeat, can be enough to keep you from being offered the job you want.

Don't doubt for a minute that defaulting on student loans has become an abhorrent experience for the defaulter. The good news is that more graduates are becoming aware of the default nightmare, evidenced by the 9.6 percent rate for fiscal 1996 (the most recent year available at press time) in comparison to 1990 when the default rate peaked at 22.4 percent.

Avoiding Default: The Who, What, When, Where, and How

As he considered his repayment dilemma, Kenneth worried first about *to whom* he must repay his education loans, which totaled $17,125. During college, Kenneth had been casual about money and never kept records of his loans, which meant he had little idea whom he should contact to start the repayment ball rolling.

Clueless and realizing that he was way behind the curve on lending lore, Kenneth decided to read, as soon as he could, a couple of books about debt repayment. One of the books he chose was *Take Control of Your Student Loans* by attorneys Robin Leonard and Shae Irving, cited at the end of this chapter.

In the meantime, Kenneth began rooting through his grubby collection of financial aid records for paperwork, receipts, promissory notes, check stubs, and award letters (which often note the original lender and guarantee agency). Oops! Kenneth was alarmed to realize that he'd trashed everything but his loan checks. The current written material on student loans from the U.S. Department of Education helped some, but it didn't clear up everything. A mix of repayment options and even the names of loans had changed since Kenneth borrowed his first school funds. Now what?

To add to his confusion, students may also receive loans from a variety of sources, including banks, schools, and state agencies. Federal laws specify the terms for buying, selling, collecting, and repaying Federal Stafford and other federally sponsored loans. But policies for repayment of nonfederal loan programs vary from lender to lender.

Even when he received his first bill, Kenneth couldn't figure out whose money he would be paying back or who should be called if he ever needed short-term assistance. So Kenneth turned to his old benefactors: his college's financial aid counselors. Some financial aid offices can find out who services your loan; others can connect you with your state's loan guarantee agency or nonprofit guarantee organization. Guarantors can help you locate your loan servicer.

Lenders are required by law to clue in borrowers (not in default) when selling loans or hiring a servicer to collect and process loan payments. If you didn't save all such documents and if you think you're now in default, contact your college or the U.S. Department of Education Debt Collection Services for Student Loans at 800-621-3115.

Words to know in debt management

Knowing these terms can help you navigate your sea of debt:

✔ **Accrued interest:** Interest that increases in value from any unpaid principal balance of a loan.

✔ **Anticipated graduation date:** The date that you expect to graduate; your school must verify this date on your loan application to determine when you must begin repayment.

✔ **Capitalization of interest:** The practice of adding interest to the principal amount rather than making interest payments. This method increases both the total amount you owe and your monthly payments.

✔ **Consolidation:** The practice of combining loans into a single loan. Federal consolidation loans may include a variety of federal loan programs.

✔ **Default:** Delinquent or insufficient payment on an education loan within an agreed upon period of time.

✔ **Deferment:** A period of time when you're allowed to delay or postpone making payments on the principal and/or interest on your educational loan.

✔ **Delinquency:** When loan payments are late or missed. After 180 days of delinquency, the loan goes into default. Delinquency gets reported to credit bureaus and can limit your ability to obtain credit.

✔ **Forbearance:** Temporary postponement or reduction of your loan payments. During forbearance, interest continues to accrue.

✔ **Grace period:** A scheduled period of time allowed, (normally when you drop below being enrolled as half-time status) before you, the borrower, are required to begin making payments on your student loan.

✔ **Guarantee fee:** A fee paid to the state agency or nonprofit organization that guarantees a Stafford or PLUS issued by a private lender under the Federal Family Education Loan Program (FFELP). The guarantee protects lenders against the risk that a loan will not be repaid due to a default, bankruptcy, death, disability, or school closure.

✔ **Half-time:** Federal rules generally require that you enter repayment six months after you leave school or drop below half-time enrollment, which is usually at least 6 semester hours or 9 quarter hours per term; 12 semester hours or 18 quarter hours per year; or 12 hours per week. Some schools may set higher requirements for half-time enrollment.

✔ **Origination fee:** A charge that helps defray the feds' cost for subsidizing federal education loans.

✔ **Prepayment:** Making your loan payments ahead of schedule. For federal education loans, you may prepay your debt in full or in part at any time without any penalty.

✔ **Principal:** The total balance of your loan on which interest is charged.

✔ **Repayment agreement:** A form lenders provide that arranges repayment. The form lists the amount borrowed, the amount of monthly payments, and the date payments are due.

✔ **Serialization:** When you combine several loans into one loan payment but the original terms of your loan agreements do not change.

✔ **Secondary market:** Some lenders sell their loans to secondary markets that have authorization to participate in student loan programs. Your loan may be sold without your permission or prior notification, but your lender will inform you of the sale after the transaction. Nothing on your end changes except that you send payments to and communicate with the secondary market or its loan servicer. If you want additional loans, however, contact your original lender.

✔ **Servicers:** Some lenders, including many colleges and universities, pay these organizations to collect and process loan payments. Unless you're in default, your lender will tell you if your loan gets transferred to a servicer. Your payments go to the servicer, but are otherwise unchanged. Inform your servicer of any change in address.

✔ **Tax offset:** When defaulted borrowers lose their state or federal income tax refunds.

✔ **Variable interest:** Interest rates that change according to a market-sensitive index.

Test repayment plans before you jump in

Kenneth finally uncovered the mystery lenders — it turned out that he had several loans. Actually, he discovered not the lenders but the names of the servicers who handled his loans. Like all student borrowers, Kenneth learned he had a number of options for reducing his monthly payments. Until he eyed the fine print in each option, he'd just assumed he was on the hook for giant payments forever. These are the options from which Kenneth (and you, too) could choose:

✔ **Standard, 10 years, equal payments option:** This plan carries the highest monthly payment, but you can overcome your debt faster and pay less in interest. You pay the same amount each month for ten years if you have a fixed loan, and a fluctuating amount if you have a variable rate.

✔ **Long-term, 12–30 years, equal payments option:** When tiny monthly payments are your speed, you pay for a longer period, up to 30 years. You pay the same amount each month, and you could end up paying twice the original amount of your loan.

✔ **Graduated repayment plan, unequal payments option:** If your starting income is low but expected to increase on a regular basis, this more graceful method may ease your payment pangs. Payments start low and increase every two or three years for the next 10 to 30 years. Interest charges remain high for the first several years.

Federal education loans, including Stafford, SLS, PLUS, Federal Consolidation Loans, and some private loans, offer graduated repayment terms that vary from servicer to servicer. Some loan servicers, including giant Sallie Mae, which acquires educational loans from lenders, allow you to make interest-only payments for the first two to four years; after that period, you must pay principal and interest.

✔ **Income-based repayment plans, unequal payments option:** Monthly payments are tied to your income. The flexibility to increase or decrease payments when your income bobs up and down is available under the *income-contingent repayment plan for direct government loans* or under the *income-sensitive repayment plan for guaranteed loans.*

Read the fine print

Kenneth decided to check out the last option: the *income-contingent repayment plan* offered by the Federal Direct loan program, which lets you base your payment on your annual income, the amount you owe, and other factors, such as family size. The monthly installment amount cannot exceed 20 percent of your discretionary income, which is defined as the adjusted gross income (AGI) you report on your federal tax return minus the poverty-income figure for your household size as determined by the U.S. Department of Health and Human Services. If you're married, you must report the income for your spouse. Every five years, you must sign a waiver allowing the Internal Revenue Service to disclose your AGI to the U.S. Department of Education. The direct loan servicer sends you an authorization form that you must sign and return.

Under direct loan rules, your repayment may be less than the accruing interest. Unpaid interest, subject to a limit equal to 10 percent of your initial loan balance, can be capitalized (that is, added to your principal balance), requiring you to pay interest on interest. Any additional unpaid interest is added to your total loan balance. If you have any leftover debt after 25 years, the federal government will forgive the remaining balance, and under laws, the feds will *not* tax the amount forgiven as if it were regular income.

The guaranteed loan program offers an income-sensitive repayment option that also bases the monthly payment on the borrower's income. Repayment schedules vary from servicer to servicer, but many plans typically set the maximum payment at 4 percent of your monthly income, as long as that payment amount covers the accruing interest. No loan forgiveness is available, and the lender does not need to access your tax return.

Tax break means paying back student loans at less cost

Thanks to the Taxpayer Relief Act of 1997, you or your family maybe able to take a deduction for part or all of the interest paid each year on your student loan. The deduction only works for the first 60 months of repayment, which need not be consecutive months. Maximum deductions: $2,000 in 2000, $2,500 in 2001, and so on. Income-adjusted limits for individuals are $40,000, phasing out completely at $55,000; for families, $60,000, phasing out at $75,000.

(This means that if you're single, the amount of tax deduction you can claim dips at $40,000 per year income and disappears entirely at $55,000; if married, the deduction dips at $60,000 and disappears at $75,000.) The tax break is good for most educational loans. Check the tax law's fine print on this one. (Current Congressional discussions at time of publication are likely to expand this tax break.)

Kenneth calculated that the last three options (the long-term equal payments option; graduated repayment plan, unequal payments option; and the income-based repayment plans, unequal payments option) would reduce his monthly payments but would also increase his total interest costs over the duration of the loan. Well, in this case, he thought, paying a bundle in interest couldn't be helped. On the brighter side, Kenneth had managed to land a part-time job at a dinner theater and was now thinking especially hard about a graduated repayment plan or an income-based repayment plan. Then a friend mentioned consolidation as a strategy.

Use a life preserver: Consolidate

As Kenneth surveyed his options for the zillionth time he realized that he had such a collection of loans that he could end up mailing four different checks each month — for a lead weight total of $1,189 per month. As with many recent grads, Kenneth's debt was so high that he wanted to minimize early payments. (According to estimates, roughly 1.176 million graduates consolidated their debts in 1997.) Treading water in his young, uncertain career, Kenneth found the option of tying all his loans into one and making lower payments ultimately the most appealing choice.

After you graduate, you should consider consolidation as an option. Consolidation plans allow you to pay off your balance (depending on its size) in from 10 to 30 years. Consolidated loans are available for both Federal Direct and Guaranteed loans and are eligible for equal-installment, graduated, and income-based repayment loans. Examine the pluses and minuses Kenneth factored into his decision to consolidate.

Consolidation can help in these situations:

✔ Your payments overstress your bare-bones budget under the preceding payment plan options.

✔ You're trying to pay off the balance on your credit cards, which charge higher interest rates than student loans. Often, these rates exceed 17 percent.

✔ You're trying to save money to start a business or return to school.

Consolidation can hurt, however. When you consolidate just to lower your payments, you end up paying quite a bit more in interest over the life of your loan. For example, a $49,000 loan paid off in 10 years could total $71,341, assuming an interest rate of 8 percent. However, paying off the same loan in 25 years could total $113,457.

Many debtors consolidate to avoid keeping track of multiple loans. If you choose consolidation for its simplicity, plan to pay off the debt within 10 years or expect to pay up to three times the amount of your loan. Consider these alternative conveniences:

✔ Authorize lenders to withdraw monthly payments from your checking account; Sallie Mae discounts .25 percent off your interest for this authorization.

✔ Make at least 48 on-time loan payments; most lenders will lower your interest rate on eligible Federal Stafford loans.

✔ Ask a servicer to buy your loans and combine the payments without changing their terms, a treatment referred to as *serialization*. While servicers are not required to buy or sell your loans for this purpose, you should force the issue. It's to your advantage to simplify your loan repayments.

✔ Ask your loan servicer to coordinate payment due dates.

Loans you can consolidate

When you want to consolidate your loans after considering the additional expenses, your next step is to double-check that your loans qualify for consolidation. Normally, you must leave school before your loans qualify. The following types of loans can be consolidated:

✔ **Federal loans**

• Auxiliary Loans to Assist Students (ALAS)

• Federal Direct Loans

• Federal Family Education Loans: Stafford, PLUS, and/or SLS

• Federal Insured Student Loans (FISL)

- Federal Perkins Loans
- Health Professional Student Loans (HPSLs)
- Loans for Disadvantaged Students (LDS)
- National Direct Student Loans (NDSL)
- Nursing Student Loans (NSL)

✔ **Defaulted loans**

Certain federal loans, such as Guaranteed Student loans and Direct loans, may be consolidated if you meet the terms and conditions for doing so. If you are in default on a federal student loan, you can consolidate if you agree to repay under the income-contingent repayment plan (ICRP). If you don't want to repay under the ICRP, you must make three consecutive monthly payments to your current loan holder under a satisfactory repayment arrangement (discussed later in this chapter). For more information, call the U.S. Department of Education Loan Consolidation Network about consolidation of loans at 301-443-1540.

Caveats for consolidation loans

Think twice about consolidating subsidized Federal Stafford Loans with other loans, including unsubsidized Federal Stafford, SLS, and PLUS loans. Doing so will sacrifice potential interest subsidy benefits on your subsidized Stafford loans should you later decide to return to school or seek a deferment.

Avoid consolidating Perkins loans as well, and keep the low 5 percent interest rate, unless lenders can promise you that it will pull down the total interest rate on your consolidation loan. If you consolidate the Perkins loan with other loans, including subsidized Federal Stafford loans, you lose all subsidies.

The following resources are your best bets for obtaining more information about loan consolidation; most offer interactive calculators to assess payment obligations:

✔ **U.S. Department of Education Loan Consolidation Network:** Offers detailed free information and application packet. Contact the network at 800-557-7392; www.ed.gov/studentaid.

✔ **U.S. Department of Health and Human Services:** Lists consolidating lenders and current rates and information. Contact the department at 301-443-1540; www.hrsa.dhhs.gov/refinance.

✔ **Sallie Mae:** Major consolidator's Web site provides free debt management software. Contact Sallie Mae at 800-524-9100; www.salliemae.com.

> ✔ **USA Group:** Nation's largest student loan guarantor and administrator will consolidate if they have at least one of your loans. Contact USA Group at 800-382-4506; www.usagroup.com.
>
> ✔ **Citibank:** International bank will consolidate if it holds at least one of your loans. Contact Citibank at 800-967-2400 or 800-845-1297 (TDD); www.citibank.com/student.

Suppose you do a consolidation deal and then think of other student loans that you'd like to fold into the big package? You can do it if you act within 180 days.

When Facing Default: To Come Up for Air — Defer or Forbear

Michelle, who defaulted on her loans, was at her wits' end. She'd lost her credit, her car, and her tax refund. She'd spent her savings and was living on credit cards that were almost maxed out. After her lender bombarded her with telephone calls, letters, and e-mails, a collection agency was hounding her in court and billing her. Speaking of big, high waves, for Michelle it was tsunami time!

Michelle needed a guardian angel — or at least a savvy counselor who didn't crack wise about how naïve she'd been. She was wondering if Della Reese moonlighted when she and Kenneth happened to meet at the local sweat palace and exchanged condolences while riding matching life cycles. Kenneth, who now considered himself as something of an expert on handling student loan repayment, offered the following suggestion.

"If you can't make a payment, contact the servicer of your loans and explain your situation. In some cases, you may be eligible for a deferment or forbearance. In other words, you can ask for mercy!"

He continued with an explanation of short-term relief in the form of deferment and forbearance.

Many loan providers and laws show understanding when the situation is truly out of your hands. But be aware that you may not be eligible for some deferment options because eligibility is related to your track record in a specific loan program.

Kenneth's choice

After reading books, visiting loan consolidation Web sites, and talking with his loan servicers, Kenneth made an executive decision: He would consolidate his loans. And because his income would be uncertain in his career field (theater, film, performing arts), Kenneth chose an income-based repayment plan.

After he'd made the decision and taken action, Kenneth felt a huge weight lifted from his shoulders. He almost called a few friends to celebrate until he remembered, "Oh yeah, I shredded that crummy credit card that gets 19.9 percent on cash advances."

Deferments and forbearance are typically granted for personal financial hardship that may include dependents or because you're helping your country and you're not making a lot of money. Reasons vary by loan — federally sponsored or private — but deferments and forbearance are often granted in these categories:

- You're still enrolled in school.
- You're participating in a graduate fellowship program.
- You're unemployed and facing serious economic hardship.
- You're parenting young children.
- You have a temporary disability or have entered a rehabilitation program for individuals with disabilities.
- You're a member of the armed forces or a law enforcement body.
- You're employed in community service, health care, teaching, or other work benefiting underserved populations.

Deferment: A postponement

Deferment is a period of time during which your lender puts your payments on hold. You escape interest charges if your monies come from a subsidized Stafford loan or Perkins loan; if not, you're still responsible for interest that accumulates during this time.

Most private, state, and university loans can be deferred while you're in school or in your grace period, typically six to nine months. After you enter repayment, deferment becomes much harder to get, unless you're a medical student completing an internship or residency. Because provisions for deferment vary among schools, contact your school's financial aid office or your state loan servicing center. If you have other loans, such as federally sponsored loans, contact your loan holder for information about canceling or deferring payments.

Here are the nuts and bolts of getting deferment:

- ✓ **Filling out the right forms:** Even if you meet all the requirements for deferment, you must still request it. Servicers defer payments only if you're not in default, so do your best to keep making payments while you await deferment. Some servicers even provide retroactive deferment to cover past-due payments in lieu of default. Contact your loan holder and ask for deferment forms (which you can also download from Web sites). The representative you speak with should note in your file that you've requested such documents, in case your bills become due while you await deferment.

  After you have your deferment request forms, read and complete them carefully — don't skip the fine print. Attach all documentation required to verify your eligibility.

- ✓ **Saving copies of all correspondence to your lender:** A few weeks after you send your request, contact your lender to double-check that it arrived and is being processed. Ask when to expect a response. Most deferment applications take between four and six weeks to process.

- ✓ **Recertifying deferments:** Some types of deferments require you to reapply every six to twelve months. For example, you may need to recertify a deferment granted for a temporary disability. Ask your loan servicer, financial aid counselor, or guarantor for details on how to maintain your deferment.

Forbearance: A pricier postponement

What if you don't qualify for deferment? Some lenders will *forbear* your payments — they postpone or temporarily lower them, but your interest continues to build up. Forbearances can last as long as three years; ask your lender how long you can forbear.

To come up for air when you feel like you're drowning financially, request forbearances on low-interest loans first. Forbearance request forms (available from your loan servicer) typically require information about your income and expenses. Remember, forbearances are generally granted at the loan servicer's discretion.

Lenders must allow forbearance if your loan payments exceed 20 percent of your monthly income and in cases of natural emergencies and disasters. Poor health, personal problems, or financial hardship are normally causes for forbearance.

The deferment/forbearance debate

If you have a choice, go for the deferment.

Although both waivers temporarily postpone the payments on your loans, the differences between deferment and forbearance for federally backed loans as described in the following sections, show clear advantages for deferment.

Eligibility requirements

Deferment and forbearance differ in eligibility requirements in the following ways:

- **Deferment:** You generally qualify for a deferment if you're in school at least half-time (including certain rehabilitation training or graduate fellowship programs), unemployed, or experiencing an economic hardship. If, at the time you obtained your Direct loan, you had an outstanding balance on a federal education loan made before July 1, 1993, you may be eligible for additional types of deferments related to your education status (or the education status of the student for whom you borrowed a PLUS loan). You may also be eligible based on your public service status, your parental status as a working mother, or a temporary total disability.

- **Forbearance:** Generally, you may qualify for a forbearance if you're willing but unable to make loan payments due to poor health or serious money problems. You can also qualify if you serve in a medical or dental internship or residence, serve under the National and Community Service Trust Act of 1993, or are making required payments on federal student loans that are equal to or greater than 20 percent of your total monthly gross income.

Interest charges

Interest charges are also applied differently in a deferment and a forbearance.

Interest is not charged on subsidized loans during a deferment; however, interest *is* charged on subsidized loans during a forbearance.

Interest is charged on unsubsidized and PLUS loans during both deferment and forbearance. All unpaid interest is *capitalized* (held over until the loan is due, so you don't have to come up with the interest money while you're cash-poor on postponement status, but you end up paying the interest as part of the principal later on).

Surprise! There Is Life after Default

After listening intently to Kenneth's discussion of deferment and forbearance, Michelle spoke up, noting that while she appreciated Kenneth's concern, he really hadn't given her any outs for a default: "This is all very interesting, and I know I should have gone to my loan servicers and lenders long before now, but it's too late. Maybe you've forgotten, but I have defaulted! I don't think I qualify for deferment or forbearance any more. I'm an outlaw in the loan repayment complex. A company I wanted to work for just ran a credit check and then didn't hire me. And while they didn't say so, I'm pretty sure it was because of my default. What now, wise owl?"

"Maybe it's not too late to get your life back on track," Kenneth replied. Why don't we talk about it at the cybercafe across the street?"

After ordering coffees, Kenneth and Michelle moved to one of the computers where search engines revealed a couple of useful Web sites:

- ✔ **Debt Collection Service Guide to Defaulted Student Loans** (www.ed.gov/studentaid): A U.S. Department of Education page that discusses student loan defaults.

- ✔ **Adventures in Education: Paying for School** (www.adventuresineducation.org/paying): A site of the Texas Guaranteed Student Loan Corporation that discusses options for defaulted borrowers.

After spending 30 minutes looking over the escape hatches she might employ, Michelle's eyes lit up. "You're right. Maybe I'm not dead in the water," she beamed at Kenneth.

Michelle discovered that she and other defaulters could look into the following options:

- ✔ **Loan Consolidation:** See "Use a life preserver: Consolidate" earlier in this chapter.

- ✔ **Loan Forgiveness:** See Chapter 22.

- ✔ **The Satisfactory Repayment Arrangements Program:** This program for federally sponsored loans restores your Title IV benefits (such as federal grants and federal student loans) as a defaulted borrower so that you can get additional financial aid. Unfortunately, it doesn't clean up your credit record (until seven years after you make all amends) — your default sticks out like a sore thumb. You have to make six consecutive monthly payments of a reasonable and an affordable amount; the size of the payments are determined after considering the balance on your account and your ability to pay. This program is a good start. Not all loan defaults are eligible for this program. Check with your loan servicer or guarantor to find out if you qualify.

✔ **The Loan Rehabilitation Program:** The rehabilitation program is a much better deal for the long term because it does remove your loan from a default status and wipes out any derogatory entry on your credit record as reported by the loan guarantee agency.

In addition, you get your Title IV benefits back — re-establishment of your student loan benefits, including deferments, repayment options, forbearance, and so on. The hitch is that you have to make 12 consecutive monthly payments of a reasonable and an affordable amount instead of six — so it takes longer to help you survive.

When a loan comes out of default after you make the 12 consecutive payments, it then gets sold to a loan holder. At that point, arrange for one of the flexible payment options discussed earlier in this chapter. *You are starting over from scratch, no longer a defaulted borrower.* (Follow up to make sure the default is erased from your credit record, a task your loan holder can facilitate.)

The bad news is that you may not be eligible to participate in the Loan Rehabilitation Program; to find out, contact the guarantee agency that guaranteed your student loan.

Michelle was ready to call it a day and turn off the computer when Kenneth clicked on the *...For Dummies* Web site (`www.dummies.com`) and caught a snippet of a sample chapter from *College Financial Aid For Dummies*. They read the following two sections:

Failure to pay costs money

Collection fees are paid for by the defaulter — you. These agencies may collect interest on the added amount due plus other charges, such as for mail and phone expenses, credit reporting expenses, bank charges, and even file maintenance fees.

To avoid sinking yourself even deeper into the debt quagmire, contact the holder of your loan immediately and negotiate a reasonable and affordable repayment plan. If you can offer to repay your balance in a lump sum or over a few months, your collector may let up.

Guarantors help identify borrowers who are in default, and the federal government receives the money. The IRS applies the refund monies against the amount owed by you. If your loan is in default, the lender is paid an insurance claim and is effectively out of the picture.

If the U.S. Department of Education, a collection agency working for that department, or a guarantee agency holds your loan, your tax refund may go straight to them. If you owe $25 or more and have made no payment in the last 90 days, the collector can notify the IRS that your loan is in default, and the IRS may decide to keep part or all of your refund to apply to the debt that you owe.

For the 20 days following this notice, you can request (in writing) copies of your loan documents and payment records. For the following 65 days, you can request a repayment schedule or review of your file (an in-person or telephone review is possible). To halt an intercept of your return, present any evidence of the following:

✔ You've repaid the loan.

✔ You're making payments according to an agreement you made with the collector.

✔ You're in deferment or forbearance.

✔ You filed for bankruptcy and the case remains open.

✔ Your loan was discharged due to bankruptcy.

✔ You meet any of the aforementioned criteria for loan cancellation.

✔ The loan is not yours.

✔ Your signature on the loan was forged.

✔ You dropped out of school and are awaiting a refund.

✔ Your school closed or the loan was falsely certified.

When you're headed for court, contact an attorney immediately; regulations for collecting debts vary by state. Just like any other debt, college loan default can mean that you lose your property if the judgment is against you.

Compromise can be done

After all the notices and warnings from collectors, can you possibly get them to compromise? Yes! If you agree to certain payments, loan holders may forget about your collection costs and up to 30 percent or more of the principal and interest with approval from the agency's director.

A Happy Ending

Two months later, Kenneth and Michelle met again by chance. "How'd everything turn out?" Kenneth asked.

"Excellent, considering the situation," Michelle answered. "Thanks in large part to you, I might add. What a relief! Now I know what to do if a default riptide threatens to pull me under again."

"Great for the future, but what about right now?"

The born-again borrower clasped her hands and continued, "I contacted my lender and told them the truth — that I was overextended, uninformed about what to do, and afraid."

"They agreed to let me cut back on my payments (extending the loan schedule) so that I can qualify for the *Satisfactory Repayment Arrangements Program*. We have the understanding that if I make my payments for a year I can move into the *Loan Rehabilitation Program*."

"Yes, I know I could be a grandmother by the time I finish paying my loan in 20 years and that it costs a lot more in the long term. But I need a breather. And I'm going to pay off the loan much faster if I can — maybe I'll get a second job and put it all toward the loan."

Kenneth raised the issue of loan forgiveness.

"I'm looking into that, too. I'd like to have a big chunk of my loan written off," Michelle acknowledged. "I'll do it if I can find the right job that carries a loan forgiveness benefit."

"Did you consolidate your loans," Kenneth asked.

"No, I only had one loan, so that wasn't an option."

Kenneth smiled, paused reflectively, and said, "You know, Michelle, since you got that default monkey off your back, you look more relaxed, not stressed out. Why don't we celebrate with dinner tonight? I'll buy. I've got a two-for-one coupon at the Bargain Belly-Up Grill."

We can't guarantee that you'll end up with a date like Kenneth and Michelle when you square your loans, but we do promise that you can get out of the sea of debt and back into the swim of life.

Additional resources

Take Control of Your Student Loans, by Robin Leonard and Shae Irving. NoloPress, 1999; $19.95; bookstores or call 800-992-6656; www.nolopress.com.

Paying for School, by the Texas Guaranteed Student Loan Corp., www.adventures ineducation.org/paying. Includes downloadable forms for many types of deferment.

Various federal government student loan Web sites, www.ed.gov/studentaid; also www.easi.ed.gov.

Student Loan Repayment FAQs, by PHEAA (Pennsylvania Higher Education Assistance Agency). An overview in a Q&A format of federally sponsored repayment, www.pheaa.com/borowers/solution.htm.

10 Ways to Cut the Cost of Repaying Student Loans, by the USA Group, www.virtual-loan-office.com/media/10ways.htm.

Part VI
The Part of Tens

The 5th Wave   By Rich Tennant

"Someone put a financial aid form in our tip cup."

In this part . . .

A ...*For Dummies* book without The Part of Tens is like a software company without a home page. This part sums up ten tips for just about every stage of the financial aid process — locating and winning aid, cutting expenses, uncovering well-kept secrets about the application process, avoiding pricey mistakes, and screening out scams. Use this important information to get every cent you can.

Chapter 24

Ten Ways to Grow Your Own Opportunities

· ·

In This Chapter

▶ Making your own breaks

▶ Aiming local spotlights on you

▶ Turning good works into good money

· ·

*T*his chapter focuses on individual actions you can take and choices you can make to grow free-money crops on the fields of financial aid. Perhaps none of these ten suggestions are startling news, but a timely reminder to plow, seed, and water your chances can't hurt.

Raise Your Class Rank

Recognition for reaching the top of your class is nice . . . but money gets you through school. Sources aplenty automatically award financial aid to classroom achievers whose rank in class is as high as an elephant's eye. A few examples follow:

> ✔ **Bard College,** Annandale-On-Hudson, New York, gives first-year students in the top 10 percent of their high school class a tuition discount.

> ✔ **The North Dakota Merit Scholarship Program** provides tuition scholarships to in-state students who rank in the top 20 percent of their high school class. Contact your high school counseling center for more details and an application.

> ✔ **The State of Iowa Merit Scholarship Program** gives financial assistance to Iowa seniors who rank in the upper 15 percent of their class and have strong SAT scores.

> ✔ **The Whiteside Scholarship Fund Trust** in Duluth, Minnesota, rewards Duluth students who rank in the top 10 percent of their high school class with scholarships.

Cultivate Good Grades

Granted, other criteria can win you college funds, but without a stellar grade point average, you'd be ineligible for programs like these:

- ✔ **The National Honor Society Scholarship Awards Program,** sponsored by the National Association of Secondary School Principals in Reston, Virginia. This program requires candidates to meet national minimum requirements to qualify for membership in their local high school National Honor Society. Each school may nominate two chapter members who've demonstrated that they have outstanding scholarship, among other requirements. The 250 award recipients receive $1,000 each.

- ✔ **The Education Foundation of the National Society of Professional Engineers Regional Scholarships** in Alexandria, Virginia. This program awards scholarships to students who plan to study engineering in college and who sport a 3.0 GPA during their last two years of high school, among other requirements. Awards vary between $1,000 per year to four-year, full-tuition scholarships.

Test Your Test-Taking Skills

If you're not the type to blank out under pressure, test your mettle for money in academic competitions. Many merit-based scholarships consider test scores, but this one bases eligibility on them.

The National Merit Scholarship Program and National Achievement Program are the largest academically competitive scholarship programs in the United States. Each year, more than 3,000 scholarships are awarded among 5,000 finalists and an additional 650 scholarships go to African American students. Fifteen hundred of these awards are one-timers of $1,000; 1,500 are four-year awards for the same amount or more.

Competition is abundant, but if you win, your harvest is more abundant than the $1,000 awards. As we note in Chapter 10, schools that value lustrous reputations lure National Merit winners with a bumper crop of financial aid awards.

To qualify, take the Preliminary Scholastic Aptitude Test (PSAT), which is the National Merit Scholarship Qualifying Test (NMSQT), usually given in your junior year of high school. Ask your high school guidance counselor for details. Finalists are chosen based on scores. Go study your head off.

Plant Career Seeds in High School

You'd never guess that acting in school plays or painting still-life oils could be a cash cow grazing in your future. But interests you develop during your high school years that cast light on what you want as a college major or career may lead to scholarship dollars. Following are work examples:

- **Communicative arts (theater, film, speech, radio, television, broadcasting, music, and dance)** scholarships are sponsored by the Educational Theater Association/International Thespian Society. You need a 2.7 G.P.A., but your academic record doesn't count in the judging. Criteria include acting, interviewing with the judges, and activities with your thespian club in high school. Each year about ten scholarships worth $1,000 each are awarded.

- **Graphic arts (design and illustration)** scholarships are offered by the National Scholarship Trust Fund of the Graphic Arts. This program offers awards to high school students and college undergraduates who wish to pursue a career in graphic communications. Finalists are selected based on SAT/PSAT scores, transcripts, recommendation letters, and the application and other materials. In excess of 160 awards ranging between $500 and $4,000 go to winners annually.

Rake in Contest Cash

Millions of dollars go out sponsors' doors each year to students who have honed their hobbies, activities, and talents to a competitive level. Check out this sampling of rewards that students can win for having fun:

- **The American Legion National High School Oratorical Contest** yields good money for students who can think and speak well. You must pen an essay and present it in several levels of competition. Regional-level winners receive $1,000 each. National winners receive $18,000 for first place, $16,000 for second place, $14,000 for third place, and $12,000 for fourth place. Contact your local Legion Post or your state's department headquarters of the American Legion.

- **Guideposts Youth Writing Contest** is a nonfiction contest that pays better than many professional writers earn for similar work. Sponsored by *Guideposts* magazine, the rules invite high school juniors and seniors to write about their most memorable and inspiring true experience. The judges assess the originality of the writing, sincerity of the author, and the values of kindness, spirituality, fairness, and morality. Annually, 30 students win between $1,000 and $4,000. No pulp fiction in this award.

✔ **The Voice of Democracy Audio-Essay Contest** is sponsored by the Veterans of Foreign Wars of the United States and its Ladies Auxiliary, in cooperation with the National Association of Broadcasters. Thirty winners each year take home awards ranging from the first prize of $20,000 to finalists who receive $1,000 each. A different patriotic theme is selected each year and assigned to contestants who broadcast the theme and move up through a series of competitive tiers, ending in a big, flashy finale in Washington, D.C.

Dig in Your Backyard

A lot of cash for your college stay is buried in your own hometown, county, or state. Create your own version of going native by making a list of local sources you can hit up for scholarships, such as these:

✔ Trusts

✔ Philanthropic organizations

✔ Service clubs

✔ Civic groups

✔ Chambers of commerce

✔ School boards

✔ Immigrant rights groups

✔ Religious organizations

✔ Youth organizations

✔ Professional organizations

Sometimes, you can get money chiefly for living in the chunk of geography you call home! Your school guidance counselor and librarian should be able to give you a big assist in this effort.

After a thorough scouting of what's lurking around your neck of the woods, you can find sources like these that other students may not have noticed:

✔ The **California Masonic Foundation** hands out more than $200,000 to Californians in undergraduate programs.

✔ The **Chautauqua Region Community Foundation, Inc.,** bestows financial aid to residents of Allegheny, Chautauqua, and Cattaragus counties, New York.

✔ The **Colorado Masons Benevolent Fund Association** awards scholarships to Colorado high school grads who plan to attend in-state colleges.

- ✔ The **Ebell of Los Angeles Scholarship Endowment Fund** allots grants to students from Los Angeles county who reside in and attend college in the county.

- ✔ The **Horace Smith Trust Fund** rewards students who've graduated from high school in Hampden County, Massachusetts.

- ✔ The **Jennie G. and Pearl Abell Education Trust** helps out students who are Clark County, Kansas residents and graduates of Clark County high schools.

- ✔ The **Paul Stock Foundation** sponsors students who live in the Cody, Wyoming area with grants to attend college.

Till the Vineyards of Volunteerism

While doing good works through volunteering in community service activities, you build career skills and leadership experience. As if that's not enough, a number of organizations return the favor with scholarships toward your education. Let these several examples inspire you to get in touch with your finer feelings:

- ✔ **Soroptimist Foundation's Regional Youth Citizenship Awards** chooses scholarship recipients on the basis of service, dependability, leadership, and sense of purpose. Academic criteria (grades, test scores) aren't considered. The foundation gives over 50 scholarships worth several hundred dollars each, plus one $2,000 international award.

- ✔ **Tylenol Scholarship Fund** recognizes students who provide leadership in community and school activities. What counts? School awards, academic record, activities, and honors are considered. Each year, 500 scholarships worth $1,000 each and ten $10,000 awards are passed to upstanding students.

- ✔ **U.S. Senate Youth Program, William Randolph Hearst Foundation** acknowledges students who have been elected to leadership offices in their high school student governments. This program distributes 104 awards annually at $2,000 each.

- ✔ **The Toyota Community Scholars Program** recognizes 100 students each year who show dedication to community service as well as academic leadership. This award was launched in 1997 with a bang of big bucks: The four-year awards range from $10,000 to $20,000. To be considered, you must have initiated or been actively involved in a service program that addresses a school or community need.

Sprout a Job in the School Financial Aid Office

A part-time, student assistant job in the school financial aid bank vault can expose you to how awards are figured and how students win them. Just by working in this office you pick up nuances you may otherwise miss. Your close contact with the office's inner workings can unveil the perfect financial aid for you.

Land a Job in the Alumni Office

The alumni office offers student assistants opportunities to find out which alumni are helping financially strapped students complete their education. As an added benefit, you can get to know alums, who, scouting their alma maters for talent, may offer you a job after graduation.

Spread the Word That You Need a Sponsor

Are you a pleasant, sincere, hard-working, deserving person? If so, you may be able to find yourself a sponsor who will pay part or all of your way through college.

You think such generosity doesn't happen? Multimillionaire Eugene Lang is well known for backing not just a single student but entire classes with his "I Have a Dream Project," which has now spread to more than 20 cities. Lang began with sixth-grade students at a Harlem school in New York City, promising that he'd take care of college if they graduated from high school.

To find your own sponsor, you can't be shy about asking teachers, friends, professionals, and community leaders to recommend potential sponsors and, if possible, introduce you to them.

A Washington D.C. student whom Dr. Davis counseled turned sponsor search into an art by passing out self-marketing packets containing a transcript, recommendation letters, and award letters to potential sponsors. The student received several partial sponsorships.

If you are lucky enough to find a sponsor, be sure to keep in touch and say thanks.

Chapter 25

Ten Strategies for Cutting College Costs

In This Chapter

▶ Cramming four years into three

▶ Getting a head start in high school

▶ Considering two-year colleges

▶ Limiting your lifestyle

*1*f you would welcome the gift of a financial chainsaw to cut down tall college costs, cast your eyes on the approaches identified in this chapter. Some of these strategies require a financial or academic about-face, while others call for minor changes in lifestyle.

Study in Bulk

Most students finish school in four or five years, but Bill Thomas, a Pennsylvania State veteran, graduated in three. How? He carried 20 hours per semester and attended summer and winter school. Even though summer and winter tuition cost more per unit, his total tab was below the usual four-year bill. Thomas entered the job market ahead of his class and found an entry-level administrative job that helped him pay off his loan debt fast. Consider overloading courses if your school allows it.

Double Up High School and College

Your high school may allow you to take as many as 12 semester hours of college-level courses before you graduate from high school. You may have to meet certain selection criteria or your hours of attendance may be limited. The most popular money-saving route is to enroll in a community or public college and build up units that can transfer to any university.

Swap AP Courses for College Classes

If you score a 3.0 or better in Advanced Placement (AP) courses, the credits usually substitute for first-year general education courses at the vast majority of U.S. colleges. You must pass an Advanced Placement test in the subject, administered by the Education Testing Service of Princeton, NJ; the tests are given throughout the U.S. By replacing first-year courses that count toward a college degree with AP courses, you can save $10,000 to $12,000 at a public college and $24,000 to $30,000 at a private college.

Get a Bargain at Two-Year Colleges

Two-year community colleges are among the best buys in higher education. Their courses cost about half those of four-year institutions, and the first two years of general education courses are roughly the same no matter where you attend college. *All in all, when money's a problem, beginning your studies at a community college is your best answer.*

Note: Most community colleges coordinate their curriculum with senior institutions, but check that your four-year college or university will accept the credits you earn at a two-year institution. The question to ask an admissions counselor at a four-year institution (from which you plan to graduate one day) is which of your two-year courses will transfer for full credit. Get the counselor to sign the agreed-upon list of transferable courses. Students have been known to accept a verbal agreement that certain courses would transfer for credit, only to find out later that the courses would not transfer and the authorizing college official had left the institution.

Choose a Lower-Cost School

Okay, we admit the pedigree from a prestigious university such as Sarah Lawrence and Brandeis looks pretty slick on your wall, but you should realize that you're paying for a brand name and the contacts you make on campus.

Magazines such as *Money* and *U.S. News & World Report* annually report on bargain schools — such as Berea College in Kentucky, Missouri Southern State, and Cooper Union in New York — where tuitions are free or modestly priced and the educational standards are high.

Work at Co-op Education

Wouldn't you love some hands-on experience so that you can use your learning and not be considered a raw rookie after you graduate? Cooperative education programs allow you to do just that. You study some, work some, and study some more throughout your college experience. You earn money as you go. More than 900 colleges operate cooperative education programs that typically take five years to complete undergraduate degrees. For more information, read *A Student-Parent Guide to Cooperative Education,* free from the National Commission for Cooperative Education, 360 Huntington Ave., 384CP, Boston, MA 02115; 617-373-3770; www.co-op.edu.

Get a Job

Granted, working part-time and attending college can take all your energy and time — but more students than ever must choose between doubling up work and school or financially doubling over in pain. If you think that idea is exhausting, hear this: Countless students, many of whom are parents, hold full-time jobs and study at night school or through distance-education programs. For more information, see the section on distance education later in this chapter and Chapter 11 for more about jobs.

Test Out or Get Credit for Life Experience

Many schools spare you a pile of course work — between 30 and 60 credit hours of it — if you can prove you know the material well enough not to need the course. Ask at your college admissions office about obtaining credits for passing tests or relevant life experience. Tests are modestly priced at $44 each. For example, you could escape a $600 computer competency course if you can get life experience credit (such as job experience or military service using computers) or take the school's computer competency exam.

Information for Candidates, a free booklet, explains testing out. Get it from College-Level Examination Programs, P.O. Box 6600, Princeton, NJ 08541-6600; 609-771-7865; www.collegeboard.org. Click Directory of Services.

Consider Low-Cost Distance Learning

Many online and study-at-home courses cost as much as on-campus studies. But persistent research can connect you to reputable classes for pennies on the dollar. Harvard College, for example, in its distance-education program, offers an online college-level calculus course for under $100. Such a deal! Are you a self-starter?

Quell Spending Urges

College students tend to ease bookworm stress with shopping sprees. Well-meaning parents spring for new wardrobes, cars, and dorm supplies, forgetting that materialistic trappings rarely improve higher learning. The frugal rule: Don't buy anything until you know you need it. Here are some money-saving suggestions:

- ✔ **Clothes:** Until you see what your classmates are wearing, don't make over your closet. A surprising amount of money is wasted on a new college wardrobe only to have a parent drag it home to store. The best wardrobe investments you'll make during college will be the graduation cap and gown and the suits you'll need to go on job interviews.

- ✔ **Textbooks:** Don't automatically believe the book list; talk to your instructor long before the first day of class and find out which books you should have first. College bookstores often have exclusives on assigned textbooks, so try to buy them used. If a course requires an especially pricey book and you don't expect you'll ever read it after this semester, see if you can borrow it from the library. Sell back any textbooks you don't plan to use again.

- ✔ **Transportation:** Some college towns are so well designed that you won't need a car most of the time. A friend's car, a bus, a subway, or a taxi can come in handy occasionally, but the expense of purchasing, maintaining, parking, and fueling your own car can eat up sparse dollars. Consider saving your money — perhaps for your dream car much, much later.

- ✔ **Living expenses:** Limit long-distance calls and air travel and watch for special deals during off-hours or off-season. Watch for student discounts on everything, including movie tickets. Put every practical need (like socks, bookshelves, umbrellas) on a wish list and share it with relatives near major holidays. Check for special discounts for low-income families from utilities companies.

If you're as preoccupied as most students, you may think that take-out food costs the same as grocery store food and saves you all the prep time. But $8 meals twice a day add up to $448 per month — and that's skipping a meal! Buy staples in bulk when they're on sale, and use an electric frying pan for quick feeds. Save your money for when you need the positive reinforcement you get from occasionally dining out.

Another food cost you can reduce is the college meal plan you choose. Most students eat between 10 and 15 meals a week at school and often leave school on weekends. Parents, worried about junior starving, tend to pay for a plan that includes 21 meals a week. You could save $700 or so a year by cutting back on plans that include uneaten meals.

Chapter 26

Ten Facts That Financial Aid Counselors Don't Tell You

In This Chapter

▶ Smoking out hidden loan policies

▶ Figuring out the insider's financial aid game

▶ Planning — so you don't have three weeks of eating beans

*I*f you thought that you solved the financial aid enigma but somebody came up with an answer you didn't like, you're probably missing a piece of the aid puzzle that no one told you existed. Here are ten points that you may have overlooked.

Loans: Verify, Not Certify

A Direct loan is made by a college acting as the lending agency with funds provided by the federal government. By contrast, a Stafford loan is made by a private-sector lender, such as a bank.

If a college participates in the Direct loan program (not all colleges do), the college may not participate in a privately sponsored loan program, such as the CitiAssist loan from Citibank.

Why is that? Some private lenders typically require the school to use lots of red tape when certifying you as a student.

In short, private-loan certification means a raft of tedious paperwork. Of course, a college's financial aid staff isn't going to volunteer that they aren't anxious to add certifying you for a private loan to their already long days.

So why would you even want a private loan instead of a Direct loan handed out by the college? You may not have a choice; either you choose a private loan or no loan at all. Many students face this situation.

Your answer: Don't spin your wheels lining up a loan only to find out that your college is unwilling to do the paperwork to make it happen. Determine whether your college "certifies" or "verifies" before you start looking for private lenders.

Verify? Verification is much simpler than certification and is illustrated by such programs as the Achiever Loan by Key Bank (800-KEY-LEND). In calling for verification, the private lender asks only that the college accept and cash its check if the student is registered; if not, all the school has to do is return the check to the private lender. A few but growing number of outside lenders no longer require a college to "certify"; they require a college to merely "verify."

Zero Aid Now, Zero Aid Later

If you don't win financial aid for your first year from your college, you may not win any later. Many private colleges' policies stipulate that first-year aid winners get priority at reapplication time. Leftover funds go to new incoming students — which means that those unlucky enough not to win financial aid during their first year may be completely out of the financial aid loop unless there is a change in circumstance. If your school emphasizes first-year financial assistance over all other levels of aid, throw extra energy and time into finding financial assistance from the get-go.

Fine Print: Oops, Money Is Missing

Many colleges advertise that they meet 100 percent of need; what they don't tell you is that they do so by packaging in parent loans to meet the gap between need and the award.

Some colleges keep mum on what's called a *gapping policy* — a harmless-looking term that means they don't meet 100 percent of your need; instead, they award part of it but leave a gap that they expect your family to fill. Gapping doesn't seem so harmless anymore. For example, assume the annual college cost is $26,000 and your demonstrated need is $18,000. Suppose you receive an award package of $14,000. You're left with a need gap of $4,000, which is filled with PLUS loans to parents (see Chapter 7) or cash out of thin air. Your parents must begin repayment on loans after you're in school a couple of months.

State Colleges Keep Gift Aid at Home

The gift aid (aid that you don't need to repay) pouring forth from the financial aid offices of some state colleges seems to have in-state residents' names on it. The type of aid awarded to out-of-state students tends to be limited to self-help (loans and jobs) unless the student is eligible for a Federal Pell grant.

Note that this trend applies only to financial aid office generosity, not to special scholarships awarded by departments in the colleges. Department faculty are more likely to aim for excellence without regard to whether you're an in-state or out-of-state student.

You Can't Win without Losing

If you win financial aid from outside your institution, expect to lose some of your school's award. Although your dear alma mater may not publish policies about third-party awards, as soon as your financial aid office hears of one, they're likely to deduct at least some of that amount from the college award.

After you notify your financial aid office (and yes, you must), negotiate to keep both awards. If they must deduct some money, ask that the amount be subtracted from your college loan or work-study, not from free money.

You Can't Have It All

Reserve Officers' Training Corps (ROTC) tuition benefits — which may pay up to 100 percent of college costs — are viewed by schools as an outside scholarship (see Chapter 17). If you receive another outside scholarship that totals more than the cost of tuition, fees, books, and supplies, the excess is taxable income. College financial aid personnel aren't obligated to tell you that you can't have it all.

Student Loans Beat Folks' Bad Credit

Mom and Dad don't qualify for a Federal PLUS loan because of their credit rating; big bummer. But the financial aid office may not tell them that you, their child, can still qualify for an additional, unsubsidized Federal Stafford loan with a lower interest rate — up to $4,000 for each of the first two undergraduate years of college, and $5,000 for each of the second two undergraduate years. Apply for this low interest loan in your name for better cash flow and a longer grace period between graduation and repayment.

More Info Requested? Watch What You Say

The financial aid office requests additional information to measure your ability to qualify for institutional aid. You thought you'd filled out all the forms, but your financial aid office asks you to fill out one more — "for their records." But the questions seem far too detailed to be simply FYI:

- What is the equity on the parents' home?
- In the event of a separation or divorce, what is the noncustodial parent's income, assets, and debts?
- Will the noncustodial parent help with college expenses?
- How many cars do the parents own (including year, model, value, and debt)?
- Will the student drive to school? If so, how much is the car worth?
- How much of the student's college expenses will the parents cover?
- What is the cash value of the parents' life insurance policies, retirement accounts, and so forth?
- Are any siblings holding any money in their accounts for the student?
- How much money will the student earn during the summer after graduating from high school?

What they're not telling you is that they may adjust your Institutional Expected Family Contribution (IEFC) based on internal guidelines that assume additional funds are available for college based on the value of assets not used in the Federal Methodology formula. Don't hesitate to ask what the office will use the information for so that you can target your responses to their queries without volunteering unrelated information.

Financial Aid Folks Push the Override Button

Though nobody behind the financial aid office desk wants to admit it, financial aid directors have unadvertised powers to make what is called a *professional judgment* in the event of additional facts and conditions.

Because of this leeway, new, documented information on employment, income, assets, and other variables that can seriously affect your family's ability to pay college expenses may change your award for the better. Don't hesitate to send letters of appeal along with hefty documentation (see Chapter 9).

If your college uses the College Scholarship Service Profile, the financial aid counselors can still make their own judgment calls as they evaluate family assets. For example, some colleges assess 35 percent of the value of the car the student drives to school as an increase in the Institutional Expected Family Contribution (IEFC). If the student's income tax form shows interest income, even if you don't list assets on the financial form, some financial aid offices figure you made an investment somewhere big enough to make that much interest. Some financial aid offices consider part of the family's retirement account as available assets that could pay for college.

Three Weeks to Live Aidless

Even if you win pocket money, don't expect to pick up your check and buy books, supplies, or food on the first day of school. Many schools disburse living expense funds after the third week of school, or after the last day you can ask for a refund.

Bring enough cash to cover books (prices are usually available through the bookstore's book list), supplies, food, housing, and transportation.

Chapter 27

Ten Top Blunders That Lighten Your Wallet

· ·

In This Chapter

▶ The mistake that too many beginners make

▶ The data request you shouldn't ignore

▶ Why being too polite hurts you

· ·

*M*istakes happen: A sleepy-headed florist goofed and filled an order celebrating the opening of a new business with a funeral arrangement of flowers in a basket labeled *Rest in Peace*.

After the basket was delivered, about two seconds passed before the angry business owner was on the telephone to the florist complaining about the obvious mix-up. "How dare you send me this unlucky floral arrangement! What were you thinking?" the business owner raged.

"I'm sorry for the foul-up," the florist replied, " but rather than getting ticked off, you should think about this: Somewhere in this city a funeral is taking place and they received flowers with a banner saying *Congratulations on Your New Location*."

Yes, mistakes happen. But one of that magnitude need not wipe out your chances of getting all the financial aid help you need.

This chapter describes ten errors — nothing flashy, but oh, so common — that can be fatal to your hopes for college money.

Waiting Until You're Enrolled to Ask for Aid

For any college that you're even thinking about favoring with your presence, ask about financial aid policies *before* you apply.

Don't hang back waiting to be admitted to a college before filing your financial aid request forms. Too many beginners make this mistake.

One explanation may be that students worry that the money-first, enrollment-second formula is asking for rejection. Maybe so, if you're applying to the small but growing number of financially stretched colleges where paying customers get the sunny front rooms while financial aid basket cases get the gate.

By contrast, most schools still look at other factors — the whole you — before finding out if you come with cash-batteries included.

Another reason not to wait for admission before pursuing financial aid is that a college's admission timeline and its financial aid timeline are not necessarily entwined.

Take steps to be present and accounted for when the money is handed out:

- ✔ For payment purposes, obtain financial aid information and respond on the financial aid timeline.
- ✔ For enrollment purposes, obtain admission information and respond on the admission timeline.

Refusing to Spend Cash on the College Scholarship Service Profile

In Chapter 3, we describe the CSS Profile application form that many select private colleges require you to fill out before they award financial aid. Even when you're tired of scribbling on forms, the request for Profile data is one you can't afford to ignore.

Typically, expensive schools require the Profile. It costs you about $20 to provide a Profile application to each school you select that uses this form. So, if you apply to six high-cost schools, you pay about $120 for Profile application processing.

When they hear the cost, students may say they can't pay the processing fee, so they don't apply to the Profile-requiring schools. Big mistake in flashing lights and buzzing bells. If payment is a problem, ask your guidance counselor for a fee waiver for at least one of the schools of choice. Then pay the processing fees and get on with the task of looking for college money — you'll get a gigantic return on your investment. If any one of the Profile-using colleges comes through for you, you're looking at a swap of about $120 for a return of more than $25,000 for a year's cost of attendance or more than $100,000 for a degree.

Think of it this way: One Profile fee is the cost of two big pizzas. Don't eat pizza this month.

Applying Too Late for Mid-Year Aid

When you plan to start college in mid-year or to transfer in mid-year, apply for financial aid as if you're starting in the fall semester. Here are the reasons:

- ✔ You must meet deadlines; January to April deadlines won't reopen to accommodate your later start.
- ✔ You must reserve money before it's all given away for the year.

When you receive an award letter, all you need to do is indicate that you're accepting for the mid-year term. If you wait until the fall to apply for the spring or mid-year, you'll probably get only federal loan money and perhaps a Pell grant. You may not get free money from your state, your college, or private scholarships.

Misunderstanding Your SAR

Part I of your Student Aid Report (SAR) contains a letter explaining what you need to do to receive aid. Often, the SAR says, "Based on this information, it appears that you are not eligible to receive a Federal Pell Grant."

This is the point at which some students go wrong. They interpret the sentence to mean "It appears that you are not eligible to receive financial aid for college." Nope, that's not what it means.

Think of a suit with lots of pockets. The correct interpretation of the SAR statement is that you cannot receive aid out of the Pell grant "pocket." You may be able to receive aid from the state's pocket, the college's pocket, the federal government's loan pocket, or some other pocket. You just won't get money out of the pocket marked "Federal Pell Grant."

Not Bringing Your SAR Up to Par

Dragging your feet on reviewing your initial SAR for errors — especially in your Social Security number, correct listing of colleges, and the first bachelor's degree statement — can cause lots of problems:

✔ Check your Social Security number. If it's wrong on your SAR, you'll be missing in action in a college's financial aid office because that's how the office keeps track of you. If the office can't find you on the computer, you don't exist on campus.

✔ Make sure that all the colleges you've targeted are listed on your SAR. If a school is missing, call the Federal Student Aid Information Center (800-433-3243) to report the omission. The center will ask for your SAR's release number located in the top-right corner of the front page, so have it ready. If a school doesn't get your SAR, you don't get the money at that school.

✔ Review to see if you made a mistake by saying that you did "receive your first bachelor's degree." Amazingly, many students think that a high school diploma is a first bachelor's degree. If you already have a first bachelor's degree, you automatically become ineligible for Federal Pell Grants, Federal Supplemental Educational Opportunity Grants, and most state grants. Wow, what a mistake!

Correct your SAR and get the aid for which you qualify.

Skipping Verification Paperwork

Colleges, by federal regulation, are required to verify by random sample the eligibility for 30 percent of the students filing for aid.

That's why colleges send students a standard verification form that requires them to identify each family member listed as a household resident and any untaxed income, as well as submit the student's and parents' tax forms and W-2 statements.

Many families pitch a fit because they believe they're being audited in the same way that the IRS audits taxes. Wrong. A verification is not an audit; instead, it's an effort to provide quality control to the financial aid process.

Not infrequently, the student or parents did err in completing their paperwork with the outcome that they become more, not less, eligible for aid.

Don't sweat verification. You can't prevent it, and it may actually do you some good. On the downside, if you fail to respond to the verification process when asked, you can kiss your federal aid goodbye.

Mixing Up Transcripts

Still another federal regulation can pop up and bite you in the aid. College financial aid offices often can't award federal money to students who have previously attended a postsecondary institution until the FAT (Financial Aid Transcript — see Chapter 3) is received from the previous college(s). The FAT maybe required even if you never received financial aid in the past.

When a student with selective listening skills hears the question "Have you submitted your Financial Aid Transcript," that student may hear only the word *transcript*. The student says, "Sure, I had the registrar at my last school send that already," when what was really sent was the academic transcript.

An academic transcript reports grades; a Financial Aid Transcript reports money.

Realize that your aid may be held for ransom until your college receives your Financial Aid Transcript(s).

Not Saying Yes to All Colleges

Accepting or regretting college offers is not akin to accepting or regretting social invitations. You are polite when you quickly turn down parties that you're pretty sure you won't attend. You are foolish when you quickly turn down colleges that you're pretty sure you won't attend.

Say yes to all offers. Yes, *all* offers! You can sort them out later. You may have to appeal for more aid later, but right now, accept what the school has offered.

You need time to sit back, weigh your offers, and make your decisions. Saying no too quickly leads to aid gone astray because someone else received the money you threw away.

Taking Automatic Renewal for Granted

It took you a whole year to get the kinks out of your understanding of financial aid, and now you have to start again for the second year.

Too bad — but financial aid, unlike admissions, is not automatically re-newed. Financial aid is an annual event.

Pick up financial aid packets from your college's financial aid office to continue or initiate awards for next year. A number of colleges do in fact initiate aid renewals automatically, but they have no responsibility if your renewal slips between the cracks.

One lucky little reminder: The federal government sends out renewal FAFSAs (which are really SARs from the previous year in disguise) to cue you that the time is here to start the process all over again. Flash — renewal FAFSAs are now on the Web. See Chapters 3 and 20 for details about using use the online FAFSA option.

Not Reapplying after a Turndown

Just because you didn't get federal money or a state scholarship one year doesn't mean you're ineligible forever. Eligibility can boomerang as a result of changes in income, parents' marital status, revisions in assets and savings, a sibling entering college, fresh money in a college's resources, and even because the student and parents have learned to play the financial aid game better.

Don't confuse advice to keep trying for federal and state aid with the advice in Chapter 26: "Zero aid now, zero aid later." This observation relates to the college's own aid. For institutional scholarships, you may not get aid after your first year if you weren't awarded aid as an incoming student.

Work to avoid flubs that will certainly leave you flabby in the financial aid department. The exercise of planning helps all your moves. It's like lifting weights on the inside.

Chapter 28

Ten Ways to Avoid Financial Aid Fakes and Frauds

In This Chapter

▶ Spotting the biggest, baddest scams

▶ Believing "free money" promises can cost you

*M*ost phony financial aid operators are true scam artists, but few may just be seriously incompetent entrepreneurs who mean well but victimize you with their ineptitude (see Chapter 14). No matter, these tricksters fool even the smartest people with a rich variety of come-ons, including the "satisfied customer" testimonial that invites you to get yours. Like this:

Ann Smith won $499,000 in scholarships; so can you!

Who is Ann Smith? Ann Smith may be a figment of the scam artist's imagination. Or Ann Smith may be the lead charlatan's kid sister. Don't be taken in by the testimonial fakery of financial aid fraud artists who promise collegiate versions of get-rich-quick schemes.

Their scams pull in large fees that range between $500 and $1,500 for information — often worthless — that you can get elsewhere for free.

Undeniably, finding money to help you pay for college does cost something, if only postage, paper, and your Internet bill. Nevertheless, you shouldn't need financial aid just to apply for financial aid. To help you spot the differences between legitimate services and bottom-feeders, we've compiled this list of ten scams and signs of scams.

Recognize Low-Life Lingo

Knowing financial aid frauds' hallmark jargon can spare you a wasted expense. Examine the service's sales pitch for any version of the following:

- ✔ *The scholarship is guaranteed or your money back.*
- ✔ *We just need your credit card or bank account number to hold this award.*
- ✔ *Just give all your information; we do all the work.*
- ✔ *I can get anyone financial aid.*
- ✔ *You can't get this information anywhere else.*
- ✔ *Act now; awards are disappearing fast.*
- ✔ *$6.6 million in scholarship funds go unused each year.*

The last claim about unused scholarships has a kernel of truth. The problem is that unused scholarships are usually reserved for children and/or employees of a given corporation or some other requirement — such as being a left-handed, Irish-Mexican, first son whose major is Russian literature at an Ivy League university — that you can't fulfill.

What abuses does this low-life lingo lead to? Once you fork over money for a scholarship search or help, scam artists may use your credit card number for unauthorized purchases and debits to your account. Or if you pay by check, a scamster may use your bank account number and forge checks to withdraw funds. When you're uncertain but decide to go ahead, the best way to pay is by money order.

Be Clear-Eyed about Free Seminars

If you open your mail to find an invitation to a free financial aid seminar or counseling help for assistance, be aware that the seminar may really be a sales pitch for investment and insurance products. These are not scams unless the providers imply that you have to purchase a financial product before you become eligible for student aid.

Other free seminars are staged by unsavory promoters pretending to be financial aid consulting services that seek unreasonable heavy fees (such as $200 a quarter to "guarantee" scholarship money, which is nonsense). Or they want to sell you overpriced computerized scholarship search services (free Web-based scholarship databases have overtaken commercial scholarship services). Or they are peddling overpriced student loans.

Some scholarship groups really turn up the heat in pressuring you to sign up right now by insisting that you have only a few days to do so, or you'll lose your scholarship. Or they claim you have only a few days to agree before all the deadlines are missed for applying for financial aid. Some may call in the late spring and summer to claim that as you didn't get enough aid from your school and they can provide you a "guaranteed" scholarship for the fall.

Nuggets of useful truth may emerge from free seminars. But don't sign anything on the spot before you check things out.

Pay an Application Fee? For What?

Some scholarship programs charge an application fee. Avoid these people.

Paying money to get money usually means no money.

Scholarship swindlers pull a disappearing act after they've skimmed enough money, but long before they've accumulated a significant number of complaints with a local Better Business Bureau and moved on only to operate under another name. Others get your bank account or credit card number, lay low, and make an unauthorized withdrawal when you're not looking.

Say Phooey to Phony Processing Fees

Frauds may require a "setup" fee *in advance* to process your loan application. Other in-advance phoney-balonies are "application fee," "origination fee," and "insurance fee." Real loan providers charge origination and insurance fees at the time you get their money, not before. They often deduct those charges from your award.

Duck Dubious Guarantees

Tricky scholarship "consultants" often "guarantee" their services, claiming you'll win a scholarship or get your money back. (They don't say what year you'll get it back.) They usually get you to okay some fine print that only promises to *match* you to sources — the rest is up to you.

Some "guarantees" are even more fraudulent. The guarantee promises you $100 to $3,000 or a U.S. Savings Bond providing you can *prove* you were turned down by every scholarship address the search service provides.

No matter how good the database, for a consumer to hear back from each scholarship sponsor to which the consumer wrote for an application is virtually unheard of. Add the no-reply factor to the probability that many of the addresses are bad to begin with, and you understand why a consumer can never prove he or she was turned down by 100 percent of the potential scholarship givers.

When a third party claims it can guarantee someone else's money, this is a serious sign of a scam. The only person or group that can guarantee anything is the person or group that is giving away the money.

Don't Ring Costly 900 Numbers

The prefixes 900 and 976 cost you dollars per minute just for talking — or listening to some scammer's long-winded spiel. Legitimate programs typically have a toll-free 800 or 888 number or a straightforward telephone number beginning with the area code.

Even a few supposedly toll-free 800 or 888 numbers are programmed to switch you over to a fee-charging 900 number after you're connected; the law requires that the caller be notified when this happens, so listen carefully to what is said when you call an 800 or 888 number.

One more comment about 800 or 888 numbers that really are toll-free: Don't assume an 800 number is a sign of a reputable scholarship service. Anyone can arrange for an 800 or 888 line.

Avoid Quirky Contests

Some scammers publicize contests that exact an entry fee. Others require specific research or information as an entry requirement for a chance to win a scholarship, such as a law essay, which is a cheap way to collect legal documentation. Another example: A magazine asks students to submit articles for its first issue on speculation. The purpose is to avoid paying for freelance work. Adding insult to injury, the magazine charges each entrant $15 for the submission.

Don't Pay for Free Information

Some tricksters get you to pay for database access that you can get for free in high school counseling offices and college financial aid offices. For example, California college financial aid offices connect students with a Pell grant database; some proprietary services, however, try to charge you for this access.

Many schools offer services like the College Board's Fund Finder, which may give you more listings than you'll ever have time to write to.

Upshot: Private financial aid services that claim to link you to private organizations have the same access to the same databases as your school guidance or financial aid office.

Spot Phony Consultants

A real dramatist, this fraud peddler poses like a real expert, charges you a consulting fee, and offers you empty advice. See Chapter 14 for ways to scope out the real experts.

Heed These Red Flags

Any of the following red flags may be the tip-off to a less-than-honest organization. The more signals you get, the more tightly you should hold onto your wallet:

- **The mail-drop address.** Good private financial aid counselors usually list a street address on their letterhead. Some tricksters try to disguise a box number as a suite number. This masquerade could be the tip-off to a fraud. At press time, postal authorities are requiring that a private mailbox be designated "PMB" followed by the box number, as in Name, PMB000, street address, city, state, and zip code. But protest by private mailbox holders has prompted a Congressional bill to cancel this policy.

- **Official looking name or logo.** Take notice of official-looking promotional literature. The organization or implied government agency may not exist. A flyer for "The National Federation for Free Money," complete with a federal-like insignia and seal, could be too good to be true. In fact, we made up the name. This is an old scam, but it pops up every few years.

- **Notification by telephone or e-mail.** Beware the telephone call or e-mail message urging you to apply for a given scholarship. There's usually a catch that costs. Real scholarship providers are so swamped with requests that they don't have the time or need to contact potential recipients who have not applied.

- **A super-easy entry.** One scam organization mailed thousands of postcards to senior high school students, promising free money. The scammers also pulled most of the other fake deals mentioned in this chapter.

✔ The scammers' real agenda was to obtain credit card and checking account numbers from money-hungry students, who bit on the fraud and expected financial aid checks in return for handing over their fiscal information.

✔ What the students actually received — if anything at all — was a hodgepodge listing rife with outdated, misaddressed, and nonrelevant organizations, plus a whopping $175 in credit card charges.

Never believe a hoaxer who claims that landing financial aid is so easy that simple contact information will be enough to make a total stranger hand you greenbacks. Scholarship sponsors always want specific and personal data, such as hobbies, memberships, fields of study, personal statements, achievements, and honors.

Don't Think You're Too Smart to Get Fooled

Hundreds of intelligent — even brilliant — students each year get taken in by obvious scams because they're desperate to enter college or pay off debts.

Angela (not her real name), a Washington, DC, graduate English student, confessed that when she was a month away from her baccalaureate (*cum laude*, *with a specialty in critical thinking*), she handed over 50 hard-earned dollars to a complete stranger who promised her substantial graduate grants. She never heard from the stranger again — and she learned a critical lesson in thinking.

Check it out

When you have doubts about an offering, you can check it out with the following:

✔ **National Fraud Information Center**
P.O.Box 65868
Washington, DC 20035
800-876-7060 or 202-835-0159
www.fraud.org

✔ **Federal Trade Commission "Scholar Scam"**
P.O. Box 99-6
Washington, DC 20050
202-FTC-HELP (382-4357)
TDD (202) 326-2502
202-326-3128
www.ftc.gov

Resource Guide

· ·

In This Guide
▶ Pages and pages of the best scholarships
▶ Awards listed by convenient categories
▶ Glossary
▶ Sample forms

· ·

*O*nce upon a time in a decade far, far away, the 1980s, Mike Hayes graduated from Rochelle (Illinois) High School wondering how he could come up with the $28,000 he needed to attend four years at the University of Illinois.

Then Mike had a brainstorm — why not go after 2.8 million pennies from heaven? Why not just ask people around the country to each send him a penny? Mike wrote a syndicated newspaper columnist asking the columnist to publish a nationwide plea for one-cent donations. Readers responded with vigor — some even sent donations up to $100. When the story appeared in *People* magazine, Mike had received more than 77,000 letters containing in excess of $26,000.

The idea probably wouldn't work the second time around, so don't try it. Go after free money scholarships instead!

Scholarships by the Score

As you review the following scholarships, refer to your *Personal Financial Aid Inventory* (see Chapter 10) to make sure that you don't have to pinch pennies because you missed a money tree.

The following awards are only a fraction of the nation's 300,000 scholarship pool. But they are substantial and worth going after. Categories include the following:

✔ Academic achievement and leadership

✔ College major or career objective

✔ Organizations (whose members are students or parents)

✔ Individuals with disabilities

- ✔ Heritage
- ✔ Minorities
- ✔ Religious affiliations
- ✔ Women

ACADEMIC, MERIT, LEADERSHIP

Bard College

Annandale-on-Hudson, NY 12504
V: 914-758-6822
No. Awards: varies
Award Amount: varies
Deadline: February 15
Features: Bard college will give first year students who rank in the top ten of their high school class a discount on tuition. These students will be charged only as much tuition as they would have paid had they gone to their state-supported school. Each student must maintain a "B" average in college.

Duluth Superior Area Community Foundation (See Local-Minnesota)

Elks National Foundation

2750 North Lakeview Avenue
Chicago, IL 60612-1889
V: 773-755-4728
I: www.elks.org
No. Awards: 1,300
Award Amount:
National: two $30,000; two $16,000; two $12,000; 494 $4,000
State: 1,585 $800 (renewable for all four years)
Deadline: January 15
Features: High school seniors who are U.S. citizens and have an interest in furthering their education. Must have financial need. Applicant must be in the top 5 percent of senior class. Based on leadership abilities.

International Brotherhood of Teamsters (See Organizations)

Jostens Foundation Leader Scholarship Program

Citizen's Scholarship Foundation of America
P.O. Box 297
St. Peter, Minnesota 56082
V: 507-931-1682
No. Awards: 200
Award Amount: $1,000
Funds Available: $200,000
Deadline: Dec. 10
Features: Graduating high school seniors who demonstrate good leadership abilities. Also open to students in U.S. territories and Department of Defense schools.

Long and Foster Scholarship Program (See Local-Washington, D.C.)

Meliora Grant (See Local-California)

National Association of Secondary School Principals (NASSP)

Department of Student Activities
1904 Association Drive
Reston, VA 22091
V: 703-860-0200

National Honor Society Scholarship Awards Program
No. Awards: 250
Award Amount: $1,000
Funds Available: Approximately $250,000
Deadline: January 28
Features: High school seniors who are members of NHS. Must have high class rank and GPA. Applicant must also send transcript, writing sample, and recommendations with application. Scholarship packets are mailed to NHS Adviser in November. National Selection Committee convenes in April, and winners are announced in May.

Principals Leadership Award (PLA)
No. Awards: 150
Funds Available: $1,000
Deadline: December 10
Features: One student from the senior class of each school is nominated by the principal. All school winners receive a certificate of merit and are considered semifinalists. At the national level, school winners compete on the basis of their application. Scholarship packets are mailed to principal in October. National Selection Committee convenes in February and winners are announced by NASSP in April in conjunction with National Student Leadership Week.

North Dakota Merit Scholarship Program (See Local-North Dakota)

Soroptimist Foundation's Regional Youth Citizenship Awards

2 Penn Center, Suite 1000
Philadelphia, PA 19102-7508
V: 215-557-9300
I: www.soroptomist.org
No. Awards: 50 regional awards, one international award
Award Amount: $1,250 one international award is $2,000.
Funds Available: $300,000
Deadline: December 15
Features: Students are selected who have been recommended for this award based on the student's service, dependability, leadership, and sense of purpose. Academic criteria such as grades, SAT scores, class rank, or GPA are not considered for this award.

State of Iowa Merit Scholarship Program (See Local-Iowa)

The Toyota Community Scholars Program

Toyota Motor Sales, USA Inc.
19011 South Western Avenue
P.O. Box 2991
Torrance, CA 90509-2991
V: 310-618-4459 or 310-618- 4167
No. Awards: 100
Award Amount: $10,000-$20,000, renewable
Deadline: December 1

Features: High school applicants should have a consistent record of academic excellence, be active in school programs, and be recognized as a leader by his/her peers and instructors. Applicants must be actively involved in a service program that addresses a school or community need. This is a merit scholarship and demonstrated financial need is not a prerequisite. Notification is made in April.

Tylenol Scholarship Program

Tylenol Scholarship Fund
Citizens Scholarship Foundation
of America, Inc.
1505 Riverview Rd., P.O. Box 88
St. Peter, MN 56082
V: 507-931-1682
No. Awards: 510
Award Amount: (500) $1,000, (10) $10,000
Funds Available: $600,000
Deadline: January 15
Features: The awards are given to undergraduates who are first-year students, sophomores, and juniors or who will be enrolled at an undergraduate institution in the fall. Students must be U.S citizens or permanent residents. These scholarships are awarded based on transcript, academic achievement, school and community leadership activities, and personal statement.

Urban League Scholar (See Organizations)

U.S. Senate Youth Program

The William Randolph Hearst Foundation
90 New Montgomery St., Suite 1212
San Francisco, CA 94105-4504
V: 415-543- 4057 or 800-841-7048
No. Awards: 2 or more per state for a total of 104
Award Amount: $2,000
Funds Available: varies
Deadline: Sept./Oct., but actual date varies by state
Features: High school junior or senior elected to a student office. Must attend public or private school in state where parent or guardian legally resides. Permanent residents of the United States only. Also open to U.S. students attending Department of Defense schools overseas. This scholarship is based on leadership abilities.

AGRICULTURE/ HORTICULTURE/ EVIRONMENT

California Farm Bureau Federation (See Local-California)

Cargill, Inc.

Cargill, Inc.
P.O. Box 9300
Minneapolis, MN 55440
V: 612-742-6201

Cargill Community Scholarship
No. Awards: 150
Award Amount: $1,000
Funds Available: $150,000
Deadline: Feb. 15, postmarked
Features: High school seniors who are U.S. citizens and are enrolling for two to four years in vocational schools, universities, and colleges. Students must live within communities where Cargill has a facility. Recipients of this scholarship get $200 for their school library.

Cargill Scholarship for Rural America
No. Awards: 250
Award Amount: $1,000
Funds Available: 250,000
Deadline: Feb. 15, postmarked
Features: High school seniors who are U.S. citizens from farm families. Applicant must be enrolling in two- or four-year colleges or vocational schools.

Moorman Scholarships in Agriculture

Moorman Manufacturing Company (MMC)
Contact the Dean's office at your university or College of Agriculture
No. Awards: 93
Award Amount: $1,000, renewable
Funds Available: varies
Deadline: varies with each college
Features: Applicant must be interested in pursuing careers in agriculture.

National Council of State Garden Clubs Scholarships

National Council of State Garden Clubs, Inc.
4401 Magnolia Avenue
St. Louis, MO 63110-3492
V: 314-776-7574
No. Awards: 32

Award Amount: $3,500
Funds Available: over $112,000
Deadline: March 1
Features: Applicants must be junior or senior undergraduates and graduate students majoring in horticulture, floriculture, forestry, landscape design, botany, biology, plant pathology, agronomy, environmental concerns, city planning, land management, and/or allied subjects. Applicants must apply through state where they are permanent residents. Students must be nominated by home state's Garden Club and enrolled at a four-year institution, maintaining a minimum 3.0 GPA.

Rockefeller State Wildlife Scholarship (See Local-Louisiana)

APPLIED SCIENCES/ AUTOMOTIVE

Automotive Educational Fund

Automotive Hall of Fame, Inc.
21400 Oakwood Blvd.
Dearborn, MI 48124-4078
V: 313-240-4000
No. Awards: varies
Award Amount: $250-$2,000
Deadline: June 30
Features: Applicants must be in undergraduate degree programs and sincerely interested in pursuing automotive careers. Scholarships are awarded to candidates who are at least sophomores in college, although they may apply in their freshman year. Students must be enrolled full-time (minimum of 12 credit hours per term) for the full year. Financial need is considered but is not necessary. Students may apply for a scholarship at any time after January 1. Only one graduate scholarship is available at the University of Michigan. Most of the available scholarships are designated for undergraduate upperclassmen.

DeVry Institute of Technology

Contact the Director of Admissions at the nearest DeVry Institute, located in Phoenix, AZ; Fremont, Long Beach, and Pomona, CA; Alpharetta and Decatur, GA; Chicago and DuPage, IL; Kansas City, MO;

Long Island City, NY; North Brunswick, NJ; Columbus, OH; Dallas TX, and in Canada: Calgary, AB, and Mississauga and Scarborough, ON

DeVry Institute Bachelor's Degree Scholarships
No. Awards: 36
Award Amount: up to $14,510, renewable
Deadline: continuous

Features: Applicants must be students who have completed associate's degree to begin study at DeVry. Students must be enrolled in technical institutions and maintain a minimum GPA of 3.3. For study in electronic engineering technology, technology management, computer information, business, telecommunications, or accounting. Open to non-U.S. citizens.

DeVry Scholarships
Contact high school guidance counselor or the director of Admissions at the DeVry Institute you plan to attend.
No. Awards: 120
Award Amount: $8,263-$29,685, renewable
Deadline: March 18
Features: Applicant must be a high school graduate and begin studies at a U.S. DeVry Institute the same year. Student must be a U.S. citizen or permanent resident. Minimum SAT scores is 530 Math and 270 Verbal. Minimum ACT score is 22.

Fred Duesenberg Memorial Scholarship (Car Restoration)

McPherson College
1600 E. Euclid
P.O. Box 1402
McPherson, KS 67460
V: 316-241-0731
I: www.mcpherson.edu
No. Awards: varies
Award Amount: varies
Deadline: May 1
Features: Contact the college department of restoration technology for dates and criteria for this scholarship created by TV personality Jay Leno, that awards one all-expenses paid scholarship for a second-year auto restoration student at McPherson College. McPherson College is the only college in the U.S. that offers an associate degree program in car restoration technology.

ARTS

ARTS — Arts Recognition and Talent Search of the National Foundation for Advancement in the Arts

800 Brickell Avenue, Suite 500
Miami, FL 33137
V: 305-377-1140
T: 800-970-ARTS
I: www.nfaa.org
No. Awards: varies
Award Amount: varies
Funds Available: Scholarships totaling approximately $3 million; cash awards totaling approximately $300,000 (1st Place: $3,000; 2nd Place: $1,500; 3rd Place: $1,000)
Deadline: June 1, early; October 1, regular deadline
Features: High school seniors or 17- or 18-year-olds as of December 1 of the year of application. U.S. citizens or permanent residents only (except for ARTS Jazz applicants, who are accepted internationally). Open to U.S. citizens studying abroad. Based on dance, music, music/jazz, theater, visual arts, writing, photography, and voice. Applicants who are in the advanced level will attend a final judging session in Miami, Florida, at all expenses paid.

Association/International Thespian Society

Director of Festival and Convention
International Thespian Society
2343 Auburn Ave.
Cincinnati, OH 45219
V: 513-421-3900
No. Awards: 10
Award Amount: $1,500
Funds Available: $15,000
Deadline: May 15
Features: Scholarships are sponsored by the Educational Theatre Association. The scholarship is based on the applicants' thespian ability including acting, interviewing with the judges, and activity with a thespian club while in high school. A GPA of 2.7 is required for entry, but academic record is not part of the judging.

The Elizabeth Greenshields Foundation Grants

1814 Sherbrooke Street West, Suite 1
Montreal, Quebec H3H 1E4 Canada
V: 514-937-9225
I: egreen@total.net
No. Awards: 40-50
Award Amount: $10,000 Canadian funds
Funds Available: Approximately $500,000
Deadline: none

Features: The purpose of the Foundation is to aid talented artists in the early stages of their careers. Awards are limited to candidates working in the following: painting, drawing, printmaking and/or sculpting — abstract or non-representational art is precluded by the terms of the Foundation's charter. Applicants must have already started or completed training in an established school of art and/or demonstrate, through past work and future plans, a commitment to making art a lifetime career. Open to nationals of any country, without regard to age, sex, color, religion, or ethnicity. The foundation is not a school and does not conduct any classes. Applicants may write or call. This scholarship is worldwide and there is no age limit.

Longy School of Music Scholarship

Longy School of Music
One Follen Street
Cambridge, MA 02138
V: 617-876-0956 ext. 530
I: www.longy.edu
No. Awards: approximately 95 (which is about 80 percent of the students who apply)
Award Amount: up to 75 percent tuition
Funds Available: $350,000
Deadline: March 15

Features: Applicant must be a full-time degree or diploma student (undergraduate or graduate) at the Longy School of Music aiming to study composition, orchestral instruments, piano, voice, opera, organ, early music. Based on financial need, audition, perfor-

mance experience, and academic background. Nationality and residency unrestricted.

National Scholarship Trust Fund of the Graphic Arts

Graphic Arts Technical Foundation
200 Deer Run Road
Sewickley, PA 15143
V: 412-741-6860
No. Grants: 356
Award Amount: $500-$1,500, renewable
Deadline: March 1 for high school students, April 1 for undergraduates
Features: Full-time students who are U.S. citizens and are interested in graphic arts careers; minimum GPA 3.0.

ATHLETICS/GOLF

FINA/Dallas Morning News All- State Scholar-Athlete Team Scholarship (See Local-Texas)

Francies Ouimet Scholarship Fund

190 Park Road
Weston, MA 02193
V: 781-891-6400
No. Awards: varies
Award Amount: $500-$5,000
Funds Available: varies
Deadline: December 1
Features: This four-year renewable scholarship is for students who work three years in Massachusetts as caddies, or in pro shops or golf course operations. This scholarship is not for persons who are golfers. Applicants who do not meet the basic criteria for eligibility as described will not be given a reply.

Gloria Fecht Memorial Scholarship Fund (See Women)

Golf Course Superintendents Association of America

1421 Research Park Drive
Lawrence, KS 66046-3859
V: 785-832-4445 or 800-472-7878 Ext: 622

CSAA Legacy Award
No. Awards: 10
Award Amount: $1,500
Funds Available: varies

Deadline: April 15

Features: Applicants must be children or grandchildren of GCSAA members who have been active for five or more consecutive years. Students must be studying a field unrelated to golf course management. Applicants must be enrolled full-time at an accredited institution of higher learning, or in the case of high school seniors, must have been accepted at such an institution for the next academic year.

GCSAA Scholars Program
No. Awards: varies
Award Amount: $500-$3,500
Funds Available: varies
Deadline: June 1
Features: Applicants must be outstanding graduate or undergraduate students who are planning careers as golf course superintendents. Applicants must be enrolled in a recognized undergraduate program in a major field related to golf/turf management. Undergraduate applicants must have successfully completed at least 24 credit hours or the equivalent of one year of full-time study in an appropriate major.

GCSAA Watson Fellowships
No. Awards: varies
Award Amount: $5,000
Funds Available: varies
Deadline: Oct. 1
Features: Applicants must be aiming towards master's and doctoral degrees in fields related to golf course management. The goal of this program is to identify tomorrow's leading teachers and researchers.

The Scotts Company Scholars Program
No. Awards: varies
Award Amount: $500-$2,500
Funds Available: varies
Deadline: March 8
Features: Students are selected for paid summer internships and an opportunity to compete for a limited number of financial aid awards. Applicants must be pursuing careers in the greens industry and be graduating high school seniors, or collegiate freshmen, sophomores, or juniors who have been accepted at an accredited university, college, or junior college for the next academic year. One of the primary goals of the program is to seek promising students from diverse ethnic, cultural, and socioeconomic backgrounds.

Women's Western Golf Foundation Scholarship (See Women)

BUSINESS

Appraisal Institute Education Trust Scholarship

Appraisal Institute Education Trust
875 North Michigan Avenue, Suite 2400
Chicago, IL 60611-1980
V: 312-335-4100
I: www.realworks.com/ai
No. Awards: 30
Award Amount: $2,000-$3,000
Deadline: March 15
Features: Applicants must be graduate or undergraduate students majoring in real estate appraisals, land economics, real estate, or allied fields. Minimum 3.5 GPA required. Applicant must be enrolled at a two-year or four-year institution. U.S. citizens only. Applicants may reapply.

Burlington Northern Sanat Fe Foundation Scholarship (See Minorities)

John L. Carey Scholarship

American Institute of Certified Public Accountants
1211 Avenue of the Americas
New York, NY 10036
V: 212-596-6221
I: www.aicpa.rg
No. Awards: 5
Award Amount: $5,000
Funds Available: $25,000
Deadline: April 1
Features: Liberal arts degree holders who have been accepted, or are in the process of applying, to a graduate program in accounting that will allow them to take CPA examination at an institution where the business administration program is accredited by the AACSB or ACBSP. Renewable for one year, provided satisfactory scholastic progress is maintained.

Duracell Scholarship and Internship Program (See Minorities)

Executive Women International Scholarship Program

Executive Women International
515 South 700 East, Suite 2E
Salt Lake City, UT 84102
V: 801-355-2800
I: www.excecutivewomen.org
No. Awards: 130
Award Amount: up to $10,000
Deadline: March 1
Features: Applicants must reside within the boundaries of one of the 34 participating chapters, enter that local contest, and be available for interview. Applicants must be high school juniors enrolling at a four-year institution. Students must be planning careers in any business or professional field of study that requires a four-year degree. Include self-addressed, stamped envelope for application forms.

Harry A. Applegate DECA Scholarship Award

Distributive Education Clubs of America (DECA)
1908 Association Drive
Reston, VA 20191
V: 703-860-5000
No. Awards: 30-40
Award Amount: $1,000
Deadline: 2nd Monday of March of each year
Features: Active DECA member pursuing full-time, two- or four-year study in marketing, merchandising, or management in an accredited institution offering those programs of study. This scholarship is based on merit.

IMA/Stuart Cameron and Margaret McLeod (SCMS) Society Student Scholarship

Institute of Management Accountants
10 Paragon Drive
Montvale, NJ 07645-1760
T: 800-638-4427
I: www.imanet.org
No. Awards: 38
Award Amount: $2,000 - $3,000
Deadline: February 1
Features: Applicants must have junior, senior, or master's degree enrollment status majoring in financial management, management, or accounting.

National Society of Accountants Scholarship Foundation

1010 North Fairfax Street
Alexandria, VA 22314
V: 703-549-6400
I: www.nsacct.org
No. Awards: 30
Award Amount: $500-$1,000, renewable
Deadline: March 10
Features: Applicant must enroll in college as an accounting major. U.S. or Canadian citizens must be enrolled in a U.S. school. Maintaining a B average is prerequisite for scholarship renewal.

State Farm Companies Foundation Exceptional Student Fellowship

State Farm Companies Foundation
One State Farm Plaza, SC-3
Bloomington, IL 61710-0001
V: 309-766-2039
No. Awards: 50
Award Amount: $3,000
Deadline: Feb. 15
Features: At time of application, student must be enrolled full-time in college with junior or senior status. Applicants must be majoring in a business-related discipline or computer science with a GPA of 3.60. Applicants must be U.S. citizens who are nominated by the head or dean of the department or school. Application requests should be made between November 1 and February 1.

COMMUNICATIONS

Academy Foundation of the Academy of Motion Picture Arts and Sciences

Academy of Motion Picture Arts and Sciences Student Academy Awards
8949 Wilshire Boulevard
Beverly Hills, CA 90211-1972
V: 310-247-3059
No. Awards: up to 12
Award Amount: $1,000 - $2,000 nonrenewable
Deadline: April 1
Features: Applicants must be majoring in communications or film-making. Eligible applicants must have made a dramatic/documentary/or animated film of up to 60 minutes within the structured curriculum of the accredited college or university.

The American Legion National High School Oratorical Contest

National Americanism Commission
P.O. Box 1055
Indianapolis, IN 46206
V: 317-630-1249
I: www.legion.org
No. Awards: 57
Award Amounts: (54) $1,500.
State, county, and local scholarships,
(one) $18,000; (one) $16,000; (one) $14,000
Funds Available: $129,000
Features: Students in 9th-12th grades who
are less than 20 years of age (as of the
national contest date); U.S. citizens only.
Also open to U.S. students studying abroad
(in some locations). On the contest date,
which varies, students must demonstrate
great public speaking abilities and prepare
speeches on an assigned topic. Students
should contact the local American Legion
post or the above address.

Broadcast Education Association National Scholarships

1771 N. Street NW
Washington, DC 20036-2891
V: 202-429-5354
I: www.beaweb.org or
fweaver@nab.org
No. Awards: 15
Award Amount: $1,250 to $3,000, not
renewable
Funds Available: $33,000
Deadline: January 15
Features: Applicants must be full-time
college students ready for the junior,
senior, or graduate level and enrolled at
accredited colleges or universities where
at least one department is a BEA institutional member. Students must show
potential to be outstanding media
professionals and make superior academic
progress. Awards must be used exclusively
for college costs. Winners are announced
each spring.

Chicago Association of Black Journalists Scholarship (See Minorities)

Community College Scholarship (See Local-California)

Cox Enterprises Scholarship

National Association of Hispanic
Journalists
1193 National Press Building
Washington, DC 20045
V: 202-662-7178
No. Awards: 6
Award Amount: $1,000
Funds Available: $6,000
Deadline: Feb. 28
Features: Full-time student with academic
excellence and a demonstrated interest in
journalism career. Open to high school
seniors, undergraduates, and graduate
level students pursuing careers in
journalism.

Dow Jones Newspaper Fund

P.O. Box 300
Princeton, NJ 08543
V: 609-452-2820 or 800-DOW-FUND
I: www.dowjones.com/newsfund
Business Reporting
No. Awards: 12
Award Amount: paid internship plus
$1,000 scholarship to students returning to
full-time college studies
Deadline: Nov. 15
Features: Must be college sophomores or
juniors in writing field. Business reporting
is open only to minority sophomores and
juniors. Application forms are available
only September 1 to November 1.

Editing Intern Program
No. Awards: up to 100
Award Amount: Summer wages plus
$1,000
Funds Available: varies
Deadline: Nov. 15
Features: U.S. citizen who is or will be full-
time college junior, senior, or graduate
student to work as copy editors at daily
newspapers, on-line newspapers, and
financial news services. Applications are
available Aug. 15 through Nov. 1.

Harold E. Ennes Scholarship Fund

Society of Broadcast Engineers, Inc.
8445 Keystone Crossing, Suite 140
Indianapolis, IN 46240
V: 317-253-1640
I: www.sbe.org (click on ennes button)
No. Awards: up to 2
Award Amount: up to $1,000
Funds Available: varies

Deadline: July 1
Features: Applicants must have a career interest in the technical aspects of broadcasting and must be recommended by two members of the SBE. Preference will be given to members of SBE. Send a self-addressed, stamped envelope for application forms.

Institute for Humane Studies Fellowship

4084 University Dr. Suite 101
Fairfax, VA 22030-6812
V: 703-934-6920
I: www.osfl.gmu.edu/ihs/
No. of Awards: approximately 60
Award Amount: up to $18,500
Deadline: December 31

Features: Applicants may be enrolled in undergraduate or graduate studies majoring in communication, economics, history, humanities, literature, English, writing, political science, or social sciences. Only applicants enrolled at a four-year institution are eligible. U.S. citizenship is not required.

National Scholarship Trust Fund of Graphic Arts Program

200 Deer Run Road
Sewickley, PA 15143
V: 412-741-6860
I: www.gatf.lm.com
No. Awards: 356
Award Amount: $500 - $1,500 renewable
Deadline: March 1 for high school students; April 1 for undergraduate students
Features: Applicants must be first, second, or third year students, enrolled full-time in a two- or four-year college and aiming for a career in graphic communications. U.S. citizenship plus 3.0 GPA required.

The Optimist International Oratorical Contest

Contest Project Coordinator
4494 Lindell Boulevard
St. Louis, MO 63108
V: 314-371-6000 Ext: 228
No. Awards: 108
Award Amount: (54) $1,500 (male students) and (54) $1,500 (female students)

Funds Available: $162,000
Features: This scholarship is based on the applicant's ability to prepare and present a speech within a timed period. Contestants must give a 4-5 minute presentation on a pre-assigned topic. The contest year is October 1 to the next September 30.

Harry S Truman Scholarships

Harry S Truman Scholarship Foundation
712 Jackson Place, NW
Washington, DC 20006
V: 202-395-4831
I: www.truman.gov
No. Awards: 75 to 85
Award Amount: $30,000 for graduate studies
Deadline: Feb. 1
Features: Awarded to college juniors who wish to pursue a career in government or public service. Applicant must attend a four-year institution and be a U.S. citizen. The student must be nominated by a college or university faculty or administrative staff person.

Voice of Democracy Program

VOD Contest
406 West 34th Street
Kansas City, Missouri 64111
V: 816-968-1117
I: www.vfw.org
No. Awards: 56
Award Amount: $1,000-$20,000
Funds Available: up to $132,000
Deadline: Nov. 1
Features: High school students in grades 9 -12 who are U.S. citizens. Applicant must prepare a short patriotic essay. The theme is different each year. Contact local VFW Post to enter.

FOOD SERVICE

Institute of Food Technologists

221 North LaSalle Street, Suite 300
Chicago, IL 60601
V: 312-782-8424
I: pgpagliuco@ift.org

IFT Freshman Scholarship
No. Awards: 16
Award Amount: approximately $1,000 - $5,000

Funds Available: $16,000
Deadline: March 1

Features: Based on academic merit. Must be high school senior or graduate entering college for the first time in a program in food science/technology that meets IFT undergraduate curriculum minimum standards. Nationality unrestricted. Notification is made in April. Applicant must be enrolled in an IFT approved food science program.

IFT Graduate Scholarship
No. Awards: 33
Award Amount: $1,000-$5,000
Funds Available: $96,000
Deadline: Feb./March

Features: Applicant must be graduate student in food science related research. Based on academic merit. Nationality unrestricted.

IFT Junior/Senior Scholarship
No. Awards: 64
Award Amount: $1,000 - $5,000
Funds Available: $72,000
Deadline: Feb. 15
Features: Applicant must be junior or senior in college studying food science/technology that meets IFT undergraduate curriculum minimum standards. Based on academic merit. Nationality unrestricted. Notification April 15. Applicant must be enrolled in an IFT approved food science program.

IFT Sophomore Scholarship
No. Awards: 23
Award Amount: approximately $1,000 - $5,000
Funds Available: varies
Deadline: March 1
Features: Applicant must be sophomore in college studying food science/technology that meets IFT undergraduate curriculum minimum standards. Based on academic merit. Nationality unrestricted. Notification is made in April. Applicant must be enrolled in a IFT approved food science program.

National Restaurant Association Educational Foundation

250 South Wacker Drive, Suite 1400
Chicago, IL 60606-5834
V: 312-715-1010 or 800-765-2122

ProManagement Scholarship
No. Awards: Approximately 120 (up to 5 recipients per school)
Award Amount: $850
Deadline: Nov. 15 and May 1
Features: Applicant must be enrolled in a ProManagement Partner School or in home-study ProManagement course and have successfully completed at least two ProManagement courses. Applications available at school in September and February.

Undergraduate Scholarship
No. Awards: 50
Award Amount: Average award $2,000
Deadline: March 1
Features: Applicant must be a senior in high school with a minimal G.P.A. of 2.75, worked at least 250 hours in the restaurant or hospitality industry, and must be accepted to a hospitality related post-secondary institution.

United Food & Commercial Workers International Union Scholarship

United Food & Commercial Workers International Union
1775 K Street, NW
Washington, DC 20006-1598
V: 202-223-3111
No. Awards: 7
Award Amount: $1,000 renewable for four years
Funds Available: $28,000
Deadline: December 31
Features: Must be high school senior, U.S. citizen, under age 20, and member or child of member of UFCW in good standing for one year. Minimum GPA: 3.5 on a 4.0 scale.

HEALTH

American Association of Critical-Care Nurses (AACN) Educational Advancement Scholarships for Undergraduates

101 Columbia
Aliso Veijo, CA 92656-1491
V: 949-362-2000
I: www.aacn.org
No. Awards: varies
Award Amount: $1,500
Funds Available: varies
Deadline: May 15

Features: Applicants must be current AACN or NSNA members, licensed as registered nurses, enrolled in NLN-accredited baccalaureate degree program in nursing with junior status, have a cumulative GPA of 3.0, and currently work in a critical-care unit or have worked in a critical-care unit for at least one year in the last three years. Previous recipients are eligible to reapply, but may receive no more than a total of $3,000. Members of the Board of Directors, Education Committee, and AACN staff are ineligible. Different awards are available for graduate and BSN students.

American Foundation for Pharmaceutical Education

One Church Street, Suite 202
Rockville, MD 20850
V: 301-738-2160

AAPS-GLAXO-AFPE Gateway Scholarship Program
No. Awards: 4
Award Amount: $5,000
Funds Available: $20,000
Deadline: Jan. 28
Features: Undergraduate in last three years of a B.S. or Pharm. D. program in accredited college of pharmacy or a baccalaureate degree program in a related scientific field of study with at least one full academic year remaining.

GLAXO-WELCOME-AFPE First Year Graduate Scholarship
No. Awards: up to 8 first year graduates
Award Amount: $5,000
Deadline: varies
Features: Final year of pharmacy college degree program or recent pharmacy college graduate and continuing pursuit of graduate or professional degree (not Pharm. D) in pharmaceutical sciences (Ph.D.) but also business administration, law, public health, engineering, and related areas. Applicants must be U.S. citizens or have permanent resident status.

AMBUCS Scholarships

P.O. Box 5127
High Point, NC 27262
V: 336-869-2166
I: www.ambucs.com
No. Grants: Over 400

Award Amount: $500-$1,500, not renewable; one scholarship of $6,000
Funds Available: varies
Deadline: April 15
Features: Applicants must be enrolled in accredited programs in physical therapy, occupational therapy, or speech-hearing. For upperclassmen or graduate students in good scholastic standing (at least 3.0 GPA) who plan to enter clinical therapy in the U.S.; U.S. citizens only; financial need required. Forms must be filed online.

American Business Club Living Endowment Fund

P.O. Box 5127
High Point, NC 27262
V: 336-869-2167
I: www.ambucs.com
No. Awards: varies
Award Amount: $500 - $2,500
Funds Available: $250,000
Deadline: April 15
Features: Applicants must be college juniors, seniors, or graduates in physical therapy, occupational therapy, speech and hearing therapy. Students must be U.S. citizens with a GPA of at least 3.0. Awards are based on financial need, commitment to local community, demonstrated academic accomplishment, compassion integrity, and career objectives. Award winners are announced in June.

Foundation of American College Healthcare Executives Albert W. Dent Student Scholarship (See Minorities)

ADA Dental Assisting Scholarship Program (See Minorities)

ADA Dental Hygiene Scholarship Program (See Minorities)

ADA Dental Laboratory Technology Scholarship (See Minorities)

Dental Student Scholarship Program

ADA Endowment and Assistance Fund, Inc.
211 East Chicago Avenue 17th Floor
Chicago, IL 60611
V: 312-440-2567
No. Awards: 25
Award Amount: $2,500
Deadline: July 31

Features: Entering second year and attending dental school accredited by Commission on Dental Accreditation. A cumulative GPA of 3.0 in required. Must show minimum financial need of $2,500. Notification of scholarship awards is made in the fall.

Foundation of American College Healthcare Executives Foster G. McGaw Student Scholarship

Foundation of American Healthcare Executives
1 North Franklin Street, Suite 1700
Chicago, IL 60606
V: 312-424-2800
No. Awards: varies
Award Amount: $3,000
Deadline: March 31
Features: Applicant must be U.S. or Canadian citizen and a Student Associate of the American College of Healthcare Executives, who is enrolled full time and in good standing in graduate program in healthcare management accredited by any regional accrediting association. Applicant must not be a previous recipient.

National Society, Daughters of American Revolution

1776 D Street NW
Washington, DC 20006
V: 202-879-3292

Irene and Daisy MacGregor Memorial Scholarship
No. Awards: varies
Award Amount: $5,000, renewable
Deadline: April 15

Features: Applicants must be U.S. citizens and obtain a letter of sponsorship from a local DAR chapter. Applicants must be students who have been accepted into or who are pursuing an approved course of study either in psychiatric nursing (graduate level) or studying to become a medical doctor (pre-med does not qualify) at accredited medical schools, colleges, or universities. This application is conducted without regard to race, religion, sex, or national origin. Men also qualify.

Send a self-addressed, stamped envelope for application. Only completed applications submitted in one package will be considered. No records are returned. Annual transcript required for renewal. Notification is made in June.

Alice W. Rooke NSDAR Scholarship
No. Awards: varies
Award Amount: $5,000
Deadline: April 15
Features: Applicants must be U.S. citizens and attend an accredited college or university in the U.S. All applicants must obtain a letter of sponsorship from a local DAR chapter. Applicants must be accepted into or already pursuing an approved course of study in medicine (pre-med does not qualify) at an approved, accredited medical school, college, or university. This application is conducted without regard to race, religion, sex, or national origin. Men also qualify. Send a self-addressed stamped envelope for application. Only completed applications submitted in one package will be considered. No records are returned. Annual transcript required for renewal. Notification is made in June.

New York Life Foundation Scholarship for Women in Health (See Women)

NSNA Frances Tompkins Breakthrough to Nursing Scholarship for Ethnic People of Color (See Minorities)

The Foundation of the National Student Nurses Association, Inc.

555 W.57th Street, Suite 1327
New York, NY 10019
V: 212-581-2215
I: www.nsna.org
No. Awards: varies
Award Amount: $1,000-$2,000
Deadline: Jan. 31, postmarked
Features: Applicants must be currently enrolled in state-approved school of nursing or pre-nursing program leading to an associate or baccalaureate degree, diploma, or a generic doctorate or master's degree. Some area of specialty must also be acknowledged. Awards are based on academic achievement, financial need, and involvement in nursing student organizations and community activities

related to health care. All factors are equally weighed. Students must submit copies of their recent nursing school and college transcripts or grade reports and a $10 processing fee along with completed applications. NSNA members must submit proof of membership. Application forms are available from September through January by sending a self-addressed, legal-size envelope with 55 cents postage. Applications are available on the Web site. Recipients are notified by March.

Physician Assistants Foundation Scholarship

Physician Assistants Foundation
950 N. Washington Street
Alexandria, VA 22314-1552
V: 703-836-2272
I: www.aaapa.org
No. Awards: 40-50
Award Amount: $2,000 or 3,000
Funds Available: varies
Deadline: Feb. 1
Features: Any AAPA student member attending a physician assistant program accredited by the Commission on Accreditation of Applied Health Education Programs (CAAHEP), or its predecessor, Committee on Allied Health Education Accreditation (CAHEEA), is eligible to apply (includes provisional accreditation). Students may apply for AAPA membership at the same time of scholarship application. If applicants are unsure if their programs are accredited by CAHEEA/CAAHEP, they should consult the program director. No exceptions are made on this requirement. Applications are judged on the basis of financial need, academic record as a PA student, extracurricular activities, and future goals. All applicants are notified in May of the status of their application. The official announcement of recipients is made at the AAPA Annual Conference.

Procter & Gamble Oral Health/ADHA Institute Scholarship Program

ADHA Institute Scholarship Program
444 North Michigan Avenue, Suite 3400
Chicago, IL 60611
V: 312-440-8900
I: www.adha.org
No. Awards: 25

Award Amount: $1,000-$1,500
Funds Available: $25,000
Deadline: June 15

Features: Applicant must be a full-time, first-year dental-hygiene student in the U.S. and show evidence of community service and leadership. Applicant must have a minimum cumulative GPA of 3.3. Nationality and residency are unrestricted. Notification is in September.

Lupus Foundation of America, Inc. Research Grants Program

1300 Piccard Drive, Suite 200
Rockville, MD 20850
V: 301-670-9292

Gina Finzi Memorial Student Summer Fellowships for Research
No. Awards: 10
Award Amount: $2,000
Funds Available: $20,000
Deadline: Feb. 1
Features: The purpose of these awards is to foster an interest in lupus erythematosus through the conduct of basic, clinical, or psychosocial research under the supervision of any established investigator. Undergraduate, graduate, and medical students are eligible to apply. However, preference is given to students with a college degree. All applicants will be reviewed by the LFA Medical Council. Each research fellowship will be competitively reviewed NIH-style and ranked by a member of the Peer Review Committee. Award notification is expected in April.

Research Grants Program
No. Awards: varies
Award Amount: $15,000/year for two years
Deadline: April 1

Features: Applicants must be junior investigators (Ph.D.s and M.D.s with assistant professor and below rank, if in academic medicine) to support biomedical research related to finding the cause(s) and/or cure for lupus erythematosus. Each research grant proposal will be competitively reviewed NIH-style and ranked by members of Peer Review Committees, including members of the LFA Medical

Council and/or outside experts in the field of proposed study. Award date is late — October 1st.

Undergraduate Scholarship Program (UGSP) for Individuals from Disadvantaged Backgrounds

National Institutes of Health (NIH)
Grants Information Office
Division of Research Grants/NIH
Bethesda, MD 20892
V: 301-402-0853 or 800-528-7689
No. Awards: 10-15
Award Amount: up to 20,000
Deadline: March 31
Features: Applicants must be individuals from disadvantaged backgrounds planning to pursue undergraduate degrees in the biomedical/behavioral sciences. Must be U.S citizens, nationals, or permanent residents. Must work for NIH for 12 months for each year awarded. Applicants must be full-time students enrolled at accredited four-year institutions and interested in biology, biophysics, nursing, nutrition, pre-medicine, psychology, biochemistry, chemistry, or chemical engineering. This program is highly competitive.

Wyeth-Ayerst Scholarship for Women in Graduate Medical Program (See Women)

LANGUAGES (ASIAN, SLAVIC. MIDDLE EASTERN)

National Security Agency (NSA) Undergraduate Training Program

National Security Agency
9800 Savage Road, Suite 6840
Attn: 5234-UTP
Ft. Meade, MD 20755-6840
V: 410-854-4725 or 800-669-0703
No. Awards: varies between 5-25
Award Amount: Pays tuition and fees for four years; provides summer work, year-round salary and a job upon graduation
Deadline: Nov. 30 of student's high school senior year

Features: Must be high school senior entering first year of college, U.S. citizen; minimum SAT 1100, minimum ACT 25. Studying electrical engineering, computer engineering, computer science, mathematics, Slavic languages, Asian languages, or Middle Eastern languages. Must demonstrate leadership. Minorities are encouraged to apply. Minimum GPA 3.0. Call for applications the first week in September.

LOCAL RESOURCES

Alaska

Howard Rock Foundation Scholarship Program

Howard Rock Foundation
1577 C Street, Suite 304
Anchorage, AK 99501
V: 907-274-5400
No. Awards: varies
Award Amount: $2,500 for undergraduate students, $5,000 for graduate students
Features: Applicant must be enrolled in a member organization of Alaska Village Initiatives and enrolled in an accredited four-year undergraduate or graduate program. Must be a full-time student for entire scholarship period, majoring in a field of study that promotes economic development and quality of life in rural Alaska. Based on financial need. If a student begins studies later than fall of the year applied for, the scholarship will be awarded in part unless student enrolls full-time during summer term. Must have high school diploma or equivalent and maintain good academic standing. Alaska Village Initiatives Board of Directors and staff, HRF Board of Directors and staff, and immediate families are ineligible. Obtain application from Cirl Foundation, 2600 Cordon St. #206, Anchorage, AK 99503.

California

California Farm Bureau Federation

C.F.B. Scholarship Foundation
2300 River Plaza Drive
Sacramento, CA 95833
V: 916-561-5500
No. Grants: approximately 27
Award Amount: $1,500-$2,000, renewable
Deadline: March 1

Features: California residents who are U.S. citizens and are planning to study agriculture at a four-year California college or university can apply.

California Masonic Foundation
1111 California Street
San Francisco, CA 94108-2284
V: 415-776-7000
No. Awards: varies
Award Amount: $500 – $40,000 (over four-year period
Funds Available: $200,000
Deadline: February 28
Features: This foundation awards college scholarships to high school seniors who are U.S. citizens and residents of California. Students must have a GPA of 3.0 or higher. The application must be requested in writing. December 1 through January 31.

Community College Scholarship
Sacramento Bee
P.O. Box 15779
Sacramento, CA 95852
V: 916-321-1000
I: sacbee.com
No. Awards: 5
Award Amount: $1,000-$3,000
Funds Available: up to $15,000
Deadline: mid-March
Features: Applicants must be enrolled in a community college and wish to pursue a career in mass media. Students must live in Sacramento, Calif., circulation area and have a minimum 3.0 cumulative GPA; McClatchy full-time employees and their family members are ineligible. Notifications are made in May.

Ebell Scholarship (and) Charles N. Flint Scholarship Fund
743 S. Lucerne Blvd.
Los Angeles, CA 90005
V: 323-931-1277
No. Awards: varies
Award Amount: $2,000 for a ten month period
Features: Must be at least a college sophomore to be considered.The Fund awards scholarships to college students who are permanent residents and attend college in Los Angeles County, Calif. The student must also be a registered voter and maintain a GPA of 3.25.

Gloria Fecht Memorial Scholarship Fund (See Women)

Colorado
Colorado Masons Benevolent Fund Association
7955 East Arapaho Court
Suite 1200
Englewood, CO 80112-1362
V: 303-290-8544
No. Awards: varies
Award Amount: varies
Funds Available: $275,000
Features: This association awards scholarships to graduates of high schools in Colorado who will attend college in-state. Applications are available only from Colorado high schools.

Florida
Bright Futures Scholarship Program
Florida Department of Education
Office of Student Financial Assistance
325 West Gaines Street, 255 Collins
Tallahassee, FL 32399-0400
V: 888-827-2004
Features: Students with high school GPAs of 3.5 to 4.0 will receive up to $1,500 per year. Students must be Florida residents and must attend a state university, college, or vocational school and registered with the Bright Futures program.

Illinois
Golden Apple Scholars of Illinois
Golden Apple Foundation
8 S. Michigan Avenue, Suite 700
Chicago, IL 60603
V: 312-407-0006
I: www.goldenapple.org
No. Awards: 100
Award Amount: $5,000, renewable for four years
Deadline: August 31
Features: Applicant must be nominated by teacher, counselor, principal, or other non-family adult during student's junior year in high school. Must complete a written application and provide ACT scores and transcripts. Recipients must earn a bachelor's degree at one of 27 Illinois participating universities; must obtain Illinois teacher certification and teach for at least five years in an Illinois school designated in need by Perkins Title One

listing and state test scores. Must participate in four summers of Summer Institute and meet conduct standards while in program. 200 finalists are chosen in fall; 100 recipients are selected in February.

Iowa

State of Iowa Scholarship Program
Iowa College Student Aid Commission
200 Tenth Street, 4th Floor
Des Moines, IA 50309-3609
V: 515-281-3501
I: www.state.ia.us/collegeaid/icsac/index.htm
No. Awards: varies
Award Amount: varies
Features: This program recognizes high school students who graduate in the top 15 percent of their class. An Iowa State Scholarship application is required along with ACT and/or SAT scores. Applications and information are available in the local high school.

Kansas

Jennie G. and Pearl Abell Education Trust
717 Main St.
P.O. Box 487
Ashland, KS 67831
V: 316-635-2228
No. Awards: varies
Award Amount: varies
Features: The Abell Trust awards numerous grants to Clark County, Kansas, high school senior students in varying amounts. Kansas college and university budgets are used as a basis to determine the awards. The student must show demonstrated need. The funds can be used at any school of higher education in the United States. The student must maintain 12 semester hours of study with a GPA of 2.0. Awards are renewable each year for four-or five-year programs.

Louisiana

Rockefeller State Wildlife Scholarship
State of Louisiana
Office of Student Aid Financial Assistance
Scholarship Section
P.O. Box 91202
Baton Rouge, LA 70821
V: 225-388-3087

T: 800-259-5626
No. Awards: 30
Award Amount: $1,000 for 7 years, must apply each year
Deadline: April 15

Features: Applicants must be Louisiana residents attending a public college within the state and studying wildlife, forestry, or marine sciences full-time at a two-year or four-year institution. Must have a minimum GPA of 2.5 and have taken the ACT. Open to non-U.S. citizens. Applicants need to fill out the FAFSA form. This scholarship is renewable for up to five years as an undergraduate and two years as a graduate student. Failure to maintain eligibility will result in permanent cancellation of the scholarship and may result in repayment of all funds received plus interest.

Massachusetts

Horace Smith Trust Fund
114 Main Street
Box #3034
Springfield, MA 01101
V: 413-739-4222
No. Awards: varies
Award Amount: varies
Funds Available: over $700,000
Features: This fund was established to award scholarships to residents and students who have graduated from high schools in Hampden County, Massachusetts.

Minnesota

Duluth Superior Area Community Foundation
Whiteside Scholarship Fund
618 Missabe Bldg.
227 W. 1st Street
Duluth, MN 55802
V: 218-726-0232
No. Awards: varies
Award Amount: $2,400 to $4,200
Features: All applicants must be graduates of Duluth, Minnesota, high schools and rank in the top 10 percent of the high school class. A 2.75 GPA is required for freshman year; renewal applicants must maintain a 3.0 GPA for sophomore and

junior level. Scholarships for local colleges are given in the amount of $2,400. Renewal applicants who choose college locations outside Duluth Superior, Minnesota, receive $4,200.

New Hampshire

Abraham Burman Charity Trust
P.O. Box 608
Dover, NH 03820-4103
No. Awards: varies
Award Amount: varies
Funds Available: $30,000
Features: This local trust provides grants to students who reside in the New Hampshire community.

New York

Chautauqua Region Community Foundation Inc.
21 East 3rd Street, Suite 301
Jamestown, NY 14701
V: 716-661-3390
No. Awards: varies
Award Amount: $100 to $3,000
Features: The Foundation awards grants to primarily residents of Chautauqua County, New York. Awards are renewable each year, but students must reapply.

Meliora Grant
University of Rochester, Director of Admissions
Rochester, NY 14627
V: 716-275-3226
I: www.rochester.edu
No. Award: varies
Award Amount: $5,000
Features: Open to N.Y. residents who are admitted to the University of Rochester.

North Dakota

North Dakota Merit Scholarship Program
North Dakota University System
600 East Boulevard Ave.
Bismarck, ND 58505-0230
V: 701-328-2960
I: www.nodak.edu
No. Awards: varies
Award Amount: varies

Features: The North Dakota Scholarship Program provides tuition scholarships to students who have outstanding academic records. Each high school senior student must rank in the upper 20 percent of the high school class. Applications and information are available in each high school counseling center.

Texas

FINA/Dallas Morning News All-State Scholar-Athlete Team Scholarship
FINA Oil and Chemical Company
P.O. Box 2159
Dallas, TX 75221
V: 800-555-FINA Ext. 4
No. Awards: 12-32
Award Amount: $500-$4,000
Deadline: Dec. 15
Features: The purpose of this scholarship is to honor Texas high school students who excel in athletics, academic achievement, and leadership qualities, and who participate in other school and community activities. Candidates should be seniors in Texas high schools who have lettered in varsity sports. Anyone may nominate an eligible senior. To become finalists, applicants must have been varsity letter winners in a UIL approved sport, have a high school average of at least 90 percent, and be in the top 10 percent of the graduating class. This scholarship is based upon academic achievements and honors, community service, and leadership. Forty finalists are chosen. Contact high school coaches, principals, or counselors, or call or write for application forms.

Washington, D.C., Virginia, and Maryland

Long and Foster Scholarship Program
Long and Foster Real Estate, Inc.
11351 Random Hills Road
Fairfax, VA 22030
V: 703 359-1500
No. Awards: 50
Award Amount: $1,000
Funds Available: $50,000
Deadline: March 1
Features: Limited to students living in Virginia, Maryland, and Washington, D.C. Applicants must be high school seniors and U.S. citizens who are preparing to attend four-year colleges or universities.

Any area of academic study is acceptable. Students should be academically strong and have records of participating in school activities as well as having held positions of leadership and responsibility. All applicants must document their demonstrated financial need. Students should develop listings of participation in community service groups and work experiences.

Wyoming

Paul Stock Foundation
P.O. Box 2020
Cody, WY 82414
V: 307-587-5275
No. Awards: 50
Award Amount: varies
Features: Foundation sponsors students with grants in varying amounts to attend college. The student must show demonstrated need and must be a Wyoming resident.

MINORITIES/ HERITAGE/ DISABILITIES

ADA Endowment and Assistance Fund, Inc

211 East Chicago Ave.
17th Floor
Chicago,IL 60611
V: 312-440-2567

Dental Assisting Scholarship Program
No. Awards: Up to 25
Award Amount: $1,000
Funds Available: varies
Deadline: September 15
Features: Applicant must be U.S. citizen, full-time student in respective dental program, and have minimum 3.0 GPA. Must be African American, Hispanic, or Native American.

Dental Hygiene Scholarship Program
No. Awards: Up to 25
Award Amount: $1,000
Funds Available: varies
Deadline: Aug. 15
Features: Applicant must be U.S. citizen, full-time student entering second year and attending dental hygiene program

accredited by the Commission on Dental Accreditation with a 3.0 minimum GPA. Students must be African American, Hispanic, or Native American.

Dental Laboratory Technology Scholarship
No. Awards: Up to 25
Award Amount: $1,000 (one year awards)
Deadline: Aug. 15
Features: Applicant must be U.S. citizen entering full-time, first year at a dental laboratory technology school accredited by Commission on Dental Accreditation. GPA 2.8 minimum. Must be African American, Hispanic, or Native American. Applicants must demonstrate a minimum financial need of $1,000. Students awarded a full scholarship from another source are ineligible. Notification of scholarship is made in the fall.

American Council of the Blind Scholarships

American Council of the Blind
1155 15th Street, NW, Suite 720
Washington, DC 20005
V: 202-467-5081
T: 800-424-8666
No. Awards: 30
Award Amount: $1,000-$4,000
Deadline: March 1
Features: Must submit certification of visual status. To be legally blind, the applicant must have a visual acuity of 20/200 or less in the better corrected eye and/or 0 degrees or less visual field. Applicant must be accepted in an accredited postsecondary school. Undergraduates must send in high school transcripts; graduate students must include undergraduate transcripts. Telephone interviews are made in May.

American Society for Microbiology

1325 Massachusetts Avenue, NW
Washington, DC 20005
V: 202-942-9295
I: Fellowships-careerinformation @asmusa.org

Minority Graduate Research Fellowship
No. Awards: varies
Award Amount: $12,000, renewable
Deadline: May 1
Features: Applicant must be minority that is underrepresented in the sciences, full-time sophomore or junior with independent

study experience, major in microbiology or related science. Minimum GPA of 2.0 to renew.

Minority Undergraduate Research Fellowship
No. Awards: Not specified
Award Amount: Up to $2,000
Deadline: June 1
Features: Must have completed first college year, be ASM student in the sciences, and be a member of an underrepresented minority including African American, Hispanic, Native American, and Native Pacific Islander.

AMS Minority Scholarship

American Meteorological Society
Attn: Fellowship Scholarship Coordinator
45 Beacon Street
Boston, MA 02108-3693
V: 617-227-2426 x235
I: www.ametsoc/AMS
No. Awards: varies
Award Amount: $3,000 (for 2 years)
Deadline: February 12
Features: Must be minority student entering first year of college; must plan to pursue career in the atmospheric or related oceanic and hydrologic sciences.

Armenian Students' Association of America, Inc.

395 Concord Avenue
Belmont, MA 02478
V: 617-484-9548
I: www.asainc.org
No. Awards: 30
Award Amount: $500-$ 2,500
Deadline: Feb. 15
Features: Applicant must be of Armenian ancestry, be a full-time student who is at least a freshman attending a four-year accredited college or university in the U.S., demonstrate financial need, have good academic performance, show self-sufficiency, and participate in extracurricular activities. Submit an application fee of $15 with completed application.

AWIS (American Women in Science) Educational Awards (See Women)

Burlington Northern Santa Fe Foundation Scholarship

American Indian Science & Engineering Society
5661 Airport Boulevard
Boulder, CO 80301
V: 303-939-0023
I: www.colorado.edu/AISES
No. Awards: 5 new students awarded each year, totaling 19 students annually
Award Amount: $2,500 for 4 years or 8 semesters, whichever occurs first
Funds Available: $47,500
Deadline: March 31
Features: Applicants must reside in Arizona, Colorado, Kansas, Minnesota, Montana, North Dakota, New Mexico, Oklahoma, Oregon, South Dakota, Washington, or California. Applicant must also be a high school senior and at least one fourth American Indian. Certificate of Indian blood is required. Eligible disciplines: science, business, education, and health administration.

Business Reporting (See Communications)

California Teachers Association Martin Luther King, Jr. Scholarships

Human Rights Department
1705 Murchison Drive
P.O. Box 921
Burlingame, CA 94011-0921
V: 650-697-1400
No. Awards: varies
Award Amount: varies, depends on individuals' demonstrated need
Deadline: February 16
Features: Based on financial need. Applicant must be ethnic minority, member or dependent of member of CTA or Student CTA, and pursuing degree or credential for teaching-related career in public education. Scholarships vary annually depending on members' voluntary contributions and applicants' financial need. Applications are available each January.

Casualty Actuarial Society/ Society of Actuaries/ Joint SAS/SOA Minority Scholarship

475 North Martingale Road, Suite 800
Schaumburg, IL 60173
V: 847-706-3500

I: www.soa.org
No. Awards: varies
Award Amount: $500-$2,000
Deadline: May 1
Features: Applicants must be Native American, African American, or Hispanic and enrolled at a two-year or four-year institution. Students must be planning careers in actuarial science and mathematics. Applicant must be U.S. citizen. Number and amount of awards vary with merit and financial need.

Chicago Association of Black Journalists Scholarship

Chicago Association of Black Journalists
P.O. Box 11425
Chicago, IL 60611
V: 312-409-9392
No. Awards: varies
Award Amount: $1,000
Features: Applicant must be minority, full-time junior, senior, or graduate student enrolled in an accredited college or university in the Chicago metropolitan area; major in print or broadcast journalism.

Duracell Scholarship and Internship Program

National Urban League, Inc.
120 Wall Street
New York, NY 10005
V: 212-558-5450
No. Awards: 5
Award Amount: up to $10,000
Features: Must be minority, junior or sophomore student pursuing full-time studies towards bachelor's degree at accredited U.S. institution of higher learning; interested in engineering, sales or marketing, manufacturing operations, finance, or business administration. Must rank within the top 25 percent of class and maintain ranking throughout participation. Must be interested in summer employment with Duracell between junior and senior years, at a location to be selected by Duracell.

The EAR Foundation Minnie Pearl Scholarship Program

1817 Patterson St.
Nashville,TN 37203
V: 615-329-7807
I: www.theearfound.org

No. Awards: varies
Award Amount: $2,000; four year; renewable
Deadline: February 15
Features: Applicants must be high school seniors with a 3.0 GPA. Students must have a significant bilateral hearing loss and must be of mainstreamed hearing-impaired status. All applicants must have been accepted at accredited two- or four-year colleges, universities, or technical schools; plan to attend full time; and be U.S. citizens.

Electronic Industries Foundation Scholarship Program

Electronic Industries Foundation
2500 Wilson Boulevard Suite 210
Arlington, VA 22201
V: 703-907-7400
I: www.eig.org/eif
No. Awards: 6
Award Amount: $30,000
Deadline: Feb. 1
Features: Financial aid must clearly offset impact of disability on applicant's goals. Candidate must have a disability as defined by the Americans with Disabilities Act of 1990, be accepted at an accredited four-year college or university at time of award, and pursuing a degree in electrical engineering, industrial manufacturing, industrial engineering, physics, electromechanical technology, mechanical applied sciences, or similar field directly related to the electronics industry. Please send a self-addressed, stamped envelope.

Foundation of American College Healthcare Executives Albert W. Dent Student Scholarship

1 North Franklin Street, Suite 1700
Chicago, IL 60606
V: 312-424-9388
I: www.ache.org
No. Awards: varies
Award Amount: $3,500
Deadline: March 31
Features: Applicant must be a U.S. or Canadian citizen minority group member, and a Student Associate of the American College of Healthcare Executives. He or she must be a full-time undergraduate in a healthcare management program leading

to a graduate program accredited by any regional accrediting association in the U.S. Applicant must not have previously been a recipient.

Foundation of the National Student Nurses Association, Inc

555 W. 57th Street, Suite 1327
New York, NY 10019
V: 212-581-2215
I: www.nsna.org

Ethnic Scholarship
No. Awards: varies
Award Amount: $1,000-$2,000
Deadline: Jan. 15
Features: Applicant must be American Indian, African American, or Asian with financial need, majoring in health services administration. Applicant must enclose a self-addressed stamped envelope with 2 oz. postage for more information and application forms.

NSNA Frances Tompkins Breakthrough to Nursing Scholarship for Ethnic People of Color
No. Awards: varies
Award Amount: $1,000-$2,500
Deadline: Jan. 31, postmarked
Features: Applicants must be minority students who are currently enrolled in a state-approved school of nursing or pre-nursing in a program leading to an associate or baccalaureate degree, a diploma, or a generic doctorate or master's degree. Awards are based on academic achievement, financial need, and involvement in nursing student organizations and community activities related to health care. All factors are weighed equally.

Imasco Scholarship Fund for Disabled Students

Association of Universities and Colleges of Canada
350 Albert Street Suite 600
Ottawa, Ontario K1R 1B1 Canada
V: 613-563-3961
I: www.aucc.ca
No. Awards: 10 minimum
Award Amount: $5,000
Funds Available: $20,000 minimum
Deadline: June 1
Features: Must be undergraduate with a disability who is pursuing a degree at Canadian degree-granting institution; must be Canadian citizen or have lived in Canada for at least two years as a permanent resident.

Kosciuszko Foundation, Domestic Grants Office

15 East 65th Street
New York, NY 10021
V: 212-734-2130
I: www.kosciuszkofoundation.org

Kosciuszko Foundation Tuition Scholarship
No. Awards: between 65-110
Award Amount: $1,000 - $5,000
Deadline: Jan. 16
Features: Applicant must be of Polish heritage to apply for scholarships for study in all areas. Those of non-Polish heritage must be studying Polish subjects. Student must be full-time junior/senior undergraduate or graduate in the United States. The majority of scholarships are for graduate students. There is a limited number of scholarships for third and fourth year undergraduates. Financial need is considered. Open to U.S. citizens or permanent residents only. Minimum GPA is 3.0. This scholarship is competitive.

Year Abroad Program at the Jagiellonian University at Krakow
No. Awards: 10
Award Amount: cost of tuition, dormitory, and partial living expenses
Features: Applicant must study Polish language, history, literature, and culture in Poland. Candidate must be enrolled at a U.S. college or university entering third or fourth year of undergraduate study or enrolled in a master's or doctoral program. Open to U.S. citizens or permanent residents only. Minimum GPA is 3.0. This scholarship is competitive.

MANA, a National Latina Organization (See Women)

Mattinson Endowment Fund Scholarship for Disabled Students

Association of Universities and Colleges of Canada
350 Albert Street Suite 600
Ottawa, Ontario K1R 1B1 Canada
V: 613-563-1236
No. Awards: varies
Award Amount: $2,500
Funds Available: varies

Deadline: June 1
Features: Applicant must be disabled undergraduate; Canadian citizen or have lived in Canada for at least two years as a permanent resident. Scholarship winners will be notified by August 31. Winners must submit to the Association of Universities and Colleges of Canada confirmation of registration to the educational institution.

National Achievement Scholarship Program for Outstanding Negro Students

1560 Sherman Avenue, Suite 200
Evanston, Illinois 60201-4897
No. Awards: approximately 600
Award Amount: $2,000 National Achievement Scholarships; corporate-sponsored scholarship amounts vary
Deadline: PSAT/NMSQT test date (in late October)
Features: African Americans who take the PSAT/NMSQT usually no later than 11th grade and plan to enroll in a bachelor's degree program; U.S. citizens only.

National Association for the Advancement of Colored People

4805 Mt. Hope Drive
Baltimore, MD 21215-3297
V: 410-358-8900

Agnes Jones Jackson Scholarship
No. Awards: varies
Award Amount: varies
Deadline: April 30
Features: Membership required in NAACP at time of application. Applicant must be a full-time student enrolled at accredited U.S. institution, and recommended (in letter form) by president of NAACP branch, Youth Council or College Chapter, a member of Executive Committee, a member of National Board, a member of SCF Trustees, or an NAACP employee (except those on the Agnes Jones Jackson Scholarship Committee). Graduating high school seniors must have a cumulative GPA of at least 2.5 on a 4.0 scale, undergraduate college students a 2.0, and graduates a 3.0. Only open to U.S. citizens. NAACP employees are ineligible. Recommendation letter should specify sender's title and be on letterhead if possible. Recipients must compete for scholarship renewal. Most recent GPA, NAACP

participation, other civil rights activities, and academic awards will be considered. Award may be reduced or denied based on insufficient enrollment (less than full-time) or NAACP participation.

Sutton Education Scholarship
No. Awards: Not specified
Award Amount: $1,000 undergraduate students; $2,000 graduate students
Features: Must be full-time college student majoring in education and NAACP member. Graduating seniors may also apply. Minimum cumulative GPA: undergraduates, 2.5; graduates, 3.0. Candidates must be U.S. citizens.

Roy Wilkins Scholarship
No. Awards: Not specified
Award Amount: $1,000
Features: Must be graduating high school senior and NAACP member. The minimum GPA is 2.5. Applicant must be U.S. citizen and full-time student.

Willems Scholarship
No. Awards: Not specified
Award Amount: $2,000 undergraduate students; $3,000 graduate students
Features: Applicant must be male, NAACP member, and student majoring in engineering, chemistry, physics, or mathematical science. The minimum GPA is 3.0 for graduate students. Applicants who are graduating seniors or undergraduates must have a minimum GPA of 2.5. Candidates must be U.S. citizens and full-time college students.

National Association of Black Accountants (NAB) Scholarship Program

7249-A Hanover Parkway
Greenbelt, MD 20770
V: 301-474-NABA ext. 114
No. Awards: over 40
Award Amount: $1,000-$6,000
Deadline: December 31
Features: Applicant must be an undergraduate or graduate business student, current member of National Association of Black Accountants. Applicants must also be of an ethnic minority. Based on GPA, involvement in NABA, financial need, and ability to overcome adversity.

National Association of Colored Women's Clubs Hallie Q. Brown Scholarship Fund

5808 Sixteenth Street, NW
Washington, DC 20011
V: 202-726-2044
No. Awards: varies
Award Amount: varies
Deadline: March 31
Features: Applicant must be minority student, U.S. citizen, and recommended by member of National Association of Colored Women's Clubs. Applicant must be a full-time student in undergraduate studies. Based on financial need. This scholarship is awarded every two years. Applicants must get scholarship packets through members of National Association of Colored Women's Clubs.

National Consortium for Graduate Degrees for Minorities in Engineering and Science, Inc. GEM PHD Science Fellowship

P.O. Box 537
Notre Dame, IN 46556
V: 219-631-7771
I: www.nd.edu/~gem
No. Awards: 200 at $20,000-$40,000 for masters; 30 at $60,000-$100,000 for PhD
Award Amount: $11,000,000
Deadline: Dec. 1
Features: Applicants must be U.S. citizens who are American Indian, Mexican-American, African American, Puerto Rican, or Hispanic. Applicants must be graduate students studying life science, mathematics, or physical science and enrolling for doctoral study at a participating GEM institution. Minimum 3.0 GPA is required.

National Italian American Foundation

1860 19th Street, NW
Washington, DC 20009
V: 202-387-0600
No. Awards: varies
Award Amount: $2,000 (minimum)
Deadline: May 31
Features: Open to Italian-American students of all college majors currently enrolled or entering college who are permanent residents of the U.S. Criteria for selection include academic merit, financial need, and community service.

Nicaraguan and Haitian Scholarship Program

Office of Student Financial Aid
Florida Department of Education
325 W. Gains St.
255 Collins
Tallahassee, FL 32399
V: 888-827-2004
No. Awards: 2
Award Amount: $4,000-$5,000
Deadline: July 1, postmarked
Features: Applicant must be a Nicaraguan or Haitian citizen or must have been born in Nicaragua or Haiti and currently living in Florida. Student must meet Selective Service registration requirements and have a cumulative high school GPA of at least 3.0 on a 4.0 scale or a 3.0 cumulative GPA for all college work attempted. Candidate must also demonstrate service to the community. Applicant must not owe a repayment of a grant under any state or federal grant or scholarship program. Student must not be in default on any federal Title IV or state student loan program unless satisfactory arrangements to repay have been made. Also, student must be enrolled at a State University System institution for an minimum of 12 credit hours of undergraduate study or 9 credit hours of graduate study. This award is not renewable. However, a person who has received the award may reapply in succeeding years.

Open Society Institute — Supplementary Grant Burma Program

400 W. 59th St.
New York, NY 10019
V: 212-548-0632
I: www.soros.org
No. Awards: approximately 300
Award Amount: average award $6,000
Deadline: May 15
Features: Unrestricted study at all college levels in the U.S.; must be between age 18 and 40 and a Burmese citizen. Grant to address the needs of Burmese students whose college education was disrupted as a result of their active participation in pro-democracy movement of 1988.

Parke-Davis Epilepsy Scholarship Award

c/o IntraMed Educational Group
1633 Broadway, 25th Floor
New York, NY 10019
T: 800-292-7373
No. Awards: 16
Award Amount: $3,000
Deadline: March 1
Features: Must be currently under a physician's care for epilepsy; a high school senior who has applied to a college or university; or a currently enrolled freshman, sophomore, or junior college student; or a college senior who has applied to graduate school. Must have achieved in academics and participated in extracurricular activities. Notification will be made in April.

Sacramento Bee Minority Media Scholarship

Sacramento Bee
P.O. Box 15779
Sacramento, CA 95852
V: 916-321-1791
I: www.sacbee.com
No. Awards: 8 to 12
Award Amount: $1,000-$4,000
Funds Available: $20,000
Deadline: March 15
Features: Applicant must live in Sacramento circulation area, and be a first-year college student who has interest in pursuing a career in mass media. Minimum 3.0 cumulative GPA; McClatchy full-time employees and their family members are ineligible. Notifications are in May.

Undergraduate Scholarship Program (UGSP) for Individuals from Disadvantaged Backgrounds (See Health)

Undergraduate Scholarship Program

Amoco Foundation, Inc.
200 East Randolph Drive
Chicago, IL 60601
V: 312-856-6306
Students should check with university department offices or student financial aid office for funds donated by Amoco.

Wasie Foundation Scholarship

Wasie Foundation
First Bank Place, Suite 4700
601 Second Avenue South
Minneapolis, MN 55402
V: 612-332-3883
No. Awards: approximately 60
Award Amount: $1,000-$10,000
Funds Available: $250,000
Deadline: March 15
Features: U.S. citizen of Polish ancestry attending specified Minnesota institutions; based on financial need, academic ability, extracurricular activities, and personal qualities.

ORGANIZATIONS/ MEMBERSHIPS

Armed Forces Communication and Electronics Association Educational Foundation (AFCEA)

4400 Fair Lakes Court
Fairfax, VA 22033-3899
V: 703-631-6149
T: 800-336-4583 ext. 6149
I: www.afcea.org

AFCEA ROTC Scholarship Program
No. Awards: 90
Award Amount: $ 2,000
Funds Available: $180,000
Deadline: April 1
Features: The purpose of this scholarship is to encourage and reward outstanding and deserving students in the ROTC program. Applicants must be U.S. citizens enrolled in an ROTC program who are sophomores or juniors at the time of application. Students must be working toward a degree in electronics, electrical, aerospace, or communications engineering, mathematics, physics, or computer science or technology. Candidates must also be of good moral character, have proven academic excellence, and demonstrate motivation and potential for completing a college education and serving as an officer of the Armed Forces of the United States. This scholarship is distributed equally among the Army, Navy/Marine Corps, and Air Force ROTC programs. Notification of winners will be made in June.

General Emmett Paige Scholarship
No. Awards: 20
Award Amount: $2,000
Funds Available: $20,000
Deadline: March 1

Features: The purpose of this scholarship is to promote excellence in scientific and engineering education. Applicants must be U.S. citizens enrolled in an accredited four-year college or university in the U.S. and working toward a bachelor's degree in electrical engineering, electronics, communications engineering, mathematics, computer technology, or physics. Minimum GPA is 3.4. Military affiliation is necessary. Veterans, active duty personnel, spouses, or dependents are eligible. Application forms are available from school ROTC units or by contacting the Administrator of Scholarships and Awards at the AFCEA after November. Veterans entering college as freshmen may apply; all others must be sophomores or juniors at time of application.

General John A. Wickham Scholarship
No. Awards: 10
Award Amount: $2,000
Funds Available: $20,000
Deadline: May 1
Features: The purpose of this scholarship is promote excellence in scientific and engineering education. Applicants must be U.S. citizens enrolled in an accredited four-year college or university in the U.S. and working toward a bachelor degree in electrical engineering, electronics, aerospace, or communications engineering, mathematics, computer technology, or physics. Minimum GPA is 3.4. Military affiliation is not necessary. Application forms are available by contacting the Administrator of Scholarships and Awards at the AFCEA. Must be a sophomore or junior at time of application.

Air Force Aid Society National Headquarters Education Assistance Department
General Henry H. Arnold Education Grant Program

1745 Jefferson Davis Hwy., No. 202
Arlington, VA 22202
V: 703-607-3072 or 800-429-9475
I: www.afas.org
No. Awards: 5,000 total
Award Amount: $1,500
Funds Available: $7.5 million
Deadline: 3rd Friday in March
Features: Applicants must be dependent sons and daughters of Air Force members in one of the following categories: active duty and Title 10 reservists on extended active duty (all other Guard and Reserve are not eligible); retired due to length of active duty service or disability, or retired Guard; Reserve age 60 and receiving retirement pay; widows of Air Force members. Applicants must be enrolled or accepted as full-time undergraduate students in a college, university, or a vocational/trade school whose accreditation is accepted by the Department of Education. Students must maintain a minimum GPA of 2.0. Applicants who are recipients of previous grants must demonstrate satisfactory progress by promotion in school grade level.

General Henry H. Arnold Education Grant Program

Air Force Aid Society Education Assistance Department
1745 Jefferson Davis Highway, Suite 202
Arlington, VA 22202
V: 703-607-3072
No. Grants: 5,000
Award Amount: $15,000
Funds Available: $5.7 million
Deadline: varies
Features: Applicant must be high school graduate accepted as a full-time college undergraduate at a college, university, or vocational/trade school with accreditation issued by the U.S. Department of Education. Minimum GPA: 2.0 (on a 4.0 scale). Applicant must be dependent child of Air Force member in the following categories: active duty and Title 10 reservists on extended active duty through award disbursement date; Retired Guard/Reserve (age 60 and older), or retired due to length

of active duty or disability; Deceased while active or retired, (or) must be spouse of Active duty member or Title 10 Reservists on extended active duty; eligible spouses must live and attend school in the continental U.S., and be legally married to member at time of application and award disbursement. Notification will be made in June.

Air Force Sergeants Association AFSA/ AMF Scholarship Program

Airmen Memorial Bldg.
5211 Auth Road
Suitland, MD 20746
V: 301-899-3500
I: staff@afsahq.org
No. Awards: approximately 50
Funds Available: $500-$3,000
Deadline: April 15
Features: Applicants must be single, dependent children, including legally adopted children, of Air Force Sergeants Association members or members of the Association's Auxiliary. Applicants must be high school graduates or in-college students. Based on academic ability, character, leadership, writing ability, and potential for success. Financial need is not a consideration. Must have 3.5 GPA and SATs above 1100. Pre-freshmen who have not previously attended college and in-college freshmen who will not have completed one full-year of college work by the end of the next spring semester or quarter must submit their SAT results. Request application forms by sending a self-addressed, postage paid ($1.47), #9x12 envelope.

Alaska Village Initiatives (See Local-Alaska)

American College of Healthcare Executives Albert W. Dent Student Scholarship (See Minorities)

American Federation of State, County, and Municipal Employees, AFL-CIO

1625 L Street, NW
Washington, DC 20036
V: 202-429-1250
TTY: 202-659-0446

AFSCME Family Scholarship
No. Awards: 10
Award Amount: $2,000
Funds Available: $20,000
Deadline: Dec. 31
Features: Applicants must be graduating high school seniors who are children of active AFSCME members. Notification is made by March 31.

AFSCME Union Plus Credit Card Award Program
No. Awards: varies
Award Amount: $500-$4,000
Funds Available: $250,000
Features: Applicants must be members, spouses, and children (includes foster, stepchildren, and adopted). Applicants must be accepted into an accredited postsecondary institution including community colleges, trade, and technical schools. Must submit high school transcript, SAT or ACT scores, and present one reference and 500 word essay. Excludes members' children in graduate school. Members need not be credit card holders, but must have AFL-CIO union affiliation.

American Indian Science & Engineering Society

5661 Airport Boulevard
Boulder, CO 80301
V: 303-939-0023
I: www.colorado.edu/AISES

A.T. Anderson Memorial Scholarship
No. Awards: varies
Award Amount: $1,000 for undergraduates, $2,000 for graduates
Funds Available: approximately $220,000
Deadline: June 15
Features: Applicant must be an AISES member ($10 fee); American Indian/ Alaskan Native (minimum 1/4 and or recognized by tribe) full-time student at an accredited institution. Minimum GPA is 2.0. Certificate of Indian blood is required. Eligible disciplines: medicine, natural resources, math and science secondary education, engineering, and sciences. This award is nonrenewable. Students must reapply each year.

EPA Tribal Lands Environmental Science Scholarship
No. Awards: 88-100
Award Amount: $4,000
Funds Available: $350,000
Deadline: June 15

Features: Applicant must be a college junior, senior, or graduate student and enrolled full-time at an accredited institution. Eligible majors: biology, botony, chemical and civil engineering, chemistry, entomology, environmental economics and sciences, hydrology and related sciences. Certificate of Indian blood is not required. This award is nonrenewable. Students must reapply each year.

American Postal Workers Union

1300 L Street, NW
Washington, DC 20005
V: 202-842-4268

E.C. Hallbeck Memorial Scholarship Program
No. Awards: 10
Award Amount: $1,000 for four years
Deadline: March 1, postmarked
Features: Applicant must be a high school or corresponding secondary school senior during application and plan to attend an accredited college of choice. Student must be a son, daughter, stepchild, or legally adopted child of an active or deceased member of American Postal Workers Union. Winners are judged on the basis of school records, personal qualifications, SAT/ACT scores, and total family income.

Vocational Scholarship Program
No. Awards: varies
Award Amount: $1,000 for three years or until completion of course
Deadline: March 1, postmarked
Features: Applicant must be a high school or corresponding secondary school senior during application and plan to attend an accredited college of choice. Student must be a son, daughter, stepchild, or legally adopted child of an active or deceased member of American Postal Workers Union. SAT/ACT scores must be submitted.

Baptist Life Scholarship Benefit

Baptist Life Home Office
8555 Main Street
Buffalo, NY 14221
V: 716-633-4393 or 800-227-8543
No. Awards: 20
Award Amount: $500 full-time student, $250 part-time student
Funds Available: $10,000
Deadline: May 31

Features: Candidates must be insured on a Baptist Life Association permanent life insurance certificate, term life insurance certificate, or annuity issued at least one year prior to May 31 of the scholarship application year. Good character and standard entrance level grades required.

Burlington Northern Santa Fe Foundation Scholarship (See Minorities)

California Teachers Association Scholarship

P.O. Box 921
Burlingame, CA 94011-0920
V: 650-697-1400
I: www.cta.org
No. Awards: 25
Award Amount: $2,000
Funds Available: Approximately $ 50,000
Deadline: Feb. 15
Features: Applicant must be dependent child of active, retired-life, or deceased members and must major in higher education.

Civitan International Foundation

Attn: Scholarship Administrator
P.O. Box 13074
Birmingham, AL 35213-0744
V: 205-591-8910
No. Awards: Approximately 40
Award Amount: $1,000 to $1,500
Deadline: January 31
Features: Each candidate must be a Civitan (or a Civitan's immediate family member) and must have been a Civitan for at least two years and/or must be or have been a Junior Civitan for no less than two years. Scholarships are awarded to students pursuing careers which help further the ideals and purposes of Civitan International as embodied in its Creed. Candidates must be enrolled in a degree or certificate program at an accredited community college, vocational school, four-year college or graduate school. If a candidate is not pursuing graduate studies, full-time attendance is required. Send a self-addressed, stamped envelope with postage to cover a 2 oz. U.S. mailing.

Coast Guard Mutual Assistance Education Grants

Coast Guard Mutual Assistance
c/o Commandant (GZMA)
2100 2nd Street, SW
Washington, DC 20593
V: 202-267-1683
No. Awards: 80
Award Amount: $500
Features: Must be dependent child of
Coast Guard member in one of the
following categories: active duty and Title
10 reservists on extended duty; retired due
to length of active duty service or
disability or retired reserve age 60;
deceased while on active duty or retired
status. Must be accepted as a full-time
undergraduate at a college, university, or
vocational/trade school whose accreditation the Department of Education has
accepted. Minimum GPA 2.0. Previous
grant recipients must re-apply and
demonstrate satisfactory progress; those
not qualified to compete for grants may be
eligible for CGMA-sponsored loans.

International Association of Fire Fighters W. H. "Howie" McClennan Scholarship

1750 New York Avenue, NW
Washington, DC 20006
V: 202-737-8484
No. Awards: Approximately 10
Award Amount: $2,500, renewable
Funds Available: $25,000
Deadline: Feb. 1
Features: Based on financial need,
aptitude, promise, and academic achievements. Must be child or legally adopted
child of fire fighter who died in the line of
duty and who was a member in good
standing of the International Association of
Fire Fighters — AFL-CIO-CLC at the time of
death. Applicant must plan to attend an
accredited university, college, or school of
higher learning in the U.S. or Canada.
Transcripts of grades, recommendations
from two teachers, and a 200-word
statement indicating reasons for continuing education required.

Japanese-American Citizens League National JACL Scholarship

1765 Sutter Street
San Francisco, CA 94115
V: 415-921-5225

I: www.jacl.org
No. Awards: over 31
Award Amount: $1,000-$5,000
Funds Available: $70,000
Deadline: March 1 for entering freshmen
April 1 for current college students
Features: Applicant or parents must be a
National JACL member.

MANA, a National Latina Organization (See Women)

National Association of Plumbing-Heating-Cooling Contractors Delta Faucet Scholarship Program

180 S. Washington Street
P.O. Box 6808
Falls Church, VA 22040-1148
V: 703-237-8100 or 1-800-533-7694
No. Awards: 6 (nonrenewable)
Award Amount: $2,500
Funds Available: About $15,000
Deadline: June 1
Features: Student applicant must be
recommended by a family member, friend,
employee, or NAPHCC member and must
plan on entering field within plumbing,
heating, or cooling. The student may be a
high school senior planning to attend a
four-year accredited college or a current
college student. Provide high school or
college transcripts, recommendation
letters from a principal, counselor, or
dean, from the NAPHCC sponsor, and a
completed application with black and
white photo.

International Brotherhood of Teamsters Scholarship Fund

25 Louisiana Avenue, NW
Washington, DC 20001
V: 202-624-8735
No. Awards: 25
Award Amount: (10) $1,500, renewable for
four years totaling $6,000; (15) $1,000 nonrenewable
Deadline: February 26
Features: Must be child or grandchild of
active, retired, disabled, or deceased
member of the International Brotherhood
of Teamsters who has been or was a
member for at least 12 months. Financial
dependents (that is, stepchildren and
wards) of Teamsters' members are eligible
if the member contributes in excess of 50
percent of the applicant's financial support

and if the applicant is a financial dependent of the member for federal income tax purposes. Applicants must be ranked in the top 15 percent of their high school class, have or expect to have excellent SAT or ACT scores, and be able to demonstrate financial need. Recipients are selected by an impartial committee of university admissions and financial aid directors on the basis of scholastic achievement, aptitude, personal qualifications, and financial need. Students participating in concurrent enrollment programs, whereby they attend college courses prior to completion of their high school requirements, must apply the year before they begin full-time college course work. Students may apply during senior year.

National Society of the Daughters of the American Revolution

1776 D Street NW
Washington, DC 20006-5392
V: 202-879-3292

American History Scholarship
No. Awards: varies
Award Amount: $2,000 renewable
Deadline: February 1
Features: Applicants must be U.S. citizens and attend an accredited college or university in the U.S. All applicants must obtain a letter of sponsorship from a local DAR chapter. Applicants must be graduating high school seniors who will be majoring in American History. This application is processed without regard to race, religion, sex, or national origin. Send a SASE for application. Only completed applications submitted in one package will be considered. No records are returned. Annual transcript required for renewal. Only state winners are eligible for judging on the Division level. Division level first and second place winners are judged on the National level. Notification is made in June.

D.A.R. Lillian and Arthur Dunn Scholarship
No. Awards: varies
Award Amount: $1,000, renewable
Deadline: April 15
Features: Applicants must be U.S. citizens and attend an accredited college or university in the U.S. All applicants must obtain a letter of sponsorship from a local

DAR chapter. Applicants must be graduating high school seniors whose mothers are current members of NSDAR (no other relationship qualifies). Each application is processed without regard to race, religion, sex, or national origin. Send a self-addressed, stamped envelope for application. Only completed applications submitted in one package will be considered. No records are returned. Annual transcript required for renewal. Notification is made in June.

D.A.R. Enid Hall Griswold Memorial Scholarship
No. Awards: varies
Award Amount: $1,000
Deadline: Feb. 15
Features: Applicants must be U.S. citizens and attend an accredited college or university in the U.S. All applicants must obtain a letter of sponsorship from a local DAR chapter. Applicants must be entering junior or senior year of college and majoring in either political science, history, governmental, or economics. Each application is processed without regard to race, religion, sex, or national origin. Send a self-addressed, stamped envelope for application. Only completed applications submitted in one package will be considered. No records are returned. Annual transcript required for renewal. Notification is made in June.

D.A.R. Idamae Cox Otis Scholarship
No. Awards: varies
Award Amount: $1,000
Deadline: Feb. 15
Features: Applicants must be U.S. citizens and attend an accredited college or university in the U.S. All applicants must obtain a letter of sponsorship from a local DAR chapter. Applicants must be graduates of Kate Duncan Smith or Tamassee DAR Schools. Applications are handled through the respective school scholarship committees. Each application is processed without regard to race, religion, sex, or national origin. Send a self-addressed, stamped envelope for application. Only completed applications submitted in one package will be considered. No records are returned. Notification is made in June.

D.A.R. Longman-Harris Scholarship
No. Awards: varies
Award Amount: $2,000, renewable
Deadline: April 15
Features: Applicants must be U.S. citizens and attend an accredited college or university in the U.S. All applicants must obtain a letter of sponsorship from a local DAR chapter. Applicants must be graduating seniors of Kate Duncan Smith DAR School. Each application is processed without regard to race, religion, sex, or national origin. Send a self-addressed, stamped envelope for application. Only completed applications submitted in one package will be considered. No records are returned. Annual transcript required for renewal. Notification is made in June.

J.E. Caldwell Centennial Scholarship
No. Awards: varies
Award Amount: $2,000
Deadline: April 15
Features: Applicants must be U.S. citizens and attend an accredited college or university in the U.S. All applicants must obtain a letter of sponsorship from a local DAR chapter. Applicants must be outstanding students pursuing a course of graduate study in the subject of historic preservation. This application is processed without regard to race, religion, sex, or national origin. The fund has been made possible through the J.E. Caldwell Company, official jewelers of the NSDAR, in honor of the DAR Centennial. Send SASE for application. Only completed applications submitted in one package will be considered. No records are returned. Notification is in June.

The Sons of Norway Foundation

C/O Sons of Norway
1455 West Lake Street
Minneapolis, MN 55408
V: 612-827-3611
T: 800-945-8851

Nancy Lorraine Jensen Memorial Scholarship Fund
No. Awards: varies
Award Amount: no less than 50 percent for one term (quarter or semester) and no more than 100 percent of the tuition for one year
Deadline: March 1, postmarked

Features: Applicant must be a U.S. citizen not younger than 17 and not older than 35 on the date that the scholarship application is submitted. Candidate must be a female member or the daughter or granddaughter of a member of the Sons of Norway, provided that such membership shall have been of at least three years duration on the date the application is submitted. Employment at the NASA Goddard Space Flight Center, Greenbelt, MD, may be substituted in lieu of Sons of Norway. Student must be a full-time undergraduate who has completed at least one term (quarter, semester) of studies majoring in chemistry, physics, or chemical, electrical, or mechanical engineering. The applicant must have attained at least a 1200 SAT score or an ACT score of at least 26. Grants awarded are jointly payable to the student and the institution of learning. Any applicant may receive three awards during undergraduate study.

King Olav V Norwegian-American Heritage Fund
No. Awards: varies
Award Amount: $250-$3,000
Available Funds: $15,000
Deadline: March 1, postmarked
Features: Any American, 18 years of age or older, who has demonstrated a keen and sincere interest in the Norwegian heritage and/or any Norwegian who has demonstrated an interest in American heritage, who now desires to pursue further heritage study at a recognized educational institution (arts, crafts, literature, history, music, folklore, and the like) is eligible to apply for a scholarship/grant. Based on GPA, participation in school and community activities, work experiences, education and career goals, and personal and school preferences. No faxed copies will be accepted. *Please note:* The King Olav V Norwegian American Heritage Fund receives a large number of applications and only those that fulfill the above eligibility requirements will go to the scholarship committee for consideration. Applicants may expect to be notified approximately one to two months after the deadline for submission. Checks are made payable jointly to the applicant and his/her school and must be endorsed by both.

PACE International United Paperworker Union Scholarships

PACE International Union
P.O. Box 1475
Nashville, TN 37202
V: 615-834-8590
No. Awards: 22
Award Amount: $1,000
Funds Available: $22,000
Deadline: March 15
Features: Applicants must be high school seniors who are children of active members in good standing. Winners are limited to two awards per region. Upon receipt of a completed and accepted preliminary application form, a supplemental packet of forms is sent to the applicant.

United Food & Commercial Workers International Union Scholarship (See Food Service)

Urban League Scholar

University of Rochester, Director of Admissions
Rochester, NY 14627
V: 716-275-3221 or 888-822-2256
I: www.rochester.edu
No. Award: varies
Award Amount: $6,000 or greater, depending on demonstrated need
Features: This scholarship is offered through the local Urban League Community offices. Applicants must be nominated by the local Urban League members. The award can be used only at the University of Rochester.

SCIENCE/ ENGINEERING

AMS (American Meteorological Society) Minority Scholarship (See Minorities)

Armed Forces Communication and Electronics Association General Emmett Paige and General John A. Wickham Scholarships (See Organizations)

AT&T ESP Scholarships (See Minorities)

AWIS Educational Awards (See Women)

Bausch & Lomb Science Award

Bausch & Lomb Science Award Committee
P.O. Box 270251
Rochester, NY 14627
V: 716-275-3221
F: 716-461-4595
I: www.rochester.edu
No. Award: one per school
Award Amount: $24,000 over 4 years, amount varies based on need
Deadline: Jan. 15
Features: The purpose of this scholarship is to recognize outstanding achievement in the sciences by high school students. Applicants must be selected as Bausch & Lomb medal winners during the junior year of high school. Only students selected by the high school faculties are eligible.

BPW Loan Fund for Women in Engineering Studies (See Women)

Canadian Society of Exploration Geophysicists

510 5th Street, SW #905
Calgary, Alberta T2P 3S2 Canada
V: 403-262-0015
I: www.cseg.org
No. Awards: varies
Award Amount: $1,500 in Canadian funds
Deadline: July 15

Features: Nationality is unrestricted. Applicants must be undergraduate students with above average grades or graduate students at a Canadian college or university pursuing a career in exploration geophysics in industry, teaching, or research.

Duracell Scholarship and Internship Program (See Minorities)

Electronic Industries Foundation Scholarship Program (See Minorities)

National Consortium for Graduate Degrees for Minorities in Engineering GEM-PHD Science Fellowships (See Minorities)

National Security Agency (NSA) Undergraduate Training Program (See Languages)

National Society of Professional Engineers — Regional Scholarships

NSPE Education Foundation
1420 King Street
Alexandria, VA 22314-2794
V: 703-684-2800
I: www.nspe.org
No. Awards: varies
Award Amount: $1,000-$2,000
Deadline: Dec. 1
Features: High school seniors who are U.S. citizens and are interested in studying engineering. This scholarship program is handled by each state organization. Student applicants must contact the state office for specific information.

The Sons of Norway Foundation Nancy Lorraine Jensen Memorial Scholarship Fund (See Organizations)

The SPE Foundation Scholarship Fund

The SPE Foundation
14 Fairfield Drive
Brookfield, CT 06804
V: 203-740-5434
No. Awards: varies
Award Amount: Up to $4,000
Deadline: Dec. 15
Features: Full-time undergraduate students at two- or four-year college or technical schools and have demonstrated interest in plastics industry. Must be majoring in or taking courses beneficial to career in plastics industry which would include but not be limited to plastics engineering, polymer science, chemistry, physics, chemical engineering, mechanical engineering, industrial engineering, and business administration.

Undergraduate Scholarship Program (See Minorities)

Undergraduate Scholarship Program (UGSP) for Individuals from Disadvantaged Backgrounds (See Minorities)

Woods Hole Oceanographic Institution Summer Student Fellowship

Woods Hole Oceanographic Institution
Clark 223, MS 31, Education Office
Woods Hole, MA 02543
V: 508-289-2709
I: www.whoi.edu
No. Awards: varies
Award Amount: $4,000 for a 12 week program
Deadline: February 16
Features: Applicants must be in junior or senior year of undergraduate course work studying biology, chemistry, physics, or geology, with an interest in ocean sciences, oceanographic engineering, or marine policy. Application requests may be made in October.

Xerox Award

University of Rochester, Director of Admissions
Rochester, NY 14627
V: 716-275-3221
F: 888-822-2256 or 800-281-6203
I: www.rochester.edu
No. Award: varies
Award Amount: $6,000 minimum, amount varies based on need
Deadline: Jan. 15
Features: The purpose of this scholarship is to recognize outstanding achievement in the sciences by high school students. Only students selected by their high schools are eligible.

TEACHING/ EDUCATION

Business & Professional Women's Foundation (See Women)

California Teachers Association Scholarship (See Organizations)

Canadian Society of Exploration Geophysicists (See Science)

Golden Apple Scholars of Illinois (See Local-Illinois)

Leopold Schepp Foundation

551 Fifth Avenue, Suite 3000
New York, NY 10176
V: 212-986-3078
No. Awards: varies
Award Amount: varies
Deadline: May or December of each year

Features: Applicant must be U.S. citizen or permanent resident, undergraduate (up to the age of 30) or graduate student (up to the age of 40), who wants to pursue education in the United States or abroad. Based on financial need. Finalists may be asked to go to New York for an interview at their own expense.

Phi Delta Kappa, Inc., Scholarship Grants for Prospective Educators

P.O. Box 789
408 North Union Street
Bloomington, IN 47402
V: 812-339-1156
No. Grants: 43-47
Award Amount: (1) $2,000 award; others $1,000
Deadline: Jan. 31
Features: High school seniors in upper third of class who plan to pursue a teaching career; based on scholastic achievement, school and community activities, recommendations, and essay. Applications are only available at local chapters. Applicants may send self-addressed stamped envelope for listing of closest chapters.

WOMEN

American Women in Science (AWIS) Educational Awards

National Headquarters
1200 New York Avenue, NW, Suite 650
Washington, DC 20005
V: 202-326-8940
No. Awards: 12-15
Award Amount: $500-$1,000
Deadline: Mid January

Features: Must be female student who is enrolled in any life science, physical science, social science, or engineering program leading to a Ph.D. Non-U.S. citizens must be enrolled in a U.S. institution of higher education. Winners traditionally are at the dissertation level of their graduate work. Funds are available for study in the U.S. and abroad. Notification is in May.

Business & Professional Women's Foundation

2012 Massachusetts Avenue NW
Washington, DC 20036
V: 202-293-1100
I: www.bpwusa.org

Career Advancement Scholarship Program
No. Awards: 50
Award Amount: $500 to $1,000
Funds Available: $50,000
Deadline: April 15

Features: Applicant must demonstrate critical need for financial assistance ($30,000 or less for a family of four). Must be 25 or older, U.S. citizen, officially accepted into an accredited program or course of study at a U.S. institution (including institutions in Puerto Rico and the Virgin Islands), expecting graduation 12 to 24 months from date of grant, and planning precisely how to use desired training to upgrade skills for career advancement, career change, or re-entry to the job market. Must study teacher education certification, computer science, paralegal studies, business studies, humanities, social science, engineering or for a professional degree (J.D., D.D.S., M.D.). This scholarship does not cover studies at the doctoral level (Ph.D.), correspondence courses or non-degree programs.

BPW Loan Fund for Women in Engineering Studies
No. Awards: Not specified
Deadline: April 15
Annual Loan: Up to $5,000
Features: Applicant must demonstrate financial need. Must be U.S. citizen, have academic and/or work experience records that show career motivation and the ability to complete studies. Must have written notice of acceptance for enrollment at a school accredited by the Accreditation Board of Engineering and Technology. Studies may be full- or part-time, but applicant must carry at least six semester hours or equivalent each semester for which the loan is requested. Seven percent interest per annum begins immediately

after graduation. Loans are repaid in twenty equal quarterly installments commencing 12 months after graduation.

BPW/Sears-Roebuck Foundation Loan Fund
No. Awards: varies
Award Amount: up to $2,500
Deadline: April 15
Features: Applicant must demonstrate financial need. Must be U.S. citizen, have academic and/or work experience records that show career motivation and the ability to complete studies. Must have written notice of acceptance for enrollment at a school accredited by the American Assembly of Collegiate Schools of Business. Studies may be full or part-time, but the applicant must carry at least six semester hour or the equivalent during each semester for which the loan is requested. BPW Foundation and Sears-Roebuck employees are ineligible.

New York Life Foundation Scholarship for Women in Health Professions
No. Awards: varies
Award Amount: $500-$1,000
Funds Available: $50,000

Features: Applicants must demonstrate financial need for assistance (defined to be $30,000 or less for a family of four). Applicants must be undergraduates in one of the healthcare fields and must be females over age 24, officially accepted into an accredited course of study at a U.S. institution (including Puerto Rico and the Virgin Islands), and expecting to graduate within 12 to 24 months from date of grant. Scholarships are awarded for full-time or part-time study.The purpose of this award is to assist women seeking the education necessary for entry or re-entry into the work force or advancement within a career in the healthcare field. This scholarship does not cover graduate or doctorate studies, correspondence courses, or non-degree programs. New York Life Insurance Company officers and their immediate family members are ineligible. All awards are granted by BPW Foundation's Financial Aid Committee.

Wyeth-Ayerst Scholarship for Women in Graduate Medical Program
No. Awards: 25
Award Amount: $2,000
Funds Available: $50,000
Deadline: April 15
Features: Applicant must demonstrate financial need for financial assistance (defined to be $30,000 or less for a family of four). Must be female over age 24, officially accepted into an accredited course of study at a U.S. institution (including Puerto Rico and the Virgin Islands), expecting to graduate within 12 to 24 months from date of grant, and have a clear plan for applying training towards career advancement or change, or to enter or re-enter the job market. Must be studying in emerging health field of biomedical research, medical technology, pharmaceutical marketing, public health, or public health policy. Only open to full-time graduate students.

Daughters of the Cincinnati Scholarship Program

Daughters of the Cincinnati
122 East 58th Street
New York, NY 10022
V: 212-319-6915
No. Awards: 10-12 new awards each year, 38-42 annual awards altogether
Award Amount: varies
Funds Available: varies
Deadline: March 15
Features: Applicant must be daughter of a career officer commissioned in the Regular Army, Air Force, Navy, Coast Guard, or Marine Corps (active, retired, or deceased), and a high school senior. Scholarships are awarded based on merit and need for up to four years. The student must plan to attend an accredited institution of higher education.

Daughters of Penelope National Scholarship Award

Daughters of Penelope National Headquarters
1909 Q Street, NW, Suite 500
Washington, DC 20009
V: 202-234-9741
No. Awards: varies
Award Amount: $1000-$1,500
Funds Available: varies
Deadline: June 20, postmarked

Features: Applicant must be high school graduate, undergraduate, or college graduate female. Applicants must be accepted or enrolled at a college, university or accredited technical school. Student must have a member of the immediate family or legal guardian (court appointed) in the Daughters of Penelope or the Order of Ahepa, in good standing for a minimum of two years, or be a member in good standing for two years of the Daughters of Penelope or the Maids of Athena. (Immediate family means father, mother, or grandparent.) College graduates must be accepted or be currently enrolled in M.S., M.B.A., Ph.D., D.D.S., M.D., or other university post-graduate degree program. College students must also be enrolled for a minimum of 9 units per academic year. Former recipients of the DOP National Scholarship Program are ineligible.

Executive Women International Scholarship Program

Executive Women International
515 South 700 East, Suite 2F
Salt Lake City, UT 84102
V: 801-355-2800
No. Awards: 130
Award Amount: up to $10,000
Deadline: January 31

Features: Applicants must enter the contest of the local chapter and be available for interview. Applicants must be high school juniors planning to enroll at a four-year institution. Students must be planning careers in any business or professional field of study that requires a four-year college degree. Applicants must reside within the boundaries of a participating chapter. There are 34 chapters in America. U.S. citizenship is not required. Include self-addressed, stamped envelope for application forms.

Gloria Fecht Memorial Scholarship Fund Women's Southern California Golf Association

Gloria Fecht Foundation
402 W. Arrow Highway, Suite 10
San Dimas, CA 91773
V: 619-562-0304
I: www.womensgolf.org/wsga/scholar/
No. Awards: 20-30
Award Amount: $1,000 - $3,000
Funds Available: $45,000 +
Deadline: March 1
Features: Applicants must be female residents of Southern California, prove financial need, be active in extracurricular activities, meet entrance requirements, plan to enroll in an accredited four-year university, and have an active interest in golf. Minimum 3.0 GPA. Application available online.

Kappa Kappa Gamma Foundation

P.O. Box 38
Columbus, OH 43216-0038
V: 614-228-6515
I: www.kappa.org

Scholarship/Fellowship/Grants
No. Awards: varies
Award Amount: varies
Deadline: Feb. 1
Features: Must be a member of Kappa Kappa Gamma. Send self-addressed, stamped envelope for more information and an application. Please note chapter membership on your request. Graduate students need to state whether studying full-time or part-time.

Scholarships and Fellowships
No. Awards: Not specified
Award Amount: Average award $1,000; includes educational expenses
Deadline: Feb. 1

Features: Must be a female member of the granting agency; at undergraduate, graduate, or postgraduate level. Nationality and residency unrestricted. Notification is in the spring.

Ladies Auxiliary of the Fleet Reserve Association (LAFRA) Scholarship

c/o Fleet Reserve Association
125 N. West Street
Alexandria, VA 22314
V: 703-683-1400
I: www.fra.org
No. Awards: Approximately 5
Award Amount: $500-$2,500
Deadline: April 15
Features: Applicant must be daughter or granddaughter of Naval, Marine Corps, active Fleet Reserve, Fleet Marine Corps Reserve, Coast Guard Reserve, or Coast Guard personnel, retired with pay or deceased. Send self-addressed, stamped envelope.

MANA, a National Latina Organization

1725 K Street NW #501
Washington, DC 20006
V: 202-833-0060 Ext.14
I: www.hermana.org
No. Awards: varies
Award Amount: varies
Deadline: April 1
Features: Applicants must be female MANA members of Hispanic heritage and enrolled full time in an accredited college or university. Criteria given special consideration are academic achievement, financial need, commitment and contributions to Hispanic issues and Hispanic women's progress. Send self-addressed, stamped envelope for application.

Margaret McNamara Memorial Fund

World Bank
1818 H Street, NW Rm. Q5-080
Washington, DC 20433
V: 202-473-5804
No. Awards: 6
Award Amount: $9,000

Features: Applicant must be a female at least 25 years old by December 31 and from a selected developing country, but living in the U.S. and studying at an accredited U.S. institution when she applies and during the period the grant covers. Must have a record of service to women and/or children in the applicant's home country and must plan to return to that country

roughly two years after date of award. Based on financial need. Students who meet all criteria should write to the above address, listing name, address, country, and institution where they are enrolled. Permanent U.S. residents and relatives or spouses of staff members of any institution in the World Bank group are ineligible.

The Sons of Norway Nancy Lorraine Jensen Memorial Scholarship Fund (See Organizations)

Women's Western Golf Foundation Scholarship

Women's Western Golf Foundation
393 Ramsay Road
Deerfield, IL 60015
V: 847-945-0451
No. Awards: 20
Award Amount: $2,000, renewable for four years
Funds Available: up to $40,000
Deadline: March 1
Features: Academic merit, financial need, excellence of character, and interest or involvement in the sport of golf. Skill in golf is not required. Must be high school senior female intending to graduate in the year of application and U.S. citizen. Must meet college entrance requirements and plan to enroll in an accredited college or university. Complete preliminary application and the Federal Student Aid Report between January 1 and March 1. Student must have submitted the Free Application for Federal Student Aid (FAFSA). Minimum GPA 3.0. *Deadline to request preliminary applications is March 1.* Final application will be sent later. Must send a self-addressed, stamped envelope for application and information.

Glossary of Financial Aid Terms

The college money system has become so complex it needs its own glossary. We very much appreciate the kindness of the National Association of Student Financial Aid Administrators in allowing us to use theirs.

Acronyms

ADC	Aid to Dependent Children	**INS**	Immigration and Naturalization Service
AFDC	Aid to Families with Dependent Children	**IPA**	Income Protection Allowance
AGI	Adjusted Gross Income	**IRS**	Internal Revenue Service
AY	Academic Year	**ISIR**	Institutional Student Information Record
BA	Bachelor's Degree		
BIA	Bureau of Indian Affairs	**LDS**	Loans for Disadvantaged Students (health professions)
COA	Cost of Attendance		
CSS	College Scholarship Service	**MDE**	Multiple Data Entry
CPS	Central Processing System	**NDSL**	National Defense/Direct Student Loan (now known as Federal Perkins Loan)
DHHS	Department of Health and Human Services		
ED	U.S. Department of Education	**NHSC**	National Health Service Corps
EIC	Earned Income Credit	**NSLDS**	National Student Loan Data System
EDE	Electronic Data Exchange		
EFA	Estimated Financial Assistance	**NEISP**	National Early Intervention Scholarship and Partnership Program
EFC	Expected Family Contribution (also FC, Family Contribution)		
EFN	Exceptional Financial Need Scholarships (health professions)	**NSSP**	National Science Scholars Program
FADHPS	Financial Assistance for Disadvantaged Health Professions Students	**NSL**	Nursing Student Loan
		OSFAP	Office of Student Financial Assistance Programs, U.S. Department of Education
FAFSA	Free Application for Federal Student Aid		
FAT	Financial Aid Transcript	**PC**	Parental Contribution
FDLP	Federal Direct Loan Programs	**PCL**	Primary Care Loan Program (health professions)
FFELP	Federal Family Education Loan Programs		
		SAR	Student Aid Report
FM	Federal Methodology	**SAP**	Satisfactory Academic Progress
FNAS	Federal Need Analysis System	**SC**	Student Contribution
FPLUS	Federal PLUS (Parent) Loan	**SDS**	Scholarships for Disadvantaged Students
FSEOG	Federal Supplemental Educational Opportunity Grant		
		SSIG	State Student Incentive Grant
FWS	Federal Work-Study	**VA**	Veterans Affairs, Department of
GPA	Grade Point Average		
GSL	Guaranteed Student Loan		
HHS	Department of Health and Human Services (also abbreviated DHHS)		
HPSL	Health Professions Student Loan		

Definitions

Academic Credit: The unit of measurement an institution gives to a student when he/she fulfills course or subject requirement(s) as determined by the institution.

Academic Year: This is a measure of the academic work to be accomplished by a student. The school defines its own academic year, but federal regulations set minimum standards for the purpose of determining student financial aid awards. For instance, the academic year at a term school must be a least 30 weeks of instructional time in which a full-time undergraduate student is expected to complete at least 24 semester or trimester hours or 36 quarter hours or 900 clock hours.

Acceptance Form: The written acknowledgment by the student of receipt of an award letter. The form usually provides for acceptance of offered aid, possible declination of all or part of the package, and some means of requesting an appeal, if that is desired, to modify the award. Frequently, acceptance letters and award letters are combined into a single document.

Adjusted Gross Income (AGI): All taxable income as reported on a U.S. income tax return.

Amnesty Applicant: An individual who entered the U.S. without proper documentation, or illegally, who was eligible to apply for temporary (and eventually, permanent) resident status under provisions of the Immigration Reform and Control Act of 1986.

Assets: Cash on hand in checking and savings accounts; trusts, stocks, bonds, other securities; real estate (excluding home), income-producing property, business equipment, and business inventory. Considered in determining expected family contribution (EFC) under the regular need analysis formula.

Assistantship: A type of student employment; usually refers to teaching assistant positions which are available to students.

Award Letter: A means of notifying successful financial aid applicants of the assistance being offered. The award letter usually provides information on the types and amounts of aid offered, as well as specific program information, student responsibilities, and the conditions which govern the award. Generally provides students with the opportunity to accept or decline the aid offered.

Award Year: An award year begins on July 1 of one year and extends to June 30 of the next year. Funding for Federal Pell grants and campus-based programs is provided on the basis of the award year. For example, a student is paid out of funds designated for a particular award year, such as the 2000-2001 award year.

Bachelor's Degree (BA): The degree given for successful completion of the undergraduate curriculum at a four-year college or a university. Also called baccalaureate degree.

Base Year: For need analysis purposes, the base year is the calendar year preceding the award year. For instance, 1999 is the base year used for the 2000-2001 award year. The Free Application for Federal Student Aid (FAFSA) uses family income from the base year because it is more accurate and easier to verify than projected year income.

Budget: The estimated cost of attendance for a student at an institution; usually includes tuition, fees, books, supplies, room, board, personal expenses, and transportation. Other expenses may be included. (See also *Cost of Attendance*.)

Bureau of Indian Affairs (BIA) Grants: A grant program for enrolled members of a tribe (Indian, Eskimo, or Aleut) pursuing an undergraduate or graduate degree at an accredited postsecondary institution. In order to be eligible for a BIA grant, students must show financial need as determined by the institution they are attending.

Business Assets: Property that is used in the operation of a trade or business, including real estate, inventories, buildings, machinery and other equipment, patents, franchise rights, and copyrights. Considered in determining a family's expected contribution (EFC) under the regular need analysis formula.

Byrd Scholarship: A federally sponsored, merit-based scholarship for academically outstanding high school students.

Campus-Based Programs: The term commonly applied to those U.S. Department of Education federal student aid programs administered by institutions of postsecondary education. Includes: Federal Perkins Loan, Federal Supplemental Educational Opportunity Grant (FSEOG), and Federal Work-Study (FWS).

Cancellation of Loan: The condition that exists when a Federal Perkins Loan (or NDSL) borrower has fulfilled requirements to permit cancellation of, or "writing off," a designated portion of the principal and interest.

Central Processing System (CPS): The computer system to which the student's need analysis data is electronically transmitted by the FAFSA processor or MDE. The central processing system performs database matches and calculates the official Expected Family Contribution (EFC) and sends out the Student Aid Report (SAR) to the student and an Institutional Student Information Record (ISIR) to the school.

Citizen/Eligible Non-Citizen: A person who owes allegiance to the United States. Most state and federal financial aid programs are considered domestic assistance programs and are available only to U.S. citizens, U.S. nationals (including natives of American Somoa or Swain's Island), or permanent residents of the U.S., or those who are in this country for other than temporary purposes. Citizens of the Marshall Islands, the Federated States of Micronesia, and the Republic of Palau are eligible for Federal Pell grant, FSEOG, and FWS only.

Collection Agency: A business organization that accepts, from schools and lenders, loan accounts that have become delinquent or are in default, and attempts to collect on those accounts. A fee is charged for the service.

Commercial Lender: A commercial bank, savings and loan association, credit union, stock savings bank, trust company, or mutual savings bank. Can act as a lender for the Federal Family Education Loan Program (FFELP).

Community Service: The National and Community Service Trust Act of 1993 established the Corporation for National Service, which offers educational opportunities through service to American communities. The three programs assist persons who serve communities before, during, or after postsecondary education by rewarding them with educational benefits. Awards may be used to pay for past, present, or future educational expenses, including repayment of portions of their federal education loans.

Commuter Student: A student who does not live on-campus, or in institutionally owned or operated housing; typically, "commuter" refers to a student living at home with his or her parents, but can also mean any student who lives off-campus.

Cost of Attendance: A student's cost of attendance includes tuition and fees, room and board expenses while attending school, and allowances for books and supplies, transportation, loan fees (if applicable), dependent care costs, costs related to a disability, and other miscellaneous expenses. In addition, reasonable costs for a study-abroad program and costs associated with a student's employment as part of a cooperative education program may be included. The cost of attendance is estimated by the school, within guidelines established by federal regulations. The cost of attendance is compared to a student's Expected Family Contribution (EFC) to determine the student's need for aid.

Defaulted (Federal Perkins Loan): A loan for which the borrower failed to make an installment payment when due and such failure persisted (not cured either by payment or other appropriate arrangements). The Secretary of Education considers a loan discharged in bankruptcy not to be in default.

Default (Federal Stafford, Direct Loan, Federal PLUS, or Direct PLUS Loan): The failure of a borrower to make an installment payment when due, or to meet other terms of the promissory note under circumstances where the Secretary of Education or the pertinent guarantee agency finds it reasonable to conclude that the borrower no longer intends to honor the obligation to repay.

Deferment of Loan: A condition during which payments of principal are not required, and, for Federal Perkins and subsidized Federal Stafford and Direct Subsidized Loans, interest does not accrue. The repayment period is extended by the length of the deferment period.

Departmental Scholarship: An award of gift assistance that is specifically designated for a recipient in a particular academic department within the institution.

Dependent Student: A student who does not qualify as an independent student and whose parental income and asset information is used in calculating expected family contribution (see also *Independent Student*).

Direct Loan Program (Direct Loans): The collective name for the Direct Subsidized, Direct Unsubsidized, and Direct PLUS Loan programs. Also referred to as William D. Ford Federal Direct Loan Program.

Direct PLUS Loan Program (Parent Loan): Long-term loans made available to parents of dependent students. The government provides the funding. Interest rates are linked to 52-week Treasury bill rates, but may not exceed 9 percent. May be used to replace EFC.

Direct Subsidized and Direct Unsubsidized Loan Program: Long term, low interest loans administered by the Department of Education and institutions. The government is the source of funding. Variable interest rate not to exceed 8.25 percent. Direct Unsubsidized Loans can be used to replace EFC.

Disbursement: The process by which financial aid funds are made available to students for use in meeting educational and related living expenses. Funds may be disbursed directly to the student or applied to the student's account.

Disclosure Statement: Statement explaining specific terms and conditions of student loans, such as interest rate, loan fees charged, gross amount borrowed, and so on. Disclosure statements must accompany each loan disbursement.

Educational Benefits: Funds, primarily federal, awarded to certain categories of students (veterans, children of deceased veterans or other deceased wage earners, and students with physical disabilities) to help finance their postsecondary education regardless of their ability to demonstrate need in the traditional sense.

Educational Expenses: See *Budget* and *Cost of Attendance*.

Electronic Data Exchange: The Department of Education's service for sending and receiving application information electronically to the CPS.

Eligible Institution: An institution of higher education, or a vocational school, or a postsecondary vocational institution, or a proprietary institution of higher education which meets all criteria for participation in the federal student aid programs.

Eligible Program: A course of study that requires a certain minimum number of hours of instruction and that leads to a degree or certificate at a school participating in one or more of the federal student financial aid programs described in this handbook. Generally, to get student aid, a student must be enrolled in an eligible program.

Employment Allowance: An allowance to meet expenses related to employment when both parents (or a married independent student and spouse) are employed or when one parent (or independent student) qualifies as a surviving spouse or as head of a household. Used in need analysis formula for parents and student, if eligible.

Enrolled: The completion of registration requirements (other than the payment of tuition and fees) at the institution the student is or will be attending; a correspondence school student must be accepted for admission and complete and submit one lesson to be considered enrolled.

Enrollment Status: At those institutions using semesters, trimesters, quarters, or other academic terms and measuring progress by credit hours, enrollment status equals a student's credit hour workload categorized as either full-time, three-quarter-time, half-time, or less-than-half-time.

Entitlement Program: Program which is funded sufficiently to ensure that all eligible applicants are guaranteed to receive maximum authorized awards. As long as the student applicant meets all the eligibility requirements and is enrolled in an eligible program at an eligible institution, he or she will receive the award for which eligibility has been established.

Estimated Financial Assistance: The amount of student financial aid a student may expect from federal, state, school, or other resources, including grants, loans, or need-based work programs.

Exceptional Financial Need Scholarship (EFN): Scholarship program for students studying to earn a doctorate in allopathic or osteopathic medicine or dentistry.

Exceptional Need: An eligibility criterion in the FSEOG and Federal Perkins Loan Programs. Exceptional need for FSEOG is defined in statute as the lowest expected family contributions at an institution. The law does not define the term for the Federal Perkins Loan Program. The definition of exceptional need varies from school to school.

Expected Family Contribution (EFC): The amount a student and his or her family are expected to contribute toward the student's cost of attendance as calculated by a congressionally-mandated formula known as Federal Methodology.

FAFSA Express: Electronic method for students to apply directly to the Department of Education for Title IV aid using a PC and a modem.

Federal Family Education Loan Programs (FFELP): The collective name for the Federal Stafford (subsidized and unsubsidized) and Federal PLUS Loan programs. Funds are provided by private lenders and guaranteed by the federal government.

Federal Methodology: Formula, defined in statute, and used to determine an expected family contribution (EFC) for Federal Pell grants, campus-based programs, FFEL programs, and Direct loan programs.

Federal Pell Grant: A grant program for undergraduate students who have not yet completed a first baccalaureate or bachelor's degree. For many students, Federal Pell grants provide a foundation of financial aid to which other aid may be added.

Federal Perkins Loans: Formerly known as the National Direct Student Loan Program, or NDSL. One of the campus-based programs; a long term, low interest (5 percent) loan program for both undergraduate and graduate students with exceptional financial need. The school is the lender and the loan is made with government funds.

Federal PLUS Loans: Long-term loans made available to parents with good credit history of dependent students. Interest rates are linked to 52-week Treasury bill rates, but may not exceed 9 percent. May be used to replace EFC.

Federal Stafford Loan Program (subsidized and unsubsidized): Long term, low interest loans administered by the Department of Education through private lenders and guarantee agencies. Formerly known as Guaranteed Student Loans (GSLs). Variable interest rate, not to exceed 8.25 percent. Unsubsidized Federal Stafford Loans may be used to replace EFC.

Federal Supplemental Educational Opportunity Grant (FSEOG): One of the campus-based programs; grants to undergraduate students with exceptional financial need who have not completed their first baccalaureate degree and who are financially in need of this grant to enable them to pursue their education. Priority for FSEOG awards must be given to Federal Pell grant recipients with the lowest EFCs.

Federal Work-Study Program (FWS): One of the campus-based programs; a part-time employment program which provides jobs for undergraduate and graduate students who are in need of such earnings to meet a portion of their educational expenses. The program encourages community service work related to the student's course of study.

Fellowship: A grant of money for post-graduate study which may require teaching or research.

Financial Aid Administrator (FAA): An individual who is responsible for preparing and communicating information pertaining to student loans, grants or scholarships, and employment programs, and for advising, awarding, reporting, counseling, and supervising office functions related to student financial aid. He or she is account-able to the various publics which are involved; is a manager or administrator who interprets and implements federal, state, and institutional policies and regulations; and is capable of analyzing student and employee needs and making changes where necessary.

Financial Aid Award: An offer of financial or in-kind assistance to a student attend-ing a postsecondary educational institu-tion. This award may be in the form of one or more of the following types of financial aid: a non-repayable grant, and/or scholarship, and/or student employment, and/or repayable loan.

Financial Aid Package: A financial aid award to a student comprised of a combination of forms of financial aid (loans, grants and/or scholarships, employment).

Financial Aid Transcript: A form used by postsecondary institutions to collect data about any financial aid awards that a student received at other educational institutions.

Financial Assistance for Disadvantaged Health Professions Students (FADHPS): Scholarship program for allopathic and osteopathic medical students and dental students from disadvantaged backgrounds who demonstrate exceptional need for financial assistance.

Financial Need: The difference between the institution's cost of attendance and the family's ability to pay (that is, expected family contribution). May be expressed in the formula: COA - EFC = Need.

Forbearance: Permitting the temporary cessation of repayments of loans, allowing an extension of time for making loan payments, or accepting smaller loan payments than were previously scheduled.

Foreign Student: A student belonging to or owing allegiance to another country. Foreign students are not eligible for the basic federal programs, although there are categories of eligible non-citizens who owe permanent allegiance to the United States and are eligible for student aid.

Free Application for Federal Student Aid (FAFSA): The original input document (aid application) of the Department of Education's need analysis system. The application filled out and filed by a student that collects household and financial information used by the federal govern-ment to calculate the Expected Family Contribution (EFC).

Full-Time Student: Generally, one who is taking a minimum of 12 semester or quarter hours per academic term in institutions with standard academic terms, or 24 clock hours per week in institutions which measure progress in terms of clock hours.

G.I. Bill Benefits: Special assistance provided by the federal government to eligible veterans for the purpose of financing education or training programs.

Gift Aid: That form of financial aid which does not require repayment or require that work be performed.

Grace Period: The period of time that begins when a loan recipient ceases to be at least half-time and ends when the repayment period starts. Loan principal need not be paid and, generally, interest does not accrue during this period.

Graduate or Professional Student: A student enrolled in an academic program of study above the baccalaureate level at an institution of higher education.

Grant: A type of financial aid that does not have to be repaid; usually awarded on the basis of need, possibly combined with some skills or characteristics the student possesses.

Guaranteed Student Loan (GSL) Programs: Previous collective name used for the Federal Family Education Loan Programs.

Guaranty Agency: A state agency, private, non-profit institution, or organization which administers a student loan insurance program.

Health Professions Student Loan (HPSL) Program: A long term, low interest loan program designed to assist students in specific health professions disciplines.

Income Protection Allowance: An allowance against income for the basic costs of maintaining family members in the home. The allowance is based upon consumption and other cost estimates of the Bureau of Labor Statistics for a family at the low standard of living.

Independent Student: A student who has attained age 24, or who has not attained age 24 but (a) is an orphan; (b) is a ward of the court; (c) is a veteran; (d) is married or is a graduate or professional student; (e) has legal dependents other than a spouse; or (f) presents documentation of other unusual circumstances demonstrating independence to the student financial aid administrator.

Institutional Student Information Record (ISIR): A federal output record that contains the student's EFC as calculated by the Central Processing System (CPS) and all the financial and other data submitted by the student on the FAFSA. The ISIR can be received electronically by schools that participate in the Electronic Data Exchange (EDE) system. (See also *Student Aid Report.*)

Legal Dependent (of Applicant): A natural or adopted child, or a person for whom the applicant has been appointed legal guardian, and for whom the applicant provides more than half support. In addition, a person who lives with and receives at least half support from the applicant and will continue to receive that support during the award year. For purposes of determining dependency status, a spouse is not considered a legal dependent.

Legal Guardian: An individual appointed by a court to be a legal guardian of a person and who is specifically required by the court to use his/her own financial resources to support that person. For 2000-2001, the legal relationship must continue beyond June 30, 2001 for the legal guardian to be considered a parent for the purposes of completing the FAFSA.

Loan: An advance of funds which is evidenced by a promissory note requiring the recipient to repay the specified amount(s) under prescribed conditions.

Loans for Disadvantaged Students (LDS): A federal loan program designed to assist disadvantaged students enrolled in specific health professions disciplines.

Military Scholarships: Reserve Officer Training Corps (ROTC) scholarships available for the Army, Navy, and Air Force at many colleges and universities throughout the United States. These scholarships cover tuition and fees, books and supplies, and include a subsistence allowance.

Multiple Data Entry (MDE): The procedure which allows for the incorporation and transmission of FAFSA data elements so that applicants can apply for Federal Pell Grants and other financial assistance by completing one form. The need analysis service key enters the student's FAFSA data into a computer system and then transmits the data to the Central Processing System. Students receive their eligibility notification directly from the Central Processing System.

Multiple Data Entry (MDE) Servicer: An organization contracted by the Department of Education to provide the means for a student to apply for federal student aid; also known as the FAFSA processor.

National Direct Student Loan (NDSL): Former name of the Federal Perkins Loan Program.

National Early Intervention Scholarship and Partnership (NEISP) Program: Grants provided to states to encourage states to provide financial assistance and support services to low-income and disadvantaged students interested in pursuing higher education.

National Health Service Corps (NHSC) Scholarships: Scholarship program for students who pursue full-time courses of study in certain health professions disciplines, and are willing to serve as primary care practitioners in underserved areas after completing their education.

National Science Scholars Program (NSSP): Science scholarship available to undergraduate students.

National Student Loan Data System (NSLDS): A national database of Title IV loan data and selected Title IV grant data.

National of the United States: A citizen of the United States or a non-citizen who owes permanent allegiance to the United States.

Need Analysis: A system used to estimate a student applicant's need for financial assistance to help meet his/her educational expenses. Need analysis consists of two primary components: (a) determination of an estimate of the applicant's and/or family's ability to contribute to educational expenses; and (b) determination of an accurate estimate of the educational expenses themselves.

Nursing Student Loans (NSL): Loans available to nursing students attending approved nursing schools offering a diploma, associate degree, baccalaureate, or graduate degree in nursing.

Overpayment: Any amount paid to a student which is in excess of the amount he/she was entitled or eligible to receive.

Packaging: The process of combining various types of student aid (grants, loans, scholarship, and employment) to attempt to meet a student's need.

Parent: The student's biological mother or father, legal guardian, or adoptive parent.

Parent Loans: See *Federal PLUS Loans* or *Direct PLUS Loan Program.*

Parents' Contribution: A quantitative estimate of the parents' ability to contribute to postsecondary educational expenses.

Part-Time Student: One who attends an institution on less than a full-time basis as defined by the institution.

Paul Douglas Teacher Scholarship: A scholarship program administered by the states to enable and encourage outstanding high school graduates who demonstrate an interest in teaching to pursue teaching careers at the elementary and secondary levels.

Postsecondary School: Technically, this term refers to any educational institution providing educational services beyond the level of high school. In daily usage, the term is often used to refer to non-higher educational institutions such as proprietary schools, trade and technical schools, and a range of nontraditional educational facilities as well as colleges and universities.

Presidential Access Scholarships: Scholarship available to undergraduate students who are eligible for Federal Pell grants and who demonstrate academic achievement.

Primary Care Loan: Loans to assist allopathic medical and osteopathic medical students who intend to engage in primary care residency and practice.

Privacy Acts: Those collective statutes that serve to protect an individual from the release of specified data without the individual's prior written consent.

Professional Student: A student in a professional school, such as a law school student or medical school student. (See also *Graduate Student.*)

Promissory Note: The legal document that binds a borrower to the repayment obligations and other terms and conditions which govern a loan program.

Reauthorization: A Congressional review process intended to refine authorized federal programs to ensure they meet the needs of the populations they are intended to serve.

Refund: The amount due a student who withdraws or fails to pursue his/her course of study when funds have been paid to the institution. When an institution determines that a student is due a refund, if that student has received financial aid funds, a portion of the refund must be allocated to the program(s) from which the student received aid.

Regular Student: A person who is enrolled or accepted for enrollment at an institution of higher education for the purpose of obtaining a degree or certificate.

Renewal FAFSA: The version of the FAFSA that students may use if they applied for federal financial aid the previous award year. If a student is among those allowed to complete a Renewal FAFSA, it will be sent directly to him or her by the FAFSA processor or the school.

Repayment Schedule: A plan, which should be attached to the promissory note at the time a borrower ceases at least half-time study, which sets forth the principal and interest due on each installment and the number of payments required to pay the loan in full. Additionally, it should include the interest rate, the due date of the first payment, and the frequency of payments.

Resident Student: A student who does not live at home (with parents or guardian) during the academic year. An off-campus resident student is one who does not live in the institutionally provided housing. An on-campus resident student is one who lives in housing facilities owned and/or maintained by the institution.

Resources: Resources include, but are not limited to, any: (a) funds the student is entitled to receive from a Federal Pell grant, regardless of whether the student applies for it; (b) Stafford (GSL) loans; (c) waiver of tuition and fees; (d) grants, including FSEOG and ROTC subsistence allowances; (e) scholarships, including athletic and ROTC scholarships; (f) fellowships or assistantships; (g) insurance programs for the student's education; (h) long term loans, including Federal Perkins and Direct loans, made by the institution; (i) earnings from need-based employment; (j) veterans benefits; and (k) any portion of other long term loans, including Federal PLUS or Direct loans, state-sponsored, or private loans, not used as a substitute for the EFC.

Satisfactory Academic Progress: The progress required of a financial aid recipient in acceptable studies or other activities to fulfill a specified educational objective.

Scholarship: A form of financial assistance which does not require repayment or employment and is usually made to students who demonstrate or show potential for distinction, usually in academic performance, at the institution.

Scholarships for Disadvantaged Students (SDS): A federal scholarship program designed to assist disadvantaged students enrolled in certain health profession disciplines.

School Year: See *Academic Year.*

Self-Help Assistance: Funds provided through the work and effort of the student, including savings from past earnings, income from present earnings, or a loan to be repaid from future earnings.

Self-Help Expectation: The assumption that a student has an obligation to help pay for a portion of his/her education. (See also *Student Contribution.*)

Simplified Needs Test: An alternate method of calculating the expected family contribution for families with adjusted gross incomes of less than $50,000, who have filed, or are eligible to file, an IRS Form 1040A, 1040EZ, or 1040TEL, or are not required to file an income tax return. Excludes all assets from consideration.

State Student Incentive Grant (SSIG): State scholarship/grant assistance for postsecondary students with substantial financial need.

Statement of Educational Purpose: Statement included on the FAFSA signed by the student financial aid recipient indicating his or her agreement to use all financial aid funds awarded for educational or educationally related purposes only.

Student Aid Report (SAR): A federal output document sent to a student by the CPS. The SAR contains financial and other information reported by the student on the Free Application for Federal Student Aid (FAFSA). That information is entered into the processing system, and the SAR is produced. The student's eligibility for aid is indicated by the EFC, which is printed on the front of the SAR. (See also *Institutional Student Information Record.*)

Student Budget: See *Cost of Attendance.*

Student Contribution: A quantitative estimate of the student's ability to contribute to postsecondary expenses.

Student Financial Aid: Funds awarded to a student to help meet postsecondary educational expenses. These funds are generally awarded on the basis of financial need and include scholarships, grants, loans, and employment.

Taxable Income: Income earned from wages, salaries, and tips, as well as interest income, dividend income, business or farm profits, and rental or property income.

Temporarily Totally Disabled: With regard to a student loan borrower, this means an injury or illness which prevents an individual from attending an eligible institution or to be gainfully employed for an extended period of time. With regard to the borrower's spouse or dependent, this means an injury or illness, established by an affidavit of a qualified physician, that requires the borrower to provide care such as continuous nursing (or other similar service) that prevents the borrower from obtaining gainful employment.

Three-Quarter-Time Student: A student who is carrying at least a three-quarter time academic workload as determined by the institution at which the student is enrolled, and which amounts to at least three-quarters of the workload of a full-time student.

Title IV Programs: Those federal student aid programs authorized under Title IV of the Higher Education Act of 1965, as amended. Includes, among others, the Federal Pell Grant, Federal Supplemental Educational Opportunity Grant, Federal Work Study, Federal Perkins Loan, Federal Stafford Loan, Federal PLUS, Direct Loan, Direct PLUS, and SSIG.

Totally and Permanently Disabled:
Unable to engage in any substantial gainful activity because of a medically determinable impairment that is expected to continue for a long and indefinite period of time or will result in death.

Truth-in-Lending Statement: The document provided to loan recipients that delineates the interest rate and other information relative to the loan the student has received. The use of the statement is required by the Consumer Credit Act.

Undergraduate Student: A student who has not achieved the educational level of a baccalaureate or first professional degree.

Unmet Need: The difference between a student's total cost attendance at a specific institution and the student's total available resources, including financial aid.

Untaxed Income: All income received that is not reported to the Internal Revenue Service or is reported but excluded from taxation. Such income would include but not be limited to any untaxed portion of Social Security benefits, Earned Income Credit, welfare payments, untaxed capital gains, interest on tax-free bonds, dividend exclusion, and military and other subsistence and quarters allowances.

Verification: A procedure in which a school checks the information a student reported on the FAFSA, usually by requesting a copy of signed tax returns filed by the student and, if applicable, the student's parent(s) and spouse. Schools must verify students selected for verification by the federal central processing system, following procedures established by federal regulations. Many schools also select students for verification in addition to those selected by the central processing system.

Veteran: A person who has served on active duty in the Army, Navy, Air Force, Marine, or Coast Guard, or was a cadet or midshipmen at one of the service academies, and who was discharged other than dishonorably. Veterans are considered to be independent. There is no minimum length of service requirement.

Veterans Educational Benefits: Assistance programs for veterans and service persons for education or training.

Vocational Rehabilitation: Programs administered by state departments of vocational rehabilitation services to assist individuals who have a physical or mental disability which is a substantial handicap to employment.

Ward of the Court: A person who is under the care of the court.

Free Application for Federal Student Aid

OMB 1840-0110   *July 1, 2000 — June 30, 2001 school year*

Step One: For questions 1-37, leave blank any questions that do not apply to you (the student).

1-3. Your full name (as it appears on your Social Security card)

1. LAST NAME   2. FIRST NAME   3. M.I.

FOR INFORMATION ONLY   **DO NOT SUBMIT**

4-7. Your permanent mailing address

4. NUMBER AND STREET (INCLUDE APARTMENT NUMBER)

5. CITY (AND COUNTRY, IF NOT U.S.)   6. STATE   7. ZIP CODE

8. Your Social Security Number   XXX - XX - XXXX

9. Your date of birth   MONTH / DAY / YEAR 1 9

10. Your permanent telephone number   AREA CODE

11. Do you have a driver's license?   Yes ○ 1   No ○ 2

12-13. Driver's license number and state   12. LICENSE NUMBER   13. STATE

14. Are you a U.S. citizen? Pick one. **See Page 2.**
   a. Yes, I am a U.S. citizen. .... ○ 1
   b. No, but I am an eligible noncitizen. Fill in question 15. ○ 2
   c. No, I am not a citizen or eligible noncitizen. .... ○ 3

ALIEN REGISTRATION NUMBER

15. A

16. Marital status as of today
   I am single, divorced, or widowed. ○ 1
   I am married. ○ 2
   I am separated. ○ 3

17. Month and year you were married, separated, divorced, or widowed   MONTH / YEAR

For each question (18 - 22), please mark whether you will be full time, 3/4 time, half time, less than half time, or not attending. Mark "Full time" if you are not sure. See page 2.

	Full time	3/4 time	Half time	Less than half time	Not attending
18. Summer 2000	○ 1	○ 2	○ 3	○ 4	○ 5
19. Fall semester or quarter 2000	○ 1	○ 2	○ 3	○ 4	○ 5
20. Winter quarter 2000-2001	○ 1	○ 2	○ 3	○ 4	○ 5
21. Spring semester or quarter 2001	○ 1	○ 2	○ 3	○ 4	○ 5
22. Summer 2001	○ 1	○ 2	○ 3	○ 4	○ 5

23. Highest school your father completed   Middle school/Jr. High ○ 1   High school ○ 2   College or beyond ○ 3   Other/unknown ○ 4

24. Highest school your mother completed   Middle school/Jr. High ○ 1   High school ○ 2   College or beyond ○ 3   Other/unknown ○ 4

25. What is your state of legal residence?   STATE

26. Did you become a legal resident of this state before January 1, 1995?   Yes ○ 1   No ○ 2

27. If the answer to question 26 is **"No,"** give month and year you became a legal resident.   MONTH / YEAR

28. Most male students must register with Selective Service to get federal aid. Are you male?   Yes ○ 1   No ○ 2

29. If you are male (age 18-25) and not registered, do you want Selective Service to register you?   Yes ○ 1   No ○ 2

30. What degree or certificate will you be working towards during 2000-2001? **See page 2** and enter the correct number in the box.

31. What will be your grade level when you begin the 2000-2001 school year? **See page 2** and enter the correct number in the box.

32. Will you have a high school diploma or GED before you enroll?   Yes ○ 1   No ○ 2

33. Will you have your first bachelor's degree before July 1, 2000?   Yes ○ 1   No ○ 2

34. In addition to grants, are you interested in student loans (which you must pay back)?   Yes ○ 1   No ○ 2

35. In addition to grants, are you interested in "work-study" (which you earn through work)?   Yes ○ 1   No ○ 2

36. If you receive veterans' education benefits, for how many months from July 1, 2000 through June 30, 2001 will you receive these benefits?

37. Amount per month? $

DRAFT – 2/16/99   Page 3

For 38-52, if you (the student) are now married (even if you were not married in 1999), report both your and your spouse's income and assets. Ignore references to "spouse" if you are currently separated, divorced, or widowed. If the answer is zero or the question does not apply to you, enter 0.

38. For 1999, have you filed your IRS income tax return or another tax return listed in **question 39**?

    a. I have already filed. ◯ ₁   **b.** I will file, but I have not yet filed. ◯ ₂   **c.** I'm not going to file. (Skip to question 45.) ◯ ₃

39. What income tax return did you file or will you file for 1999?

    a. IRS 1040 .... ◯ ₁   **c.** A foreign tax return. See Page 2. .... ◯ ₃

    b. IRS 1040A, 1040EZ, 1040Telefile ...... ◯ ₂   **d.** A tax return for Puerto Rico, Guam, American Samoa, the Virgin Islands, the Marshall Islands, the Federated States of Micronesia, or Palau. See Page 2. ...... ◯ ₄

40. If you have filed or will file a 1040, were you <u>eligible to file a 1040A or 1040EZ</u>? See page 2.   Yes ◯ ₁ No/don't know ◯ ₂

41. What was your (and spouse's) adjusted gross income for 1999? Adjusted gross income is on IRS Form 1040–line XX; 1040A–line XX; or 1040EZ–line X. $ ☐☐,☐☐☐

42. Enter the total amount of your (and spouse's) income tax for 1999. Income tax amount is on IRS Form 1040–line XX plus XX; 1040A–line XX; or 1040EZ–line XX. $ ☐☐,☐☐☐

43. Enter your (and spouse's) exemptions. Exemptions are on IRS Form 1040–line XX, or on Form 1040A–line XX. For Form 1040EZ, **see page 2.**   ☐☐

44. Enter your Earned Income Credit from IRS Form 1040–line XX; 1040A–line XX; or 1040EZ–line XX. $ ☐☐,☐☐☐

45-46. How much did you (and spouse) earn from working in 1999? Answer this question whether or not you filed a tax return. This information may be on your W-2 forms, or on IRS Form 1040–lines X, X, and X; 1040A–line X; or on 1040EZ–line X.   **You (45)** $ ☐☐,☐☐☐   **Your Spouse (46)** $ ☐☐,☐☐☐

47. Go to page 8 of this form; complete the column on the left of **Worksheet A**; enter student total here. $ ☐☐,☐☐☐

48. Go to page 8 of this form; complete the column on the left of **Worksheet B**; enter student total here. $ ☐☐,☐☐☐

49. Total current balance of cash, savings, and checking accounts $ ☐☐,☐☐☐

For 50-52, if net worth is one million or more, enter $999,999. If net worth is negative, enter 0. $ ☐☐,☐☐☐

50. Current <u>net worth</u> of <u>investments</u> (<u>investment value</u> minus <u>investment debt</u>) See page 2. $ ☐☐,☐☐☐

51. Current <u>net worth</u> of business (<u>business value</u> minus <u>business debt</u>) See page 2. $ ☐☐,☐☐☐

52. Current <u>net worth</u> of investment farm (Don't include a farm that you live on and operate.) $ ☐☐,☐☐☐

Step Two: If you (the student) answer "Yes" to any question in Step Two, go to Step Three. If you answer "No" to every question, skip Step Three and go to Step Four.

53. Were you born before January 1, 1977? .... Yes ◯ ₁ No ◯ ₂

54. Will you be working on a degree beyond a bachelor's degree in school year 2000-2001? .... Yes ◯ ₁ No ◯ ₂

55. As of today, are you married? (Answer yes if you are separated, but not divorced.) .... Yes ◯ ₁ No ◯ ₂

56. Are you an orphan or ward of the court or were you a ward of the court until age 18?................ Yes ◯ ₁ No ◯ ₂

57. Are you a <u>veteran</u> of the U.S. Armed Forces? See page 2. .... Yes ◯ ₁ No ◯ ₂

58. Answer **"Yes"** if: (1) You have children who receive more than half of their support from you; **or** (2) You have dependents (other than your children or spouse) who live with you and receive more than half of their support from you, now and through June 30, 2001. ...... Yes ◯ ₁ No ◯ ₂

Step Three: Complete this step only if you answered "Yes" to any question in Step Two.

59. How many people are in your (and your spouse's) <u>household</u>? See page 7.   ☐☐

60. How many in question 59 will be <u>college students</u> between July 1, 2000, and June 30, 2001? See page 7.   ☐

Now go to Step Five. (If you are a graduate health profession student, you may be required to complete Step Four even if you answered "Yes" to any questions in Step Two.)

Step Four: Please tell us about your parents. See page 7 for who is considered a parent.
Complete this step if you (the student) answered "No" to all questions in Step Two.

For 61 - 75, if the answer is zero or the question does not apply, enter 0.

61. For 1999, have your parents filed their IRS income tax return or another tax return listed in **question 62**?

a. My parents have already filed. ○ 1   **b.** My parents will file, but they ○ 2   **c.** My parents are not going to ○ 3
have not yet filed.   file. (Skip to question 68.)

62. What income tax return did your parents file or will they file for 1999?

a. IRS 1040 .... ○ 1   **c.** A foreign tax return. **See Page 2.** .... ○ 3
b. IRS 1040A, 1040EZ, 1040Telefile ...... ○ 2   **d.** A tax return for Puerto Rico, Guam, American Samoa, the Virgin Islands, the ○ 4
Marshall Islands, the Federated States of Micronesia, or Palau. **See Page 2.** ......

63. If your parents have filed or will file a 1040, were they <u>eligible to file a 1040A or 1040EZ</u>? See page 2.   Yes ○ 1   No/don't know ○ 2

64. What was your parents' adjusted gross income for 1999?
Adjusted gross income is on IRS Form 1040–line XX; 1040A–line XX; or 1040EZ–line X. $ ☐☐☐,☐☐☐

65. Enter the total amount of your parents' income tax for 1999. Income tax amount is on
IRS Form 1040–line XX plus XX; 1040A–line XX; or 1040EZ–line XX. $ ☐☐☐,☐☐☐

66. Enter your parents' exemptions. Exemptions are on IRS Form 1040–line XX or
on Form 1040A–line XX. For Form 1040EZ, **see page 2.**   ☐☐

67. Enter your parents' Earned Income Credit from
IRS Form 1040–line XX; 1040A–line XX; or 1040EZ–line XX. $ ☐☐☐,☐☐☐

68-69. How much did your parents earn from working in 1999? Answer this **Father/** $ ☐☐☐,☐☐☐
question whether or not your parents filed a tax return. This information **Stepfather (68)**
may be on their W-2 forms, or on IRS Form 1040–lines X, XX, and XX; **Mother/** $ ☐☐☐,☐☐☐
1040A–line X; or on 1040EZ–line X. **Stepmother (69)**

70. Go to page 8 of this form; complete the column on the right of **Worksheet A**; enter parent total here. $ ☐☐☐,☐☐☐

71. Go to page 8 of this form; complete the column on the right of **Worksheet B**; enter parent total here. $ ☐☐☐,☐☐☐

72. Total current balance of cash, savings, and checking accounts $ ☐☐☐,☐☐☐

For 73–75, if net worth is one million or more, enter $999,999. If net worth is negative, enter 0.

73. Current <u>net worth</u> of <u>investments</u> (<u>investment value</u> minus <u>investment debt</u>) **See page 2.** $ ☐☐☐,☐☐☐

74. Current <u>net worth</u> of business (<u>business value</u> minus <u>business debt</u>) **See page 2.** $ ☐☐☐,☐☐☐

75. Current <u>net worth</u> of investment farm (Don't include a farm that your parents live on and operate.) $ ☐☐☐,☐☐☐

76. Parents' marital status as of today? (Pick one.)   Married ○ 1   Single ○ 2   Divorced/Separated ○ 3   Widowed ○ 4

77. How many people are in your <u>parents' household</u>? **See page 7.**   ☐☐

78. How many in question 77 (except for your parents) will be
<u>college students</u> between July 1, 2000, and June 30, 2001? **See page 7.**   ☐☐

   STATE

79. What is your parents' state of legal residence?   ☐☐

80. Did your parents become legal residents of the state in question 79 before January 1, 1995?   Yes ○ 1   No ○ 2

   MONTH   YEAR

81. If the answer to question 80 is "No," give the month and year legal
residency began for the parent who has lived in the state the longest.   ☐☐ / ☐☐☐☐

82. What is the age of your older parent?   ☐☐

Step Five: Please tell us which schools should receive your information.

For each school (up to eight), please provide the federal school code. Indicate your housing plans for the first four schools you list. Look for the federal school codes at your college financial aid office, on the Internet at http://www.ed.gov/offices/OPE, at your public library, or by asking your high school guidance counselor. If you cannot get the federal school code, write in the complete name, address, city, and state of the college for only the first four colleges you list.

Federal school code	OR	Name of college	College street address and city	State	Housing Plans
83. FIRST SCHOOL CODE					**84.** on campus ○ 1 / off campus ○ 2 / with parent ○ 3
85. SECOND SCHOOL CODE					**86.** on campus ○ 1 / off campus ○ 2 / with parent ○ 3
87. THIRD SCHOOL CODE					**88.** on campus ○ 1 / off campus ○ 2 / with parent ○ 3
89. FOURTH SCHOOL CODE					**90.** on campus ○ 1 / off campus ○ 2 / with parent ○ 3
91. FIFTH SCHOOL CODE	**92.** SIXTH SCHOOL CODE	**93.** SEVENTH SCHOOL CODE		**94.** EIGHTH SCHOOL CODE	

Step Six: Please read, sign, and date.

By signing this application, you agree, if asked, to provide information that will verify the accuracy of your completed form. This information may include a copy of your U.S. or state income tax form. Also, you certify that you (1) will use federal student financial aid only to pay the cost of attending an institution of higher education, (2) are not in default on a federal student loan or have made satisfactory arrangements to repay it, (3) do not owe money back on a federal student grant or have made satisfactory arrangements to repay it, (4) will notify your school if you default on a federal student loan, and (5) understand that **the Secretary of Education has the authority to verify income reported on this application with the Internal Revenue Service.** If you purposely give false or misleading information, you may be fined $10,000, sent to prison, or both.

95. Date this form was completed.

MONTH | DAY / 2000 ○ or 2001 ○

96. Student signature

1 **FOR INFORMATION ONLY.**

Parent signature (one parent whose information is provided in Step Four.)

2 **DO NOT SUBMIT.**

97-98. Your **father's** Social Security Number and last name

96. FATHER'S SSN: X X X – X X – X X X X
99. FATHER'S LAST NAME: FOR INFORMATION ONLY

99-100. Your **mother's** Social Security Number and last name

100. MOTHER'S SSN: X X X – X X – X X X X
101. MOTHER'S LAST NAME: FOR INFORMATION ONLY

If this form was filled out by someone other than you, your spouse, or your parent(s), that person must complete this part.

Preparer's
Name and Firm _____

Address _____

101. Social Security # ⬜⬜ – ⬜⬜ – ⬜⬜⬜⬜
OR
102. Employer ID # ⬜⬜ – ⬜⬜⬜⬜⬜⬜⬜

103. Signature and Date 1 _____

SCHOOL USE ONLY
D/O ○ 1   Federal School Code ⬜⬜⬜⬜⬜
FAA SIGNATURE
1

MDE USE ONLY
Special Handle ⬜ – ⬜⬜⬜⬜⬜

CSS/FINANCIAL AID
PROFILE® 1999-2000   **Application**

Section A - Student's Information

1. How many family members will the student (and spouse) support in 1999-2000? <u>Always include the student and spouse.</u> List their names and give information about them in Section M. See instructions.

2. Of the number in 1, how many will be in college at least half-time for at least one term in 1999-2000? Include yourself.

3. What is the student's state of legal residence?

4. **What is the student's citizenship status?**

   a. ₁ ○ U.S. citizen (Skip to Question 5.)

   ₂ ○ Permanent resident (Skip to Question 5.)

   ₃ ○ Neither of the above (Answer 'b' and 'c' below.)

   b. Country of citizenship?

   c. Visa classification?
   ₁ ○ F1   ₂ ○ F2   ₃ ○ J1   ₄ ○ J2   ₅ ○ G   ₆ ○ Other

Section B - Student's 1998 Income & Benefits

If married, include spouse's information in Sections B, C, D, and E.

5. The following 1998 U.S. income tax return figures are (Fill in only one oval.)

   ₁ ○ estimated. Will file IRS Form 1040EZ, 1040A, or 1040TEL. Go to 6.

   ₂ ○ estimated. Will file IRS Form 1040. Go to 6.

   ₃ ○ from a completed IRS Form 1040EZ, 1040A, or 1040TEL. Go to 6.

   ₄ ○ from a completed IRS Form 1040. Go to 6.

   ₅ ○ a tax return will not be filed. Skip to 10.

Tax Filers Only

6. 1998 total number of exemptions (IRS Form 1040, line 6d or 1040A, line 6d or 1040EZ - see instructions.)

7. 1998 Adjusted Gross Income from IRS Form 1040, line 32 or 1040A, line 16 or 1040EZ, line 4 (Use the worksheet in the instructions, page 3.) $ _____ .00

8. a. 1998 U.S. income tax paid(IRS Form 1040, line 46 or 1040A, line 25 or 1040EZ, line 10) $ _____ .00

   b. 1998 Hope Scholarship Credit and Lifetime Learning Credit from IRS Form 1040, lines xx and xx (Use the worksheet in the instructions, page x .) $ _____ .00

9. 1998 itemized deductions (IRS Form 1040, Schedule A, line 28. Write in "0" if deductions were not itemized.) $ _____ .00

10. 1998 income earned from work by student (See instructions.) $ _____ .00

11. 1998 income earned from work by student's spouse $ _____ .00

12. 1998 dividend and interest income $ _____ .00

13. 1998 untaxed income and benefits (Give total amount for year.)

    a. Social security benefits (See instructions.) $ _____ .00

    b. AFDC/ADC or TANF (See instructions.) $ _____ .00

    c. Child support received for all children $ _____ .00

    d. Earned income Credit (IRS Form 1040, line 56a or 1040A, line 29c or 1040EZ, line 8a) $ _____ .00

    e. Other - write total from instruction worksheet, page 4. $ _____ .00

14. 1998 earnings from Federal Work-Study or other need-based work programs plus any grant and scholarship aid required to be reported on your U.S. income tax return $ _____ .00

Section C - Student's Assets

Include trust accounts only in Section D.

15. Cash, savings, and checking accounts $ _____ .00

16. Total value of IRA, Keogh, 401k, 403b, etc. accounts as of December 31, 1998. $ _____ .00

17. Investments (Including Uniform Gifts to Minors. See instructions.)

What is it worth today?	What is owed on it?
$ _____ .00	$ _____ .00

18. Home (Renters write in "0".) $ _____ .00 $ _____ .00

19. Other real estate $ _____ .00 $ _____ .00

20. Business and farm $ _____ .00 $ _____ .00

21. If a farm is included in 20, is the student living on the farm?   Yes ○ ₁   No ○ ₂

22. If student owns home, give

    a. year purchased 1 9 _ _   b. purchase price $ _____ .00

Section D - Student's Trust Information

23. a. Total value of all trust(s) $ _____ .00

    b. Is any income or part of the principal currently available?
    Yes ○ ₁   No ○ ₂

    c. Who established the trust(s)?
    ₁ ○ Student's parents   ₂ ○ Other

Section E - Student's 1998 Expenses

24. 1998 child support paid by student $ _____ .00

25. 1998 medical and dental expenses not covered by insurance (See instructions.) $ _____ .00

Section F - Student's Expected Summer /School-Year Resources for 1999-2000

	Amount per month	Number of months
26. Student's veterans benefits (July 1, 1999 - June 30, 2000.)	$ .00	

27. Student's (and spouse's) resources
(Don't enter monthly amounts.)

	Summer 1999 (3 months)	School Year 1999-2000 (9 months)
a. Student's wages, salaries, tips, etc.	$ .00	$ .00
b. Spouse's wages, salaries, tips, etc.	$ .00	$ .00
c. Other taxable income	$ .00	$ .00
d. Untaxed income and benefits	$ .00	$ .00
e. Grants, scholarships, fellowships, etc. from sources other than the colleges or universities to which the student is applying (List sources in Section P.)		$ .00
f. Tuition benefits from the parents' and/or the student's or spouse's employer		$ .00
g. Contributions from the student's parent(s) for 1999-2000 college or university expenses		$ .00
h. Contributions from other relatives, spouse's parents, and all other sources (List sources in Section P.)		$ .00

Section G - Parents' Household Information - See page 5 of the instruction booklet.

28. How many family members will your parents support in 1999-2000? ☐
Always include the student and parents
List their names and give information about them in Section M.

29. Of the number in 28, how many will be in college at least
half-time for at least one term in 1999-2000? Include the student. ☐

30. How many parents will be in college at least half-time in 1999-2000?
(Fill in only one oval.)
₁ ○ Neither parent ₂ ○ One parent ₃ ○ Both parents

31. What is the current marital status of your parents?
(Fill in only one oval.)
₁ ○ single ₃ ○ separated ₅ ○ widowed
₂ ○ married ₄ ○ divorced

32. What is your parents' state of legal residence? ☐

Section H - Parents' Expenses

		1998	Expected 1999
33. Child support paid by the parent(s) completing this form	33.	$ .00	$ .00
34. Repayment of parents' educational loans (See instructions.)	34.	$ .00	$ .00
35. Medical and dental expenses not covered by insurance (See instructions.)	35.	$ .00	$ .00
36. Total elementary, junior high school, and high school tuition paid for dependent children			
a. Amount paid (Don't include tuition paid for the student.)	36.	$ .00	$ .00
b. For how many dependent children? (Don't include the student.)		☐	☐

Section I - Parents' Assets - If parents own all or part of a business or farm, write in its name and the percent of ownership in Section P.

	What is it worth today?	What is owed on it?
37. Cash, savings, and checking accounts	$ .00	
38. Total value of assets held in the names of the student's brothers and sisters	$ .00	

	What is it worth today?	What is owed on it?
39. Investments	$ .00	$ .00
40. a. Home (Renters write in "0". Skip to 40d.)	$ .00	$ .00

b. year purchased 1 9 ☐ c. purchase price $ .00

d. Monthly home mortgage or rental payment $ .00
(If none, explain in Section P.)

	What is it worth today?	What is owed on it?
41. Business	$ .00	$ .00
42. a. Farm	$ .00	$ .00

b. Does family
live on the farm?
Yes ○₁ No ○₂

	What is it worth today?	What is owed on it?
43. a. Other real estate	$ .00	$ .00

b. year purchased 1 9 ☐ c. purchase price $ .00

CSSEV2 4-15-99

Section J - Parents' 1997 Income & Benefits

44. 1997 Adjusted Gross Income (IRS Form 1040, line 32 or 1040A, line 16 or 1040EZ, line 4) $ _____ .00

45. 1997 U.S. income tax paid (IRS Form 1040, line 46, 1040A, line 25 or 1040EZ, line 10) $ _____ .00

46. 1997 itemized deductions (IRS Form 1040, Schedule A, line 28. Write "0" if deductions were not itemized.) $ _____ .00

47. 1997 untaxed income and benefits (Include the same types of income & benefits that are listed in 55 a-k.) $ _____ .00

Section K - Parents' 1998 Income & Benefits

48. The following 1998 U.S. income tax return figures are (Fill in only one oval.)

₁ ○ estimated. Will file IRS Form 1040EZ, 1040A, or 1040TEL. Go to 49.
₂ ○ estimated. Will file IRS Form 1040. Go to 49.
₃ ○ from a completed IRS Form 1040EZ, 1040A, or 1040TEL. Go to 49.
₄ ○ from a completed IRS Form 1040. Go to 49.
₅ ○ a tax return will not be filed. Skip to 53.

Tax Filers Only

49. 1998 total number of exemptions (IRS Form 1040, line 6d or 1040A, line 6d or 1040EZ - see instructions)   **49.** ⊔⊔

50. 1998 Adjusted Gross Income (IRS Form 1040, line 32 or 1040A, line 16 or 1040EZ, line 4)   **50.** $ _____ .00
Breakdown of income in 50

   a. Wages, salaries, tips (IRS Form 1040, line 7 or 1040A, line 7 or 1040EZ, line 1)   **50. a.** $ _____ .00

   b. Interest income (IRS Form 1040, line 8a or 1040A, line 8a or 1040EZ, line 2)   **b.** $ _____ .00

   c. Dividend income (IRS Form 1040, line 9 or 1040A, line 9)   **c.** $ _____ .00

   d. Net income (or loss) from business, farm, rents, royalties, partnerships, estates, trusts, etc. (IRS Form 1040, lines 12, 17, and 18). If a loss, enter the amount in (parentheses).   **d.** $ _____ .00

   e. Other taxable income such as alimony received, capital gains (or losses), pensions, annuities, etc. (IRS Form 1040, lines 10, 11, 13, 14, 15b, 16b, 19, 20b and 21 or 1040A, lines 10b, 11b, 12, and 13b or 1040EZ, line 3)   **e.** $ _____ .00

   f. Adjustments to income (IRS Form 1040, line 31 or 1040A, line 15) see instructions.   **f.** $ _____ .00

51.   **a.** 1998 U.S. income tax paid (IRS Form 1040, line 46, 1040A, line 25 or 1040EZ, line 10)   **51. a.** $ _____ .00

   b. 1998 Hope Scholarship Credit and Lifetime Learning Credit from IRS Form 1040, lines xx and xx (use the worksheet in the instructions, page x.)   **b.** $ _____ .00

52. 1998 itemized deductions (IRS Form 1040, Schedule A, line 28. Write in "0" if deductions were not itemized.)   **52.** $ _____ .00

53. 1998 income earned from work by father/stepfather   **53.** $ _____ .00

54. 1998 income earned from work by mother/stepmother   **54.** $ _____ .00

55. 1998 untaxed income and benefits (Give total amount for the year. Do not give monthly amounts.)

   a. Social security benefits received   **55. a.** $ _____ .00

   b. AFDC/ADC or TANF (See instructions.)   **b.** $ _____ .00

   c. Child support received for all children   **c.** $ _____ .00

   d. Deductible IRA and/or Keogh payments (See instructions.)   **d.** $ _____ .00

   e. Payments to tax-deferred pension and savings plans (See instructions.)   **e.** $ _____ .00

   f. Amounts withheld from wages for dependent care and medical spending accounts   **f.** $ _____ .00

   g. Earned Income Credit (IRS Form 1040, line 56a or 1040A, line 29c or 1040EZ, line 8a)   **g.** $ _____ .00

   h. Housing, food and other living allowances (See instructions.)   **h.** $ _____ .00

   i. Tax-exempt interest income (IRS Form 1040, line 8b or 1040A, line 8b)   **i.** $ _____ .00

   j. Foreign income exclusion (IRS Form 2555, line 43 or Form 2555EZ, line 18)   **j.** $ _____ .00

   k. Other - write in the total from the worksheet in the instructions, page 7.   **k.** $ _____ .00

WRITE ONLY IN THE ANSWER SPACES. DO NOT WRITE ANYWHERE ELSE.

Section L - Parents' 1999 Expected Income & Benefits
If the expected total income and benefits will differ from the 1998 total income by $3,000 or more, explain in Section P.

56. 1999 income earned from work by father $ _____ .00

57. 1999 income earned from work by mother $ _____ .00

58. 1999 other taxable income $ _____ .00

59. 1999 untaxed income and benefits (See 55a-k.) $ _____ .00

CSSRV2 4-3-98

Section M - Family Member Listing – Give information for all family members entered in question 1 or 28. List up to seven family members in addition to the student. If there are more than seven, list first those who will be in school or college at least half-time. List the others in Section P. Leave shaded sections blank.

60.	Full name of family member	Use codes from below.	Age	Claimed by parents as tax exemption in 1998?		1998-99 school year				1999-2000 school year			
				Yes?	No?	Name of school or college	Year in school	Scholarships and grants	Parents' contribution	Attend college at least one term full-time / half-time		College or university Type	Name
1	You - the student applicant			○	○			$					
2				○	○			$		1 ○	2 ○		
3				○	○			$		1 ○	2 ○		
4				○	○			$		1 ○	2 ○		
5				○	○			$		1 ○	2 ○		
6				○	○			$		1 ○	2 ○		
7				○	○			$		1 ○	2 ○		
8				○	○			$		1 ○	2 ○		

Write in the correct code from the right. → 1 – Student's parent 2 – Student's stepparent 3 – Student's brother or sister 4 – Student's husband or wife 5 – Student's son or daughter 6 – Student's grandparent 7 – Student's stepbrother or stepsister 9 – Other

Write in the correct code from the instructions on page 8.

Section N - Parents' Information (to be answered by the parent(s) completing this form)

61. Fill in one: ○ Father ○ Stepfather ○ Legal guardian ○ Other (Explain in P.)

a. Name _____ Age |__|__|

b. Fill in it: ○ Self-employed ○ Unemployed - Date: _____

c. Occupation _____

d. Employer _____ No. years ___

e. Work telephone |__|__|__| – |__|__|__| – |__|__|__|__|

f. Retirement plans: ○ Social security ○ Union/employer ○ Civil service/state ○ IRA/Keogh/tax-deferred ○ Military ○ Other

62. Fill in one: ○ Mother ○ Stepmother ○ Legal guardian ○ Other (Explain in P.)

a. Name _____ Age |__|__|

b. Fill in it: ○ Self-employed ○ Unemployed - Date: _____

c. Occupation _____

d. Employer _____ No. years ___

e. Work telephone |__|__|__| – |__|__|__| – |__|__|__|__|

f. Retirement plans: ○ Social security ○ Union/employer ○ Civil service/state ○ IRA/Keogh/tax-deferred ○ Military ○ Other

Section O - Information About Noncustodial Parent (to be answered by the parent who completes this form if the student's biological or adoptive parents are divorced, separated, or were never married to each other)

63. a. Noncustodial parent's name: _____
Home address _____
Occupation/Employer _____

b. Year of separation |__|__| Year of divorce |__|__|

c. According to court order, when will support for the student end? |__| |__| Month Year

d. Who last claimed the student as a tax exemption? _____ Year? |__|__|

e. How much does the noncustodial parent plan to contribute to the student's education for the 1999-2000 school year? (Do not include this amount in 27g.) $ _____ .00

f. Is there an agreement specifying this contribution for the student's education? Yes ○ No ○

Section P - Explanations/Special Circumstances Explain any unusual expenses such as high medical or dental expenses, educational and other debts, child care, elder care, or special circumstances. Also, give information for any outside scholarships you have been awarded. If more space is needed, use sheets of paper and send them directly to your schools and programs (please print)

Certification:

All the information on this form is true and complete to the best of my knowledge. If asked, I agree to give proof of the information that I have given on this form. I realize that this proof may include a copy of my U.S. state, or local income tax returns. I certify that all information is correct at this time, and that I will send timely notice to my schools or programs of any subsequent change in family income or assets, financial situation, college plans of other children, or the receipt of other scholarships or grants.

Student's signature _____
Student's spouse's signature _____
Father's (stepfather's) signature _____
Mother's (stepmother's) signature _____

MAIL COMPLETED APPLICATION TO: COLLEGE SCHOLARSHIP SERVICE P.O. BOX 4004 MOUNT VERNON, IL 62864-8604

Date completed: |__|__| |__|__| Month Day 1 ○ 1998 2 ○ 1999

CSS Use Only
W
Y
P
S

CSSPv4 5-7-98

FINANCIAL AID TRANSCRIPT

PART I: To be completed by the STUDENT.

Instructions: If you ever attended another postsecondary institution, you **must** complete Part I of this form and submit it to the Financial Aid Office of that institution. Federal regulations require that a Financial Aid Transcript request be sent to *every* institution you previously attended, regardless of whether you received aid to attend that institution.

Name _____ Social Security # _____
      Last   First   M.I.   Maiden
Name used at previous institution (if different from above) _____

Student's Address: _____

I request that the Financial Aid Office at

_____

which I attended from _____ to _____ provide the information requested in Part II to the institution shown to the left.

I ☐ did   ☐ did not receive aid while a student at this institution.

(Fold here for window envelope)

Student's Signature (optional): _____

PART II: To be completed by the STUDENT FINANCIAL AID OFFICE at the previous institution.

Complete either: • Sections A, B and F; OR
                • Sections A, and C through F.

SECTION A   Other Institutions Attended (Everyone must complete this section).

The institution has information indicating the student attended institutions other than this institution.

☐ No, our records show no previous institution attended.
☐ Yes, our records indicate that the student has attended the following institutions: _____
_____

SECTION B   To be completed if the institution is not completing Sections C, D, and E.

The information requested in Sections C, D, and E is not provided because:

☐ The student neither received nor benefited from any Title IV aid while at this institution.
☐ The transcript pertains solely to years for which the institution no longer has and is no longer required to keep records under the Title IV recordkeeping requirements.

If you have completed Section A and checked one of the reasons in Section B, and are not required to provide any other information, skip Sections C, D, and E, and complete Section F. Otherwise, proceed with Section C.

SECTION C   Complete the first statement and check all others that apply.

1. The student first received Title IV aid at this institution for award year: _____ through: _____
                                                            mo/yr   mo/yr

2. Check all that apply:
   ☐ The student received increased Federal Perkins Loan/NDSL at this institution due to Expanded Lending Option or study abroad.
   ☐ The student received increased FSEOG at this institution due to study abroad.
   ☐ The student had an outstanding balance on an NDSL at this institution on July 1, 1987, *which is still outstanding as of today's date.*
   ☐ The student had an outstanding balance on a Federal Perkins Loan/NDSL at this institution on October 1, 1992, *which is still outstanding as of today's date.*
   ☐ The student owes a refund due to overpayment on a Federal Pell Grant, FSEOG or Federal Perkins Loan/NDSL at this institution.
   ☐ The student is in default on a Federal Perkins Loan/NDSL/Income Contingent Loan (ICL) at this institution.
   ☐ The institution is aware that the defaulted Federal Perkins Loan/NDSL/ICL has been discharged in bankruptcy.
   ☐ The institution knows the student owes a refund due to overpayment on SSIG received for attending this institution.
   ☐ The institution knows that the student is in default on a Federal Family Education Loan (FFEL) or a Federal Direct Student Loan (FDSL) received for attendance at this institution (including consolidation loans).
   ☐ The institution is aware that the defaulted FFEL or FDSL has been discharged in bankruptcy.

Revised 4/11/94

For ALL federal aid programs: When indicating totals, deduct any refunds, repayments, or Federal Pell Grant recoveries which have been returned due to an overpayment or student withdrawal. Do NOT deduct Federal Perkins Loan/NDSL and ICL prepayments or payments made according to a repayment schedule.

Sources of Assistance	Current Year Amounts 19__ – ___	Cumulative Total (include current year)
Federal Pell Grant: Total Disbursement		xxxxxxxx
Scheduled Award (full time, full year)		xxxxxxxx
Does the school expect to make additional disbursements to the student after this transcript is signed? If so, indicate when:_____	xxxxxxxx	xxxxxxxx
FSEOG		xxxxxxxx
Income Contingent Loans (Report ICL separately even if merged with Federal Perkins/NDSL funds. ICL does not count toward Federal Perkins/NDSL aggregates.)	xxxxxxxx	
Federal Perkins/NDSL Loans		
Federal SLS Loan or PLUS Loan (ALAS) (borrowed by the student)		
Federal PLUS/Federal Direct PLUS Loan (borrowed by parents for the student)		xxxxxxxx
SSIG/State Grant/Other aid* (optional – identify each)		

* If this school participates in health professions aid programs through the Department of Health & Human Services, include them here.

List the loan period and amount for each of the following Title IV loans received for attendance at this institution. Include current loans.

Subsidized and Unsubsidized Federal Stafford/Federal Direct Stafford Loan			Additional Unsubsidized Federal Stafford/Federal Direct Stafford Loan (Include only amounts which exceed Federal Stafford/Federal Direct Stafford Loan eligibility for independent or graduate students, or dependent students whose parents cannot borrow PLUS)		
Loan Period	Grade Level	Amount	Loan Period	Grade Level	Amount

Authorized Signature _____ Date _____

Typed Name _____ Title _____

Name of Institution _____

Address _____

_____

Telephone _____

COMMENTS _____

_____

Form developed by the National Association of Student Financial Aid Administrators.

Revised 4/11/94

Index

IDG BOOKS WORLDWIDE
BOOK REGISTRATION

We want to hear from you!

Visit **http://my2cents.dummies.com** to register this book and tell us how you liked it!

- ✔ Get entered in our monthly prize giveaway.

- ✔ Give us feedback about this book — tell us what you like best, what you like least, or maybe what you'd like to ask the author and us to change!

- ✔ Let us know any other *...For Dummies®* topics that interest you.

Your feedback helps us determine what books to publish, tells us what coverage to add as we revise our books, and lets us know whether we're meeting your needs as a *...For Dummies* reader. You're our most valuable resource, and what you have to say is important to us!

Not on the Web yet? It's easy to get started with *Dummies 101®: The Internet For Windows® 98* or *The Internet For Dummies®,* 5th Edition, at local retailers everywhere.

Or let us know what you think by sending us a letter at the following address:

...For Dummies Book Registration
Dummies Press
7260 Shadeland Station, Suite 100
Indianapolis, IN 46256-3917
Fax 317-596-5498

BESTSELLING
BOOK SERIES